THE NEW SLAVE NARRATIVE

The New
Slave Narrative

THE BATTLE OVER REPRESENTATIONS
OF CONTEMPORARY SLAVERY

Laura T. Murphy

Columbia University Press
New York

Columbia University Press
Publishers Since 1893
New York   Chichester, West Sussex
cup.columbia.edu
Copyright © 2019 Columbia University Press
All rights reserved

Cataloging-in-Publication Data is available from the Library of Congress.
ISBN 978-0-231-18824-1 (cloth: alk. paper)
ISBN 978-0-231-18825-8 (pbk. : alk. paper)
ISBN 978-0-231-54773-4 (e-book)

LCCN 2019002799

∞

Columbia University Press books are printed on permanent and durable acid-free paper.
Printed in the United States of America

Cover design: Milenda Nan Ok Lee
Cover art: Yinka Shonibare CBE, Girl Balancing Knowledge III, 2017. © Yinka Shonibare
CBE. All Rights Reserved, DACS/Artimage 2019. Image courtesy James Cohan Gallery.
Photo: Stephen White.

CONTENTS

vi

CONTENTS

ACKNOWLEDGMENTS

My most humble gratitude goes first, of course, to the thousands of survivors of contemporary forms of slavery around the world who have courageously shared their narratives in the hopes that many millions of others will not have to. Special thanks go to Minh Dang, Shamere McKenzie, and James Kofi Annan as well as several other less public survivor-activists whose stories are not included in this book but who have been generous and engaging interlocutors as I have worked on this issue.

I am enormously grateful that the writing of this book was supported by research leaves that bookended its creation—the first words creeped across a blank screen during a pretenure research leave funded by Loyola University New Orleans, and the first draft of the manuscript was then completed on sabbatical while I was the John G. Medlin Jr. Fellow at the National Humanities Center. Final revisions were completed while on a British Academy Visiting Fellowship at the Rights Lab at the University of Nottingham. In between those critical moments of intense reflection, Loyola generously provided me with research funding through the Carter, Bobet, and Marquette faculty research grants.

Any book is the distillation of a thousand excellent conversations. I have many people to thank for those engaging exchanges, which were just as likely to happen on a conference panel as over lunch, coffee, or drinks.

Thanks to my Africanist colleagues who have been discussing these ideas with me for a decade now: Ato Quayson, Steph Newell, Gaurav Desai, Adeleke Adeeko, Esther deBruijn, Dan Magaziner, Pallavi Rastogi, Matt Brown, Teju Olaniyan, Matt Omelsky, Ainehi Edoro, Kirk Sides, Madhu Krishnan, Cajetan Iheka, Carli Coetzee, Jacob Dlamini, Luise White, and all the participants of the Bloods Lab at Princeton. I appreciate the sometimes heated but always generative debates I have with my slavery and human rights studies colleagues—Kevin Bales, Zoe Trodd, alix lutnick, Melissa Gira Grant, Joel Quirk, Joey Slaughter, Eleni Coundouriotis, Elizabeth Goldberg, Alexandra Schulthies Moore, and Jim Stewart. At the National Humanities Center, I spent many lunches sorting through these ideas with an incredible interdisciplinary group of scholars. Special thanks to Nancy Hirschmann, Harleen Singh, Andrea Williams, Hollis Robbins, Tera Hunter, Libby Otto, Kimberly Jannarone, Tsitsi Jaji, Emily Levine, Jose Amador, Todd Ochoa, David Cory, and the Nineteenth-Century Working Group, each of whom helped add nuance to this project. Many other great scholars, colleagues, and friends have contributed to the conversation; thanks to Carol Ann MacGregor, Julia Lee, Erin Dwyer, Andy Lewis, Lelia Gowland, and Jason Allen.

At Loyola, I am grateful to all my colleagues in the English Department, especially those who have responded to this work: Hillary Eklund, Christopher Schaberg, Tim Welsh, Kate Adams, John Biguenet, Danny Mintz, and Sarah Allison. Ashley Howard pored over the near-final drafts of most of these chapters even when her hands were super full. My brilliant research assistants at Loyola—Amelie Daigle, Jasmine Jackson, Lauren Stroh, and Marley Duet—have spent the last few years reading new slave narratives and providing feedback on my ideas, as have the students in my Twenty-First-Century Slavery and Abolition and Slave Narratives, Past and Present courses. My sincere thanks go to Provost Maria Calzada and John Biguenet for supporting this work without fail.

I have presented sections of this book at events at Yale University, the University of Toronto, Kwara State University, Eichstätt-Ingolstadt University, University College London, the University of Wisconsin, Princeton University, the University of Oklahoma, Tulane University, the University of Nevada Las Vegas, Louisiana State University, Lehigh University, Tougaloo University, Rockhurst University, Simpson College, College of the Holy Cross, and the University of New Orleans. The ideas were put to the test at the Bloods Lab hosted by Carli Coetzee and Jacob Dlamini at Princeton University and at the Slavery, Memory, and Literature symposium hosted by Mads Anders Baggesgaard, Madeleine Dobie, and Karen-Margrethe Simonsen at L'Ecole des Hautes Etudes en Sciences Sociales. Thanks to those who invited me and to their generous colleagues and students who asked the difficult questions that were instrumental in developing my thinking on this project.

Thanks to the anonymous reviewer of my earlier collection of new slave narratives, who recommended writing a full critical study of the genre, as well as to the generous anonymous reviewers of this book, whose challenges and provocations were enormously helpful in sharpening my arguments. My gratitude also goes to my editor, Philip Leventhal, for believing in this project and for his tremendously useful advice in the final revisions. Thanks to Abby Graves for her keen and sensitive copyediting and to Ina Gravitz for an index that helped me see my own ideas anew.

To my extraordinary krewe in New Orleans—the Howangs, the Peterae, the Larklunds, CAM, Jerry, and the Birds—you are my family and constant companions in all things worth doing. And to Rian Thum, my eternal thanks; every page here is marked by your tireless, in-house collegiality.

Sections of chapters 1 and 2 were previously published in different forms in *Slavery and Abolition*, and chapter 3 was previously published in the *Cambridge Journal of Postcolonial Inquiry*. They are reprinted here with permission.

A NOTE ON LANGUAGE

While almost no one today would argue that forced labor does not exist in the global economy, scholars and advocates are engaged in fierce debates regarding the language we use to describe it. It is important from the outset to explain the choice of some terms that will appear in this book.

Some scholars protest that the word "slavery," as it describes contemporary forms of forced labor, is being utilized out of context, without precision, and in ignorance of the gravity of the experiences of people who were enslaved in the antebellum United States. Critics often stress that use of the term "slavery" outside the fifteenth-to-nineteenth-century transatlantic context (and often, even more narrowly, outside the African American context) insensitively risks diminishing the experiences and legacy of transatlantic slavery.[1] Tryon P. Woods argues that "the slave is paradigmatically black" and suggests that the appellation "modern slavery" is indicative of "an ahistoricism symptomatic of our anti-black world."[2] For these critics, the word "slavery" has been inextricably sedimented in a particular moment and in the particular form of legalized and racialized chattel slavery of the antebellum United States in much the same way the word "holocaust," though it predates World War II, is now largely understood as synonymous with the Holocaust in Germany in the 1940s. I contend that these critiques disregard the fact that slavery has taken many forms throughout human history and that it both pre-dates and postdates the very aptly described "peculiar" institutions of chattel slavery that existed in the Americas.

The reticence to use the term "slavery" is furthermore a response to three (sometimes overlapping) phenomena that have been justifiably criticized by scholars and activists alike. First, some critics decry the inappropriately sensationalized, overly expansive, or nebulous use of the term as it is used in media and some scholarship. They argue that when activists and writers take the word out of context and use it with little commitment to precision, proponents of the term often misidentify low-wage labor, kidnapping, sexual assault, human smuggling, and other forms of terror as "slavery."[3] Second, many progressive thinkers are critical of self-professed "Radical Feminists" who believe that all sex work is exploitation and who therefore equate sex work to slavery in a labored attempt to mobilize the gravity of the word "slavery" to their own cause of prostitution abolition. Critics argue that this approach not only undermines the agency of women engaged in sex work but deliberately deracializes slavery and turns attention away from marginalized members of society to focus on "white slavery" and the protection of white feminine fragility.[4] This approach to the term justifiably offends advocates for sex workers' rights and confounds labor rights, immigrant rights, and sexual-assault victim advocates. And last, other critics suggest that the term "slavery" should not be used because some antislavery activists have been irresponsible in their implementation of antislavery projects, and thus the use of the term in the contemporary context itself has been tainted.[5] In many of these cases, the evidence of the term's abuse is indeed well documented and convincing; however, these critics unnecessarily conflate the term "slavery" itself with its misuse and the people who work in the name of it, which puts undue limits on the use of language simply because some people have employed the term and worked in its name irresponsibly.

The anxiety around the term is certainly not misplaced. The term "slavery" has a unique gravity that cannot and should not be disassociated from the distinctive experience that results from the intentional and typically violent subjugation of a person's agency, labor, and rights simultaneously. People do use the word "slavery" to exaggerate, to invoke a metaphor, or to add weight to claims of oppression even when they are not describing slavery per se. However, removing the word from the realm of discourse does a disservice to people who are indeed enslaved today. To remove the term "slavery" from use in contemporary contexts forces us to use euphemism to describe genuine situations of slavery worldwide, undermining our ability to describe precisely and critique rigorously the corrupted systems of labor exploitation that result in the absolute subordination of one person's labor power to another person's or corporation's benefit. As Claude Meillassoux suggests, the term "slavery" has been applied to an extraordinarily heterogeneous body of situations—some of which include legal institutionalization, cultural acceptance, lifelong captivity, transferable property rights in persons, open markets, and many others that do not include any of those characteristics—and, as a result, there has been significant debate over the legal and sociological parameters of slavery, both historically and in the contemporary context.[6] I argue, however, that to use this word consciously, consistently, and precisely is crucial, as it does indeed conjure the experiences of nineteenth-century transatlantic slavery so familiar to American citizens, as well as the experiences of the many millions of other people throughout human history who have suffered under a wide variety of forms of involuntary forced labor around the world. This includes legalized and racialized chattel slavery like that practiced in the United States in the nineteenth century, but it also incorporates other less institutionalized or shorter-term forms that have been practiced in other times and places. I use this word because the term "slavery" and the experiences it evokes accurately describe situations of forced labor that remain a largely hidden but nonetheless perniciously pervasive aspect of global capitalism in the twenty-first century. Using the word "slavery" explicitly and literally ensures that we are not hiding behind euphemism and thereby avoiding addressing the consequences of a global system of trade that continues to rely on slavery.

In this book, I use "slavery" or "slave narrative" to describe only the experiences or life stories of people who use the term "slavery" to describe their own experiences. I never call someone "a slave," opting instead for "enslaved person" as a way of pointing to experience over essence. This sometimes results in somewhat inelegant phrasing such as "narratives of formerly enslaved people," but I prefer that over projecting that name onto someone as an identity, even for those who identify their experiences as "slavery." In one case in which a survivor has used the term "slavery" to describe her experiences in print but then has advocated against using that word, I have indicated that in the text, as I have in the case of a survivor who was compelled to use the word "slavery" by a publisher but explicitly protested against it in the pages of her book.

I use the term "trafficking" to refer exclusively to the particular crime as it is defined in the law in the particular country in question. In the United States, that describes forced labor, including forced sex work, and any engagement in the sex trade by minors. It is distinct from slavery in that it can include consensual sex work involving minors and may at times include fraudulent or coercive labor conditions that are not tantamount to forced labor and in which people can elect to walk away. As often as possible, I use the terms that survivors use to describe their own experiences and ideas, but in discussions of antislavery and anti-trafficking advocacy, I intentionally employ the term that most closely describes the violations that their activism specifically addresses. I never use the word "slavery" inaccurately to describe consensual, voluntary work, except in cases where I am quoting the self-identification of a survivor of trafficking.

Because both "slavery" and "trafficking" are used to characterize a wide variety of experiences, are sometimes used interchangeably and indiscriminately in the field, and are used to describe people's personal experiences, I may cite these terms even when they do not conform to the precise definitions that I typically use in my scholarship in order to honor the terms used by the survivors and activists discussed herein and always when employing a direct quotation. In much of chapter 3, I use "trafficking" when I discuss the body of post-2010 narratives because, though the authors all describe their experiences as both trafficking and slavery, their overarching concern is with domestic minor sex trafficking, and their ambivalences about agency, choice, and volition are part of what is at stake in the argument.

Throughout this book, where I refer to what is colloquially and legally known as "prostitution," I will use the phrase "sex work," "commercial sex," or "sexual labor." Though I am committed to respecting the wishes of survivors regarding the language we use and the politics we espouse in addressing modern slavery, there is significant debate about the phrase "sex work." I use the term "sex trafficking" when I am describing the crime discussed above, but "sex work" or "sexual labor" to describe labor that is sometimes exploited by sex traffickers, just as I would use "construction work" or "agricultural labor" when describing industries that labor trafficking affects. As this book is focused on slavery, I am necessarily concerned about labor—forced labor in particular. Thus, any discussion of slavery in the sex industry inherently suggests that sex can be a form of labor and that it can be performed voluntarily or involuntarily like any other form of labor. Most of the survivors of sexual enslavement here disagree with my logic on this point, as they argue that their experiences were so demeaning, dehumanizing, and involuntary that the valor of the word "work" cannot possibly be attributed to it. However, the involuntary work enslaved people have performed for all of human history has included the most demeaning and dehumanizing labor. Furthermore, it is my contention that if sex cannot be considered work, then it can never be considered slavery. Without the labor aspect, the experiences described here might be called rape, domestic abuse, or kidnapping. Labor is a necessary condition of slavery. Insofar as I can honor the ideas of survivors on this point without losing precision, I have done so by describing each individual's experience using the terms they employ. I have only used the infelicitous phrase "sex slavery" or the term "prostitution" in quoting others, however, because they have been used in such salacious and sensationalized ways that they carry an evaluative and judgmental weight inappropriate to scholarly discourse; I instead tend to use "sexual enslavement" or "forced sex work."

As this book attests, the discourses of slavery change over time, and these debates are far from settled in these pages. Nonetheless, I think these discussions and the continual refinement of the way we describe one another and our experiences is critical to both ethical activism and engaged scholarship.

PREFACE

> Slavery has been fruitful in giving itself names . . . and it will call itself by yet another name; and you and I and all of us had better wait and see what new form this old monster will assume, in what new skin this old snake will come forth next.
>
> —FREDERICK DOUGLASS, "THE NEED FOR CONTINUING ANTI-SLAVERY WORK" (1865)

I first learned of the existence of contemporary forms of slavery in January 2004. Taking a break from a pile of nineteenth-century slave narratives that I was reading for my research on the transatlantic slave trade, I began scrolling through articles in the *New York Times Magazine*. I happened upon an article titled "The Girls Next Door" by Peter Landesman. I was immediately enraged by the carelessness with which Landesman wrote. His article opened with a description of a house that was being used as a way station for women coming into the United States to work in the sex industry. Landesman asserted, "They weren't prostitutes; they were sex slaves." Taken aback by what I considered an egregiously sensationalized journalistic expression, I continued reading, and I quickly encountered an ominously familiar image: "The police found a squalid, land-based equivalent of a nineteenth-century slave ship, with rancid, doorless bathrooms; bare, putrid mattresses; and a stash of penicillin, 'morning after' pills and misoprostol, an antiulcer medication that can induce abortion. The girls were pale, exhausted and malnourished."[1]

A land-based equivalent of a nineteenth-century slave ship?! I could not fathom how Landesman could so callously compare any experience in the twenty-first-century United States to the captivity and enslavement of Africans in the transatlantic trade. I immediately thought of Olaudah Equiano's description of the tightly packed cargo hold of the ship in which he was transported through the Middle Passage to the United States. He wrote of that horrific scene that it was "absolutely pestilential":

The closeness of the place, and the heat of the climate, added to the number in the ship, which was so crowded that each had scarcely room to turn himself, almost suffocated us. This produced copious perspirations, so that the air soon became unfit for respiration, from a variety of loathsome smells, and brought on a sickness among the slaves, of which many died, thus falling victims to the improvident avarice, as I may call it, of their purchasers. This wretched situation was again aggravated by the galling of the chains, now become insupportable; and the filth of the necessary tubs, into which the children often fell, and were almost suffocated. The shrieks of the women, and the groans of the dying, rendered the whole a scene of horror almost inconceivable.[2]

Despite Equiano's extraordinary ability to paint such a painstakingly vivid though nonetheless stark image of that confined space on which he was introduced to his own captivity, he reminds us that the suffering and even the very fact of the cargo hold was nearly inconceivable in Equiano's own time. Such inhumane conditions are especially inconceivable today, more than two hundred years after the abolition of the slave trade that was the impetus for that ghastly voyage. And thus, it was only anger that urged me to continue reading after encountering Landesman's hyperbolic analogy to the slave ship.

While it did not exonerate him for the insensitive slave ship analogy (even the *New York Times* admitted that the article was rhetorically problematic) or other misconceptions and exaggerations he perpetuated, what I read in the rest of his article did indeed justify the literal evocation of the word "slavery." The article outlined the routes of migration used by human smugglers to transport Central American and Eastern European women and girls to find work in the United States. Though many of the women believed they were coming to the United States to work in restaurants or in the nurseries of wealthy families (and, no doubt, many others did), the women whose stories he told were instead held captive in fetid apartments in New York or in the arid reed groves of Southern California, where organized criminals forced them to serve the sexual demands of countless men. When the women tried to escape, the traffickers beat them mercilessly. And though the earnings gained through their labors were likely significant, their employers did not pay them a penny for their work.

Slavery.

I searched for other reports of contemporary slavery and found accounts of people who had been forced to pick cotton in Uzbekistan, mine minerals and gems in Tanzania, stitch clothes in Chinese prison labor camps— all without pay, under threat of violence, without a plausible means of escape. I set aside the stack of nineteenth-century slave narratives I had been poring over and began learning about their twenty-first-century counterparts.

Over the next few years, I volunteered and consulted for a number of nonprofits that work to address contemporary slavery. I also shifted my academic focus to study this contemporary iteration of a problem that has haunted all of human history. I met many survivors in the course of that work. Many of those survivors wanted to tell their stories in an effort to effect change, while others preferred silence. Those who did feel empowered by sharing their stories found eager and diverse audiences of activists, scholars, and journalists who were seeking evidence for their claims that slavery still exists in the United States and around the world. In the last two decades, I have witnessed the rise of a cadre of prominent and powerful survivor-activists. They have insisted on their significance in the shaping of a reinvigorated twenty-first-century antislavery movement, which has, in turn, both amplified their voices and co-opted them. This book, then, tells the story of the ways those survivors have reinvigorated the use of the word "slavery" to effect a reemergence of the slave narrative and the antislavery movement.

The slave narrative has a long tradition, as does the study of that tradition. Some of the earliest known slave narratives were published in the 1760s in the United States. By 1849, as the production of slave narratives was reaching a fevered pitch in the United States, the *Christian Examiner* magazine included a review by a minister named Ephraim Peabody about first-person testimonies that he called "narratives of fugitive slaves," for which he said the nation had garnered the "mournful honor of adding a new department to the literature of civilization."[3] These "most remarkable productions of the age" would eventually amount to thousands of testimonies that African American studies scholars would dub the "slave narrative tradition."

Peabody described the development and characteristics of a most unfortunate genre—its conventions and tropes, its oratorical roots, and its capacity to render a complex system legible for white audiences who might deny the realities of slavery. While his review is marred by his privileged position, he is likely the first person to publish an analysis of the slave narrative as a genre and to begin to understand the way, when read together, the narratives represented not only a collective plea made up of the voices of thousands of individual fugitives but also a trenchant critique of the ideological and racialized underpinnings of slavery and freedom in the United States.

Like Ephraim Peabody, we are witnessing the emergence—or reemergence—of a genre. Publishers in the United States have churned out several new narratives of contemporary slavery each year of the last decade and a half, and many more survivors of slavery self-publish narratives, write blogs, and post their experiences on social media, all in response to a seemingly voracious desire on the part of the American public to consume narratives of extraordinary violence and exploitation. These "new slave narratives," much like their predecessors, are representative of the time we live in and can tell us as much about the predilections and investments of American culture as they can about the mechanisms of slavery today. This book reveals the striking resonances between nineteenth- and twenty-first-century slave narratives, but it is also concerned with the very peculiar cultural and political contexts that have encouraged the reemergence of the genre at this particular moment. In part, this project grew out of a frustration with the way antislavery discourse in the United States and around the world so often appropriates survivors' experiences for ends that are often at cross-purposes with the narratives themselves—waging quiet Islamophobic wars in Africa, marginalizing voluntary sex workers, profiteering for otherwise-impotent nonprofits. This book is a result of my committed and rigorous engagement, as a scholar and an activist, with the narratives of survivors of contemporary slavery in an effort to wrestle with these pervasive and divisive controversies.

It is my unflagging belief that slavery is not a subject about which a scholar should be unbiased or dispassionate. I am close to these narratives both temporally and politically, and my perspective is inflected with this immediacy. I consider myself an antislavery activist, someone who believes that slavery is a violation of fundamental human rights and who has committed my life to finding ways to make my work directly and indirectly lessen the suffering of those who have endured it. I have interacted professionally with several of the organizations discussed in this book, and I have close intellectual and personal relationships with survivors and activists who represent very different, even opposing, factions of the revivified antislavery movement. This means that at times I may be more explicit regarding my political commitments than the typical scholar, in part as a way of making clear the contentious terrain upon which the slave narrative functions in the twenty-first century. Indeed, as much as participating in a divisive movement is a seemingly unavoidable aspect of the slave narrative tradition, making those divisions transparent is a necessary aspect of the tradition of the scholar of the slave narrative.

In an effort at full disclosure, however, I want to note that I have worked with several antislavery organizations that are relevant to this project. During graduate school, I briefly interned with the American Anti-Slavery Group, whose ideological approach is critiqued in these pages, and my job for four months was to assist them in the production of a highly edited (and at times fictionalized) collection of narratives entitled *Enslaved.* I soon quit that position, however, when I learned about the anti-Islamic politics of many who worked there and was ignored in my pleas that they stop embellishing survivor narratives. I later volunteered for and made financial contributions to Free the Slaves, another nonprofit antislavery organization discussed in this text. Between 2008 and 2010, I assisted them in small writing projects, assisted in the development of a university chapter program, and visited one of their partner organizations. I have collaborated with or interacted with many other antislavery organizations in the United States and abroad in the process of my scholarship and activism over the course of the last fifteen years. The twenty-first-century antislavery movement—if it can even be described as a singular entity—is a vast and varied creature. I will not pretend to agree with everyone or suggest that I share anything in common with all the players except, perhaps, an interest in eradicating exploitative labor practices. Nonetheless, my attempt here is to present a fair and respectful critique of a movement that is fraught, divided, rapidly changing, and constantly expanding. Most importantly, my goal is to put survivor voices at the center of the discussion of this movement, even when those voices are in friction with elites in the movement, with each other, or with me.

In some instances, my definition of slavery differs from that of the new slave narrators, sometimes radically. There have been journalists and academics who have doubted the veracity of certain slave narrators' claims of enslavement in part because of these differences. Nonetheless, I will not pass judgment on whether someone qualifies as a survivor of slavery or make any claims as to the veracity of any of the texts discussed in this book. As an academic, I am much more interested in understanding the "suspicious reading" habits of those who consume the slave narrative than I am concerned about the truth of any individual narrative.[4] At the same time, as an activist and a person committed to the humane and just treatment of others, I would rather take the slight risk of believing a dissembling survivor's word than protect my own reputation by suggesting that someone's trauma was not, in fact, her own. This means that readers will not find in these pages any final discovery that puts to rest the debates as to the truth value of any individual life narrative discussed here. Instead, my aim is to suggest—through discussing this now relatively large body of texts, many of which have been critiqued for various faults, mistakes, or misrecollections—that the genre of the slave narrative is one that is always characterized by its omissions, reversals, and anxieties, a fact that is more likely rooted in the nature of slavery, the conventions of the genre, and the pressures put upon the narrators by publishers and the public than it is in the nature of any individual human who chooses to tell a story of slavery.

Along similar lines, even as I dissect the varied discourses and ideologies that influence or are even imposed upon the narratives, I will not be lured into the tempting quicksand of determining authorship in these complicated, often collaboratively authored texts. In the narratives that are explicitly ghostwritten or coauthored by formerly enslaved people and activists, it is impossible to know which of the sentiments or turns of phrase can appropriately be attributed to the first-person narrator and which to the coauthor (and, in the final chapter, the tensions in multivocal narration as a result of ghostwriting will be discussed at length). Even those narratives which are single authored or self-published have often been edited by colleagues, friends, or professionals, who may have encouraged the deployment of certain tropes or language. All the narrators, regardless of the processes of composition or publication, spoke before audiences about their experiences in slavery and were no doubt shaped by what seemed most compelling to those who attended and have often been coached by organizations regarding the most effective shape, style, and elements of their stories. None of this necessarily compromises the narrators' voices or ideas or negates the agency of the slave narrators, but it certainly does complicate them. The slave narrative is a "rich performance of the negotiations, collaborations, usurpations, and performed mysteries of form."[5] This collaborated and negotiated testimony is indicative of all life narratives—we are all constantly shaping and honing what we tell of our lives based on other people's responses and the concerns and purposes that others bring to the interactive act of communicating one's life. As a result, however, the critic is largely unable to determine when an amanuensis may have intervened in a narrative, and we cannot know when any particular conception of slavery may have been introduced to the narrators. Instead, we can interrogate the seeming tensions in the texts and use them as a window into the ideological underpinnings of slavery and antislavery discourse. Unpacking those tensions is one of the primary aims of this project.

As was the case for Peabody's research on the slave narrative, it is quite early to begin this work, and I am intellectually pained to recognize that the genre is still developing and that new narratives are written each month, which makes it difficult to make claims about the genre as a whole. It is impossible within the confines of this one book to discuss substantively all the narratives that have emerged in the last twenty years even (see the appendix for a list of all the narratives that have been considered in the formation of the ideas contained here). This book focuses, then, on outlining the generic contours of the genre as it has developed to this point and engaging in some of the most significant debates that have grown up around renewed activism against slavery. Still, what I take from Peabody's own mistakes and misjudgments is a warning that I, too, will find that some of the ideas and conclusions set forth here will seem premature at some point in the future. I eagerly look forward to that moment and to the conversations and debates that I suspect a rigorous reading of the new slave narrative will inspire.

THE NEW SLAVE NARRATIVE

INTRODUCTION

The Reemergence of the Slave Narrative in the Twenty-First Century

What was still not clear to me was that this was my first day of slavery—being forced to work for no payment but the garbage from the family's dinner and an occasional beating from Giemma's big cattle whip.

—FRANCIS BOK, *ESCAPE FROM SLAVERY* (2003)

I often found myself wondering if Dred Scott had endured the same cruelties to which I had been subjected as a child slave on the impoverished island of Haiti. . . . I wondered if slavery had stolen every moment of his childhood, as it had mine. I wondered if, like me, he had been taken away from his family as a toddler, never to lay eyes on them for the next thirty years. I struggled to interweave the history of slavery in the United States with my own background, because child slavery was then, and is *to this moment*, being practiced in all areas of Haiti.

—JEAN-ROBERT CADET, *MY STONE OF HOPE* (2011)

But often reporters want a "sexy project," something hot, to wake up the readers and viewers. They ask me to talk about my past—if not, how will they convey the importance of the work we're doing? That's one of the reasons I decided to write this book. Perhaps it will stop me from having to tell my story over and over again, because repeating it is very difficult.

—SOMALY MAM, *THE ROAD OF LOST INNOCENCE* (2009)

According to his autobiography, Piol Buk was enslaved at the age of seven when a band of unfamiliar men descended on the village market and began torturing and murdering his neighbors. He writes, "How did I feel? People always ask me how I felt at that moment, and all I can answer is that I had never felt such terror, confusion, and helplessness before—or again. . . . I felt so many feelings at once that I suddenly felt nothing. My entire body and mind turned numb as I waited to be killed."[1] Terrified, Buk managed to coax his body to run. But a man spotted him before he could hide, and he was captured, thrown over the back of a horse, and carried to a distant, unknown land.

For the following ten years, Buk was held captive by a family who claimed to own him, though he had never known it was possible for one human being to own another. This cruel "owner" and his family spoke an incomprehensible language, beat Buk at the slightest offense, and treated him as if he were equal to the animals he was forced to tend from before dawn until well after night fell. He soon learned why the family he served refused to call him by his given name and referred to him only as *abeed* instead—"it meant both 'black person' and 'slave,'" he recounts.[2] Enslaved, he was not allowed to speak to other people from his homeland, and he was forbidden to practice any of his cultural traditions while in the service of these cruel masters.

Buk constantly dreamed of escaping, but his initial attempts were thwarted by his owners' persistent surveillance and his own inability to navigate the landscape. He tells us in the book-length narrative of his life, "I soon realized that, while the pain and fear came and went, the one thing that never seemed to go away was the ache of wanting to escape this place where I was forced to work and live like an animal."[3] When he finally managed to escape by running away from the field where he was sent to tend animals, the first people he turned to for help—the police—reenslaved him. After another dangerous escape, he found a succession of kind people who were willing to assist his long route to freedom, which eventually led him to Boston. There, his generous new friends, members of local faith communities and activists in the antislavery movement, encouraged him to write what he titled his "true story" with the help of a ghostwriter, and he began to speak on a lecture circuit. His autobiography, written using his Christian name, Francis Bok, motivated prominent legislators and politicians to speak out against slavery. He quickly realized that "my feelings became their feelings. My passion became theirs."[4] He became something of a celebrity and even shook the hand of the president of the United States, but he remained steadfast in his commitment to ensuring the freedom of all people who were enslaved as he had been.

Buk's story is eerily recognizable for many scholars of transatlantic slavery. It is powerfully reminiscent of Olaudah Equiano's narrative of childhood capture in Africa, Venture Smith's narrative of the surprise raid on his African village, and Baquaqua's long road of enslavement through Western Africa before he reached the shores of the Atlantic and the Middle Passage. It resonates with stories such as those told by Frederick Douglass or Harriet Jacobs of their struggles to liberate themselves and of the abolitionists who supported their routes to freedom, activism, and the publication of their memoirs. Narratives of courageous enslaved Africans and African Americans like these flourished in the late eighteenth and early nineteenth centuries in the United States and Europe, shaping the antislavery movement and influencing the legal eradication of institutionalized slavery around the world.

Indeed, much of Buk's slave narrative could have described an experience of capture and enslavement in 1787; instead, it took place two hundred years later. Francis Bok (born Piol Bol Buk) published his slave narrative titled *Escape from Slavery: The True Story of My Ten Years in Captivity—and My Journey to Freedom in America* in 2003. The story Bok tells is one that has become increasingly familiar in recent decades. Those who are enslaved today—people who are forced to work against their will for the benefit of another without the ability to walk away—are not typically subjects of the kind of institutionalized legal slavery that prevailed in the nineteenth-century United States but are often held captive in forms of slavery that are less readily recognized or remedied because their exploitation is illegal and therefore remains hidden by employers. Today's enslaved laborers work in a wide variety of legitimate workplaces—in agricultural fields, on construction sites, in quarries, in brothels, on the battlefield, in the homes of the wealthy. In the cases of slavery that have emerged in the last twenty years, employers in these familiar settings have physically and psychologically coerced people into situations of forced labor and have maintained complete control over the workers' lives and over the economic proceeds of their labor.

Bok's story and his experiences of forced labor resonated with the narratives of nineteenth-century slavery to such an extent that his editors at St. Martin's Press gave first priority on the paperback cover to the *Boston Globe* reviewer who announced the book as "a touching modern day slave narrative." Bok's narrative was written, in collaboration with a nonprofit and a coauthor, with the express intent of producing a slave narrative that would speak to contemporary forms of slavery and excite a renewed antislavery sentiment. For its gravity and legibility, his narrative relied on a slave narrative tradition that served as the foundation of earlier global antislavery movements. Scholars have identified approximately two hundred narratives authored by formerly enslaved people during the era of transatlantic slavery. In the eighteenth and nineteenth centuries, formerly enslaved people published their stories in popular magazines and oversubscribed books, including a few in Africa and Latin America; they spoke on lecture circuits in the United States, England, and Europe; they provided testimony that supported abolitionist organizations in their collective fight to end slavery. According to Frances Smith Foster, if we also count the narratives collected by the Works Progress Administration in the 1930s, there are nearly six thousand first-person narratives about the experience of slavery in the Americas, ranging from short interviews to four-hundred-page published tomes.[5] The voices and the written words of formerly enslaved people were wielded as political power, and that power was used to emancipate millions of others who suffered in bondage and later under Jim Crow. From Briton Hammon's *Narrative of the Uncommon Sufferings, and Surprizing Deliverance of Briton Hammon, a Negro Man*, published in Boston in 1760, to the Works Progress Administration narratives, which include nearly 2,300 accounts told by survivors of antebellum slavery who remained alive in the 1930s, first-person autobiographical recollections of slavery have remained central to both activist efforts to eradicate slavery and to historical accountings of the past.

IF SLAVERY STILL EXISTS . . .

This book, then, emerges from a simple question: If slavery still exists, then does the slave narrative still exist? The simple affirmative answer to that question, for which Bok's narrative is clear evidence, leads immediately to others. What does it mean to tell the story of slavery in the twenty-first century? How does this "new slave narrative" take up the tropes of its predecessor, and in what ways do the material realities of the twenty-first century encourage its divergence? How has the reinvigorated use of the term "slavery" affected the ways survivors of forced labor have understood and represented their lives? How have survivors mobilized the concept of slavery and the discourse of antislavery to effect change in both their own lives and the lives of others? And in what ways have slave narratives—so central to the nineteenth-century abolitionist movement—been employed and appropriated by the newly resuscitated antislavery movement?

This book is about the discourse that has been driven by the reemergence of the concept of "slavery" as it describes contemporary forms of forced labor. It is particularly focused on the ways the experience of slavery has been articulated by those who have experienced it firsthand and the ways their narratives have been consumed and employed by antislavery advocates. Through reading these new slave narratives, it is possible to discern the way a renewed commitment to the intellectual frameworks that "slavery" provides has catapulted us into a new era, radically altering discussions of labor, rights, migration, and sex. This book charts, analyzes, and critiques some of those discursive transformations. I do not seek to answer the question "What is contemporary slavery?" Nor do I attempt to quantify the problem, describe or analyze its mechanisms, determine its relevance in the economy, or tell a comprehensive history of the antislavery movement. This book aims instead to provide a careful analysis of the new slave narrative and its production, circulation, influence, and co-optation. In doing so, I undertake the crucial task of examining the discourses of modern slavery that make possible the articulation of the economic, political, and power relations that undergird slavery as well as those that animate contemporary antislavery activism.

As the first extended study that reads this diverse range of texts describing forced labor in the late twentieth and early twenty-first centuries as the reemergence of the genre of the slave narrative, this book provides a framework for analyzing the autobiographical representation of contemporary forms of slavery contextualized within the contemporary literary, political, religious, cultural, and commercial circumstances that have encouraged the genre's renaissance as well as within the history of slavery and the slave narrative.[6] The analysis interweaves three significant threads: (1) the description and analysis of the tropes, themes, forms, and aesthetic conventions of the new slave narrative; (2) a historical approach that both connects the new slave narrative to the eighteenth- and nineteenth-century tradition of slave testimony and contextualizes it within the animating forces of contemporary antislavery advocacy; and (3) a critique of the deployment and sometimes exploitation of these narratives by activists, the media, and cultural producers for their own political goals and audiences. In the process, I describe the contours of the new slave narrative, arguing that the genre found fertile ground in the early twenty-first century through a confluence of seemingly unrelated cultural forces, including the voyeurism of the "memoir boom," the academic and popular resurgence of the discourse of "slavery," the birth and rapid expansion of a nonprofit antislavery industry, post-9/11 anti-Muslim sentiments, and a growing conservative campaign for "family values" and against sex work.

I argue that it is no coincidence that the new slave narrative begins to flourish as a means of promoting a wide variety of political causes in the first years of the twenty-first century because the contemporary antislavery sphere in which it circulates is a product of a curious and precarious alliance that emerges from a unique political atmosphere. The issue of modern slavery uncomfortably unites the international aid community, liberal human rights activists, and antioppression activists with an extensive network of Christian evangelicals, a small group of radical Zionists, and freedom-obsessed neoliberals. This book seeks to analyze the complex political terrain upon which these narratives are operating and, in doing so, interrogate the precarity of the very freedoms their narrators seek. In the final analysis, the study of these memoirs as slave narratives reveals that the politics of genre are as central to our understanding of slavery, freedom, and abolition in our time as they were in the nineteenth century.

This book is very much concerned with the way the life narratives of people of color, people from the Global South, and women are circumscribed by the production values, political investments, and prurient interests that have always drawn Western audiences to the slave narrative.[7] Which lives get narrated for publication, which survivors are held up as exemplars, and which forms, experiences, and durations of slavery are considered worthy of our concern are determined by a publishing apparatus that seems committed to the dissemination of individualist, capitalist values through the publication of what Leigh Gilmore calls "neoliberal life narratives," which represent the potential and the necessity of individual uplift.[8] As such, those who are survivors of slavery and seek publication of their life narratives must establish themselves first as having lived lives worth reading. To do that, new slave narrators must conform to certain generic expectations, which may or may not allow them to conform to the realities of their lived experiences. As will be demonstrated throughout this book, for women and people of color—who make up the vast majority of victims of contemporary slavery—the radical dissonance between the expectations of masculinist subjectivity that are so central to life narratives and the realities of their lives and politics typically leads to silence or to a very complex relationship to the narration of one's life. Of course, the narrative of uplift that is common to the autobiography belies the capitalist structures that make slavery possible, collective resistance inconceivable, and systemic injustice invisible. As a result, many of the narratives, even while conforming to certain genre conventions, necessarily provide alternative visions of freedom, agency, and activism that are in tension with the form and structure of the narrative, which seem bent toward the exultation of freedom and individual subjectivity.

THE REEMERGENCE OF A GENRE

Because there is no doubt that people who are enslaved, like all other humans, have told life stories either in personal or public settings throughout human history, Joe Lockard contends in his review of Bok's narrative that the slave narrative never died.[9] In that people were enslaved throughout the twentieth century and spoke and wrote about their experiences, he is certainly correct. People we might now consider enslaved—including Japan's "comfort women," conscripted laborers in colonial West Africa, "coolie" laborers from South Asia, and migrants forced into unpaid domestic and agricultural labor worldwide—certainly shared their life experiences with others and protested their work conditions in the twentieth century.[10] While slavery itself is not new—indeed forms of slavery persisted worldwide throughout the years between the Great Depression and the end of the Cold War—few if any sustained first-person narratives have mobilized the language of slavery and the conventions of the slave narrative as a political weapon as the nineteenth-century slave narrators did.

In the late 1990s and early 2000s, however, as a renewed social movement resurfaced to respond to this human rights issue that came to be commonly known as "modern slavery," survivors of forced labor began to write first-person, nonfiction life narratives revealing the details of experiences they deemed slavery. At least forty-one book-length narratives (written by thirty-six distinct authors) depicting experiences of contemporary forms of slavery have been published since that time, and three edited collections add more than 150 shorter narratives to the archive.[11] If we count all the book-length, nonfiction, first-person narratives; the shorter narratives included in the edited collections; and other first-person testimonies collected in court documents, public records, or online fora, at least three hundred narratives of contemporary slavery have been published since 1991. The published long-form narratives currently in circulation were written by people who were enslaved in Sudan, Nigeria, Uganda, Cambodia, North Korea, Hungary, Iraq, Syria, Thailand, Lebanon, Yemen, Haiti, France, England, and the United States. The labor they depict takes place on farms and battlefields, in hotels and private homes. The majority of them were originally published in the United States and Britain, in express pursuit of the abolition of forced labor and sexual enslavement.[12] These narratives were written as testaments to the fact that slavery exists in every part of the world and takes shapes that are both familiar and unfamiliar to scholars of transatlantic slavery.

Until recently, these twenty-first-century slave narratives have been read as human rights narratives, "maternal melodramas," child soldier narratives, or stories of sexual exploitation and abuse.[13] Collecting and analyzing these first-person narratives of forced labor under the rubric of the slave narrative recognizes the claims of their authors that what they are experiencing and testifying to is, in fact, slavery. What unite the first-person life narratives studied here are the narrators' explicit depictions of their experiences as enslavement not only through asserting the compulsory and dehumanizing nature of the labor but also by explicitly describing their experiences as "slavery" or comparing their lives to those of the historical slave narrators. In the epigraph that opens this chapter, Francis Bok reveals that he understood the word "slavery" to be a discovery—something that he boldly declares his experience to have been today but that was inconceivable to him when he was first captured. To assure us that this was no childish mistake, he offers up as evidence the fact that the family who held him captive actually called him "abeed," the Arabic word for slave, from the moment he arrived. Mobilizing the word "slavery" empowers Bok and the other new slave narrators to come to terms with their experiences of labor subjugation and enables them to articulate the nearly incomprehensible violence that was inflicted on them. The very victims of forced labor themselves evoke the language, the generic conventions, and the history of slavery and the slave narrative as a way of accurately describing their experiences, making their lives legible, and inspiring activist momentum for a renewed antislavery agenda. Intrigued by their self-identification, I aim to analyze the implications of this development.

In an effort to analyze the deliberate deployment of the idea of slavery and the renewed investment in the genre of the slave narrative and to lay a foundation for future study of the genre, I have decided to focus exclusively on texts in which authors self-identify their experiences as slavery. This is not to suggest, however, that this list is definitive or that these are the only texts that *should* be considered slave narratives. If one were to include all those first-person, book-length memoirs in which narrators tell stories of slavery fitting a particular definition of "slavery" without invoking the word itself, the list might also include several child soldier narratives that describe forced, conscripted military service as well as a number of narratives of forced or coerced sexual labor that do not explicitly use the word "slavery" to describe those practices.[14] However, because this is an early investigation into this emerging genre and because there is such debate regarding the parameters of slavery in the contemporary context, I believe it is a useful exercise to focus attention on those narrators who self-identify their experiences as slavery. This limitation runs the risk of excluding some texts that certainly describe experiences of forced labor, but it avoids the risk of imposing the concept of "slavery" as well as the form of the slave narrative upon those writers.

In the tradition of the American slave narrative, these authors see their memoirs as activist testimonies committed to explaining and eradicating slavery around the world today. The texts studied here typically shape themselves as slave narratives in their paratextual apparatus, their narrative conventions, and in the evocation of the nineteenth-century tradition. They employ many of the same strategies, themes, tropes, and narrative devices found in antebellum American slave narratives, which were first described by critics such as Frances Smith Foster, William L. Andrews, Henry Louis Gates Jr., Sidonie Smith, John Blassingame and others.[15] As James Olney has so astutely outlined, the slave narratives of the nineteenth century followed fairly consistent structures and plot conventions, and the twenty-first-century narrators (both wittingly and unwittingly) replicate many of those trends.[16] Formerly enslaved people tell of their experiences of being captured, transported, and sold or traded like animals. As was the case in the nineteenth century, slave narrators today describe forced labor in a wide variety of fields—domestic work, agricultural labor, military service, entertainment, sex work, factory labor—and the diverse but entrenched structures of power that allowed others to maintain control over them. They paint literary portraits of the purportedly upstanding or pious community members who enslaved them as well as the subordinate and complicit captives who subverted their escapes, the suffering laborers who had given up hope, and the powerful and resistant ones who inspired them. They often thematize the liberatory potential of literacy, education, and religion, all of which were denied them in captivity. More than any other aspect of their lives in bondage, slave narrators typically linger on their persistent obsession with escape and freedom, depicting the failed plots they concocted as well as those that eventually led to a route to liberation. The generous citizens and neighbors who helped them to freedom are figured as heroes in many of the narratives, and the authors' drive to activism and public life is depicted as a necessary responsibility of freedom. The conclusions to their narratives often invoke a personal but public rededication through narrative to the eradication of injustice and inequality in the world. Their books act as material representations of their commitment to social justice.

EARLY ITERATIONS

It seems likely that it was in 1991, when Zana Muhsen published *Sold: One Woman's True Account of Modern Slavery*, a first-person account of her experience as an involuntary child bride in Yemen, that a generically self-conscious slave narrative tradition first began to resurface.[17] Though her status as "enslaved" might be debated by some, Muhsen's book marks a significant turning point in the history of the representation of slavery. It is the first book-length, first-person narrative to be published for a general readership that purports to document modern slavery in the late twentieth century that I have been able to locate. Muhsen's title alone, which indicates both that she was sold as a commodity and that she considers her situation to have been "modern slavery," reveals that she intended to invoke the gravity of the historic institution.[18] In her narrative, Muhsen, who grew up in England, writes that she "remembered Kunte Kinte, the slave in *Roots* who tried to run away from the plantation where he had been taken," aligning herself with the popular imagination of slavery and fugitive escapees in circulation in the 1970s and '80s.[19] She reflects that she "had no way of knowing how relevant [*Roots*] would be" to her own life when she first read Alex Haley's epic novel of the slave trade, but in her own autobiography, she links her life and the story told in *Roots* as a means of legitimizing her claim that forced child marriage is tantamount to slavery.[20] Though Muhsen could never be credited with a global social justice mission targeted at eradicating all slavery, she dedicated her life in freedom and the proceeds of her life story to rescuing her family members from captivity, as Venture Smith, Moses Grandy, Lunsford Lane, and so many eighteenth- and nineteenth-century slave narrators did before her.[21]

Though Muhsen's narrative gained traction in England and France and helped her gain support for liberating her sister and her children, it did not immediately inspire a new trend or renewed interest in the slave narrative tradition. Her autobiography, categorized as a women's rights narrative or a child-marriage narrative and shelved next to other sensationalized and widely disparaged memoirs such as *Not Without My Daughter*, went largely unnoticed by newly emerging antislavery advocates.[22] That, in conjunction with controversies that sprang up around Muhsen's sister's denial of her forced captivity and Muhsen's hiring of mercenaries, made her an unlikely candidate for emulation among survivors of slavery and human rights groups.[23]

Later in the 1990s, however, a diverse set of cultural and political actors emerged who designated the experiences of coerced sex work, debt bondage, conscripted military service, and other forms of forced labor as "slavery." The slave narrative was quickly mobilized as a major vehicle for circulating that shift in understanding. The slave narrative is a genre driven not solely by the fact that its protagonist narrator is held in forced labor and seeks freedom; it is equally defined by its ambition, its desire to affect an audience. As Audrey Fisch notes, "First and foremost, the slave narrative is a text with a purpose: the end of slavery."[24] The long-form slave narrative, in particular, mobilizes the gravity of the story of captivity and the word "slavery" to provoke complacent citizens and nations to action (whereas a short-form narrative might be written or told solely as a testimony for courts, asylum, or nonprofits). It capitalizes on the narrator's ability to create an identification between herself and her audience that will compel free citizens toward change and justice for those who remain unfree. Muhsen may have been relatively unique in 1991 in her usage of the term "slavery" to describe her experience of forced labor and in her attempt to ignite activism around her experience, but she was not alone for long.

In 1998 Jean-Robert Cadet's *Restavec: From Haitian Slave Child to Middle-Class American* was published, once again evoking the power of the word "slave," this time to describe the forced labor he experienced in his foster family in Haiti.[25] Cadet describes his white father's abandonment of him and his subsequent servitude to a woman named Florence who denied him his humanity and his rights. He spent his days and nights working at her command, and when he made even the slightest mistakes, he was demeaned and brutally assaulted. He was only able to escape when Florence moved to the United States, where she was no longer able to maintain her absolute control over the young boy. Cadet describes the psychological barriers he faced in his attempt to live as a free individual, but he eventually managed to turn his pain to activism for other children. Cadet's life story—of a forced domestic child laborer of African descent who fought his way out of captivity and into a role as an abolitionist—struck many as recognizably a story of slavery and closely aligned with the slave narrative tradition. For many Western audiences, it seems that slavery is most legible when the enslaved person is of African descent. Cadet was able to build a movement and start a nonprofit based on his ability to compellingly and convincingly describe slavery in the late twentieth century, which may have led to the success of his book and his activist career.

Muhsen's and Cadet's texts largely stood alone until the beginning of the twenty-first century. As Cadet's book was gaining traction in human rights circles, Bok's *Escape from Slavery* and Mende Nazer's *Slave: My True Story* were published in 2003, both explicitly evoking the concept of enslavement to describe the captivity and forced labor of Southern Sudanese children during the civil war.[26] Bok and Nazer both relate their disorientation as their villages were raided, they were sold into slavery, and they were alienated from the security and rootedness of their homes by the conflict in Sudan. Whereas Bok was forced into slavery in agriculture and herding, Nazer was made a forced domestic servant in the home of a wealthy family in Khartoum. She was only able to escape when she was sent to serve a family in London, where she managed to relay her experience to a Sudanese man she met while running errands for the family. Both Bok's and Nazer's books were published in conjunction with activists and nonprofits as concerns about the civil war in Sudan were circulating in the United States and Britain. Both authors found themselves thrust into the spotlight as conservative and liberal nonprofits alike sought to use their stories of enslavement as identifiable representations of the repressive regime of Omar al-Bashir. Both testified before governments, met with prominent officials, and spoke on lecture circuits in an effort to end both slavery and government oppression in Sudan.

Following on the success they had in supporting the publication of Bok's narrative, the nongovernmental organization American Anti-Slavery Group published a collection of shorter narratives titled *Enslaved: True Stories of Modern Day Slavery* in 2006.[27] These narratives, along with Bok's and Nazer's, were widely distributed under the moniker of "slave narratives" and inspired the publishing industry to take note of the popular potential for such narratives. In the years following the publication of Bok's narrative, survivors of varied forms of slavery began to author their memoirs as part of activist campaigns. Several narratives of conscripted child soldiering began attracting commercial audiences and popular media attention as well. While Ishmael Beah's *A Long Way Gone* (2007) does not mention slavery by name, it has been read by other critics as a narrative of enslavement and drew significant public attention to the forced captivity and labor of child soldiers. A lesser-known contributor to that conversation, Grace Akallo's *Girl Soldier* (2007), describes both forced child soldiering and sexual enslavement under the Lord's Resistance Army in Uganda during the civil war. Her book, discussed at length in chapter 3, depicts the overlap between sexual and labor enslavement for young women on the battlefield and provides an intimate portrait of harrowing escape through the desert to freedom, and it was written specifically to call attention to the plight of Uganda's children during conflict. By 2008, one of the most widely read of the new slave narratives, Somaly Mam's *Road of Lost Innocence*, was published in the United States (an earlier version with a different coauthor was previously published in France with a much more limited circulation). Mam's story opened Westerners' eyes to the conditions in Cambodia's brothels, where Mam recounted being forced to sell sex for several years as a teenager. Her book, which is the focus of chapter 5, was later indicted for inaccuracies and exaggerations. By 2010 at least eleven new slave narratives had been published in the United States, the United Kingdom, and France, representing child soldiering, forced sexual labor, domestic servitude, and child marriage around the globe. Five of those narratives were about people who were African, and another one was about Haiti, signaling the effect that race had on people's conception of slavery in the early years of the new slave narrative. Only one narrative told a story of sexual enslavement located in the United States, and another one described slavery in the United Kingdom. Before 2010, there were about an equal number of texts focused on labor as there were on sex slavery, and men's narratives, few as they may have been, were given significant public and nonprofit attention. The narratives represented a diverse conception of "slavery" and its manifestations.

Since 2011, when Rachel Lloyd's narrative of forced sexual labor, *Girls Like Us*, attracted a wide readership,[28] the trend in the slave narratives has shifted dramatically. In its second significant decade of existence, the new slave narrative moved toward narratives of exploitation in the sex trade, with increasing numbers of women from the United States and the United Kingdom taking advantage of an ever-expanding publishing terrain and a public outcry against to the domestic sexual exploitation of minor girls. After 2011, child-soldier narratives dropped off, as did child-labor narratives. Stories of men's forced labor have almost disappeared, and stories of men's forced sexual labor have never really appeared at all. The twenty-six new narratives published in the 2010s are almost exclusively written about sex trafficking, and white women from the United States and the United Kingdom currently dominate the genre. As I will discuss in chapter 4, their narratives follow a relatively conventional autobiographical plotline in which naïve life mistakes lead to horrific consequences in which they are forced to engage in the sex trade, but through incredible determination, faith, and personal responsibility, they rise from the victimization of their youth to become powerful feminist advocates. Prominent survivor activists such as Rachel Lloyd and Carissa Phelps published narratives depicting sexual captivity with major presses after 2010, while other active survivor advocates, including Barbara Amaya, Katariina Rosenblatt, and Brook Parker-Bello turned to micropresses, religious presses, and self-publishing platforms in their efforts to share their testimonies.[29] Global narratives of sexual enslavement have also been published, primarily focused on regions of the world where the United States is engaged in conflict—North Korea, Iraq, and Syria in particular. Those narratives recount young women's captivity by repressive regimes or by opportunistic bystanders who use sexual exploitation as a means of political and ethnic subordination. Their escapes typically depend on their rescue by religious or political groups who assist them in migrating to the West. Only four of the narratives published during this period depict labor trafficking exclusively, and all but one of those narratives are by women. In the years since 2010, the diversity of the archive of slavery and the slave narrative has been considerably constricted.

Nonetheless, since the publication of the two Sudanese narratives, hardly a year has gone by without the publication of at least one new slave narrative, and by 2015, several were emerging each year, encouraged by an ever-expanding publication terrain. In this book, I will be concentrating on the forty-one book-length narratives written by thirty-six individual authors that had been published through the summer of 2018 (when this book was submitted for publication), but new narratives that could potentially be included emerge regularly. Readers should consult the appendix for a list of all narratives included in this study. The book-length narratives differ from the shorter slave narratives that have been collected by nonprofits or in court testimony in that they are typically more explicitly intended by their authors to provoke a political response through the narration of a first-person experience of enslavement. Whereas the narratives presented in collections, in court proceedings, or for the use of nonprofits may have been offered by the survivor with a variety of purposes in mind—gaining asylum, accessing services, prosecuting a trafficker—the narratives composed as books have the express purpose of effecting change and thus represent a particular strain or body of slave narrative. There are many aspects of these texts that are worthy of critical pursuit, but I have foregrounded dominant areas of inquiry and debate here in this first foray. This book is meant to serve as a starting point for a discussion of the "new slave narrative" and as a transition point for the scholarship surrounding the study of the slave narrative, and as such, it cannot aim to account for all narratives and all aspects of the narratives given the constraints of publication.

This book focuses on book-length narratives because they are more deliberately shaped as slave narratives, but this must not be taken to represent all the voices of the enslaved. Book-length new slave narratives appear at this time to be a phenomenon that exists almost exclusively in the United States, the United Kingdom, and France, and even there, publication is afforded by only a small number of presses and to only a select group of survivors.[30] In the twenty-first century, as was the case in the nineteenth, the people who have been enslaved and have escaped to talk about it and who then gain access to the machinery of publication are relatively privileged, and thus they cannot be considered representative of all the people who are enslaved in the world today. "Fugitive testimony"—the memoirs of those lucky enough to escape slavery—is overrepresented in our understanding of antebellum U.S. slavery, and it certainly is of today's slavery as well. The stories that even the privileged few get to tell of their slavery and freedom are nonetheless radically constrained. Despite the wide range of voices, forms of slavery, and geographical locations that the new slave narratives represent, there are many voices that are not heard in book-length narratives and will only be locatable in the interstices of the arguments forwarded here. Perhaps it will come as no surprise that there are no book-length narratives written by people who remain enslaved today or even by survivors who are not connected to some activist or nonprofit work on slavery. There will be few international narratives published in the West by people who were enslaved in countries that are considered insignificant in respect to the major foreign policy priorities of Western nations. There are particular narratives and narrative conventions that have gained traction and that provide the details that make slavery legible in our society and that highlight particular political investments. One of the aims of this book is to make those predilections and privileges explicit in order to consider how our knowledge of slavery is constructed by a very particular set of cultural impulses and generic conventions.

WHY NOW?

The rise in publication of new slave narratives in the United States and Britain can be attributed to a constellation of phenomena that has encouraged survivors to testify and created Western audiences that are eager to learn more about contemporary forms of slavery. The issue of modern slavery made a significant claim on the attention of American scholars and activists with the publication of Kevin Bales's *Disposable People: New Slavery in the Global Economy* in 1999. Encouraged by Anti-Slavery International's continuous 150-year commitment to fighting slavery globally, Bales insisted on the use of the word "slavery" to describe forced labor in diverse environments. Though he was certainly not a pioneer in analyzing forced labor, his articulation of the most extreme forms of labor exploitation as "slavery" garnered significant interest in a public that considered slavery to have been long eradicated. In his accessible scholarly work, Bales, a sociologist, first provided statistical evidence that at least twenty-seven million people were enslaved—a number that would quickly become both a refrain and a point of contention that animated antislavery advocates in the early years of the movement's resurgence.[31] The revitalized usage of the words "slavery" and "abolition" found currency among academic, activist, and media circles. Informed by the history of abolition and the work of eighteenth- and nineteenth-century reformers such as William Lloyd Garrison and Thomas Clarkson, Bales's abolitionist argument (as well as the work of the organization that resulted from his research, Free the Slaves) was founded on close attention to the first-person testimonies and experiences of enslaved people. Though his work is a source of persistent debate within the field, before Bales's *Disposable People* was published, the issues of forced sex work and involuntary labor were often siloed in expert circles, largely discussed only in regard to the Global South, and were relatively obscure to the general public. The popularity of his work reached survivors who were often eager to tell their stories and to collaborate with Free the Slaves in the expansion of antislavery efforts in their home countries. Organizations in Asia, the Caribbean, and West Africa were simultaneously founded by survivors like Jean-Robert Cadet who used their expertise on the issue to determine strategies for addressing trafficking and promoted their own life narratives as means to raise funds. Thus it was that the popular imagination of contemporary forms of slavery in the twenty-first century largely emerged as a result of a nonprofit industry that circulated those narratives and other awareness-raising materials drawn from survivor experiences. The films and written narratives that organizations like Free the Slaves produced and scholars like Bales included in their writing represented some of the first slave narratives to reach Western audiences in nearly seventy-five years.

The sudden reinvigoration of the antislavery movement in the United States and Britain in the late 1990s and early 2000s was no doubt extraordinarily influential in precipitating this literary trend and in mobilizing the word "slavery" as a tool for engaging activist supporters. Early in the short history of this contemporary antislavery movement, most slave narrators were recruited from among antislavery organizations' contacts and were championed by particular groups. The nascent movement was eager to enlist survivors to raise awareness and rouse donor sympathies. Bok rose to prominence, for instance, through the assistance of the American Anti-Slavery Group (AASG), whose founder, Charles Jacobs, told him that his story would put "a human face on slavery in Sudan."[32] Evangelical historian Allen Hertzke gives sole credit to the "singular contribution" of Jacobs to mobilize the slave narrative to the cause of the Southern Sudanese.[33]

Within two years, Bok was a regular on the human rights lecture circuit. He testified before legislative bodies and is touted as being the first formerly enslaved person to meet a U.S. president since the nineteenth century. Bok's book was soon considered required reading for antislavery activists. AASG also supported Beatrice Fernando, a victim of forced domestic labor in Lebanon, in her efforts to launch an antislavery speaking career. She self-published her memoir, *In Contempt of Fate: The Tale of a Sri Lankan Sold into Servitude, Who Survived to Tell It*, in 2005 before she launched her own nonprofit organization called Nivasa to help enslaved domestic laborers from Sri Lanka.[34] In the next year, AASG published their own collection of shorter narratives, proclaiming in their introduction, which begins with a gesture to the nineteenth-century slave narrative, "Unfortunately, we are compelled to revive [the slave narrative] today at the dawn of the twenty-first century. Slavery persists, and survivors of human bondage must once again share their stories to awaken the public."[35] Based on their knowledge of the nineteenth-century slave narratives, AASG immediately knew the significance of including survivor voices in their campaigns, though they had no significant survivor leadership in the organization.[36] They were not alone. As was the case in the nineteenth century, the rise of the new slave narrative can largely be attributed to the rise of the new antislavery movement.[37] By 2018, there were at least 2,700 documented anti-trafficking organizations globally, and many of them employ survivor narratives as part of their advertising strategies and for advocacy purposes, though few of them employ survivors as leaders.

Another motivating factor for the production of narratives of slavery came from government and judicial bodies. At the same time that Bales was forming Free the Slaves to put pressure on slavery internationally and AASG was working in Sudan and Mauritania, other organizations were formed to advocate for foreign-national survivors in human trafficking cases that were being tried in the United States. The Coalition Against Slavery and Trafficking (CAST), for instance, was formed in 1998 in response to the El Monte case in California, which resulted in the conviction of traffickers who exploited eighty Thai immigrant laborers in the garment industry and led as well to significantly increased awareness of forced labor in the United States.[38] When the El Monte case and other major breakthrough cases were being prosecuted in California, explicit survivor testimony regarding forced labor was crucial to convincing judges that forced labor was indeed a problem on American shores. Antislavery organizations and survivors put increasing pressure on government bodies to enact laws that would address this persistent form of global oppression as well. The United Nations Protocol to Prevent, Suppress, and Punish Trafficking in Persons, Especially Women and Children was passed in 2000, strengthening previous conventions against forced labor, and the United States passed the Victims of Trafficking and Violence Protection Act (TVPA) in the same year.[39] As Congress debated the issue, legislators actively sought out the testimony of survivors.[40] The passage of the TVPA was an affirmation for survivors and their supporters that testimonies of formerly enslaved people made a significant impact on Congress and citizens alike. Whether it was Bok or Fernando or Lloyd in the United States, Nazer in England, or Cadet in Haiti, survivors began to use their life narratives as a means of influencing governmental opinion and changing laws to protect others who were suffering as they had, though not necessarily as a means of prosecuting their own traffickers (which remains quite rare in the United States and United Kingdom).

Like all life narratives, the reemergence of the slave narrative is a result of diverse legal and political circuits that determine their form. In the cases of some of the earliest new slave narratives in the United States and Britain, post-9/11 political and religious anxieties served as an impetus for nonprofits and religious presses to pursue survivors of slavery as witnesses. Indeed, as anti-Muslim sentiments became more prevalent among U.S. citizens, antislavery activism was promoted by neoliberal organizations as a supposedly nondivisive, apolitical façade for campaigns against purported Muslim oppression and persecution of Christians. Narrators were encouraged to stress the religious aspects of their experiences in slavery. Bok's narrative, for instance, is particularly insistent that the war in Sudan grew solely out of Muslim jihad against innocent Christians, reaffirming American paranoia after 9/11 that there was a conspiracy of Christian persecution at work around the globe, which Bok (following his mentor and religious activist Charles Jacobs) claims is allowed to flourish because of a purported "human rights complex" that restricts activism against Islam.[41] Faith McDonnell—a researcher with an evangelical Christian think tank and Grace Akallo's coauthor—frames *Girl Soldier* as a tale of children whose lives she believes are caught up in a deliberate anti-Christian crusade fought by Joseph Kony, the "mystic spiritist" supported by the "radical Islam" of the Sudanese government. Akallo's testimony, McDonnell suggests, serves as a "history of how God's people are answering His call to save the children of northern Uganda."[42] When the United States turned it sights on the Islamic State in the second decade of the twenty-first century, the narratives of slavery shifted to that target, with narratives of "Yazidi sex slaves" as well as Boko Haram's victims taking center stage. In this way, post-9/11 Islamophobia and related political campaigns support the publication of narratives of slavery, which in turn encourage American and British readers to identify with victims of oppression and rally behind military intervention. As will be made clear in chapter 3, these anti-Muslim politics are evidence of Gillian Whitlock's claim that autobiography can be used as a "soft weapon," which can be "easily co-opted into propaganda" that, in the case of the slave narrative, can be radically divorced from the humanitarian efforts that originally motivated the narrators to speak.[43] Vron Ware argues that women's rights issues in particular often acted as a thin veil for neoliberal prowar policies in Iraq and Afghanistan in the 2000s, which actually silenced the very women they were supposed to protect and support.[44] Contemporary slavery is similarly taken up as a pretense for Islamophobic political projects, exploiting, among other products of the survivor experience, their own life narratives. After September 11, 2001, this particular theme in the new slave narratives grew more appealing to a public that was eager to "liberate" the women and children of the Middle East and Africa from a purportedly oppressive, patriarchal Islam.

Internationally, women's rights and migrants' rights organizations had been defining and addressing human trafficking for a decade or more before the United States took up the issue at the turn of the twenty-first century. Those organizations typically addressed the exploitation of marginalized women that emerges at the nexus of economic migration and sexual labor, and central to that work were the voices of survivors. Their testimonies were instrumental in bringing about the UN protocols on the trafficking of women. The debates that are discussed throughout this book began in those early years. But their voices went largely unheard in the United States. When the United Nations and countries in the West "rebranded" sex trafficking as the new "slave trade," the notion that slavery still exists gained more traction. Increasingly, however, the focus in the West was less on the laborers' rights—which remained the focus of many international organizations— than on the policing of sexual labor domestically and abroad.[45] Major anti-trafficking campaigns flourished in the West in the first two decades of the twenty-first century as the idea took hold particularly well among Christian women who saw sex trafficking as a threat to "family values," and they sought out survivor narratives as evidence of this creeping menace. As Elizabeth Bernstein explains, there were two turns in conservative Christian ethics and liberal feminist concerns that made sex trafficking a primary target for both groups: "a secular feminist shift in focus from bad men inside the home (sexually abusive husbands and fathers) to sexual predators outside of it (traffickers, pimps, and clients), and the feminist-friendly shift of a new generation of evangelical Christians away from sexually improper women (as prior concerns with issues like abortion suggest) and toward sexually improper men."[46] As the popular figure of the nefarious trafficker grew to nearly mythological proportions within these evangelical feminist groups, narratives by survivors of sexual exploitation became a necessary justification for what Bernstein dubs the "carceral politics" of the feminist abolitionists who demanded higher criminal penalties for sex traffickers than for practically any other crime—including labor trafficking (Utah even considered the death penalty for trafficking of minors). In the 2010s, then, narratives of sexual enslavement dominated the market and proliferated at a rate previously unimagined. Survivors of domestic minor sex trafficking (sensationally dubbed "teen sex slaves") were encouraged to write their life narratives and speak at conferences, churches, colleges, and legislative hearings across the United States and the United Kingdom.

The rise of antislavery activism also coincided with the rise of the tell-all memoir and the talk show in the United States and Britain. The popularity of the self-reflective mode of the autobiography encouraged popular interest in the slave narrative in the early 2000s, much as it had in the 1830s.[47] William Zinsser dubbed the last decade of the twentieth century "the age of the memoir," and as Ben Yagoda shows and Julie Rak confirms, that "memoir boom" continued through the early 2000s as "total sales in the categories of Personal Memoirs, Childhood Memoirs, and Parental Memoirs increased more than 400 percent between 2004 and 2008."[48] Sidonie Smith and Julia Watson attribute the increased interest in memoir to rising literacy, leisure time, and income matched with a voyeuristic impulse to know about the lives of the less fortunate.[49] These global demographic trends support the popularity of both the written memoir and the television talk show, both of which employ a public therapeutic talking cure, which in turn emboldens ordinary citizens to share their extraordinary personal experiences. A self-help culture inspired by the popularity of talk shows transformed Freud's talking cure into an industry for both the for-profit and nonprofit sectors.[50] New slave narrators featured in this study were welcomed to the stages of the *Oprah Winfrey Show*, the *Tavis Smiley Show*, and the *Tyra Banks Show*.

The talk show and memoir industries deployed the narratives of survivors to reach the hearts, minds, and pocketbooks of Western consumers. In the age of the talk show, the first-person testimony creates an intimate space for what otherwise might seem to be a distant reality. The pervasiveness of Oprah's self-referential formula trained American audiences to consume first-person narratives in a way that presupposed that the narrator or guest on the stage could be any one of us. But this formula also made the process of bearing witness somewhat necessary for a situation to be consumed, understood, accessible, and known. Widely televised footage of "distant suffering" has been influential in attracting public attention to events like the World Trade Center bombings, the 2004 tsunamis in Asia, and other human tragedies that previously would not have shaken the entire globe into action and generosity but now create cosmopolitan citizenship through spectatorship and an appeal to ethical investments according to Lilie Chouliaraki.[51] Recently, an event like the kidnapping and sexual enslavement of the Chibok girls by Boko Haram, for instance, has garnered the attention of an international audience through a highly visible social media campaign, which moved people to action globally to advocate for a group of young women who might otherwise have gone unnoticed outside of Nigeria, but that sympathetic response has depended in part on the self-exposure of the girls themselves.[52] The significance of the memoir boom has not been lost on survivor activists; it encouraged a culture of testimony that reached right into the consciousnesses of survivors in such a way that Ima Matul, a young survivor of domestic slavery from Indonesia, wished to meet President Obama and Oprah Winfrey, seemingly the two pillars of power—one political and the other cultural—and she did eventually meet Obama and testify on the stage of the Democratic National Convention in 2016.[53]

As first-person narration became a staple of the human rights industry, survivors have embraced new technologies and platforms such as blogs and social media to take control of their narratives and their public lives as well as to connect with one another in less confining or generically determined discourse environments. As trafficking victims and survivors of slavery become more resistant to the usurpation by human rights groups of the "control over representation, interpretation, and dissemination" that Paul Gready describes, independent survivor networks and counseling groups have proliferated, employing an empowerment-through-storytelling strategy akin to that utilized by the anti-domestic-violence movement in the '90s.[54] The survivor-led anti-trafficking organization GEMS (Girls Educational and Mentoring Service), for instance, created a survivor leadership institute that empowers survivors to both share their stories and also refute the singular narrative of trauma that is projected upon survivors through workshops and webinars that engage survivors' full skill sets rather than simply their traumatic experiences. The National Survivor Network was similarly formed to empower survivors in an online forum through which survivors separated by great distances are able to share their experiences and expertise. More recently, the Survivor Alliance has emerged as a peer-to-peer network focused on the development of survivor leadership. After more than a decade of being asked to serve as the examples of human rights violations at the service of other people's politics, increasing numbers of survivors began establishing their own platforms upon which they were able to share life narratives in ways that both expressed their exploitation and asserted their leadership and expertise.

The varied motivating forces described above—whether humanitarian sentiments, juridical requirements, emotional appeals, political expediencies, personal healing, or activist ambitions—all mobilize the new slave narrative to illustrate and lay bare the horrific realities of a rights violation that remains an abstract historical concept to most. As a result, we must read the new slave narratives not as discreet individual narratives but as historically and contextually produced expressions of contemporary cultural discourse, which are overdetermined by political, religious, and humanitarian genre requirements. The new slave narrative is burdened by the diverse interests and stakeholders to whom a single person's life experiences must speak. In what Leigh Gilmore calls "a transactional dynamic of testimony,"[55] slave narrators must navigate the sometimes contradictory and divergent interests and investments of courts, funders, sympathetic churchgoers, human rights advocates, student activists, their families, their former colleagues, their traffickers, all the people for whom the publication of their life narrative might make a difference, and, not least, themselves. As I will suggest in this book, these external impulses often create narrative tensions that are impossible to resolve within the text of the slave narrative and reveal significant fissures within antislavery advocacy.

GENERIC TOPOGRAPHIES

In an effort to scrutinize the ways these varied influences shape the form and structure of survivor testimony, *The New Slave Narrative* begins with an in-depth generic analysis of the conventions of the new slave narrative. Literary and historical in its approach and grounded in the work of scholars of the nineteenth-century slave narrative, the first chapter outlines the contours of the genre as it has reemerged at the turn of the twenty-first century. This chapter makes a much-needed case for the inclusion of contemporary forms of slavery and the new slave narrative in the wider field of slavery studies. Titled "Making Slavery Legible," the chapter builds on the generic reading to analyze the discursive strategies that slave narrators employ to make their experiences legible as slavery more than a century after most people think slavery has been eradicated. Employing—sometimes consciously, at other times likely unconsciously—the conventions of the nineteenth-century slave narrative, the narrators make themselves visible as survivors of slavery in a context in which race is no longer a salient defining feature of slavery. Despite their commitment to legibility, however, the narrators consistently use "strategies of displacement" that obfuscate the most traumatic and revealing aspects of their experiences to project empowered images of themselves that reject the voyeuristic demands of the humanitarian pornography that drives the antislavery establishment. In this chapter, I reveal three prominent strategies that new slave narrators use to deflect the readerly gaze from their traumatic experiences and to make their unique life experiences representative of a larger cause. Through these strategies and others, new slave narrators collectively provide us with a primer in reading the slave narrative in the twenty-first century.

As was the case with the nineteenth-century slave narrative, the new slave narrative reveals that there is a profound difference between being unenslaved and experiencing freedom. The authors' critiques of the failures of freedom that they experienced in the United States and England after liberation operate as counternarratives to the images of docile captives that their traffickers *and* their antislavery collaborators have produced. In recounting the barriers to freedom and citizenship encountered poste-mancipation, the slave narrative turns less toward the "freedom narrative" that Paul Lovejoy describes and more toward a not-yet-freedom narrative. I argue in a chapter titled "The Not-Yet-Freedom Narrative" that the uto-pian vision of freedom evoked by the new slave narrators is one that pro-motes a notion of cosmopolitan mobility that transcends national borders and grants citizenship to and protects the freedom of all people of the world. Their insistence that they remain unfree postcaptivity interrogates the neo-liberal structures of "freedom" that are so prominent in the milieu in which their narratives are produced and often undermines the politics of their coauthors and nonprofit collaborators who posit Western notions of freedom as the antidote to what is figured as largely non-Western exploitation.

In a chapter titled "Blackface Abolition," I further analyze how the demands for legibility within the available discourses of slavery and free-dom circumscribe the voices of the enslaved. Focusing on one narrative (among several) of an enslaved African child that is coauthored by an advo-cate from a conservative nongovernmental organization, I interrogate the way political organizations have co-opted African narratives, depicting contemporary forms of slavery to promote crusade politics driven by a post-9/11 anti-Muslim sentiment that is not representative of the narrators' own stated concerns within their narratives. While these texts allow new slave narrators to become legible to and identifiable by politically powerful Chris-tian American reading audiences, their narratives are co-opted to suit the needs of what I dub the "blackface abolitionist" wing of the movement.

As the anxieties about global Christian persecution began to subside in the slave narratives, the religious conservative wing of the antislavery move-ment in the United States turned its sights on a new target: sex. "Sex Prob-lems and Antislavery's Cognitive Dissonance" takes on the most highly vis-ible iteration of the new slave narrative—the "sex slave" narrative—which came to prominence after 2010 and now dominates the market. The chap-ter looks at the ways new slave narrators adopt the language of "victimiza-tion" as they come to define their experiences as both "trafficking" and "slavery"; however, a closer reading of the narratives reveals pervasive cul-tural impulses toward victim blaming and a surrender to religion, which are drawn from evangelical conversion and drug rehabilitation narrative conventions. I argue that these narratives reflect a cognitive dissonance that is endemic in contemporary antislavery discourse, which pits victimization against responsibility and captivity against salvation. This chapter reveals the way antislavery activism has ignited a new era of the "sex wars" and engaged in a new moral panic. But unlike many of the academics and activists who tend to either refute the existence of voluntary sex work or elide the reality of forced sex work, both in the name of defending women's rights, the narratives written by women forced into the sex trade reveal a highly complex notion of consent and agency that transcends the loudest voices in the movement and provides a way forward for thinking about women's rights in the labor market.

It is, of course, not simply the neoliberal Christian wing of antislavery advocacy that constrains the voice of the slave narrator in the twenty-first century—humanitarian aid groups, activist journalists, and left-leaning political activists also shape and co-opt the new slave narrative. "What the Genre Creates, It Destroys" critiques the public shaming and expulsion from the human rights community of Somaly Mam, who has fallen under scrutiny as her story of being a forced child sex worker has been challenged for its authenticity. Through an analysis of what Philippe LeJeune calls "the autobiographical pact" and the ways its demands are amplified within human rights discourse communities, I suggest that Mam created composite narratives of slavery that reveal precisely how generic conventions are determined by the political terrain upon which slave narrators must operate in order to garner the attention of powerful antislavery advocates. In questioning the heightened standard of authenticity to which slave narrators are held, I argue that Mam's exile from the antislavery community is exemplary of the political turmoil within the movement that is exposed throughout the book.

There certainly are (and will be) exceptions to the generic topographies mapped in this book. The new slave narrative is a living archive, and the narrative conventions of such an archive change in response to varying cultural influences and political requirements, as genres are dynamic and subject to reinterpretation. New narratives will continue to be authored and discovered as scholars pay greater attention to contemporary slavery. Any attempt to enumerate the conventions of a genre runs the risk of reductionism, immediate obsolescence, and hyperbole. The very validity of the concept of genre has been questioned by critics from Benedetto Croce to Jacques Derrida.[56] However, while Derrida's condemnation of the prescriptive tendencies of generic analysis suggests a critical yield sign, we must only yield, recalibrate to address the prescriptive potential inherent in all literary analysis, and proceed forward to historicize and critique the literary "kinship networks" that form genres.

"Genre" is meant here to indicate a productive (rather than reductive) relationship between texts, which foregrounds genre's "reproductive history" that is characterized by "cumulative reuse, an alluvial process, sedimentary as well as migratory."[57] Attention to this constantly morphing terrain admits to both rigid cultural conventions and elastic trends in discourse that are by-products of the political and cultural contexts from which they emerge. The goal is not to create a categorical definition but to follow the lead of these formerly enslaved storytellers in their efforts to make contemporary slavery and antislavery more legible. With these risks and potentials in mind, this project's aim is to pay sustained critical attention to the new slave narrative as a literary genre, homing in on its earliest sources and conventions as well as on what it can tell us about human rights discourse in the moment of the slave narrative's rebirth.

Still, no genre lives in a vacuum determined solely by memory or a single individual's lived experience. I am as much interested in the generic conventions employed by narrators of slavery as I am with the ways slavery and freedom are mobilized in the post-9/11 moment and how the genre of the slave narrative is utilized as a "soft weapon" in culture wars and political maneuvering.[58] The introduction and the first two chapters focus largely on survivor interventions in the discourse of slavery and freedom. The third and fourth chapters investigate more explicitly the negotiations for meaning and politics that occur between survivors and the activists they work with. The fifth chapter suggests how it is that external pressures on the narratives can come to dominate our ability to hear survivor stories at all. Scholars of the slave narrative tradition might find the first chapters, in which I outline the historical continuities of the genre and highlight the developments made in the new slave narrative, most illuminating. Those who are more interested in the politics of contemporary slavery and antislavery might consider reading the book backward, starting with the final chapter on the ethics of the slave narrative and then moving through the chapters on the political fault lines of the movement as they emerge from the new slave narratives.

Despite these necessary critiques, the overall intent of the book is to be constructive and to instigate a conversation about how antislavery movements might more expansively and responsibly engage the narratives of slavery and freedom that are produced by today's slave narrators. Through this extended analysis of more than forty book-length narratives, I hope to illuminate the enormous pressures that genre conventions have put on the narratives of slavery written today and, as a result, the way those generic pressures shape what we know and how we respond to slavery—not just in the academy but on the ground. As an antislavery activist myself, however, I am not inclined to proffer an academic critique of the discourses surrounding slavery today without providing some potential way forward. Thus, the book concludes with a reflection on our critical reading practices and encourages a more sympathetic rather than suspicious form of intellectual engagement. In connecting our collegial reading practices to the aims and ambitions of the new slave narrators, I suggest that we can fight forced labor in collaborative, responsive, substantive, and effective ways.

Chapter One

MAKING SLAVERY LEGIBLE

I may try to represent to you Slavery as it is; [but] . . . Slavery has never been represented; Slavery never can be represented.

—WILLIAM WELLS BROWN, "A LECTURE DELIVERED BEFORE THE FEMALE
ANTI-SLAVERY SOCIETY OF SALEM" (1847)

One of my greatest challenges is getting people to gain insight into what it means, practically, to be a victim of trafficking. No matter how crafty and skillful a writer or an artist may be, nothing on paper can parallel the experience for its length, intensity, and emotions.

—JAMES KOFFI ANNAN, *SURVIVORS OF SLAVERY* (2014)

The slave is the "real" body, the "real" evidence, the "real" fulfillment of what has been told before. Before the slave ever speaks, we know the slave; we know what his or her experience is, and we know how to read that experience. Although we do not ourselves have that experience, we nevertheless know it and recognize it by its language. This is because the language that the slave has to speak in, finally, is the language that will have political efficacy.

—DWIGHT MCBRIDE, *IMPOSSIBLE WITNESS* (2001)

In the nineteenth century, slave narrators were compelled to provide evidence that slavery was an unjust institution and that it should be abolished. The physical presence of survivors of slavery and the narration of their life experiences were meant to act as living testimony that their humanity was undeniable, which, in turn, would cultivate a sense of moral outrage over that inhumane and oppressive institution. Though Frederick Douglass was famously asked to add "a little of the plantation manner of speech" to his public lectures in order to convince audiences of his enslavement, racialized slavery made most nineteenth-century narrators' skin color simple proof of their experience and status, though they still had to prove the severity and immorality of the institution to their audiences.[1]

Most enslaved people today, however, are not enslaved solely by dint of their race or skin color. There is no consistent or necessary physical marker of their vulnerability or exploitation. The new slave narrator can reliably assume that the general public is morally opposed to slavery, at least in abstracted or historical terms. Survivors do not typically have to assert their humanity for public audiences, even though they often report feeling dehumanized by their traffickers.[2] In every country in the world, narrators are supported by laws that make slavery illegal. On their side in convincing the public is the fact that their claims of enslavement do not necessarily call into question the very economic or political foundations of any nation or economy.[3] Instead of being enslaved within a necessarily racialized, legalized, widely accepted institution of bondage, people are typically enslaved due to their vulnerability and marginalization in a global labor market that is characterized by radical income inequality, racial prejudices, and gender discrimination and that denies the existence of slavery itself. The case formerly enslaved people make today, then, differs somewhat from nineteenth-century claims.

Formerly enslaved people now face a crisis of legibility. Though the nineteenth-century slave narrative was no doubt shaped by significant silences, elisions, and unrepresentable experiences, I suggest that the circumstances of contemporary slavery present new challenges to representation. New slave narrators must confront a crisis of legibility that grows out of public ignorance regarding the existence of slavery, a problem woefully unfamiliar to the nineteenth-century narrator whose skin was the mark of institutionalized subordination in the law. Indeed, new slave narrators struggle to be read as having been enslaved at all. This environment of skepticism promoted the development of survivor testimony that would act as "flesh-and-blood" examples of the largely hidden and illegible human rights violation of contemporary slavery. In response, slave narrators adopt the tropes and structures of the nineteenth-century slave narrative to make their enslavement legible. Their books are packaged to alert readers to slavery's twenty-first-century manifestations and to put them in stark contrast to the freedoms and rights promised to the world's citizens today. Their narratives echo the refrains of subjection, escape, and activism that are so familiar from the literary tradition of the fugitive slave, precisely in an effort to make their claims legible for American and British readers.

In our post-Freudian world, in which tell-all memoirs are more marketable than most fiction, the new slave narrative is nonetheless counterintuitively riddled with silences—especially when it comes to the bodily detail. I argue that despite the voyeuristic demands of human rights discourse, new slave narratives reveal a generic tendency against the bodily detail and toward "strategies of displacement" that authenticate slave experiences through relying on the expertise or experiences of others.[4] As they did in the nineteenth century, these strategies allow the survivor to maintain control over her narrative and, ironically, to effect an identificatory process between the reader and the survivor that elevates the singular experience of slavery to the level of mass social injustice. Through this "imaginative identification," grounded in the withholding of the bodily detail, the genre of the new slave narrative revises and interrogates our spectacular expectations of a humanitarian sentimental education so often promoted by human rights projects while making the experiences of slavery legible and sharable for activist purposes.

NAMING SLAVERY

The common perception that slavery was successfully and permanently abolished in the nineteenth century means that the enslavement of forced laborers today remains undetectable to many observers both in the United States and abroad, even when the signs of slavery are clearly observable. The majority of people enslaved today are physically abused, and yet their bodies do not necessarily bear the marks familiar to us from daguerreotypes of nineteenth-century enslaved people's whipped backs. A person may be visibly controlled by another person, may be bruised or even branded, may be laboring incessantly among family members who are relaxing, may go entirely unpaid for her work or have all of her wages stolen, and still most people would not recognize her enslavement as such because for much of the last one hundred years, people around the world have assumed that slavery has been eradicated. In many cultures, slavery is cloaked in the language of tradition or understood as the unfortunate collateral damage of business, but it is typically not recognized as "slavery." Clear signs of forced labor may be present, but they are unintelligible to the uninformed onlooker. Slave narratives take on the task of making those signs intelligible to readers.

Even when the signifiers of bondage are made explicit, people do not tend to recognize them. For Jean-Robert Cadet, for instance, the "tradition" of *restavec* fosterage in Haiti made his enslavement illegible. Hundreds of thousands of restavecs are forced child laborers, but the seeming innocence of the designation "restavec"—which simply means to "stay with" but also signifies "motherless and unwanted"—left him subject to horrible abuse and compulsory labor that he was unable to escape and that few were willing to acknowledge.[5] Despite the fact that he was toiling in inescapable forced labor, the language used to describe his status allowed people to ignore the enslavement that was visibly indicated by the scars he carried on his malnourished body, the tattered clothes he wore, and his complete subordination to his employer. Quantitative researchers call enslaved people a "hidden population" because the illicit nature of the work and/or of the employment situation makes it difficult to locate or detect laborers who are enslaved.[6] Some scholars have called contemporary slavery an "invisible crime," but narratives such as Cadet's make it clear that slavery is not invisible. It is not that enslaved people go unseen. Their narratives are filled with people seeing them and witnessing their exploitation and abuse, but when onlookers do not know that slavery exists, signs of slavery remain illegible.

This relegation of victims of enslavement (or other forms of extreme abuse) to invisibility puts the burden on the victim to come into the spotlight, whereas reconceptualizing slavery in the contemporary context as a problem of illegibility puts the onus of responsibility on the onlooker, reader, or audience. The signs are there; we simply need to learn how to read them. First-person narrative testimonies regarding the transatlantic slave trade such as Olaudah Equiano's "not only brought so-called new worlds into view, their texts also demanded a difficult and emotional engagement with them; in effect they draw the modern reader as secondary witness into being," according to Gillian Whitlock.[7] In much the same way, new slave narratives create their own audiences, teach those audiences to read slavery, and bring into being a cadre of "secondary witnesses" who might have their own platforms upon which to denounce this largely unrecognized global rights violation. As Francis Bok indicates, his book is an "attempt to offer documentation of the existence of slavery in Sudan: my life, my story, this book."[8] His story can teach us to read the signs of slavery.

Writing the new slave narrative, then, is an active effort to reeducate readers so that slavery is legible and nameable. All the narrators studied here invoke the term "slavery" within their texts to describe their experiences and to make explicit for their largely Western readers the connection between their forced labor and that of those who labored in bondage in the nineteenth century. Cadet names and then defines his bondage in no uncertain terms: "Restavecs are slave children who belong to well-to-do families. They receive no pay and are kept out of school. . . . Restavecs are treated worse than slaves, because they don't cost anything and their supply seems inexhaustible."[9] By connecting his experience to familiar definitions and histories, Cadet makes restavec slavery legible for readers. Nadia Murad, author of *The Last Girl: My Story of Captivity, and My Fight Against the Islamic State* (2017) and winner of the 2018 Nobel Peace Prize, addresses any doubts as to the reality of her enslavement by explaining that the people who held her captive and named her "slave" used that language as justification of exploitation. Murad explains that ISIS militants told her that she had no choice but to serve the sexual desires of the soldiers because she was *sabaya*. She writes, "When ISIS took over Sinjar and began kidnapping Yazidis, they called their human spoils *sabaya* (*sabiyya* is singular), referring to the young women they would buy and sell as sex slaves. . . . Yazidi girls were considered infidels, and according to the militants' interpretation of the Koran, raping a slave is not a sin."[10] Rachel Lloyd develops historical analogies to make her own experience legible as slavery to a twenty-first-century readership that may be unaware of contemporary forms of slavery. She compares her Stockholm syndrome to Olaudah Equiano's close relationship with his master Pascal, and she claims that her trafficker's behavior toward her was akin to the "paternalistic and condescending justifications of slave owners in the 1800s."[11] These writers do not hesitate to call slavery by its name, and in order to fully mobilize the power of the term, they find themselves compelled to confront readers with textbook-style definitions and brief history lessons that point to the precision with which they are mobilizing the term "slavery" regardless of the diverse venues in which they were held captive and the forms of labor they experienced.

PARATEXTUAL AUTHORIZATIONS

Even before readers confront the contents of these narratives, however, new slave narrators and their publishers are shaping expectations by packaging the books in ways that authorize the writers' claims of slavery. The narratives, from their very covers, are co-opted as propaganda for particular conceptions of slavery and the freedom that ostensibly becomes available to the narrators when they escape their lives of enslavement and either migrate to the West or exit the sex trade. In this chapter, I primarily read with the grain to attend to the narrative conventions that can be discerned across this varied field of texts and then delve into the silences of the narratives to see where narrative tensions or instances of "representational static" (as Janet Neary terms it) arise and how slave narrators take control of their narratives even when they are coauthoring the texts with amanuenses.[12] In the coming chapters, I will analyze how the narratives navigate the ideological impulses imposed on slave narrators in the twenty-first century, questioning the notions of freedom that seem so transparent on a first reading.

As was the case in the nineteenth century, the paratextual elements of the new slave narrative are designed to mark it as an authentic, verifiable, first-person testimony of slavery. Letters and "blurbs" from authorities, titles, and cover designs all contribute to this authenticating effect. The list of the generic conventions of the nineteenth-century slave narrative that slave narrative scholar James Olney published in the pages of *Callaloo* in 1984 enumerates five typical paratextual elements including (a) an engraved portrait of the author, (b) a title page that insists that the former slave is indeed author of the text, (c) an abolitionist's or a friend's testimonial that attests to the veracity of the narrative, (d) a poetic epigraph, and (f) appendices that provide documentation of the veracity of the narrative.[13] Whatever may be included in (e), "the actual narrative," the paratextual elements of the narrative provide a virtual stamp of validity and legitimacy through the testimonies of experts, abolitionists, and companions as well as the powerful rhetoric of the portrait and title. Though slave narrators in the nineteenth century were held up as examples of the brutality of slavery, white abolitionists established themselves as "experts" who had the authority to contextualize, politicize, and theorize the significance of slave lives in short addendums that were included in nearly all nineteenth-century narratives.

Paratextual elements of the new slave narrative function quite similarly. The new slave narrative often includes endorsements from expert authorities on the cover or in the front matter, a title that invokes both the brutal enslavement and ultimate freedom of the author, and an inspiring photo of the narrator. It also often includes a foreword or epilogue by an abolitionist, expert, or friend of the author. As in the traditional slave narrative, there is a fairly explicit urgency on the part of publishers and abolitionists to validate the claims of the formerly enslaved narrator through external expert authority. However, while verifying the fact of slavery and authenticating the struggle of the narrator, the commercial framing of the text is overwhelmingly upbeat and positive, a sign to readers that while they will learn of the horrors of slavery, they will also find inspiration in the very same pages.

A glance at the covers of the books reveals this tendency toward authorizing the texts as slave narratives through the positioning of slavery and freedom as diametrical opposites. The title suggests the gravity of the narrator's experience by invoking the word (or at least the concept of) "slavery," which likely comes as a surprise to contemporary readers who first encounter it. For instance, Mende Nazer's enormously popular first memoir is titled, succinctly and perhaps shockingly, *Slave: My True Story*, and the sequel is aptly titled *Freedom: A Nuba Slave's Struggle to Rediscover Her Lost Family*. Tina Okpara's narrative is titled *My Life Has a Price: A Memoir of Survival and Freedom*; on one side of the colon lies Okpara's commodification, on the other, her personal quest for freedom and her status as a survivor instead of a slave. At the same time, the titles testify to the centrality of freedom to any narrative of slavery, and freedom is often given the place of privilege and priority. Bok's title, *Escape from Slavery: The True Story of My Ten Years in Captivity—and My Journey to Freedom in America*, insists upon defining Bok's experience as slavery, but it prioritizes his escape and freedom as the defining bookends of his life story. Cadet's *Restavec: From Haitian Slave Child to Middle-Class American* invokes the word "slave" for its representational power but, like Bok's title, insists upon the journey and the end result of freedom and social mobility in America as being of equal import. Theresa Flores invokes the trope of slavery "in our own backyards" that became popular in the 2010s with her title, *The Slave Across the Street: The True Story of How an American Teen Survived the World of Human Trafficking*, whereas Barbara Amaya plays on the trope of stolen childhood innocence in slavery with her *Nobody's Girl: A Memoir of Lost Innocence, Modern Day Slavery, and Transformation*. Both titles pit the authors' enslavement against their survival and transformation. While the titles rely on appealing to the shock elicited by slavery and the commodification of human lives, they effectively mobilize pervasive anxieties about freedom in the twenty-first century to amplify their legitimization of the existence of slavery.

Further legitimating work is enacted through the endorsements printed on the back of the book and on the dust jacket cover. These expert commentaries on the value of the text pit the narrator's enslavement against her inherent freedom, her victimization against her tireless resilience. In this

THE INTERNATIONAL BESTSELLER

SOLD

One woman's true account
of modern slavery

ZANA MUHSEN

with Andrew Crofts

FIGS. 1.1.–1.4. Zana Muhsen's *Sold: One Woman's True Account of Modern Slavery* (1991), Jean-Robert Cadet's *Restavec: From Haitian Slave Child to Middle-Class American* (1998), Francis Bok's *Escape from Slavery: The True Story of My Ten Years in Captivity—and My Journey to Freedom in America* (2003), and Mende Nazer's *Slave: My True Story* (2003) were the first memoirs of contemporary forced labor to explicitly appropriate the genre of the slave narrative.

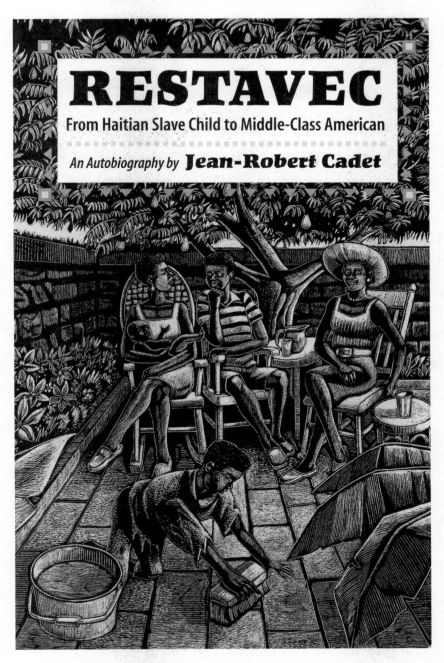

RESTAVEC

From Haitian Slave Child to Middle-Class American

An Autobiography by Jean-Robert Cadet

FIGS. 1.1.–1.4. (*continued*)

ESCAPE
FROM
SLAVERY

*The true story of my
ten years in captivity—
and my journey
to freedom in America*

FRANCIS
BOK

with Edward Tivnan

FIGS. 1.1.–1.4. *(continued)*

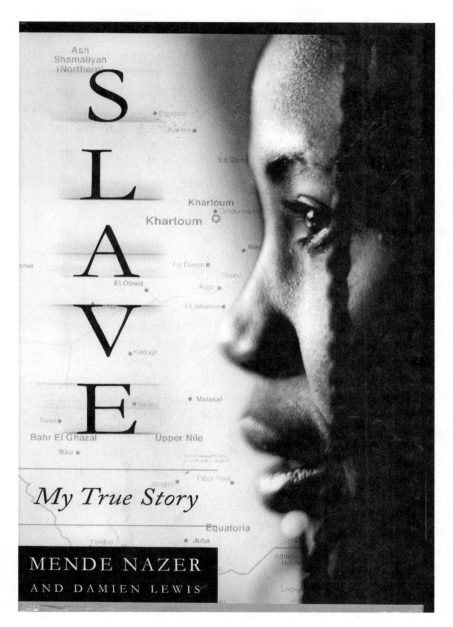

FIGS. 1.1.–1.4. (*continued*)

way, they introduce the readers to the nearly unfathomable reality of slavery but put them at ease through the readers' identification with the narrator's Promethean struggle against the greatest adversity. The back cover of Katariina Rosenblatt's *Stolen: The True Story of a Sex Trafficking Survivor* declares, "There is HOPE, even on the darkest of days," and the endorsements on most of the other texts reassert that claim. Grace Akallo's narrative *Girl Soldier* includes an endorsement from no less an authority than John Miller, then the head of the U.S. Trafficking in Persons Office, who wrote, "After meeting with child soldier slavery survivors in Uganda, I wondered if anyone could bring this moving story of horror and redemption to the world. . . . Read this book. Weep. And rejoice at Grace's incredible struggle. A moving call to prayer and action." Invoking the language and "horrors" of slavery, Miller invites us to identify with Grace's struggle and to act. Mende Nazer's *Kirkus* review, quoted on the back cover of her book, toes a similar line: "The shockingly grim story of how the author became a slave at the end of the twentieth century—mercifully, it has an ending to lift the spirit." Never willing to suggest that the tales of slavery might simply be tales of oppression and violence, these endorsements, after attesting to the reality and atrocity of contemporary slavery that can be discerned from reading the narratives, invariably highlight their redemptive narrative arcs. Alex Dupuy proclaims on Cadet's cover that his slave narrative is the "autobiography of a young man who escaped the most foreboding of circumstances and raised himself up by his bootstraps." The endorsers of Rebecca Bender's *A Roadmap to Redemption* suggest that the readers, too, can pull themselves up through reading the book. Congresswoman Linda Smith writes that Bender's book "is not only a story of hope for anyone to read, but it . . . should be the go-to book for any survivor looking to turn her tragedy into triumph." These brief windows into the narrative inevitably point to the triumphant spirit of the narrator that led her to redeem herself from indescribable suffering and bondage. They anticipate the theme of our common humanity at the heart of the narrative while exalting the individual determination and success that serve as mainstays of the first-person narrative. They dress these tales of woe in the shroud of the neoliberal dream, evoking Horatio Alger–esque self-made men, who, with a little help from some good Samaritans, can find their way to health, happiness, and prosperity as middle-class citizens of democratic nations. These external authorities not only confirm the realities of the slavery described in the pages of the books but suggest the promise of universal freedom that awaits the narrators (and the readers for whom this is also meant to be cathartic) at the end of their journeys of suffering and resilience, a freedom that the narrators themselves eventually undermine within the texts (a topic discussed at length in chapter 2).

About half of the narratives feature survivor photos that depict proud, healthy, and determined agents for change prominently positioned on either the covers or the dust jackets or within the first pages of the books. While some of the narratives that were self-published after 2010 project a variety of amateur designs on their covers, the majority of the cover images, especially those that are published by professional presses, demonstrate the strength of the narrators and allow readers to identify with and see them as honest narrators who are worthy of being heard even as they tell us stories of horrors we otherwise cannot imagine if we are to believe the blurbs. When the narrators' photographic portraits are featured on the covers of their books, they are often framed in severe, cropped, close-up headshots, with the narrators' eyes focused carefully on something offset and distant. A few of the photos are shot with some of the narrators' bodies in the frame, but the distant stares remain. Though the stare directs us to an unseen focal point outside the frame of the photo, there is something ambitious, forward-looking, and determined in the way the narrator peers into the unknown. Cover images that do not feature the gaze of ambition present a camera-focused gaze in which the narrator peers directly out of the cover at the reader, suggesting honesty and strength.

Not coincidentally, I suspect, the covers of narratives written by people of African or Middle Eastern descent are most likely to have portraits on the covers—perhaps because the enslavement of people of color is most convincing to Western readers. The cover images of Farida Khalaf's and Nadia Murad's books, for instance, echo many of the images we see of activist women from the Islamic world after 9/11 in the United States—beautiful and feminine, with confident gazes and firmly set shoulders projecting confidence.

When publishers forgo a portrait of the narrator on the front cover, the cover often includes an artistic rendering of someone who is meant to represent the enslaved person, sometimes with her back to the camera or in shadow, but often in the scene of work or bondage. That fictional image is almost always paired with a simple headshot of a proud and smiling

FIGS. 1.5.–1.8. New slave narrative cover portraits are reminiscent of those included inside the nineteenth-century narratives, through their ambitious gazes and determined body language.

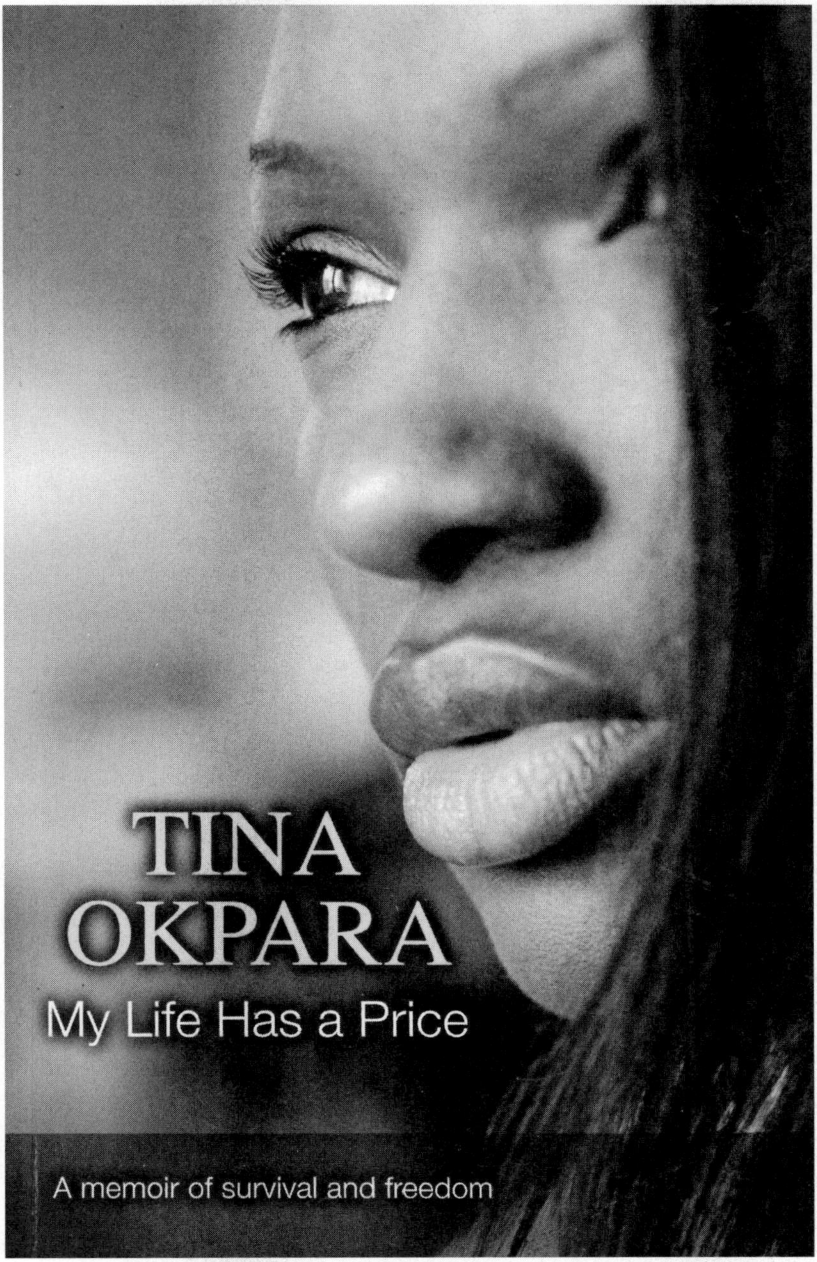

TINA OKPARA

My Life Has a Price

A memoir of survival and freedom

FIGS. 1.5.–1.8. (*continued*)

RUNAWAY GIRL

ESCAPING LIFE ON THE STREETS, ONE HELPING HAND AT A TIME

FIGS. 1.5.–1.8. (*continued*)

FATIMA
ESCLAVE À 11 ANS

TÉMOIGNAGE

Flammarion

FIGS. 1.5.–1.8. *(continued)*

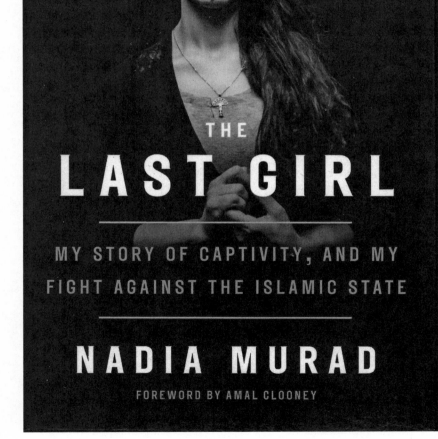

THE

LAST GIRL

MY STORY OF CAPTIVITY, AND MY
FIGHT AGAINST THE ISLAMIC STATE

NADIA MURAD

FOREWORD BY AMAL CLOONEY

FIGS. 1.9.–1.10. Portraits of women enslaved by ISIS reiterate images of strong but victimized women popular in post-9/11 rhetoric.

"A shattering, brave, enraging book but also a stirring story of survival."
—*SUNDAY EXPRESS* (UK)

THE GIRL WHO ESCAPED ISIS

This Is My Story

FARIDA KHALAF

ANDREA C. HOFFMANN

FIGS. 1.9.–1.10. *(continued)*

narrator somewhere within the dust jacket or inside the back cover, creating a before-and-after effect, emphasizing the seemingly unambiguous difference between slavery and freedom. Taken alone, the survivor's cover photo is a standard headshot pose, but read within the context of the other paratextual authorizations, rhetorical tropes are clearly discernable, and they tell a story of a person who, though enslaved, was indomitable and successful in her pursuit of freedom—freedom that could only be achieved once she escaped her oppressive captors and, not coincidentally, her country of origin.

This commercial packaging falls prey to the same co-opted authority for which the nineteenth-century abolitionists were condemned and for which much of the contemporary human rights industry is critiqued. The paratext of the new slave narrative teaches us how publishers expect audiences to read the narratives, whether they are about international or domestic experiences of enslavement. They direct the reader's attention to the reality of contemporary slavery but promise to both inform and uplift. Even as they forcefully charge the readers with a mandate to engage with the brutality of human rights violations, the materials that surround and precede the narratives of slavery compel us to read them as testimonies of triumph and freedom and to seek out the inherent subjectivity, agency, and liberty inscribed within the pages of the autobiographies. Ironically, the paratexts betray the agency of their authors. While the paratext may purport to tell the story of a self-determined individual, the majority of the publishers nonetheless rely on external, typically American authorities to authenticate the narrative and the fact of slavery for a skeptical and fickle reading audience. As was the case with the nineteenth-century narrative, these mechanisms may, in fact, render slavery visible and legible to ignorant reading audiences, but they also subordinate the messaging of the formerly enslaved to the consumable political and commercial purposes of the endorsers and publishers.

The faces of the black and brown narrators—almost exclusively women—from around the globe that dominate the covers of about half of the new slave narratives furthermore suggest the common Western differentiation between the gendered violence in the Global South and the freedoms that those same young women are afforded in the Germany, France, Britain, or the United States once they are liberated. As Wendy Hesford notes in her *Spectacular Rhetorics*, the images of determined and innocent young women that characterize human rights advertising in the twenty-first century reveal the "gendering of sympathy in the American transnational human rights industry."[14] As is the case with the images of women that Hesford focuses her work on, the paratextual packaging of the new slave narrative reveals an ideological purposiveness deliberately asserting Western notions of and opportunities for freedom, which contrast clearly with the depiction of oppressive enslavement and violation of women in the Global South.[15] This value judgment is then explicitly reinforced by the blurbs on the covers and on the insides of the texts. As we will see throughout the book, new slave narratives are often employed to assert these reductive narratives and are often co-opted as justification for military and political interventions by the United States government.

IDYLLIC ORIGINS

Once we open the book's cover and begin to read the narrative, however, the very first pages reinforce the depiction of the depravity of slavery. The new slave narrative is not typically propelled by a temporally linear narrative structure, as the nineteenth-century narrative typically was, and so the birth of the narrator is often delayed for several pages, as the narrator instead begins in medias res, often in the midst of that "scene of subjection" to which Saidiya Hartman refers, often the very moment when the narrator was made captive or was most forcefully exploited.[16] From the very first line, most narratives immerse the reader in the intense shock of forced labor, which captivates audiences precisely because of the inhumanity and the incongruity of such an experience in contemporary times. Bok, who was enslaved as a child in Sudan, opens his narrative with a line that invokes the day-to-day mundanity that was interrupted by slavery: "I have told the story many times about that day in 1986, when my mother sent me to the market to sell eggs and peanuts: the day I became a slave."[17] Nazer's first line hints at the destruction of her idyllic childhood landscape: "The day that changed my life forever started with a beautiful dawn."[18] Beatrice Fernando and Timea Nagy begin their narratives waiting to board planes that they hope will take them to a land of high-paying wages but that instead escort them into slavery. The second paragraph of Akallo's narrative is a memory of the lowest point in her enslavement: "Slowly the bitter memories flow back to me. I am in Sudan, and I have been buried among the dead. Seven months after my capture. I am no longer myself."[19] Surely publishers and ghostwriters encourage authors to introduce their narratives with shocking images of captivity in order to impress upon readers the deplorable reality of slavery in our time. Those moments provide audiences voracious for scenes of violence, violation, and exploitation with the taste of horror that will compel them to read on.

After a quick glimpse into the horrors of slavery, the text always returns to the origins of the narrator. In an effort to make the experience of slavery intelligible and believable to the readership, the new slave narrator typically establishes a sense of the originary freedoms that pre-dated captivity soon after the gripping intro has captured the mind of the reader. The trope through which the text establishes those freedoms—that of innocent birth and childhood—is resonant with the nineteenth-century narrative, which in itself is a route to legibility. Olney's most compelling observation in his *Callaloo* list of the slave narrative's generic conventions is the frequency with which slave narrators established both their existence and their essential humanity with the phrase "I was born" or with a depiction of their earliest childhood memories. Included first on Olney's list of conventions of the narrative proper, this existential claim was "intended to attest to the real existence of a narrator, the sense being that the status of the narrative will be continually called into doubt, so it cannot even begin until the narrator's real existence is firmly established."[20] The slave narrator establishes, in this quick turn of phrase, the fact that he was born of a mother and father, like all other humans, and that he was situated in a specific geographical context in the South. These two origins are significant because, of course, in the nineteenth century, children were subjected to the most severe form of subordination by mere dint of parentage and geography. The phrase "I was born" thus levels a forceful critique against the institution of slavery, indicating a moral crisis between the enslaved person's God-given status as free and his racially and governmentally determined status as slave. Though Olney does not discuss the phrase in this way, the evocation of the narrator's origins is just as much about establishing the foundational right to freedom as it is to his essential humanity.

Like the nineteenth-century slave narrator, the new slave narrator often enunciates the phrase "I was born" or recounts the moment of her birth in the process of establishing her genealogy and early childhood innocence.[21]

Somaly Mam, for instance, writes, "I was born sometime around 1970 or 1971, when the Troubles began in Cambodia."[22] Beatrice Fernando, who tells her entire story of enslavement, before going back to retrace her origins, writes, "On the west coast of Sri Lanka, north of the capital city of Colombo, lies the fishing village of Negomboa, and there, nestled among the young coconut groves, was the house my family occupied when I was born. It was December 1956."[23] Mende Nazer recalls, "When I was born, my father chose to call me Mende."[24] Another new slave narrator begins with the birth name that was refused her while she was enslaved: "My name is Evelyn Amony. I was born on November 25, 1982, in my father's village of Pawiro Ato, Pupwonya Parish, in Aitak subcounty, Gulu District, Uganda."[25] These origin tales indicate the narrators' own verifiable existence by anchoring their lives in specific locations, political situations, families, and names, calling attention to the fact that the narratives are first-person nonfictional accounts of individuals who experienced such horrific events. In all these narratives, the authors are free and blissfully unaware of the existence of slavery. American narrators also refer to their own births in the early chapters, often in humble or impoverished settings, where their youth left them equally unaware of the existence of slavery and its potential harm to their childhood innocence. If the nineteenth-century narrator was required to indicate the circumstances of his birth in order to prove his humanity, the new slave narrator points to her identifiable origins to establish not only her own existence but the fact of her inherent freedom. These origin stories establish the writers as being born in freedom, a state from which the narrators are ripped, typically as innocent children. Their innocence and freedom are then placed in stark contrast to the slavery and injustice they encounter after they are taken from their families.

In order to dramatize and authenticate their free birth, the narrators tend toward romantic depictions of the idyllic surroundings into which they were born. In the majority of the new slave narratives, the setting, though almost inevitably impoverished, is bucolic, comfortable, carefree. In the narratives depicting childhoods in the United States, the families might be dysfunctional, but the narrators still focus on their private, happy childhood innocence despite the impoverished and even abusive settings. Indeed, the typical narrator, like so many of the nineteenth-century narrators, foregrounds her childhood innocence to the horrific reality of slavery in the world and highlights her naïveté to the struggles of her family, community, and nation. But most importantly, regardless of her childhood experiences, the new slave narrator was born free.

Some of the narrators from the Global South also take readers on an anthropological journey through the cultural milieu of their childhoods, interspersed with vignettes of their typically joyful lives in their home countries as a contrast to the injustice of slavery. Just as the fifteen antebellum slave narrators who were originally from Africa were not able to assume that readers would know about their cultures or lives before slavery,[26] today's slave narrators from Iraq, Sri Lanka, or Uganda present compelling portraits of their cultures in an effort to convince readers that slavery is not endemic to their cultures and to dispel the myths that they were simply victims of their own families' avarice. Bok tells us about the little clay cows he made as a child in anticipation of becoming a powerful male elder like his cattle-owning father, convincingly portraying the cultural hierarchies he hoped to ascend to had he not been relegated to the status of slave.[27] Farida Khalaf describes the peaceful religion of the Yazidis and recalls that her father treated her as an equal to her brothers in many ways, preemptively contradicting the widely held notion that endemic gender discrimination in the Middle East made her easy prey for sexual enslavement.[28] Through these anthropological chapters, narrators are immediately able to dismiss any notions that slavery was pervasive and situate themselves in environments that embrace freedom, peace, freedom of religion, and rule of law.

The idyllic settings of childhood are matched by the promise that the narrators represented for their families as young children before they were enslaved, another testament to the injustice of their bondage and their right to freedom. Amony writes that she planned to become a doctor or nurse because she was ranked high in her class and was good in science before she was abducted by the Lord's Resistance Army in Uganda and made the wife of Joseph Kony. She was athletic, had been taught to treat people with kindness, and had many friends. Her origin story suggests a poor but happy childhood that was disrupted by the horrors of war and slavery.[29] Bok, who was a forced child laborer after being captured by mujahideen in Sudan when he was only seven years old, spends almost the entire first chapter depicting the idyllic setting in which he was raised, where his father was *ajak* (a rich man), owned a massive farm, and worked as an international trader. Bok dreamed of growing up to be just like his father, who treated him as his "special son" who would one day "do important things."[30] The nickname his father gave him, Muycharko, meant that he was like "twelve men" and would accomplish as much.[31] Mende Nazer, who was also held captive in Sudan during the war, spends the first eight chapters describing the supportive environment from which she was taken when she was enslaved. She recalls the love of her parents, the sweet kitten she had as a childhood pet, and the extraordinary bond she shared with her siblings. Her promise as a student led her to imagine becoming a doctor and going away to school, all of which she imagines would have been her rightful destiny if she had not been taken captive. In her second memoir, she writes, "The first years of my life were an idyllic time, growing up in a close-knit, loving family in our little village in the Nuba Mountains, one of the most isolated areas on earth. The Nuba tribe are a black African people famed for their body painting and wrestling, and for their prowess as warriors. We are the oldest inhabitants of Sudan, having lived there for thousands of years. It is even said that the Nuba founded the original civilisations of Egypt."[32] Nazer's childhood promise and inherent freedom were her rightful inheritance, founded in the origins of the people from whom she descended, a free people with claims to both land and power. It is striking that nearly all new slave narrators who published over this twenty-year period, regardless of geographical origin, were promising students and even family favorites before they were enslaved. Their status as children marks them as indisputably innocent of any wrongdoing that might sully their characters or their veracity; their native intelligence suggests that they were not to blame for their victimization or were merely victims who did not understand what was happening to them. There is no way to conclude that these children were guilty prisoners or that they chose the lives of servitude to which they were bonded. Their bucolic childhoods and their intellectual promise act as testaments to their veracity and to their rights to liberty.

These idyllic and auspicious origins act as material evidence of the inherent freedom that was made captive in slavery. They are the evidence that new slave narrators provide to insist that they were not slaves by nature but were enslaved by circumstance. They establish the narrators' right to freedom and mobility (both physical and social)—through the depiction of their families' power in their communities or their dedication to the narrators' education—and to the enormous potential each child had to succeed as an adult. Narrating these origins provides evidence of the narrators' fundamental right to freedom. Whereas many American-born nineteenth-century narrators were born into slavery, the twenty-first-century narrators typically remind audiences that they were born into freedom, in a state of innocence, and they do so to insist upon precisely the same claim that the nineteenth-century narrators advanced—that they have a right to their freedom despite whatever experiences they may have had in between being born as humans endowed with inherent rights and reclaiming their freedom after slavery.

SLAVERY'S CONVENTIONS

The narrator's essential humanity and freedom then stand in stark contrast to the brutal realities the narrator discovers as she matures and comes to recognize her enslavement. Often, the literal birth of the child is followed by the figurative birth of the slave in the first chapters of the narrative. As Hartman writes of the spectacle of violence that often follows the "I was born" of the nineteenth-century narrative, the scene of subjection "dramatizes the origin of the subject and demonstrates that to be a slave is to be under the brutal power and authority of another; this is confirmed by the event's placement in the opening chapter on genealogy."[33] Displaying the utter inhumanity of the system of slavery, the traditional slave narrator condemns what human beings were forced to endure under the rule of Southern law. Similarly in the twenty-first-century narrative, the scene of subjection that opens the text and the captivity scenes that often follow the "I was born" moment provide the brutal evidence of slavery. Whether it is the mujahideen attack on Bok's village, the fraudulent offer of help that runaway Carissa Phelps accepted that immediately revealed itself to be recruitment into forced sex work, or the brutality of the domestic sphere that Shyima Hall encountered when she was brought to the United States to work for a rich family, the radical shift from freedom to captivity is made transparent early in the narrative.

Once the narrative begins to depict life in captivity, many of the generic conventions are unsurprisingly determined by the very conventions of slavery itself. The central conventions of the slave narrative, past and present, always include literary sketches of the characters who populate the world of slavery—cruel slaveholders and overseers who deny the enslaved person's rights, religious slaveholders whose sadistic behaviors betray their own faith, an innocent fellow captive who is the victim of brutal abuse. The narratives depict the horrible conditions of enslavement, including the horrific "breaking-in" process that some slaveholders use to instill terror, the meager food on which enslaved people are expected to subsist, the excessive work they perform, and the commodification of their lives through either sale or transferability. These are the characters and realities that constitute slavery in all nations and across generations, and through them, the narratives of formerly enslaved people consistently depict the mechanisms of power inherent in the relationship between bonded laborer and bondsman in the twenty-first century as much as in the nineteenth.[34] The brutal conditions that serve to maintain power among the slaveholding class—the extraordinary violence, the denial of literacy and religion, the meager material rations, the numbingly redundant and excessive schedule of labor, the separation of families and loved ones, and the transfer of lives as property— are central to establishing the pathos of the narratives as well as the echo of nineteenth-century slavery that will confirm the new slave narrators' claims of enslavement. As new slave narrators make their cases for their experiences being read as slavery, these are the details that resonate with audiences who might otherwise be tempted to call the experiences simply "harsh labor conditions" or "slave-like."

The character sketches that depict the human capacity for brutality are crucial to making that claim. Cadet's "maman," Florence, is a telling example of the contradictions of the pious public life and the abusive private life endemic among slaveholders. In public, Florence styled herself as a church-going maternal figure when, in fact, Cadet knew she secretly practiced taboo traditional religions and sold sex to white men. But, more disturbingly, she beat young Cadet for even the slightest mistake, made him sleep on a pile of rags after working all day and night, and refused him his education and his communion in the Catholic church.[35] Nadia Murad's captors were devoted Muslims who nonetheless threatened to kill her regularly and forced her into sexual servitude based on her ethnic heritage and religion. Tina Okpara agreed to work for a famous professional soccer player only to find that he forced her to attend to his family's every whim, whether that was domestic labor or sex. The nefarious, Janus-faced enslaver is a trope that continues to have significant traction today as narrators attempt to explain the extremity of their experiences in slavery.

Evidence of the inherent violence of slavery is also painted into the portraits of the broken and defeated people who are enslaved alongside the narrators. Cadet witnessed his young friend René, a neighbor restavec, brutally beaten by his "family" and the police when he stole a mere two dollars.[36] Bok encountered a young Dinka boy whose legs were missing, and he was told, "That's what happens to bad boys. He tried to escape."[37] Child soldier narratives are replete with the massacre of fellow captives who pay the price for defiance. Akallo recalls in a staccato report, "A twelve-year-old girl tried to escape two weeks after our capture. Her head was smashed. This was scary. The thought of escape left me immediately."[38] In most of the narratives, facades of familial bonds, pious religious devotion, community respect, and paternal/maternal care only barely mask the constant threat and reality of violence that, in fact, maintain slavery.

The new slave narrative also provides a window into the devastating psychological effects of slavery on its victims and on the nearly obsessive focus on escape and freedom that are typical of, if not all people who are enslaved, then at least those who eventually write their life stories. Almost all the international narratives include scenes of sudden recognition, characterized by what Frederick Douglass called the "blood-stained gate, the entrance to the hell of slavery"—a moment of gratuitous violence that convinces the narrators that they are, in fact, enslaved.[39] When Francis Bok first arrived at the home of his captor, he was delighted to see other children come running out of the house, but his potential playmates called him "slave" and ruthlessly beat him with sticks in a spectacular display of their differing statuses. When the father did not stop the beating, Bok understood that he had been deemed no better than a dog and began to suspect why they kept shouting "abeed." As in the case of Douglass, that moment woke Bok from his childhood naïveté and forced him to reckon with his new reality. Similarly, even though Tina Okpara had endured working without sleep and without pay for months before she was raped by the famous soccer player who employed her, it was only in that moment of extraordinary physical subordination that she realized, "I have become a slave in his house."[40] In the American narratives of sexual enslavement, that moment of full recognition and the naming of the experience as "slavery" is often delayed until after escape, but the "blood-stained gate" moment of brutal violence is often a turning point that leads the survivors to realize that they must escape.

The moment of recognition typically leads to incessant thoughts of suicide while a successful escape seems impossible. Farida Khalaf tried to take her life several times before she was able to escape. Jean-Robert Cadet hoped each night that he—or his "mistress"—would not wake to see the next day. Grace Akallo admits to having tried to shoot herself three times. She lived in a constant battle between fearing that she would be killed by her captors and wanting to die and find peace. Rachel Lloyd actually tied the belt of her bathrobe around her neck and jumped off the balcony of her hotel only to be saved by the very person she was trying to escape.

In times when they were able to fend off the despair, these enslaved people focused on freedom. They meticulously planned routes to escape, setting aside money, food, or weapons to make their liberation possible. Beatrice Fernando plotted for weeks until she finally saw her chance at freedom in an unlocked door. She snuck out that door and jumped off a fourth-story balcony in a desperate attempt to either secure her freedom or escape her life altogether. Grace Akallo led several of her friends through the desert to freedom, risking starvation and recapture along the way. Farida Khalaf plotted for months before she and her friends were able to escape to the home of a stranger who kindly took them in and reconnected them with their families. Most of the women who were forced into the sex trade in the United States checked themselves into rehabilitation clinics or homeless shelters as a plot to break free from those who held them physically and psychologically captive.

Once free, new slave narrators depict their return to the education and religious practices that were denied them in slavery. If they are from the Global South, they typically migrate to the West—to the United States, the United Kingdom, or Germany—where they are connected with aid organizations and antislavery groups. They relate their ambitions to join the antislavery struggle in order to prevent others from being enslaved now that they have gained their own freedom. Indeed, the life of drudgery that is slavery is hardly the focus of these narratives. Instead, the majority of the narrative space is typically consumed by the narrator's persistent and often agonizing commitment to escape and freedom. It was for this same reason that Paul Lovejoy suggested that we start calling the nineteenth-century slave narrative "the freedom narrative" instead.[41] The narrative drive to freedom, far from obscuring slavery, in fact provides that stark contrast that is necessary to define the contours of slavery. It is the slave narrators' conscious and obsessive ambition to gain their freedom that makes their slavery visible. While many of us take our ostensible freedom for granted, those who are enslaved and eventually write about it tend to contemplate freedom obsessively and pursue it with every opportunity presented to them. These freedom narratives make plain the consequences and the stakes of slavery for those who experience it.

The new slave narrative, then, provides documentary, eye-witness evidence of the humanity of the enslaved and the inhumanity of those who attempt to master them, enacting a reversal of the roles prescribed by slavery. In the nineteenth century, this was a critical political motivation of the slave narrative. Today, the evidence of brutality helps to constitute for the middle-class Western reader the subjectivity of people who are often distant, sometimes by geography or class but always by experience, from the day-to-day banal realities of bourgeois life. Though their inherent humanity is typically not in question, as it was in the nineteenth century, slave narrators constitute themselves as unwilling and undeserving victims of systems that are otherwise unimaginable. In stark contrast to the images projected by their covers, their depictions of lives outside of slavery ensure that Western audiences cannot simply relegate slavery to the category of developing-world poverty and gender discrimination. They reveal that the violence and existence of slavery are just as foreign to their experience as they are to the reader's, even as they often imply that the violence is essential to other groups or environments, such as Muslims or the sex trade (as chapters 3 and 4 will demonstrate). Through aligning themselves with the reader's popular Western conceptions of freedom and invoking their surprise at the existence of slavery, they make a seemingly impossible experience intelligible for readers.

THE DETAIL OF BODILY SILENCE

Making slavery legible in the twenty-first-century context is not simply a matter of defining and using the word "slavery" or echoing familiar tropes, however. Legibility demands intimate evidence and knowledge. Judges bring formerly enslaved people to the stand, nonprofits bring them to the stage, and talk-show hosts welcome them into comfortable armchairs because, as a culture, we are desirous of that "flesh-and-blood" specimen that indicates the veracity of human rights claims. The first-person humanitarian narrative has long acted as substantiation of rights violations, but its power to convince is reliant on the establishment of verifiable truth. According to Thomas Laqueur, two rhetorical mechanisms emerged in the eighteenth century that formed the foundation of humanitarian claims to veracity in the West for centuries—attention to the specific detail that indicates specialized or intimate knowledge of a subject and the depiction of the bodily effects of suffering that are signatures of the lived experience of human violation. Both of these strategies "connect the actions of [a text's] readers to the suffering of its subject."[42] Mario Klarer claims that, as a strategy of identification, humanitarian narratives "have to be graphic in their descriptions in order to pass as truthful accounts," highlighting torture and suffering in great detail.[43] Sidonie Smith and Julia Watson, extending Laqueur's analysis to a much wider range of autobiographical texts, argue that "life narrative inextricably links memory, subjectivity, and the materiality of the body."[44] As memory and life are always embodied, so are they in the narratives of those lives. Thinking specifically of the embodiedness of the slave narrative, Gillian Whitlock writes of the scars on slave narrator Mary Prince's back: "What is taken down from Mary's lips remains suspect, but the flesh cannot lie. Testimony incarnate, which is inscribed on the body and legible to these benevolent witnesses, authenticates her story of abuse."[45] Thus, unlike the presidential autobiography or even the Horatio Alger bootstraps tale, the humanitarian narrative—the slave narrative included—is generically required to lay bare the body of the narrator. The perverse voyeurism of audiences invested in the slave narrative requires the "sadistic pleasure to be derived from the spectacle of sufferance," as Hartman puts it, and they accept no less as evidence of rights violations.[46]

Despite a cultural predilection for holding up the body as evidence of suffering, however, the slave narrative reveals a generic resistance to bodily detail. There is no doubt that, whether in the nineteenth or the twenty-first century, slaveholders mark the bodies of captives. Many forced sex workers, for instance, have been coerced to tattoo their pimps' names on their bodies, which calls to mind the branding employed in chattel slavery. Others carry scars on their bodies that act as physical evidence of their torture. However, even when formerly enslaved people do have indelible markers and personal reminders of their experiences branded on their bodies, those traces typically remain obscured in the stories they tell of their lives and inaccessible to eager audiences who hear them speak in public.

The nineteenth-century slave narrative reveals similar reservations. The narratives do depict scenes of abuse and radical exploitation, but they are often reserved and reportorial in tone. William L. Andrews suggests that though it may be counterintuitive, the nineteenth-century slave narrator was subject to a discourse regime that held subjective perspectives as suspect, and abolitionist audiences preferred instead a speaker who submitted to "objectifying himself and passivizing his voice."[47] Self-effacing narratives that concentrated on facts instead of sentiments were more highly sought after among abolitionists because they conformed to the image of the pacified slave that they wanted to project to audiences.[48] Furthermore, in the case of female narrators such as Harriet Jacobs, cultural norms prohibited divulging sexual intimacies, such that while the narratives might allude to ubiquitous sexual abuse, the scene of sexual trauma is never depicted.[49] Harriet Jacobs is particularly illuminating here; generations of scholars consistently reveal her weaponization of the enforced silences around female sexuality that she used not only to shield herself from the predations of her owner but also as a means to forge an identification strategy between herself and her largely female audiences.[50]

In the new slave narrative, the corporeal effects of slavery are also largely absent from the depiction of bondage, though they are often alluded to or elided in strategic ways. While the testimony of their physical labor and suffering would seem a likely piece of evidence of enslavement and, unlike in the nineteenth century, there now exists a vast contemporary literature of salacious "tell-all" memoirs that genuinely do tell it all, new slave narrators are unlikely to re-expose their own bodies for public consumption in their narratives. The survivor of slavery is typically not wont to dwell on the bodily details of his or her experience in spite of, and perhaps because of, the fact that the body is the space upon which enslavement was enacted.[51] The body's enslavement was all too legible to those who held them captive. The body was the site at which the captor exacted control and extracted labor. Enslaved bodies are often the subject of community gossip and public shame. They may have been held up for community inspection by family members who condemned them for the work they were forced to do. Even nonprofits, purportedly resolute in protecting and assisting survivors, often make a spectacle of the enslaved body. As was true in nineteenth-century bondage, the enslaved is always subject to the "hyperembodiness of the powerless."[52] As a result, slave narrators often keep their own bodies shrouded in a deliberate response to the overwhelming desire for them to disrobe. Nonetheless, their silences, ellipses, and gaps in memory are often the textual spaces in which we can locate the most intimate effects of slavery.

In the new slave narrative (as was often the case in the earlier tradition), it is through maintaining a studied distance from the bodily experience of slavery that survivors often enact their power over their own life narratives. In defiant response to the requisite spectacular subjugation, the nineteenth-century slave narrator "recreate[d] himself as the protagonist of his life story," according to Sidonie Smith. Similarly, the new slave narrator also "maintain[s] a controlled distance between himself in the present as writer and himself in the past as protagonist."[53] As survivor-scholar Claudia Cojocaru admitted, "The only way I could maintain some sense of control over my narrative was by withholding some of the narrative."[54] Many of the narrators express the same anxiety. Shyima Hall recounts that she would often tell people to simply do a Google search for her name to learn more about her so that she could avoid telling people the details of her experience in forced domestic labor. Doing so allowed her to put a distance between her current self and her past self and allowed the current self to have control over what others might know about her past self as well.

New slave narrators often reach the point at which a description of bodily harm seems inevitable (i.e., a scene involving the physical strains of labor, rape or other sexual abuse, or extraordinary physical abuse), but the narratives turn elusive or reportorial in that very moment. Slave narrators sometimes utilize euphemism and simile to expose the more traumatic aspects of their experiences. Amony describes her rape by Joseph Kony at the age of eleven as he did: it was her "turn to spend the night in [Kony's] house" or to "start living in Kony's house as husband and wife." Though she graphically depicts the experience of giving birth to his child only nine months later, she never describes the scenes of her sexual assault or the emotional aftermath.[55] When former child soldier Akallo was "distributed" as a concubine to one of Kony's commanders during the Ugandan civil war, she only recounts, "I felt like a thorn was in my skin as my innocence was destroyed" and says nothing more.[56] Murad was similarly "distributed," to

ISIS soldiers, and when she was first raped, she euphemistically reports, "He came at me, as he'd said he would."[57] When she approaches other moments in which she was raped, she explicitly names it rape but does not describe the experience or the humiliation that followed. Often in these most excruciatingly traumatic moments, there is a section break or paragraph break where the readers are left to imagine what happened on their own, knowing from the previous section that a scene of horror was on the tip of the narrator's tongue but was nonetheless elided in the space between the lines. For other narrators, the persistence of the abuse exacerbates any attempt at narration, and the bodily effects of long-term violence remain necessarily reduced to a report. After Beatrice Fernando recalls once that she was beaten and felt a "stinging pain as the [brush] bristles dug into my flesh," her daily abuse remains undramatized and is reduced to a brief list of offenses: "Not a single day went by without a knock on the head, a squeeze of the ear, a slap on the face or verbal abuse."[58] An exploration of the physical or emotional content of the experience is largely erased while the simple facts of the case are laid out.

Similarly, when Rachel Lloyd describes being recruited by a pimp, she impassively notes, "He rapes me, telling me that it is only fair, as he has to try it first." The simple legal fact of the sexual abuse is laid bare, but her typically dialogue-laden memories turn on that single word, "rape," at the moment of greatest violence. A few pages later, she recalls recognizing that her boyfriend was a pimp because she had "been told to call him Daddy, that he had twisted some wire coat hangers together into a 'pimp stick' to beat me, that I turned over all my money to him every night and got beaten." She does not describe the clients for whom she was compelled to perform sex acts or detail the sexual abuse she endured, and she does not expand on the persistent physical abuse either. Instead, in the next paragraph, she leaps to a more journalistic tone, describing the "average American adult" perception of a pimp. When she comes back to the personal narrative of her relationship with her abuser several paragraphs later, she passingly notes that for not behaving as expected, she got "the choking up and a smack on the side of the face, hard enough that it'll show tomorrow," indicating both the routine nature of the abuse and the bodily evidence that would have existed during her captivity, but without dramatizing the actual scene of the abuse as she does with other events in her life. Lloyd repeatedly shifts midscene like this throughout the narrative—just as events become violent or physical, she maintains control over the way her own pain is depicted and creates a distance from the spectacle of her own suffering.[59]

While many of these books are written by professional ghostwriters who deploy these elliptical strategies to great effect, the narrators who self-publish deflect from their intimate bodily and emotional trauma as well. In fact, even when survivor activists take the stage in public venues and speak extemporaneously, they resort to these same silences. Elaine Scarry has convincingly attributed the metaphorization of bodily suffering to pain's resistance to representation, and to some extent, that certainly seems to be the case in these narratives.[60] In addition, however, narrators who retreat from the bodily detail maintain control over their narratives, extracting their bodies from the frames of their narratives and subordinating that venue of their experience. Their narratives implicitly advance claims as to what constitutes appropriate and sufficient testimony of their own experiences that must be respected and understood. Their life narratives require that readers consume the aspects of the violence against victims of contemporary forms of slavery that those victims themselves deem a complete version of their experience, even when that version does not include graphic details or emotionally charged responses.[61] The bodies of survivors have been all too exposed in slavery; as free activists, they look to alternative forms of evidence to substantiate their claims of exploitation. The strategies of displacement they use to avoid the bodily detail move the frame of reference from the body of the enslaved to a more holistic portrait of the experience of enslavement, demanding a more comprehensive response than mere empathy for a single individual.

STRATEGIES OF DISPLACEMENT

If the humanitarian narrative—whether it is utilized to move the reader to a cause, to provide substantiation of a legal claim, to support a political position, or to serve as public entertainment—requires evidence to achieve its effects, the slave narrator who refuses to hold up his body as specimen must locate alternative avenues for making his enslavement legible. How do slave narrators describe their experiences if they are not willing to focus attention on the very site of the violence they endured, if they are not willing to participate in the "humanitarian pornography" that Mario Klarer describes?[62]

Slave narrators develop alternative strategies of representation that circumvent those traditional requirements of evidence. As Avital Ronell argues, "Silence offers its own syntax of testimony. Yet it runs counter to the traditional adducement of proof, the constitutive demand of cognitive discourse, the demand to prove the existence or reality of the claim one makes according to established rules, so that they can be verified by others."[63] Slave narrators speak through the very silences that pervade their texts. They regularly employ three particular strategies to substantiate claims of slavery while avoiding the bodily detail: deferral to paratextual expert authority, introduction of statistical evidence, and projection of the experience of slavery onto a vast array of supporting characters. Each of these represents a strategy of displacement that allows narrators to deflect attention from their intimate experience at the same time as it elevates the personal to the level of the political, the individual to the representative. Of course, each of the new slave narrators explores his or her experience in unique ways, and no one strategy is common to every narrative. Nonetheless, strategies of displacement both represent and obscure the experience of suffering, refusing the reader access to the intimate details of the author's life while still extending to the reader an engagement with suffering.

One strategy of displacement is the use of prefaces and appendices written by legitimating authorities who verify the survivors' claims (quite similar to those found appended to the nineteenth-century narratives). In the new slave narrative, these paratextual authorizations might include essays by expert professionals such as law enforcement agents or psychologists, as in Timea Nagy's and Theresa Flores's narratives. Cadet incorporates family testimony that gives witness to his posttraumatic symptoms. Nazer's and Muhsen's memoirs contain essays written by their ghostwriters, who testify to the validity of what they wrote in the first person for the survivor. Akallo's *Girl Soldier* is particularly reliant on the paratextual elements of the book. She includes a forward by a prominent Christian rock singer as well as one by the archbishop of the Anglican Church of Uganda, and her first-person chapters are interspersed with chapters of documentary-style evidence provided by her coauthor. As was true of its generic predecessors, the new slave narrative employs these extratextual elements to provide not only the verification of enslavement and suffering but also details that are conceived as speaking into the gaps left by survivor silence.

The deferral to external authority extends into the text of the first-person narrative as well, as the survivor employs statistics and research as proof that her experience is not an individual anomaly but part of a larger local or global trend. Lloyd's *Girls Like Us* includes extensive footnotes, and her prologue introduces UNICEF estimates of commercially sexually exploited children.[64] Before she reveals how she herself came to be counted among these statistics, she preempts her own intimate authority with scholarly evidence that her experience is a quantifiable reality, and she continues to interject scholarly material into her narrative throughout. Instead of mobilizing her bodily suffering as a means of identification for the audience, she uses the magnitude and severity of the problem as a cue that all citizens must respond to the issue. Cadet repeatedly includes sociological passages and statistics that explain the cultural and societal forces that make child labor so pervasive and invisible in Haitian society. In several scenes in which Murad depicts being sexually abused, she zooms out from the scene of her body just as she is about to be harmed in order to provide historical context for understanding ISIS or to discuss religious doctrine and how ISIS has distorted it.

In all these ways, the narratives provide respite from the terror of the moment—for the readers as well as for the narrators—and use the larger context as a strategy of displacement to indicate the larger significance of the narrators' experiences. By indicating that this first-person narrative is simply one among thousands, perhaps even millions, the author validates her own narrative within the context of a much more significant political and economic problem and expands upon the narrative effects of her own individual experience. The reference to the statistical or historical context is both a strategy of displacement and a means of making her singular experience speak for others who were left behind.

As an extension of this universalizing function, narrators, especially those who now work with survivors, also often rely on the experiences of others who were enslaved as a way to tell their own stories and to displace the violence they personally endured. Lloyd, even before she records the statistical evidence of commercially exploited youth, tells the story of an eleven-year-old girl who was trafficked on Craigslist "to adult men who ignore her dimples and her baby fat and purchase her for sex."[65] Akallo depicts the rape of countless other young girl soldiers and civilian women instead of describing her own sexual abuse, but even that depiction is not elaborate. She writes, "He undressed all the women he got from their hiding places. He beat and raped some. It seemed like hell."[66] In the midst of describing his own mistreatment as a child laborer, Cadet redirects to a portrait of the plight of young René, the childhood restavec friend who was brutally beaten for stealing two dollars.[67]

Perhaps there is comfort in sharing the stories of others when the stories of their own violated bodies alienate them and locate the experience too close to their understanding of the self. The inclusion of experiences of others promotes their horrific life experiences to the level of being representative of a larger collective of people in need. It gives meaning to their suffering. Especially when the stories they tell of others are those of people the survivor has aided in recovery, the narratives speak to the way their individual experiences can be put to a greater cause. Though the first-person narrative often allows us to see with the narrator's eyes that which we might not otherwise witness, when the accounts of slavery get too personal, become minutely individualized, or reveal the intimate details of the experiences, slave narrators often turn their narrative eyes away from the worst scenes of their own subjection and allow the experiences of others to speak.

The new slave narrative signals the slave narrator's rejection of the assumed centrality of the body in both slavery and humanitarian discourse. It is in the moment of thwarted expectation, in the scene that elicits both humanitarian impulses and a voyeuristic desire for the flesh-and-blood evidence of the horror of slavery, that new slave narrators express the power to represent their own lives as they see fit and resist captivity, both literal and figurative. Smith and Watson remind us that it is through discourse that particular "aspects of bodies become meaningful—what parts of the body are there for people to see. They determine when the body becomes visible, how it becomes visible, and what that visibility means."[68] As slave narrators attempt to make their enslavement legible, they equally control how they are seen and read. They reserve the right not to write their bodies into the narrative. They remove the captors' power over their bodies by not showing what was done to them. By robing themselves in strategies of displacement, the slave narrators model responsible avenues for engagement that renounce the voyeuristic impulses of human rights discourse. Their narratives provide a counterdiscourse for the spectacular desires that readers bring to narratives of trauma.

READING LESSONS

The process of writing a slave narrative is only the narrator's first step toward legibility. The narrator has been doubted and silenced throughout his or her life. It is only through audiences who read the narrative that the legibility has its intended effects. If the narrative ends up in a drawer or in a fire, slavery remains illegible. On the page, in our hands, slavery becomes real, and readers become witnesses to the violations the narrator endured. The slave narrative creates a condition of mutual support between the narrator and the reader. In order to bring the audience to this knowledge-informed action, the new slave narrator seeks a connection, an identification between herself and the reader to ensure the bond that might spur on action.

In these narratives, a powerful imaginative identification is attempted as the use of the nonfictional, first-person "I" of the enslaved speaker in the narrative is shared with the identity of the audience in the act of reading. As Bok recalls, "Simply by telling what happened to me I could make an emotional connection with the audience. My feelings became their feelings. My passion became theirs."[69] The power of his narrative lies in his having experienced slavery and his willingness to share that experience, even if only partially, with an audience. Even as the narrators turn away from explicit scenes of their own pain, the first-person narrative works to make readers feel implicated in the suffering of the narrator so that they are mobilized against suffering. Readers recognize the humanity of the other through imagining themselves in the survivor's position, however imperfect the identification may be.

Furthermore, when the narrators employ the strategies of displacement described here, which, instead of providing bodily evidence, prove that the narrator's individual experience is representative of a much larger group of suffering humans (whether they are other sexually exploited children or all the people enslaved in the world or perhaps even the whole of suffering humanity), they effect an identification displacement as well. While Scarry warns us that it is nearly impossible for human beings to imagine vast numbers of others, the new slave narrative attempts to bridge the gulf between the single "human face" of slavery and all those who remain enslaved.[70] As Bok describes it, "To them, slavery had been something that happened in a far-off place in Africa they rarely gave a moment's thought to. After my speech, slavery had become a person they had seen, a young Sudanese whose hand they had actually shaken."[71] This synecdochal expansion links the survivor's singular experience to the entire concept of slavery, and through that identificatory process, the reader, too, is connected to all those who are suffering in bondage. This strategic displacement can promote a sense of world citizenship and responsibility that exceeds the bounds of the personal identification with the solitary narrator who suffers.

At the same time, their narratives provide readers with interpretative lenses that make their experiences legible not merely as victims or exploited masses but as survivor activists. Here, a third level of identification is produced. As the narrator becomes an activist in the narrative, readers are not only interpellated as humans who suffer, they are privileged to identify with the one who can eradicate suffering. Joseph Slaughter calls the humanitarian the "third actor in the drama of suffering," between both the violator and the victim as well as between the one who suffers and the one who reads of suffering.[72] This intermediary position "transforms and reroutes that pathetic force into a metonymical relation between the reader and humanitarian figure who is an exemplary extension of our better angels."[73] In third-person narratives of suffering or in narratives in which humanitarians are called to aid others, the identification is with the one who responds to suffering, with the savior figure who inserts himself between violence and the violated.

In the new slave narrative, the role of survivor activist is not located in the in-betweenness of the humanitarian that Slaughter describes but instead unites the slave and the liberator, the victim and the humanitarian, in one identity. While readers are instructed to imagine the greatest depths of bondage with the narrators, they are quickly elevated to what is often figured in humanitarian literature as the greatest height—the savior. This slave-liberator identification allows the reader to empathize with the beneficent and responsible citizen-servant while still eliding the distance between the reader and the one who suffers. It continues to foreground the suffering inherent in slavery and makes a claim to the responsibility we all have as global citizens to respond. More crucially, it defies the slave-liberator dichotomy that so often characterizes both slavery and the abolitionist movements that seek to eradicate it. It marks the survivor's narrative as the source of the greatest expertise on the subject and thus provides a model for responsible activism and engagement that is not from the top down from the distant humanitarian perspective but from one who has been "slave," witness, and liberator him or herself.

Through this process, new slave narrators train readers to see survivor knowledge not merely as that of the victimized but also as that of a participant-observer, one who can speak from intimate knowledge to the larger stakes of the humanitarian cause. In the next chapter, we will see how survivors use that complex positionality to emerge from the conventions of the autobiographical uplift narrative to level rigorous critiques of the limited freedoms available to those who emancipate themselves from slavery.

Chapter Two

THE NOT-YET-FREEDOM NARRATIVE

The title of Jean-Robert Cadet's second memoir, *My Stone of Hope*, is a reference to somewhat lesser-known lines from the "I Have A Dream" speech, which Martin Luther King Jr. gave at the March on Washington in August 1963, a day he said would "go down in history as the greatest demonstration for freedom in the history of our nation." King lamented on that historic day that the United States remained a nation in which "the Negro is still not free" one hundred years after the Emancipation Proclamation.[1] Cadet's memoir recalls the inspirational lines that served as the basis for his slave narrative's title at greater length in his epigraph: "We will be able to hew, out of a mountain of despair, a stone of hope." The "stone of hope" that King holds dear here and to which Cadet alludes is aspirational, forged in the future tense. King's words were a dream for a future yet unrealized. As an emphasis on the futurity of hope, this line acted as a prelude to King's incantation of "let freedom ring," in which he mapped all the many places where freedom *would* exist in the distant utopian democracy of the United States. Those lines conclude in the future conditional:

When we allow freedom to ring—when we let it ring from every village and every hamlet, from every state and every city, we will be able to speed up that day when all of God's children, black men and white men, Jews and Gentiles, Protestant and

Catholic, will be able to join hands and sing in the words of the old Negro spiritual, "Free at last, Free at last, Thank God almighty, We are free at last!"

Not yet free, though not legally enslaved, King represented the sentiments of so many Americans of African descent—that slavery had been abolished but that freedom was yet on the horizon. And though he used the prophetic word "when" to project a sense of the inevitability of these freedoms, the sentiment declared by the spiritual remained a utopian dream that was yet a mirage. King's life work was dedicated to the effort of conjuring this freedom into reality through words and activism. That tension between the certainty of freedom's promise and the unattainability of fundamental rights is at the crux of the problem of freedom, and it is with a reference to this precarious freedom dream that Jean-Robert Cadet chooses to begin his own slave narrative.

For centuries, philosophers have tried to untangle the very same problem that Cadet and King wrestle with in regard to their own and their ancestors' enslavement by defining the essence of human freedom. Western philosophers have handed down to us a dizzying and contrary array of definitions of freedom. With few exceptions, scholars of slavery rarely delve into the intricacies of freedom, and scholars of freedom rarely engage the realities of slavery, further exacerbating the difficulty of defining freedom.[2] When the revered Western philosophers do address slavery and freedom together, the terms are employed metaphorically or metaphysically. Augustine writes that one can be free while enslaved, suggesting the transcendent nature of freedom, while remaining silent regarding the impossibility of exercising that freedom for the enslaved person. Rousseau famously opens his *On the Social Contract* with the aphorism, "Man is born free, and everywhere he is in chains," ignoring the gravity of slavery and its difference from the metaphorical restraints on human freedom outside of literal bondage.[3] Hannah Arendt describes the plight of Western philosophers of freedom well when she famously suggests that thinking of freedom "forces the mind into dilemmas of logical impossibility so that, depending on which horn of the dilemma you are holding on to, it becomes as impossible to conceive of *freedom or its opposite* as it is to realize the notion of a square circle."[4] Centuries of philosophical wrangling with the notion of freedom in the absence of a real engagement with "its opposite" have proven her correct. Many consider freedom an inherent condition of human existence, which, as Zygmunt Bauman points out, leads scholars, especially sociologists (and, I would add, historians and literary scholars), to focus on slavery, when they do, as an "artificial creation, a product of certain sociological arrangements," a perversion of the natural state instead of an inherent facet of the construct of freedom itself.[5] Orlando Patterson attributes this to the fact that freedom is a construct that is always already tacitly defined by European philosophers in opposition to and as a means of distinguishing themselves and, thereby, their unacknowledged privilege from those who are subordinated or enslaved as a result.[6] Enslaved people have no such luxury. As the slave narrative tradition and its twenty-first century manifestation both attest, though slave narrators nearly universally maintain a dogged commitment to the notion of a God-given free will, the discernment of what constitutes freedom—and the plot to gain access to it—is one of the primary conscious acts of enslaved people. They often come to realize, as does Bauman, that "freedom was born as a privilege and has remained so ever since."[7]

In studying these historically entangled lines of thought, one startling reality becomes clear. The philosophers to whom we so often turn for definitions of freedom have never themselves been enslaved. For the European philosophers of freedom, slavery was the often unnamed, unexplored exception to freedom. When King and Cadet invoke the word "freedom," they are not describing a metaphysical state but are typically referring to political freedoms including the right to vote, the right to move freely without interference, the right to participate in the body politic as equal citizens. Their conceptions of freedom were no doubt influenced by centuries of debate regarding freedom that circulated within Western culture, but their conceptions of the unequal distribution of freedom came from the lived experiences of black people in the Americas—from the life stories delivered to them from slave narratives, from the struggles of Haitian ancestors to win freedom from slavery and colonialism, from the recounting of systemic Jim Crow persecution by the generations that preceded them, and from their own and their colleagues' exclusion from political and social life in the United States.

Slave narrators are, thus, the theorists of freedom to whom we must turn if we want to escape freedom's power to obfuscate slavery and bifurcate itself from that most extraordinary challenge to its claim on human existence and consciousness.[8] Formerly enslaved people know the relationship between slavery and freedom most intimately, and that terrible knowledge acts as a unique challenge to those impediments that mark "freedom and its opposite" as practically unthinkable, as Arendt suggests. Admittedly slave narrators and their coauthors are not professional philosophers and are not likely to be steeped in academic debates regarding freedom. They are more likely influenced by political and popular discourse about freedom, and like most people, they sometimes conflate several philosophically discrete theories of freedom in their writings on the subject. However, given the slave narrative's preoccupation with freedom, slave narrators' experientially informed theories should be taken into account as we pursue the complicated question of what defines human liberty. Indeed, some of the most forceful, profound, and significant claims that slave narrators make are not about the nature of slavery but about the nature of freedom in the shadow of slavery.

There is no doubt that freedom is *the* central concern in practically all slave narratives. Paul Lovejoy has argued of the eighteenth- and nineteenth-century narratives (especially those written by people who were born outside of slavery in Africa) that "what usually are called 'slave narratives' would sometimes be better described as 'freedom narratives'" because "their stories often focus on the quest for and achievement of freedom through escape, self-purchase, or other means but always resulting in freedom."[9] As Lovejoy astutely demonstrates, a recalibration of our reading of the slave narrative in terms of freedom sheds new light on the ways slavery is experienced and represented by survivors of bondage as well as on their philosophical approaches to the nature of freedom from the standpoint of slavery.

The new slave narrative is similarly fixated on freedom's journey: on the freedom dreams that haunt slavery, the self-determined emancipation, and the exercise of hard-won liberties after captivity. Liberty, read through these elements of the narrative, is figured as an entitlement of human existence. That essential freedom is reinforced by free birth, which all the new slave narrators assert. In many ways, new slave narrators espouse a notion of freedom as essence that cannot be violated, even by slavery. Their free will inheres, even as they are forced into utter subservience. Their enslavement is figured as a perversion of God's will rather than a lack of freedom itself. Their return to a state of physical freedom is often marked, then, as merely a physical expression of what they suspected to be true all along—that no human can take their inherent freedom away.

However, while the paratextual elements of the texts as well as many of the narrative tropes and conventions of the new slave narrative might allow us to read the texts as "freedom narratives" that effectively act as defenses of liberal, Enlightenment notions of inherent freedom, the life after emancipation that is depicted in the narratives radically contradicts those premises, leaving formerly enslaved people condemned to a status of not-yet-freedom. The freedom-as-futurity evoked by Cadet's epigraph emerges in the new slave narrative in direct distinction to the simplistic blurbs, titles, and childhood nostalgia testifying to the narrators' inherent freedom in their early lives, which were discussed at length in the previous chapter.

Even as they embrace the notion of freedom handed to them by Western discourse, new slave narrators testify to the fact that there is a profound difference between being a nonslave and being free. These narrators suggest that once enslaved, emancipation from captivity becomes a precondition for freedom, but it is not sufficient for the exercise of free will. They suggest, as did Martin Luther King Jr., that freedom is always a persistent mirage of slavery, operating as a distant utopian potential. Slave narratives testify to the unattainability of the privileges of freedom that are reserved for certain social classes. Necessarily relegated to the future tense, the utopian vision of freedom evoked in the new slave narrative is one that is grounded in substantive freedoms that provide people the capacity to pursue lives they deem worth living and that embrace an expansive cosmopolitanism that transcends national borders and grants citizenship to and protects the freedom of all people of the world. In recounting the barriers to substantive, cosmopolitan freedoms encountered postemancipation, the new slave narrative suggests that we might revise Paul Lovejoy's "freedom narrative" moniker further to dub these testimonies to slavery and liberty the "not-yet-freedom narrative."

INHERENT FREEDOMS

As William L. Andrews suggests of the nineteenth-century slave narrative, the most crucial purpose of the slave narrative genre is to " 'tell a free story' as well as talk about freedom as a theme and goal of life" despite the undeniable necessity of depicting the horrors of slavery. The writing of the narratives themselves, Andrews contends, is "uniquely self-liberating, the final climactic act in the drama of their lifelong quests for freedom."[10] The new slave narrative is no different. Descriptions of work and even violence are kept relatively brief, often discussed in euphemism or through other strategies of displacement that allow the narrator to avoid the retraumatizing effects of describing their own suffering, as is discussed in the first chapter. As the bodily detail of enslavement is largely displaced in the new slave narrative, however, the journey to freedom takes center stage, and the act of writing is often celebrated as its own act of liberation. The teleological structure of the slave's life story practically requires the pitting of abject slavery against universal freedom, affirming the binaristic logic that circulates in antislavery circles and in common cultural conversations about slavery, past and present. Narrators must travel from slavery to freedom in relatively unambiguous terms in order to stress the gravity of their enslavement; an obsession with freedom is a marker of legibility when the very fact of slavery is in question.

It is useful to return to Cadet's narratives to unpack the trajectories of freedom that are depicted in the new slave narrative. Like so many of the new slave narratives, Cadet's two new slave narratives are packaged to depict a triumphant rise from slavery to freedom. *My Stone of Hope: From Haitian Slave Child to Abolitionist* projects the same Horatio Alger–style myth-making in its title as his first narrative, *Restavec: From Haitian Child Slave to Middle Class American*. Cadet's own childhood imagination for freedom, however, was primarily constructed in the moments when he heard totalitarian dictator François "Papa Doc" Duvalier's speeches appealing to Haitians' nationalist fervor by evoking the nostalgic memory of their ancestors' struggle for freedom against slavery. Cadet quotes Duvalier's speech, which he heard on Haitian Independence Day when he was a child: "Liberty, Equality, Fraternity. . . . We broke the chains of slavery to seize our own sovereignty. . . . We are proud of our freedom for which our ancestors paid in blood and in gold francs."[11] Liberty, here, is guaranteed to Haitians by dint of their ancestors' struggles against slavery. It is part of the national character that each citizen inherits by birthright. Despite the fact that Cadet was enslaved and the authoritarian Duvalier had an iron grip on his country, this notion of an inherent freedom infused Cadet with a sense of his own rights. Constantly dreaming of the privileges and liberties afforded other children in his neighborhood, Cadet maintained a distinct impression of freedom as constitutive of his human existence, even as he sometimes numbed the psychological pain of his captivity by resigning himself to the seeming inevitability of his enslavement.

The idea that generations of ancestors secured universal freedom for all permeates many of the narratives, but the source of one's essential freedom varies. Carissa Phelps attributes her freedom to "Americans [who] died for it," and Mende Nazer admires that in America, people take their freedom for granted because they were "born into it."[12] These notions of American exceptionalism are challenged by Cadet's claim of inherited freedom in Haiti (though he later appreciates its guarantees in American law) and by others like Shyima Hall, who argues that in Egypt, even though she was enslaved, it was only in subvention of the freedom that had been granted to every citizen.[13]

Though it may be enshrined in law, the theory of freedom that these narrators describe positions liberty as inalienable and transcendent of any nation or law. Undaunted by the external controls placed on his mobility and choices, for instance, Francis Bok trusted that his ability to plot his own escape was itself evidence of his inherent free will. "It was there in my thoughts—my memories of life with my family, and my dreams of escape—that I discovered freedom. Giemma and his family could beat me; they had total control of what I did every day. But they could not touch my thoughts and dreams. In my mind I was free, and it was there in that freedom that I planned my escape."[14] Similarly, Timea Nagy was submitted to the most insidious forms of psychological coercion, but she "couldn't stop formulating and comparing the different variables and possible outcomes of the most colorful escape plots conceivable."[15] Grace Akallo's escape, figured as a resurrection, reveals a similar conception of inherent freedom, but in her case, that freedom was granted to her by God's grace. Animated by an unknown hand that refused her the role of the defeated or murdered slave archetype, Akallo's body itself refused death and slavery.[16] Freedom is established as a state of mind, a way of understanding oneself as inherently free, that allows enslaved people to transcend whatever treatment they may endure and eventually empowers them to escape.

Empowered by this notion of their essential and inherited freedom, enslaved people are nonetheless undeniably and consciously aware that they must struggle for recognition of their right to self-determination. Their actions bound by slavery, an unreasonable and unlawful external inhibitor

to their ability to exercise freedom, slave narrators must pit their philosophical intuition that their freedom is inherent against the material reality of
their lives. Their inherent freedom does not allow them to transcend entirely
the binary categories of slavery and freedom that mark all enslaved people
as unfree in body if not in spirit. When Francis Bok describes his plot to
escape, for instance, his syntax often figures freedom as the opposite of slavery in dramatic rhetorical binaries. Like so many other slave narrators,
when Bok escaped, he says, he enjoyed "this strange new feeling of being
on my own, being responsible for my own choices." He proclaims, "I was
free!"[17] Here a different figuration of freedom is depicted, one in which freedom is an experience that emerges in opposition to slavery, as a release
from slavery, as a rejection of slavery. The promise of freedom regained that
is so central to Bok's narrative implies a very particular and achievable teleological destination that is determined by one's physical freedom and the
ability to make autonomous choices and to choose something other than
that which an external authority imposes. Freedom is that which is
unenslaved, at least in these early moments in the narrative. Similarly, when
Bok wonders at the slaveholder's son's autonomy and independence, he
notes, "His freedom taught me that I had none,"[18] determining his notion
of freedom on his physical captivity; however, he later revises his theory,
recalling his belief that, "I may have been a slave, but I was free to plan my
escape."[19] In this new conceptualization of freedom, slavery is not in opposition to freedom as the semichiasmic structure of that sentence might
suggest. Instead, freedom is ever present and inalienable, even when the
body and its labor are completely subjugated. These two notions of freedom
are in constant tension through the first half of his narrative.

For many of the new slave narrators, freedom is a human quality that
transcends captivity and acts as the internal fuel that drives their persistent plots to escape. At the same time, however, there remains the persistent
material reality of slavery and the challenge of its effects on freedom. New
slave narrators consistently insist that their metaphysical freedom was not
born solely of escape or rescue—rather, it was given to them by their cre-
ators and forebears; it was kept in their minds and hearts throughout their
captivity. But they must see material freedom as a distant goal nonetheless,
a destination on which they must focus singular energy. As Jeremy Waldron suggests and the new slave narrative affirms, the term freedom "may
be used to convey something about the rank or status of human beings;

on the other hand, it may be used concomitantly to convey the demand that the rank or status should actually be respected."[20] Narrators consistently point to the people moving freely around them as evidence of their claims to rights violations, as evidence of their right to the very same freedom. They do not attempt to suggest that their inherent freedoms transcend their bondage in any material way. Instead, like Bok, they highlight the conflict between their ontological freedom and their material captivity in an effort to advocate for every person's right to exercise those freedoms that are inherent.

In this way, the new slave narrative takes part in a venerable abolitionist tradition of understanding freedom as God-given and inherited while slavery is figured as a perversion. William Lloyd Garrison and other nineteenth-century abolitionists saw the institution of slavery—the denial of the rights of men—as an appropriation of a role that rightfully belonged to God: "All those laws which are now in force, admitting the right of slavery, are therefore before God utterly null and void; being an audacious usurpation of the Divine prerogative, a daring infringement on the law of nature, a base overthrow of the very foundations of the social compact, a complete extinction of all the relations, endearments and obligations of mankind, and a presumptuous transgression of all the holy commandments."[21] Moving out of the theological argument and into what we would call a rights-based approach today, Angelina Grimké contends that, "a man, is a *man*, and *as* a man he has *inalienable* rights, among which is the right to personal liberty. Now if every man has my *inalienable* right to personal liberty, it follows; that he cannot rightfully be reduced to slavery."[22] The basic inalienable right of liberty was and continues to be the foundation of abolitionist claims that people of all nations and races should be free of bondage and enslavement, but their arguments are levied precisely at that nonetheless pervasive "daring infringement" that is slavery.

NOT-YET-FREEDOM

Once they emancipate themselves, survivors of slavery in the twentieth and twenty-first centuries often expect that emancipation from oppressive slaveholders will guarantee them the essential, inherent human freedoms provided for in the Universal Declaration of Human Rights, even when they are not aware of the declaration itself. They believe in the protections guaranteed by democratic governments in Europe and North America, where they expect to find asylum. They believe the stories they heard as children of emancipated leaders like Toussaint L'Ouverture, Frederick Douglass, and even the fictional Kunte Kinte, who all rose to become leaders in the struggle for the rights of others once they were free. Postemancipation, however, formerly enslaved writers report that they are free in body and by law, but often not in practice. The notions of transcendent and inalienable freedom do not characterize slave narrators' theories of freedom developed after their physical emancipation, however. Many slave narrators quickly realize they are not able to take for granted that they will be treated as if these ostensible inherent freedoms are universally and equally distributed, even in the countries where they thought their freedom was assured by law and culture. As soon as the exhilaration of escape wears off, slave narrators' postemancipation experiences challenge their expectations of the universality of freedom.

Some of the narrators depict this sense of not-yet-freedom through a questioning of the very idea of freedom itself. Mende Nazer's first narrative poses the problem in a simple rhetorical question that she uses as the hesitant title of her final chapter: "Truly Free?" Though Nazer admits, "I often *feel* fulfilled and free and happy," this titular question reveals Nazer's uncertainty about what constitutes freedom after slavery.[23] Timea Nagy also falters in her faith in her liberation: "What was freedom, I wondered?" she writes, lamenting her incapacity to escape the cycle of enslavement that resulted from poverty and lack of options. After emancipation, she found herself doubted by police, threatened with arrest, limited in work options, and reduced to "a shadow of someone I used to know" as she cycled back into the sex industry after her escape.[24] Brook Parker-Bello, whose Evangelical memoir suggests a divine source for freedom as well as all other human experiences, nonetheless wondered after her escape, "Was I free?" and she lists a long series of impediments to her freedom: crippling fear, self-hatred, suicidal tendencies, and even homosexuality (which she denies is an authentic desire and attributes to the sexual abuse she encountered when she was trafficked).[25] Slave narrators seem to ask: If every human person is born in freedom, why did I have to fight for mine? What is this freedom for which I am fighting, and will I ever attain it? Is it ever possible to gain access to the freedoms promised by Western democracies and human rights protocols?

For Bok, a sense of trepidation regarding the accessibility of freedom comes from a recognition that in his home country, where slavery was illegal and ostensibly all citizens were free, it was impossible for a former slave to attain what he considered to be true freedom. When he escaped from slavery to a Sudanese refugee camp, his choices, mobility, and labor were unsurprisingly still controlled by the state. Bok thought his story of enslavement would help him secure his refugee status within Sudan; instead, police interrogated him for professing antigovernment sentiments by "telling people you are a slave who has escaped," and they subsequently reenslaved him themselves.[26] When he escaped that scene of bondage, he ended up in refugee camp called Jabarona, which, he notes, means "the forced place" in Arabic—a moniker that turns out to be all too apt. Bok was forced to remain there against his will, was refused the freedom of movement that he so closely associated with emancipation.[27] His sense that slavery and freedom operate in binary oppositions quickly faded. In fact, he came to realize that slavery begets slavery. Declaring that he was enslaved in a country where slavery was illegal was seen as an act of sedition. But more compelling is that fact that the police nonetheless insisted upon a present-tense formulation of his identity as slave. They complained, "You have been saying you are an escaped slave."[28] While Bok was telling a story of his *escape* from illegitimate captivity, the authorities who rounded him up thought of him as a slave by nature who had escaped. The difference between these two positions toward his forced bondage is significant, and the notion that he *was* a slave undermined any indication that he might be free by nature or might even be able to attain freedom. It is clear that the freedom that Bok anticipated was never truly his as far as the Sudanese government was concerned.

His refusal to admit and accept that he was a slave in essence was met with brutal violence and a death threat that proved that his life and freedom were of no consequence to the government. Bok admits to having lied to the police in telling them, "I never had a master, I was never a slave," but there is something critical to Bok's resistance to that label that even he and his amanuensis, Edward Tivnen, do not recognize.[29] In refusing to be labeled as a slave—either past or present tense—Bok resisted the demarcation of his identity and his subjectivity as enslaved. He refuted the power of another human to "master" him. At the same time, he was reminded that slavery and freedom are not held in a taut binary opposition. Through abject

violence, the state would not allow him his definition of or right to freedom. In their estimation, endorsed by the state, Bok had no hope of freedom; he would forever be marked as slave, even after emancipation.

Ironically, Bok was later punished for suggesting that slavery existed at
all in Sudan and was simultaneously forbidden from escaping from it. "The
government denied that there was any slavery in Sudan, and they were not
about to let a seventeen-year-old Dinka boy wander from camp to camp
telling everyone he had been a slave for ten years."[30] His story had the power
to rouse the state out of their complacency regarding the refugee camp, but
only insofar as they reasserted their power to intimidate and control the
young man. He could not legally be a slave because Sudan had prohibited
slavery by law, but he was not allowed any alternate status. He certainly was
not free to speak his mind, tell his story, defend his claims, or avoid police
surveillance.

After emancipation, new slave narrators are often left uncertain of even
the existence of freedom because their ability to exercise their free will falls
so radically short of their expectations while enslaved. Literal reenslavement
sometimes awaits the victim of contemporary forms of slavery, but even for
those who manage to break entirely free of their captors, freedom is but a
utopian vision that they can hardly conceive much less fully achieve. Some
struggle to find work and are vulnerable to reexploitation in the labor market. Many others find that their political freedoms are restricted by their
ambiguous status as formerly enslaved people, and their ability to navigate
and participate in society is severely limited and even determined by state
actors who are invisible and inscrutable. Their testimonies of not-yet-
freedom urge us to ask what this freedom, so celebrated in the West, truly
is. Beyond inherent free will, the new slave narrators describe a desire for
freedom that guarantees not only freedom from servitude to others but also
psychological independence, racial equality, self-expression, security, and
mobility (both social and geographic).

As the slave narratives collected here demonstrate, the slavery-freedom
binary immediately dissolves when the terms are defined within the context of political determinants of freedom, for the lack of physical bondage
or legal status as slave does not necessarily guarantee that someone is free
despite being declared free by law or being released from constraints.
Because their postemancipation freedoms are still restricted psychologically, socially, and politically, the stories that new slave narrators tell

reconfigure and contest commonly accepted Western notions of liberty and refute simple binaristic constructions of slavery and freedom. With this profound capacity to interrogate freedom, slave narrators produce a theory of freedom and its failures that emerges from the texts like a horrific specter.

The stories of uplift, successful emancipation, and healing placed in necessary opposition to slavery in the legitimating narratives produced by celebrities, advocates, activists, academics, and pundits imply the possibility for a finished project of emancipation, of full access to human rights outside of slavery (as discussed in a previous chapter). However, the stories the narrators tell of their postemancipation experiences betray the binaristic framings of their books, as discoveries of their not-yet-freedom erupt from the seemingly predictable path to liberty. What emerges from a generic study of the new slave narrative is that while the free origins of the narrators seem to work as a means of establishing their legitimate claims to freedom, the universal access to the practice of freedom is undermined in the chapters that describe liberation after slavery. The lived experiences of emancipation often betray the simple oppositional freedom that we find depicted in the paratextual elements of the texts or in the portraits of innocent childhood freedom that we find at the beginning of most of the narratives.

This focus on contested freedom is reminiscent of the specter of slavery that haunted fugitives from slavery in the nineteenth-century United States, even after legal emancipation. As historian Eric Foner argues, "The death of slavery did not automatically mean the birth of freedom. Instead, it thrust the former slave into a kind of no-man's-land, a partial freedom that made a mockery of the American ideal of the independent citizen. Once Reconstruction had been overthrown, as Douglass put it in 1883, African Americans remained 'only half free,' standing in 'the twilight of American liberty.'"[31] Between disenfranchisement, lack of access to education and work, convict leasing, Jim Crow laws, lynching campaigns, and even today's mass incarceration, many scholars and activists convincingly argue that American slavery simply begat new forms of slavery and repression for citizens of African descent.[32] For black and white female U.S.-citizen narrators writing in the 2010s, discrimination against sex workers, juridical punishment for their victimization, and the constant specter of retributive violence inhibit their ability to exercise their freedoms after emancipation as well, which I discuss at length in chapter 4. For many of the slave narrators of African, Middle Eastern, or Asian descent today, however, it is into this racialized and unequal distribution of freedoms in the West that they emerge as ostensibly free subjects only to confront barriers determined by their race, class, and status as formerly enslaved.

SUBSTANTIVE FREEDOMS

Formerly enslaved people—particularly those from the Global South who find refuge in purportedly democratic countries—critique the unexpectedly compromised freedom that awaits them in emancipation. The promise of freedom that the narrators infer from their childhood memories of freedom, from the humanitarian and aid workers they encounter, from the colleagues and friends who support them after they are liberated, from the news media, and from cultural discourse is revealed to be a utopian vision that remains unrealized and deferred. New slave narrators discover what Hannah Arendt asserted in her discourse on freedom: namely, that "the status of freedom [does] not follow automatically upon the act of liberation." Arendt argues that freedom requires a political sphere in which the free person operates, "into which each of the free men could insert himself by deed and word."[33] It is this political sphere to which the slave narrators aspire, and their narratives are a collective record of blocked entry. The narrators certainly do not suggest that they remain enslaved, per se, but they persistently reflect on the compromised freedom they have access to as refugees, immigrants, people of color, former sex workers, and former captives. This is why I suggest that we might just as aptly describe the slave narrative as the not-yet-freedom narrative.

We can return to Cadet as an example again here. It would be easy to read Cadet's journey to freedom as liberal, nationalist propaganda attesting to the Horatio Alger–style mythology that his cover proclaims. In both of Cadet's narratives—and, indeed, in most of the narratives—however, the conditional nature of freedom takes center stage and contradicts much of the framing and packaging that relies on the notion of inherent or even attainable freedom. His impression, reinforced by American popular culture and state propaganda alike, was that if he were to work hard, remain disciplined, and serve his country more faithfully even than people who were native U.S. citizens, he would have the right to prosperity and the pursuit of happiness. However, the subtitle of Cadet's first memoir (*From*

Haitian Slave Child to Middle-Class American) elides the fact that being an American citizen—and a self-declared middle-class one at that—did not even afford him the "negative" freedoms that he thought were promised: freedom from systematic discrimination, insecurity, injustice, and inequality. Instead, pervasive racism robbed him of all those and his positive freedoms as well, such as his freedom of movement and his freedom to prosper. By the middle of *Restavec* and from the very first pages of *My Stone of Hope*, Cadet recounts his freedom in the United States not only as a struggle—which in itself challenges his inherent freedom—but as practically unattainable. He tells us in the opening chapter that "pulling oneself up by one's own bootstraps can be a Herculean task," but he unambiguously engages in that mythic endeavor as it is intimately linked to his ability to claim the middle-class American freedom he celebrates in his first title.[34] Cadet's liberty is undermined, however, by the long reach of slavery on several intersecting fronts: social, economic, psychological, and political.

The effects of caste and status resonate across the borders from Haiti into the United States and from slavery into freedom. Though Cadet "took a course on United States government and learned that the Constitution protects everyone's political preferences,"[35] protection of his beliefs is not enough; he ironically finds that he is nonetheless socially and economically marginalized by dint of his race. He writes, "My blackness was an obstacle to obtaining the most basic necessities of life."[36] Cadet was unable to live in some apartments because he was black, and he found it difficult to find roommates who would live with him. He was paid four times less than his white counterparts because of his race, and his white colleagues told racist jokes during their breaks. Though he was no longer working under threat of violence, his participation in a free society and labor market was inhibited by racial prejudice, which kept him politically disconnected and socially alienated. When he was called derogatory names, he said that it "had the same effect on me that 'restavec' did when I was a boy."[37] For him, this was an extension of his enslavement; that it happened in the United States, where he thought his equality was assured and his enslavement erased, was a further insult. His denigration was not limited to interpersonal aggressions or microaggressions. Instead, Cadet's survivor experience was persistently mediated by the history of slavery both in his own country and in his adopted country, despite the fact that he was an officer in the U.S. Army, earned a college degree, and married a citizen. His supposed freedom was attended by the "dream deferred" of African Americans in the U.S. South. He justifiably came to believe that to be a black male in America was to be treated as inherently inferior, and to him, that resonated all too clearly with his experience of enslavement. As Bruce Dickson writes of emancipation in the nineteenth century, "The notion that one should receive the benefit from one's labor and, moreover, that one should be able to negotiate the terms under which one worked was a notion many slaves knew and valued."[38] Similarly, Cadet knew that the terms of freedom in a democracy included the right to choose his work, equality under the law, and social mobility, and he also knew when he was being denied those aspects of freedom.

What the slave narrators keenly observe is that some people have *more freedom* to pursue economic, political, and social goals. Formerly enslaved people, for reasons that often preceded their enslavement—poverty, race, social class, descent, nationality, ethnicity, gender, cultural upbringing, etc.—and as a result of their previous enslavement itself, are often cut off from those freedoms or limited in them. Bok, for instance, experienced great relief when he escaped physical bondage, but his sense of liberty was immediately compromised by his mistreatment by the police who reenslaved him and by the depravity of the refugee camps in which he was forced to reside. Bok writes, "I had experienced the relief of freedom, but I now realized that the happiness, the relaxation I felt in the camp—which was really the absence of the anxiety of my life under Giemma and then on the run—was a false sense of security."[39] The absence of being a slave or fugitive is not what constitutes "freedom" for these narrators. Bok notes that to Sudanese people of Arab descent, "we Dinka were all 'abeed' [slave]" even when they were not being held in bondage.[40] The rights to determine his own fate, to speak freely, to move at will, and to avoid captivity were not, in fact, his—not necessarily because any individual enslaved him but because his society had designated his status as subordinate and determined that he could not escape.

Being enslaved is one form of unfreedom that new slave narratives depict, but, in fact, the slave narrative is a testimony to many forms of unfreedom. For Fernando, the aftereffects of her enslavement in Lebanon traveled with her to her home country of Sri Lanka, where she was unable to pursue her dreams or even marry the man she loved. She writes, "If only I could leave this country, I kept thinking, I could find freedom, acceptance, a life without shame! . . . I began thinking that maybe Nuwan and I could be happy in a different country, in a place where we would be accepted as a couple, freed from the chains of the past. We could be happy and free! A tiny seed of hope grew in me. All we wanted now was the freedom to love each other, nothing more."[41] When she was presented with the opportunity for a skilled job that would help her escape her poverty, she thought it was an "impossible dream," but she thought that the money she would make might mean that "people would forget [her] past" and allow her to live her life as she deemed fit.[42] Emancipation presents a vicious cycle of unfreedom—her past meant that she could not pursue her dreams of sustainable paid work, but without money, she would never escape her past. Like Cadet, Bok, and Fernando, many formerly enslaved people find that they lack the mobility, legitimate paid work, and security from violence that they need to be able to secure their freedom in real terms. They are systematically excluded from what they deem real freedom by their status in society.

The narrators often describe themselves as happy after slavery, meeting the utilitarian criteria of freedom. They often find work that is meaningful to them. Several of them report the joy of earning their first paycheck or spending their own money without the consent or approval of someone else, meeting a more resources-based determination of one's access to freedom. The slave narrators realize, however, that achieving these goals— goals common to most humans—does not bring them equal access to free- dom. Neither happiness nor resources are tantamount to the freedoms the slave narrators seek. It is not simply a "negative freedom" from captivity itself that they seek, nor is it happiness or wealth. It is the freedom to pur- sue the lives they deem worthwhile without being inhibited by societal oppression. As described above, Cadet, Bok, and Fernando all encoun- tered the problem that Amartya Sen demonstrates in his *Development as Freedom*: "The freedom of agency that we individually have is inescapably qualified and constrained by the social, political, and economic opportu- nities that are available to us."[43] The inhibitors that slave narrators point to as deterrents to their freedom demonstrate a shared commitment to what Amartya Sen and Martha Nussbaum call "substantive freedoms." Sen and Nussbaum engage a "capabilities approach" in their understanding of freedom. In Sen's model, freedom is measured by the capabilities we have to exercise it. In his formulation, people are free insofar as they have the ability to pursue a life that they have reason to value.[44] While individuals may have different abilities or incomes or contexts that determine the likelihood of their accessing certain commodities or levels of happiness, in Sen's formulation, as in the slave narrators', freedom is more appropriately determined by a person's capacity to pursue the life he deems worthwhile.

As Nancy Hirschmann frames it, freedom is socially constructed in such a way that ideological and societal norms determine the access that any individual has to exercise her free will. In the case of the intimate-partner abuser that she uses as a test case, for instance, "a battered woman is up against something more than a single abuser in the social construction of her choices. Rather, the abuser derives his power to restrict his partner's freedom from the set of ideological beliefs and norms that constitute the basic tenets of patriarchy."[45] That is to say, spousal abuse is not condoned publicly, but it is promoted ideologically through patriarchal notions that circulate freely in our cultures. As with spousal abuse, social and ideological imperatives mark the unfreedom of certain races, classes, genders, and statuses as acceptable, even as the promise of freedom is celebrated as universal. And though the law may explicitly provide protection against any violent restraints on our freedom and everyone might openly condemn the practice of slavery, in reality, commonly held ideologies and beliefs about race, class, and gender as well as capitalism and individual worthiness of freedom determine who is allowed to exercise freedom.

The social mobility that slave narrators thought was guaranteed to all who worked hard and adapted to life either in freedom at home or in Western democracies reveals itself to be a mirage. Instead, their inferiority by dint of birth or past experience is socially reinforced outside of slavery, at home and abroad. They are inhibited from the pursuit of their goals because they are up against not only the power of individuals to enslave them but against the power of society and ideology to restrict freedom. Enslaved people dream of a day when they will be treated as equals, both in the eyes of the government and in the eyes of their fellow citizens. Their definitions of freedom are bound up in a right to equality, but the social, political, and economic realities of their lives betray the promise of equal access to sustainable freedoms.

"A SLAVE MENTALITY"

In addition to the not-yet-freedom that narrators describe in terms of economic and social mobility, the vast majority of the slave narrators describe a psychological afterlife of slavery, which haunts them long after they have escaped the clutches of their enslavers. Many of the slave narrators feel that their freedom is inhibited by the psychological repercussions of their experience and are persistently haunted by the real or imagined specters of their captors. These narratives of psychological haunting reveal the way trauma undermines people's capacity to access the substantive freedoms—or the ability "to choose a life one has reason to value" as Amartya Sen puts it—that the narrators seek. Slave narrators compel us to contemplate how psychological trauma might both intersect with and perhaps complicate the capabilities approach to freedom. What would it mean, for instance, if a person is unable to imagine a life that he has every reason to value? Or if he believes himself inherently incapable of attaining a life he deems worthwhile? Neil Roberts suggests that "the slave's trauma is also existential, its effects capable of distorting awareness of an agent's inherent capabilities."[46] The idea that formerly enslaved people should be able to make the choices to which they might reasonably aspire relies on their capacity to recognize their own capabilities, assuming they are not disabled by trauma.

Perhaps it is not surprising, however, that the most frequent inhibitor to freedom depicted in the narratives is demonstrably psychological trauma. Cadet, for instance, found himself unable to escape the psychological effects of slavery, which haunted him long after emancipation. "During meals I sometimes locked myself in a closet and refused to come out. Other times I would eat alone in the kitchen where I was more at ease, as if I had become a child restavec again. . . . The nightmares began to come back. Almost every night I was screaming and fighting a giant monster which caused me to kick and punch Cindy [my wife]."[47] The cover of the narrative admits to Cadet's struggle to "surmount the psychological wounds of slavery," and it was indeed a Sisyphean struggle. Cadet could not function well in public or even in familial settings, a debilitating psychosis he attributes to the "social death" (in Orlando Patterson's terms) he experienced as a restavec because he was not allowed to socialize with family and friends.[48] While he may have felt "free, renewed, and vindicated" when he finally confronted his "mistress" about the torture she inflicted on him as a child, and he indicates that his life improved some through therapy, he admits that these attempts at changing his life "were not a cure."[49] He continued to urinate in his bed long after he was an adult, a traumatic reaction he developed shortly after being enslaved.[50] His wife testifies to the nightmares he continued to have even after he had written his memoir and had undergone therapy.[51]

Cadet is not alone; the new slave narrative is a testament to the long-term psychological effects that reach into every aspect of survivor lives. Mende Nazer experienced a similar impediment to psychological freedom, recounting that "the nightmare of my years in slavery didn't end as soon as I escaped. It was just the nature of my suffering that changed."[52] She struggled to make relationships with people as an equal because "ever since my capture, everyone I'd met had been a master, a member of a master's family, a master's friend or one of their slaves."[53] Even exceedingly banal experiences, like having a meal or visiting a friend, were shaped by the social economy of slavery. She admits, "One of the most difficult things for me still is to be served in a restaurant. It just doesn't feel right."[54] Nazer's limited psychological freedom undermines the myth of social mobility in Western cultures. Though she was seemingly free to enjoy the income she earned from her free labor and to participate in the social relationships that were denied her in bondage, her ability to navigate the social terrain outside the role of the submissive servant was limited by her training and psychological trauma. As a result, she struggled to imagine any role for herself that would allow her the social mobility she sought after slavery.

Narrators recount the long reach of psychological trauma and the haunting effects of captivity that seem interminable many years after their escape. Shyima Hall echoes the vast majority of slave narrators when she writes, "I never anticipated how difficult it would be to change my mind-set from being a captive to being a free person, or how complicated life could get in the process."[55] Hall was haunted by fears of people who reminded her of her captor, of practicing a religion of her choosing, and of seemingly simple human interactions. New slave narrators read these experiences as a psychic aftereffect of slavery that restricts their ability to attain the freedoms they seek. In this way, it sometimes seems that slave narrators embrace a utilitarian view of freedom. The narrators are compelled by the belief that they should be free to be happy, that emancipation should mean escaping the trauma and psychological terrors associated with their enslavement. To be truly happy, then, seems to be the marker of their individual freedom.

Complicating matters, however, several of the narrators conflate a certain self-described psychological captivity with the many social and economic barriers they encountered to the substantive freedoms they sought after emancipation. In this way, the psychological determinants of not-yet-freedom become relevant to the narrators' calls for substantive freedoms. As is the case with Nazer's self-directed critique of her inability to function socially after slavery, many narrators find it challenging to fully place responsibility outside themselves for the harm that has been (and continues to be) done to them. Cadet writes, for instance, of the ways in which his race deterred him from accessing the social mobility he had anticipated in the United States in this way: "I seemed to be trapped by my background and the color of my skin, neither of which I could change. I felt embarrassed, isolated, confused, and out of place. I wondered if I would ever escape these horrible states of mind."[56] Internalizing his alienation from social and economic engagement as a psychological disability or a "horrible state of mind," Cadet takes on a degree of personal responsibility for what is clearly a failure of the state and society to protect his rights, even as he interrogates the racism and classism that are limiting his freedoms. Being able to exercise his freedom as a citizen is essential to Cadet's ability to attain the social mobility he seeks. His emotional response to societal limitations leaves him feeling isolated and trapped within his own haunted mind. Resigned to the possibility that his "mistress" Florence had psychologically scarred him to an extent that made happiness and sociability impossible, social mobility became his myopic focus because it was a material pursuit that existed outside his troubled psyche. As he discovered the inequities of his work and social lives after emancipation, however, Cadet admitted to himself that he "had accepted the position with the mentality of a slave."[57] He figures his trained resignation to his subordination in the labor market as a kind of "slave mentality" that he did not shake after emancipation and which was itself reinforced by the economic and political circumstances that determined his social status in the United States. This conflation of personal responsibility with the responsibilities of society, culture, or the state is instructive in thinking about how freedom is configured in the new slave narrative. On the one hand, it demonstrates the way people intellectually resign themselves to systemic problems by internalizing those problems. On the other hand, while institutional racism limited his access to economic and social freedom, his psychological trauma—from slavery and not-yet-freedom—does, in fact, limit his capacity to imagine reasonable goals and expectations for himself. He—like Nazer, Mam, Hall, and others—is inhibited in his freedom by his internalization of his relegation to the role of submissive subject.

This psychological lens puts pressure on the concept of substantive freedoms and a person's right to pursue that which he deems valuable. Does psychological trauma inhibit a person's capacity to exercise his capabilities? Nancy Hirschmann's example of the abused wife can be instructive here as well. She explains that a battered woman can internalize a sense of her own inferiority as well as the ideas that violence is endemic to relationships. She may believe that she is to blame for her spouse's violence to such an extent that her choices are inhibited and her range of choices seems limited by the psychological harm caused by the abuse. As a result, women often "choose" to stay with abusive spouses (as enslaved people often do with their enslavers), but this points to the construction of freedom and the contingencies of gender for the construction of choice.[58] For formerly enslaved people, the psychological harm done to them in bondage limits their sense of their own capabilities, their ability to function in social situations, and their sense of the range of opportunities that might be available to them as a result. Society's rejection of them for a range of reasons reinforces this internalized sense of inferiority. Their freedom is thus constructed by the societal circumstances into which they emerge as emancipated subjects, but it is also constricted by their own internalization of the ideologies that position them as slave, even after emancipation. Their experience in slavery allows them to recognize the institutional, economic, political, and social impediments to the universal inherent freedoms they imagined from childhood and in their captivity, and yet their psychological trauma inhibits their ability to believe that they have a right to desire those freedoms. When they do desire them, social interactions suggest that these freedoms are not accessible to the formerly enslaved. Thus, their ability to determine what constitutes a life worth valuing is necessarily circumscribed. This constricted experience of freedom and the limitation of choices for formerly enslaved people—especially those who are immigrants, women, or people of color—run contrary to the experiences of the white, unenslaved men they encounter, for whom the expectation and attainability of substantive freedoms is normative.

THE STATE OF FREEDOM

Perhaps ironically, given all the impediments to freedom they recount, Cadet and his fellow slave narrators embraced whatever freedoms they were allowed in the countries in which they were granted asylum or citizenship with a fervor unique to people escaping hardship in other countries. Cadet joined the army in the United States, was promoted rapidly, and went to college on a scholarship to become an officer. He became a U.S. citizen and proclaimed triumphantly that he gradually became American. He chastised a black high school student for not embracing the very same Pledge of Allegiance that he had critiqued when he was a young man. For Cadet, like many other migrant slave narrators, refuge in the West was such a relief from the strains of enslavement that he felt he must celebrate the freedoms associated with national mythologies. Tina Okpara expresses her gratitude to her country of refuge in her acknowledgements, writing, "I thank France, the country that freed me and gave me justice" because it was the French courts that eventually determined that she had been enslaved by the Okpara family (who gave her their name when they enslaved her).[59] Bok shook the hand of the president and spoke before Congress, where he was surprised that the nation's leaders would actually listen to the requests of "an ex-slave who had never been to school."[60] "Here in America," he writes, "a free country, I can tell my story, and I will keep on telling it."[61] For Nazer, that sense of trust took time to build: "Everyone kept telling me that I was safe, that no one could recapture me on the streets of London. It just wasn't possible. But it took some time for me to fully believe that England was a free country and that the authorities there would protect powerless people like me from those who I had believed were all-powerful."[62]

Practically all the narrators from the Global South who moved to the West were enormously grateful to be in a country that ostensibly guaranteed their freedom and access to empowering political mechanisms. For so many of the narrators, however, those trusts, though long fought for, were ill-founded. When Bok realized that freedom was not guaranteed to him in Sudan and it began to seem, in fact, that only slavery was guaranteed for the Dinka, his dreams turned to escaping Sudan to find a place where he could be free.[63] Bok immediately recognized in a refugee camp that he had to apply to larger national and international entities for his freedom: "She asked me why I came to Cairo, what I wanted the UN to do for me. 'I want to be free,' I told her. She asked me what country I wanted to go to. I told her that I didn't care. I wanted only to leave Mrica, I did not want to go back to Sudan. I said, 'I just want to be safe and free.'"[64] He wanted security and liberty, but his freedom was entirely contingent on being granted asylum by a sovereign state. All notions of inherent freedom or inherited freedom disappeared in the refugee camp. It was no longer a supernatural power that granted freedom—it was the state. Bok did appeal for and win refugee status, but even then, the struggle for freedom was defined by state conferral. Granted his own individual freedom by the United States, he then sought a greater freedom—freedom within his own country's borders. Bok writes,

From those historical precedents [African American and South African struggles for freedom], I have learned that no one gives a people oppressed for generations their freedom and equality without a struggle. You have to fight for it. But a poor people like the southern Sudanese cannot do it alone. They need help. And that is why my work with the AASG has become so important to me. I am in a position to ask the Americans to help us in our struggle for freedom and equality. And when we achieve those goals, I will go back to Sudan to retrieve what I lost by growing up in the north as slave: the culture and traditions of my people. For me that will be proof of my freedom. Certainly, here in America I am free. But I am still a guest.[65]

Here, there is a sense of the contingency of freedom both in the United States and in Sudan. He does not quite attain the freedoms of U.S. citizens as he is still a guest, but he still must enlist the assistance of his host country to guarantee his freedom in his own country. In this formulation of freedom, the struggle for freedom and the determination of who will hold it are fought not at the level of enslaved and slaveholder but at the level of the state.

The new slave narrator is inundated by cultural cues that indicate that freedom is a promise that is protected by democratic governments, a universal human right guaranteed by global declarations. Particularly in the years following September 11, 2001, and the bombing of the World Trade Center in New York City, when—not coincidentally, as we will see in the next chapter—the new slave narrative began to reemerge, the language of fundamental freedoms and the democratic promise to protect those freedoms took center stage. The new slave narrators regularly remark upon the extraordinary distance between Western Enlightenment aspirational promises of freedom and the extreme conditions of bare life that they encountered when they liberated themselves from enslavement. As the new slave narrative attests, even governments that purport liberty to be inalienable also maintain the purview to grant it and take it away, determine who is citizen and who is alien, distribute rights and refuse them. Nazer's attempts at gaining asylum, for instance, are evidence of the way her freedoms were severely limited even in democratic England. Nazer, who was enslaved both in Sudan and in a London suburb, sought asylum in Britain so that she could be protected from reenslavement by her former slaveholders, which she felt was inevitable if she returned home. With her enslavement known to police and to friends, Nazer believed her freedom would be protected in England even while the slaveholders remained there. In order to live a life free of the terror and literal captivity she believed would be her fate if she returned to her native Sudan, however, she had to prove to the British government that she would specifically suffer the persecution of the state. When she could not prove that, the British government refused her asylum.[66] "I believed that Britain was a democratic country that respected human rights, justice and freedom. For the first time in my life, I had started to feel safe and secure in this country. I cannot believe that the British government will now send me back to face the horrors that for certain await me in Sudan. I am shocked and shaken to the core by this asylum decision."[67] Nazer's asylum request was denied because she was found to be in no harm from state actors in Sudan—her security, her life, and her freedom were all dependent on the state's determination of the legitimacy and extent of her persecution and suffering, a determination that rested in the hands of the British government. The end of her book—as celebratory of her freedom in England as it is—is still weighted with not-yet-freed anticipation regarding her qualification for asylum, which is the only way she can return home and see her parents after decades apart. Her freedom of mobility is entirely regulated by the British government, as are her security and happiness. Though she says she "*often feels* fulfilled and free and happy," her conclusion is written in a trepidatious future tense in hopes that she will attain the utopian dream of freedom of movement: "Maybe my story will have a happy ending, after all. *Insha'Allah*—God willing."[68] Her fate in Britain's hands, she still assigns her freedom to God's will. Without state recognition of her persecution, however, Nazer could not gain permission to pursue what she considers her God-given freedom. Similarly, Tina Okpara had to thank France for granting her asylum. As an illegal immigrant, Okpara did not have the ability to fully emancipate herself without the intervention and generosity of the state. In fact, she could have been treated as a criminal for the transgressions of her captors. The fact that the state was involved in determining her status provides significant proof that liberty is not an inalienable right—that, in fact, it is a gift of the state.

Cadet sums up the precarity of state-granted freedom when he proclaims that he had not quite realized that "'liberty and justice for all' was not to be taken too literally by anyone whose skin color was similar to mine."[69] He laments, "There I was, a non-native black man trying to make his way in the 'land of the brave and the free,' only to find how the cards in U.S. society are stacked against an outsider."[70] For all these slave narrator outsiders, freedom is merely a mirage on the horizon, constantly touted as universal by those around them but accessible by successful application only. Eric Foner argues, "Abolitionists [of the nineteenth century] glimpsed the possibility that the national state might become the guarantor of freedom, rather than its enemy. At a time when the authority to define the rights of citizens lay almost entirely with the states, abolitionists maintained that emancipation would imply not simply an end to the legal status of bondage, but a national guarantee of the equal civil rights of all Americans, black as well as white."[71] Of course, as Martin Luther King Jr. proclaimed one hundred years later, that guarantee had never been made good. As is clear in Cadet's case, even well into the twentieth century, the nation did not guarantee equal rights to its black citizen, even if the law indicated it would. And for all other formerly enslaved applicants, they must apply as the suffering supplicant, indicating the not-yet-freedom inherent in a system that requires the state to approve one's freedom. The notion handed down to the world's citizens by the Enlightenment-era revolutions of Europe and the United States that the role of government is to *protect* our inherent freedoms meets a perplexing contradiction when it is the state that determines whether or not to *grant* freedom to a person.

The new slave narrative puts into stark relief the extent to which our supposedly inalienable freedoms have been ceded to the state. Formerly enslaved people recount having to apply for their rights and for their freedom. Cut off by societal, ideological, economic, and state inhibitors, many of the narrators realize that the freedom of the former slave is not taken for granted as an inherent human right but is considered a privilege defined and bestowed by the state. If a state can grant an individual rights, then the rights are no longer essential. Who is counted as human or citizen suddenly comes into play, and those who are excluded from those categories are excluded from those rights and protections. The terrifying consequence of this is that if a government can grant freedom, then it can revoke it. This is the consequence that is all too real to the former slave.

The state is unprepared for formerly enslaved subjects. There is no language for applying to be recognized as a former slave. For twenty years now, formerly enslaved people have had to create a language to describe their experiences, to make themselves legible, and to convince the governments to protect them as citizens and humans endowed with rights. Despite all the transnational conventions and national and local laws governing labor, formerly enslaved people must still demand legal protections, remedies, and freedoms that are purportedly guaranteed them by dint of being human. As a result, the former slave is in the position of persistently applying for status, for rights, for citizenship, for a place in the economy, for political engagement. New slave narrators seek shelter in places where they believe their past captivity and social status will not determine their present and future mobility, both physical and social. They expect that they will be treated as citizens of the world, guaranteed the protections of the Universal Declaration of Human Rights, which proposes that all humans have a right to the protections of states that declare their governmental function to lie precisely in the protection of people from violations of their rights. Instead, they find that an ironic twist has occurred—the protectors of rights have become purveyors of rights.

These narratives collectively reveal that freedom, while it may very well be considered inalienable in the rhetoric of the West, is rarely understood as an inherent characteristic of human experience in practical terms but instead is experienced and even sometimes distributed as a privileged status, condoned, created, and managed by the state to which formerly enslaved people, refugees, and noncitizens can make only nominal claim. People who seek to attain this "right" to "freedom" are required to mobilize powerful advocates (as Mende Nazer was required to do to attain her asylum) if they hope to attain the promise of freedom. And that freedom remains ever a promise and only a promise, ever fleeting and unobtainable—ever a mirage on the horizon.

COSMOPOLITAN FREEDOM: "HEARTS LARGER THAN WHOLE CONTINENTS"

Read together, the new slave narrators redefine freedom as a multifaceted, elusive, psychological, and political project, grounded in substantive, cosmopolitan freedoms. When the new slave narrators escaped slavery, they believed they would immediately experience freedom. But what they realized instead was that they were marginalized, liminal, stateless, exiled. This left them little room to make claims to rights. They were under the impression that they were free by nature, but they needed a state to guarantee it. Where do the stateless turn to request or exercise or protect their rights? They have to believe that despite their places of birth, there will be a place of refuge that will ensure and endorse their freedom.

But what citizenship can the formerly enslaved claim? Enslaved in their own countries and alienated from citizenship and its rights in the countries in which they seek refuge, the new slave narrators seek out alternative venues for their claims to rights only to find compromised citizenship everywhere they turn. The fact of this reality consistently refutes the conventional themes of uplift and the positive teleologies promised on the surface of the slave narrative and other human rights narratives. The new slave narrators—those from the Global South in particular—do not abandon the promise of freedom in response to the barriers they encounter. Instead, they are invested in a notion of freedom that is grounded in autonomy that transcends state sovereignty. Insofar as they are inhibited from exercising their autonomy because of the restrictions of state governments or because of the state's sovereignty over who has status within its borders, they feel as though they have been robbed of the very freedoms that those states are sworn to protect. In the face of the overwhelming power of the state to undermine their autonomy, they envision a world without borders, a world in which their mobility is not restricted by government regulation, a cosmopolitan freedom that transcends state sovereignty altogether. Collectively, the new slave narrative lodges a forceful critique of the failures of freedom in the West and the lack of the cosmopolitan, substantive freedoms about which the narrators dreamed while enslaved.

The slave narratives' critiques of state-based freedom imply an alternative definition of freedom. The narrators' vision of freedom is global; it is bounded by no specific state. Their experience of oppression allows them—essentially requires them—to transcend the national boundaries determined by states and often enforced by birth. As Mende Nazer describes this cosmopolitanism, "Where are my roots now? My real identity? Am I still a Nuba girl? Or am I a best-selling author? Am I an escaped slave, or an award-winning human rights activist? Am I Sudanese? British? Or just a citizen of the world? I am probably a hybrid of all these things."[72] They imagine the freedom to live as citizens of the world under the protection of global declarations that seek not only to eradicate slavery for all the world's citizens but to guarantee substantive freedoms for all globally. As Christien van den Anker suggests and the new slave narratives attest, if freedom from slavery is a human right, then it is imperative that we recognize and activate the "role of other governments toward people whose rights are violated by their own government."[73] She suggests that insofar as any government has a role in determining a person's freedom, its primary function should be in the role of increasing individual access to freedoms across borders. She provides evidence that trafficking and slavery are exacerbated by the restrictive regimes of migration and border crossing, making impoverished people who migrate from the Global South particularly vulnerable to restrictions on their freedoms. Embracing a "cosmopolitan approach to human rights" similar to van den Anker's, the new slave narrators promote a notion of cosmopolitan global citizenship in contrast to the long processes, applications, bureaucracies, and even literal barriers that undermine their access to the freedoms promised by the democracies in which they seek asylum as well as by their home countries. Thus, cosmopolitan mobility is essential to the notion of freedom that particularly emerges from the first decade of the new slave narrative. The narrators understand that it was their ability to move from their sites of subjection to sites of ostensible freedom that differentiates them from the millions of people who remain immobile and encumbered by the fetters of slavery.

To this end, the new slave narrators believe that those freedoms should be shared by all humans regardless of whether they are under the protection or asylum of a seemingly democratic nation or simply seek substantive freedoms in their own countries away from their captors. They promote equal access to freedom and believe that "freedom that is guaranteed for one must be guaranteed for all."[74] Indeed, for many of the slave narrators, part of their process of freedom is grounded in the notion that none of us can be free until all of us are free. Even Grace Akallo, who emerged from a grave and led her friends like disciples through the desert to freedom, admits, "I knew I was alive but not free because of my friends. I had left them in that hell."[75] She admits a sense of conflict in the unequal freedom she possessed but tried to transform it into an opportunity to make change for others: "I did not deserve the freedom I have now more than they, but there is a purpose for my freedom."[76] Farida Khalaf was similarly disturbed by her privilege even within this unequal distribution of freedoms: "For how could I enjoy my own freedom if [my mother] was still imprisoned?"[77] For people who have themselves been enslaved, the reality of captivity is all too close, and any existence of slavery is a sign that they might be brought back into slavery. It makes them ever more conscious of the barriers to their personal and political freedoms and of the significant risk of return- ing to bondage. The responsibility of the former slave becomes clear—to ensure a slave-free existence for all other humans regardless of back- ground, race, nationality, location, gender, or status. They feel bound to this responsibility.

The idea that we cannot be free if there are other people in the world who are enslaved might easily be disregarded as a trite truism. Our freedom, in fact, might be responsible for or the beneficiary of the enslavement of oth- ers, less directly than in the plantation system of the antebellum South but nonetheless significantly. However, the cosmopolitan outlook that the new slave narrators bring to the conversation is one described by Martha Nuss- baum in *For Love of Country*, in which she suggests that we "conceive of the entire world of human beings as a single body, its many people as so many limbs."[78] When this is the conception of the body politic, it is indeed conceivable that one person's freedom is dependent on the freedom of all the other people who constitute that body. The new slave narrator seems to ask, with an estimated forty million people enslaved in the world today, in every single nation on the planet, with people from all walks of life repre- sented, who among us can say that we are necessarily free?

We might conclude, then, that the most radical experience of servility inspires a vision of the most expansive notion of freedom. What the new slave narrators seem to collectively endorse is a kind of cosmopolitan, sub- stantive freedom that is granted equally to all citizens of the world. As exiles from their home countries (or, in other cases, from their families, commu- nities, benefactors, colleagues, friends, and faith-based communities), many formerly enslaved people are by necessity global citizens. In the process of developing their own ability to make a home elsewhere, this international group of formerly enslaved people came to believe that their rights should not be tied to their own nations or to any other, that their freedoms should not be guaranteed only on their native soil, that their equality should not be dependent on their race, that freedom should not be fettered by their circumstances. They emerge as global citizens more by necessity than by deliberation.

Like Martin Luther King Jr., however, the new slave narrators are burdened with the unfortunate futurity of this vision of freedom and the immediate unattainability of it. Because national borders are so deeply embedded in the ideological projects of most cultures in the twentieth and twenty-first centuries, Martha Nussbaum diagnoses such a position with a sense of "boundless loneliness." She writes, "If one begins life as a child who loves and trusts his or her parents, it is tempting to want to reconstruct citizenship along the same lines, finding in an idealized image of a nation a surrogate parent who will do one's thinking for one. Cosmopolitanism offers no such refuge; it offers only reason and the love of humanity, which may seem at times less colorful than other sources of belonging."[79] This is indeed a trap of cosmopolitan freedom for formerly enslaved subjects. On the one hand, the notion grows out of the recognition that freedoms and opportunities should be equally distributed among all the world's citizens. On the other hand, the realization that this is not what is provided for by the world's nations as they are currently construed sets a person adrift, unable to reconcile her sense of what is right with her understanding of what is real. In response, the new slave narratives return to the most transcendent, global, inherent definition of freedom while maintaining the necessity of the practical freedoms that all humans require to lead lives they deem valuable. Thus, the narratives tend to end on a bittersweet note—sorrowful optimism told in the future conditional that perhaps one day we might all be free.

Chapter Three

BLACKFACE ABOLITION

Frederick Douglass's 1855 narrative *My Bondage and My Freedom* provides critical personal insight into the influence white abolitionists like William Lloyd Garrison had on the shape and structure of his earlier life narrative and of the lectures he was invited to give while touring the United States for fourteen years. The combination of his intimate personal experience of slavery, his extraordinary intellect, and his autodidactic education in the politics and economics of the "peculiar institution" put Douglass in a unique position to provide the "philosophy" and expound upon his own sophisticated political claims. As far as many white abolitionists were concerned, however, Douglass was merely the black face of the movement, relegated to the role of illustration, instead of political philosopher. He recalls how this realization became sedimented in his understanding of his colleagues' perception of him: " 'Give us the facts,' said Collins, 'we will take care of the philosophy.' . . .'Tell your story, Frederick,' would whisper my then revered friend, William Lloyd Garrison, as I stepped upon the platform. I could not always obey, for I was now reading and thinking. New views of the subject were presented to my mind. It did not entirely satisfy me to narrate wrongs; I felt like denouncing them." Douglass's own politics were not of particular concern to eminent abolitionists like Garrison and his colleagues in the Massachusetts antislavery movement. In fact, when Douglass drew his own conclusion that the Constitution was a document that held within it the

requirement of a slave-free nation, a contention to which Garrison was ada-
mantly in opposition, Douglass was exiled, and his life story was no longer
of use to the revered white activist.

In the same year as Douglass published *My Bondage*, a small coalition
of revolutionary activists, including Gerrit Smith, James McCune Smith,
Frederick Douglass, and John Brown, splintered from the mainstream
abolitionist movement to form the Radical Political Abolitionists. They
admitted to only one ambition: the immediate emancipation through governmental decree of all enslaved people in every U.S. state. In *The Black
Hearts of Men*, John Stauffer suggests that John Brown and Gerrit Smith
transcended the pervasive sense of racial superiority among white abolitionists in that their "individual self-definitions crossed racial lines. They defined
themselves publicly by constructing authentic, intelligent, and black per-
formative selves—the wearing of a mask, so to speak—that helped them to
blur and subvert racial barriers."[1] To the New York–born African American James McCune Smith, that black mask, or "black heart" (as Stauffer
calls it), was the only way for a white American to genuinely embrace the
cause of abolition; he had to viscerally experience the shame of slavery and
forgo the sin of white privilege. That "black heart" led John Brown to sac-
rifice his own life for the cause of his black and black-hearted brethren.

Even as Douglass's fellow abolitionists were cultivating "blackhearted-
ness" as a sign of their progressive stance toward race and their spiritual
transcendence of the American sin of slavery, the black minstrel tradition
was taking root in the United States, entertaining white audiences with par-
odies of black life. Frederick Douglass wrote in the *North Star* of October 27, 1848, that minstrel shows were produced by "the filthy scum of white
society, who have stolen from us a complexion denied to them by nature,
in which to make money, and pander to the corrupt taste of their white fellow citizens."[2] Douglass knew the difference between a black heart and
blackface. Both are imbued with a peculiar desire regarding blackness. The
difference is in the motivation for and means of engaging that desire. For
the Radical Abolitionists, "the true spiritual heart was a black heart that
shared a humanity with all people and lacked the airs of superiority of a
white heart."[3] The minstrel show, on the other hand, was no spiritual
engagement with the oppressed black community. Blackface instead provided license to white actors to behave in absurd and childish ways, to perform the fop and the dandy, as if those behaviors and types were innate to

the black race. Blackface provided white minstrels a taste of the freedom of expression they imagined to be an inherent aspect of black life, even as people of African descent lived in slavery and had their own expressions entirely circumscribed by law and practice. It "conveniently rationalized racial oppression," as Eric Lott contends.[4] "Minstrelsy was an arena in which the efficient expropriation of the cultural commodity 'blackness' occurred," but it was also the cultural space in which "racial conflict and cultural exchange are negotiated between men."[5] The blackface imagination of black life was limited, not transcendent; it was a display of the radically other that merely implied the radically intimate.

But white abolitionists were not entirely free from the snares of a blackface style of engagement with the black community. Even abolitionist heroes like William Lloyd Garrison (who was, not coincidentally, the source of much of the Radical Political Abolitionists' consternation) were likely to expect a caricature of blackness from the formerly enslaved people with whom he worked, seeking out only the facade of black sentiment and thought, while maintaining white people at the core of the movement and its politics. The black former slave on the stage was a puppet, a mask for the white abolitionists' agendas. Indeed, Frederick Douglass was explicitly told to tell only his life story when on stage and to leave the "philosophizing" to the white abolitionists who surrounded him. Douglass represented the black public face of the movement, relegated to the role of exemplar instead of philosopher. Even more gallingly, he was also encouraged to put on a "little of the plantation manner" in order to convince others that his story was a legitimate contribution to the movement.[6] Douglass's life story was material to be exploited toward the political ends that the white abolitionists devised and promoted.

Despite the ambition of cultivating "black hearts," many abolitionists often exploited the life narratives that formerly enslaved people contributed to the abolitionist movement as merely living and breathing evidence of the larger political messaging that white abolitionists devised and deliberately curated. Douglass's revelation of the control white abolitionists demanded over the framing of the slave's narrative was a political claim that condemned the appropriation of black experience for white ends. It disclosed the abolitionists' regulation and management over what and how Americans learned about slavery. It called into question the agency and control that the life narrative is supposed to represent to the enslaved or to any writer who chooses to tell his or her own story. It indicted abolitionist motivations for engaging fugitives in the movement. It suggested that abolitionists had not achieved the "spiritual heart" that would allow them to identify with their black counterparts but instead had reinscribed the political and intellectual hierarchies inherited from institutionalized slavery. It accused the most prominent antislavery activists of using formerly enslaved people as the black faces of the movement while white men remained behind the mask, determining the image of blackness that was to be available to their audiences and the politics that would be communicated. Douglass essentially charged Garrison and his colleagues with being blackface abolitionists.

As the slave narrative tradition—for which Frederick Douglass is the standard bearer and most revered representative—has reemerged in the last twenty-five years, so has the accompanying apparatus of the antislavery movement and its attendant crises in the representation of bondage and freedom. As was the case in the nineteenth century, much of the political messaging that the new slave narrative promotes is packaged and framed by white activists. First-person narratives provide the evidentiary foundation upon which nonprofits, legislators, lawyers, researchers, and activists make their claims for justice. The few printed life stories of formerly enslaved people are promoted by U.S. retailers, Christian bookstores, and nonprofit e-stores, and they fund a renewed twenty-first-century abolitionist movement, but they cannot possibly provide a representative sample of the approximated tens of millions of people who are enslaved today. Instead, the subjects who are chosen to tell and publish their stories are few, and the sample group is quite deliberately selected to represent the agendas of the groups that engage in the antislavery cause. Today, it is often through nonprofit organizations, think tanks, and politicians with their own particular agendas, anxieties, and needs in mind that we learn of slavery. As we have seen in the first chapters of these books, narrative tensions in the new slave narratives reveal fissures in ideological, political, and intellectual concerns, and there is no doubt that some of those dissonances grow out of both the competing ideological claims of the antislavery movement and the competing narrative impulses of the named narrators and their amanuenses. As I will argue in this chapter, the lives and narratives that do gain public attention can sometimes be co-opted by blackface abolitionists who seek, as Garrison did, to control the narrative of slavery that is made available even in first-person narratives that are not their own. Douglass's experience of the thin line between black hearts and blackface is instructive as we consider the political implications of the genre and of antislavery discourse as it takes on twenty-first-century contours.

CRUSADE POLITICS: THE NEW SLAVE NARRATIVE FROM AFRICA

Recent statistical estimates of global slavery (as widely disputed as they may be) suggest that in sub-Saharan Africa alone, there are approximately 6.2 million people currently enslaved—that means sub-Saharan Africans account for approximately 15.4 percent of the estimated 40.3 million enslaved laborers in the world, which corresponds fairly closely to the ratio of sub-Saharan African people in the global population in general.[7] From the chattel enslavement of people in Mauritania to the debt bondage practiced in the mines of Tanzania to forced foster-child labor in Benin to child soldiering in Uganda and the sexual enslavement of women from Nigeria, we find versions of every form of slavery practiced in the world today in Africa.

Nonetheless, it is curious that victims of slavery in Africa (and other survivors of African descent) are so overrepresented among slave narrators and have so often been employed as poster children for the new abolitionist cause. African authors compose 30 percent of all book-length new slave narratives being considered here and 45 percent of those published before 2010, when the trend turned toward domestic child sex trafficking narratives (which use the language of "slavery" to define their experiences). Not insignificantly, many of the most widely disseminated of them are tales of African captivity, including, of course, Mende Nazer's and Francis Bok's memoirs but also Grace Akallo's *Girl Soldier*, Evelyn Amony's *My Name is Evelyn Amony*, Tina Okpara's *My Life Has A Price*, Bukola Oriola's *Imprisoned: The Travails of a Trafficked Victim*, Fatima's *Esclave à 11 ans*, and Henriette Akofa's *Une esclave moderne*. If we count narratives by people of African descent in the diaspora (including Jean-Robert Cadet, Brook Parker-Bello, and Mimi Crown), of course, the numbers rise even higher.

It might be that people in the West gravitate to images of slavery that depict people of African descent as its victims because of the West's history of racialized slavery. However, African settings are often employed as a convenient facade for the neoliberal political agendas and post-9/11 anti-Muslim sentiments that dominate the form and content of some of the most popular new slave narratives. Indeed, 30 percent of all the narratives involve a captor who is Muslim and corresponding anti-Islamic sentiment. This particular strain of the narratives is used to promote a crusade politics, mobilizing antislavery discourse as an irrefutably ethical facade for barely hidden agendas aimed at deposing African leaders such as Uganda's Joseph Kony and Sudan's Omar al-Bashir, dismantling Muslim governments, and promoting Christian-led U.S. policy abroad. Far more insidious than Garrison, who wanted to control the political messaging that accompanied Douglass's personal experience, white, conservative Christians who control a significant sector of twenty-first-century antislavery activism employ enslaved people's narratives as illustrations while they provide their own "philosophy" of universal Christian persecution and justified military and political engagement in Africa. In this politicized setting, some of the most widely distributed narratives are those from Africa, and the specter of blackface abolition finds its way into mainstream depictions of slavery once again as Africa becomes the battleground for an ideological war.

Many of the religiously motivated activists engaged in antislavery advocacy indicate sincerely that their inspiration for pursuing the abolition of contemporary forms of slavery is their sense of it as a fundamental duty of their faith and a legacy of their ancestors' commitment to abolition. Linda Smith, former congresswoman from the state of Washington and founder of Shared Hope International, remembers in her memoir/humanitarian narrative/religious tract *From Congress to the Brothel* that "God burdened my heart for the [trafficked] girls. I didn't know exactly what it meant or what it might require, but at that moment, I overwhelmingly knew it was my calling."[8] Faith McDonnell, religious director of the Institute for Religion and Democracy and coauthor of Grace Akallo's child soldier narrative *Girl Soldier* (discussed at length below), suggests that "the Christian community is on the cutting edge of history that is being written today. It is the history of how God's people are answering His call to help save the children of northern Uganda."[9] The framing of humanitarian commitment through the discourse of a call to "save" people (especially Africans) is typical of the white "savoir or redeemer," as described by Makau Mutua, who "protects, vindicates, civilizes, restrains, and safeguards."[10] The condescending role of the savior implies the helplessness and lack of agency of those being rescued by those who believe they are called by God and history to act.

Some contemporary abolitionists attempt to resist such critiques by invoking an inheritance of the motives of black-hearted, self-sacrificing abolitionists. For instance, Sam Brownback, a former Republican senator and governor of Kansas and current U.S. ambassador at large for international religious freedom, who has championed the abolitionist cause in the U.S. legislature, "literally sees his work on Sudan as rooted in his Kansas forebearers' agitation against American slavery,"[11] which links him to the Radical Abolitionists and to John Brown in particular. While the religiously based organizations, activists, and legislators that employ the new slave narrative as evidence for their causes trace their roots to biblical imperatives and antebellum abolitionist causes, their agendas are born of uniquely contemporary political concerns. The new slave narratives are employed as weapons in twenty-first-century ideological battles, the likes of which would be completely foreign to a slave narrator of the nineteenth century. Allen Hertzke, author of *Freeing God's Children: The Unlikely Alliance for Global Human Rights*, characterizes the new Christian abolitionist movement as being driven by a "concern for the persecuted church,"[12] which can "dramatize the plight of the 'suffering church' abroad."[13] The evangelical ambition is to "stem the pandemic of global religious persecution," by which they mean specifically Christian persecution and only very rarely that of other religions.[14]

Evangelical attention to the issue of contemporary slavery emerged from Cold War anticommunist anxieties that pit the civilized, democratic, Christian West against a nebulous and nefarious array of communists who, according to the evangelicals' argument, waged a war focused on the religious persecution of Christians.

With the end of the Cold War, conservatives sought and clearly found a new way to project their political anxieties onto national political debates. Their search for a human rights angle to their anticommunist, pro-Christian platform was answered in a variety of humanitarian causes, including the Sudanese genocide, while they kept an eye on North Korea and Cuba as the last remaining communist strongholds.[15] All along, the specter of religious persecution was used as a proxy war for run-of-the-mill Cold War anticommunist sentiments. In 1998 a broad coalition of evangelicals pressured Congress to pass the International Religious Freedom Act (IRFA), which was meant to focus on Christian persecution but eventually had to be expanded to protect all religions in order to pass.[16] Through this bill, the Christian Right put Christian persecution at the center of U.S. foreign policy. The binaristic logic of the Cold War (which itself is a legacy of colonialism) finds continued resonance among these religious activists who continue to define their political agendas in opposition to a foreign enemy.

In the years after the Cold War ended, many of old so-called cold warriors transferred their anxieties to global Islam, again often framing it in terms of religious persecution, but by the 2000s, it was also framed in the guise of antislavery activism. Indeed, some stalwarts of the Cold War era have rebranded themselves as champions of the abolitionist cause. The Institute for Religion and Democracy, for instance, which has taken up slavery in Uganda as one of its flashpoint issues, is presided over by Mark Tooley, a former CIA analyst who first became involved in the issue of religious persecution in the late 1980s when he wrote a critical report about religious funding of pro-Marxist organizations for his congregation of the United Methodist Church.[17] Perhaps the most notorious among converts to the cause of contemporary slavery is John Eibner of Christian Solidarity International (CSI), who began his career with the conservative Keston Institute, which was founded in 1969 to research religious persecution in the USSR and other communist countries.[18] Now he is the CEO of an organization that was originally founded to "smuggle Bibles and broadcast an evangelical radio show to Eastern bloc countries" and which is now (in)famous for its purported (and much maligned and discredited) cash purchases of southern Sudanese people whom CSI claims were enslaved by the mujahideen. Benjamin Skinner's investigations proved that the supposedly enslaved people were, in fact, actors and that the funds were being funneled to the Sudanese People's Liberation Army (SPLA) so that they could fight the Muslim-dominated North. Christian Solidarity International mobilized the public horror regarding the revelation of contemporary slavery to raise funds that allowed them to support covert militarized operations in Sudan.[19]

The bombing of the World Trade Center on September 11, 2001, provided even greater political impetus and elite political willpower to propel these religious anxieties to the policy level. Hertzke, who was a leader in the effort to make Christian persecution an issue at the foreign policy level, admits that "in the literature of Christian advocacy groups, in fact, we see the twin specters of militant Islam and the Communist remnant as the key threats to the faithful abroad. The September 11 attack by Islamic radicals only crystallized an emerging ecumenical consciousness among disparate Christian groups."[20] The focus on a Muslim enemy was bolstered by U.S. anxieties about national security, which provided opportunities for wider networks of religious affinity. In the years after 9/11, national security and the struggle against vague but constantly proliferating enemies became the focus of U.S. foreign and domestic policy as well as the paranoia of the average U.S. citizen.

Sub-Saharan Africa seems to represent a favored case study for the intersection of human rights concerns and the conservative agenda against socialist governance and Islamic extremism. The binaristic logic of colonialism finds continued resonance among these religious activists who continue to define their political agendas in opposition to a foreign enemy. They suggest that what Islamists do in Africa is merely a precursor for attacks they are planning and, in fact, carrying out in the West. The fear stoked by those claims justifies government military action against African enemies. In this way, as Eric Lott argues of blackface, blackness (or in this case, more specifically, Africanness and African oppression) becomes a commodity to be co-opted and marketed.[21] In the post-9/11 milieu, this means that advocacy groups that laid claim to that commodified black suffering could bring in significant funding and lucrative aid dollars that were funneled through U.S. charitable organizations such as the Institute for Religion and Democracy, Christian Solidarity International, or the American Anti-Slavery Group and justified the expansion and political influence of the military-industrial complex. Abolitionist blackface is lucrative just as blackface has been for almost two hundred years.

This abolitionist blackface is being mobilized to mask nefarious and racialized acts of intellectual and political violence that only thinly veil the anti-Muslim hatred that serves as the impetus for the publication of some new slave narratives. In this particular strain of new slave narrative, the black storyteller, the one who can be the example of slavery, is merely a mask for the politics espoused and disseminated on the abolitionist lecture circuit. By using the nonfiction, first-person testimony of formerly enslaved people, some white abolitionists are thus able to play a black masquerade, implying that their message is the authentic, genuine, legitimate product of enslaved Africans in the twenty-first century, while they infuse the narratives with their own anti-Islamic sentiments. The new slave narrative provides a striking example of how the language and processes of identification characteristic of human rights discourse are co-opted and corrupted to serve conservative political goals, which are often out of sync with the politics espoused by the narrators themselves.

Blackface functions to distort black experiences in several distinct ways. The most apparent distortion is the exoticization of imagined African attributes and black culture. It also elides the oppression that white people have enacted upon people of African descent by suggesting that black people are happy in their positions or that they are responsible for their lot in life (by, for instance, suggesting that they are lazy or stupid or inherently evil). At the same time, and perhaps counterintuitively, blackface allows white people to identify with black culture, or at least with their imaginary construction of the black experience, be it their perceived ignorant happiness, supposed uninhibited behavior, or even their very real suffering and oppression. This allows for white audiences and blackface performers to imagine themselves as joyous and playful at the same time as it allows them to adorn themselves with the persecution and othered status of people of African descent, evoking both a sympathy for the oppressed and a fear that one might fall into the same lot as the people being ventriloquized.

As we will see through the example of Faith J. H. McDonnell and Grace Akallo's *Girl Soldier: A Story of Hope for Northern Uganda* (2007), these exoticizing, exonerating, and identificatory mechanisms of blackface are precisely those that a particularly conservative religious strain of antislavery activists in the twenty-first century mobilize to replicate, evoke, and promote their own neoliberal politics. For them, the individual narrative of slavery is not one through which formerly enslaved people express their humanity or a mechanism through which they might express their own theories of slavery and freedom. Instead, for these activists, the new slave narratives are employed as what Gillian Whitlock describes as "soft weapons," texts that humanize marginalized voices but that can be appropriated and weaponized through propaganda.[22] In this way, these life narratives are "politics by other means,"[23] a compelling and seemingly unassailable human rights facade that justifies their arguments for actions that many advocates would deem human rights violations. Through closely reading this one, admittedly exaggerated, example of the co-optation of the slave narrative, we can expose this trend in the antislavery movement that largely goes unnoticed and uncritiqued.

NARRATING SLAVERY

Fifteen-year-old Grace Akallo was captured by the Lord's Resistance Army rebels in 1996 and was forced to fight in the Ugandan civil war. After emancipating herself and her friends, she founded and worked as president of United Africans for Women and Children Rights. She publicly shares her experience as a forced child soldier and advocates for other children's rights in regions that are experiencing political crises. The book that includes her first-person narrative of enslavement is composed with an unusual multivocal narration. Chapters in the book alternate between the nonfictional, historical voice of coauthor Faith McDonnell and the first-person, autobiographical voice of Grace Akallo. In her remarkably brief chapters, Akallo tells a story infused with religious significance. The narrative begins with a sort of resurrection in which she has been buried alive, but she miraculously survives and digs her way out of the shallow grave in which she was left for dead. In her resurrection, she "become[s] a skeleton that will not stay peacefully in its grave," and her story seems to allude to Jesus Christ's resurrection and its redemption of others from sin.[24] Her resurrection and redemption allow Akallo, later shaped as a modern-day Moses, to lead her friends out of the desert and into freedom from slavery. Like so many of the slave narrators who came before her as well as those who are writing today, Christian faith is at the foundation of Akallo's activism, and churches form a major support network and promoter for her career as she continues to do Moses's work of leading people out of slavery.

As is the case in nearly all the new slave narratives written by authors from the Global South, Akallo begins her narrative in medias res with a gripping narrative set during her time in captivity—in this case, a story of her near death and seeming resurrection—but then turns quickly to a narrative of her idyllic preslavery origins. She begins that origin narrative with the phrase "I was born," unknowingly echoing the nineteenth-century slave narrative tradition.[25] As I argued in chapter 1, Akallo's use of the phrase "I was born" is meant to establish her preslavery birth into freedom. Akallo's opening, and indeed the entire chapter "Safe Times with Grandpapa," establishes her as a human person imbued with dignity, rights, and freedom, enmeshed in family structures and village life. She shares stories of her innocent childhood during which she was raised in a poor but loving family in a beautiful and peaceful village. She writes, "The village I knew when

I was a child was a special place. We children felt loved and taken care of. Life could be hard, so everyone looked after everyone else."[26] It was in this idyllic environment that Akallo learned a seemingly universal morality of sharing and assisting others in a place where children never had to worry about being harmed. Akallo establishes her royal origins in the midst of her poverty, stating, "My grandfather was the son of a chief. He believed he had power to control and protect people the way his father had."[27] Having established the foundation of her existence, her humanity, her dignity, her lineage, and thus her roots in freedom and even power, she then describes her culture and practices, grounded in a lively market culture, a hard-working agricultural community, and a storytelling tradition that provides the foundation for an ethical originary world. Much like many of the approximately fifteen nineteenth-century slave narrators who wrote of their lives before slavery in Africa, these anthropological digressions are reminiscent of those found in the traditional slave narrative, providing the (still largely unknowing) Western reader with a rendering of life in Africa that establishes the universal moral values, humanity, and freedom that connect African narrators with their readers.

It is from these idyllic beginnings that Akallo is then snatched into a life of captivity and begins to establish her experience as slavery within the text. She explains that she and the other girls who were captured in her school were "led like slaves" and "taken to a life of torment."[28] She laments that they were captured on Uganda's Independence Day because it was the day she lost her own freedom. In her depiction of her time in captivity, she describes the constant forced marches they went on like slaves in a coffle and how, when they cried, they were threatened with rape or murder. Her story takes her to Sudan, where she and the other girls were forced to become child brides (or "sex slaves" in McDonnell's description) to commanders in the Lord's Resistance Army. She describes meeting LRA leader Joseph Kony, who ordered that the girls be trained to fight and forced to serve on the battlefield. She depicts her own radical depression and subsequent suicidal obsession, which seemed to her to be the only escape from captivity. Even her attempts at suicide were met with death threats from the commanders, confirming that there was no escape from the service of the LRA other than death. Here we see the definition of slavery emerge—she was held captive, compelled to work as both a forced child bride and a child soldier. She was held by extraordinary but very real violence, and her escape options were largely limited to suicide. In her descriptions of her life in Kony's army, she establishes herself as an enslaved captive.

Having established the nature of her enslavement, Akallo retreats to the vague, reportorial, metaphorized, passive, and euphemized descriptions of suffering that are relatively characteristic of slave narratives and other traumatic life narratives in which people testify to atrocities,[29] and Akallo's contributions to the text indicate those familiar displacement strategies discussed in chapter 1. In the two short chapters in which Akallo discusses the horrific conditions of her enslavement, including the brutality she was forced to inflict on others or the rape she endured, she typically turns away from specific details, writing euphemistically of violence and displacing the most traumatic experiences onto other people she knew. Though Kony commanded that the girls be taught to fight, she admits, "Hunger taught me how to fight," and she quickly notes, "We raided villages, looking for food and water," commenting on the persistence of deprivation. She discusses none of the violence that she may have taken part in or at least witnessed on those raids.[30] She worries about how she might eventually help other children who "are dragged into the bush and taught to smash people's heads and cut people's lips, hands and limbs," but she never describes committing any atrocities and rarely even describes seeing anything like that in her own life narrative.[31]

Akallo euphemistically describes the rape she endured as being "distributed" to a commander who "forced me to go to bed with him," and when he first assaulted her, she says only that she "felt like a thorn was in my skin as my innocence was destroyed."[32] Akallo was repeatedly brought before commanders to be punished, sometimes even to be executed, but she narrowly escaped in nearly every instance she reports. When she wants to evoke the constant terror of punishment, she typically turns to other children's suffering instead of her own, and in those moments, she nonetheless adopts a reportorial tone, writing in simple declarative sentences. "A twelve-year-old girl tried to escape two weeks after our capture. Her head was smashed. This was scary."[33] In the one scene in which she depicts violence in any extensive detail, she writes only, "Through the pain in my skin, I could not cry any more. I felt the earth rotating. Maybe I was going to die this time."[34] Her slave narrative is riddled with narrative gaps that signify the reduction of the physical and psychological experiences of enslavement to psychically manageable metaphors and understatement.

Whatever condemnation of the war that Akallo may reveal in her part of the narrative is directed at the commanders and the nameless and faceless child soldiers who were the perpetrators of the violence and the enforcers of her captivity, but elision of those violent actors and even sympathy with them are more often the routes she takes. Sometimes, all she reveals of the perpetrators are their specters, which lurk in the spaces of passive-voice sentences, as in the time when Akallo writes that her friend's "head was smashed," without ever accusing anyone of the violence.[35] She writes that for those who had been in the army for a long time, "constant anger made their eyes red and bloodshot. The soldiers with red and bloodshot eyes are no longer children but killers."[36] She restores humanity to them, or at least to the selves they had to shed in the process of becoming soldiers, suggesting that they were all innocent children at one time.

Even in her descriptions of meeting Kony while she was captive, she discloses absolutely no anger or even fear, describing him simply as "the leader of the rebel movement, Joseph Kony." She says that he "believed in a mix of Christianity and a mystical sort of spiritism," and in her chapter about her escape, she describes his failure as a military leader, suggesting that he was "a proud man" who was "trying to make his name great with the Sudan government." She punctuates the story of the legacy he was trying to build with a powerful single-sentence paragraph: "He left the children to die."[37] Reportorial and unemotional, she briefly condemns Kony for being a failure and a pawn of the Sudanese government, and then she quickly returns to the story of her escape. This characteristically unemotional and relatively distanced description of the suffering and terror of slavery is typical of the genre of the slave narrative.

Akallo's experience of slavery, captivity, and child soldiering, however, fills only a mere thirteen pages of the book. Like so many slave narrators, past and present, much of her focus is on the faith that sustained her through her captivity instead of on her suffering or anger and on the plans of escape and activism that her faith propelled her toward. She says that she "promised God she would never turn [her] back on Him if [she] survived."[38] Her suffering, so obscurely described, is sublimated into her higher vocation as activist, through which she can act as God's missionary to the children of Uganda. Like many other slave narrators (both in the nineteenth and the twenty-first centuries), Akallo focuses the vast majority of her narrative on her "freedom narrative," replete with tales of her miraculous escape, her commitment to her own inherent freedom, and the spiritual strength she found to lead others out of captivity. As discussed in chapter 2, however, she is left with the sense of "not-yet-fre dom" as well, as she laments that she will never be free until all her friend and fellow citizens of Uganda are also free. In this way, Akallo becomes a s: rvivor activist in that long-revered tradition—no longer one of millions who suffer, but one who stands up, so often with a spiritual purpose, to eradicate the injustice that she and the others endured. In all these ways, Akallo's own sections of the narrative of *Girl Soldier* reveal a fairly standard new slave narrative, conforming, likely unintentionally, to the conventions of the genre as it was taking shape in the years in which she wrote and over the next several years after it was published.

CO-OPTING A GIRL SOLDIER

Akallo's chapters of *Girl Soldier* mark it as a relatively representative example of the new slave narrative, and they provided the platform from which Akallo's activist career was launched. Akallo's narrative also echoes the conventions of the nineteenth-century slave narrative tradition in its reliance on a paratextual apparatus that establishes the veracity of her narrative through the voices of external authorities. As Olney writes of the nineteenth-century slave narratives, the conventions of the slave narrative "tend to turn up as often in the paraphernalia surrounding the narratives as in the narratives themselves."[39] It is critical to pay attention to the way the slave narrative is framed in order to understand how the life experiences of enslaved people are shaped and packaged for antislavery purposes.

Girl Soldier was published by Chosen Books (a division of the evangelical Baker Publishing Group), whose mission is to "help believers to better know and love the Lord Jesus Christ; to pray about the concerns that are on God's heart; to be empowered by his Spirit for ministry; to fulfill the Great Commission; and to transform their communities and their world."[40] The paratext of the book sets the scene for the spiritually transformative and identificatory experience that the publisher expects Akallo's slave narrative to render. Michael Card, a Bible teacher and musician, endorses the book as a "precious gift from two women, both uniquely qualified to speak for the suffering children of Uganda" and promises that the book will help readers imagine "the enormous monolith of the suffering of Africa."[41] This familiar, reductive vision of continental suffering is paired with a testimony from Steven Haas of World Vision International that the book is also a sign that "there is still One who understands and redeems."[42] The framing of the text significantly evokes the word "slavery" and plays on the image of suffering Africa to promote the spiritual redemption that is available to us through our engagement with Akallo's life story.

Coauthor Faith J. H. McDonnell's introduction reiterates the significance of the crisis in Uganda in terms of suffering and slavery: children are being "used as slave laborers, and girls serve the sexual lusts of older soldiers."[43] McDonnell's description of Akallo's experience as slavery taps into the rhetorical power of twenty-first-century antislavery discourse, supported by an endorsement on the cover by the former director of U.S. Trafficking in Persons, John R. Miller, who calls the book a "moving call to prayer and action" that represents the "moving story of horror and redemption" of "child soldier slavery survivors in Uganda."[44] The paratext of the book invokes the power of the term "slavery" and the tradition of the slave narrative to authorize Akallo's story as one worthy of our attention even before Akallo begins to narrate her own experience or define it.

Akallo's book is extraordinary, however, in that the voice of the external authority, which typically remains in the paratext, is woven around and practically overwhelms the narrative of her life in captivity. In fact, McDonnell's long historical sections form the primary frame of the book into which Akallo's narrative is episodically interspersed, effectively reshaping Akallo's narrative in a way that is unlike any other. Based on the paratextual apparatus of the text, it would seem that Akallo's self-representation is the central concern of *Girl Soldier*. In fact, the back cover announces, "More than 30,000 children have been kidnapped in Uganda. Now one of them has a voice." Nevertheless, the voice of this book is not solely Akallo's. The voice of this narrative is explicitly divided between Akallo's own and McDonnell's. However, Akallo's narrative constitutes only sixty-four of the 225 pages of the book. Akallo's chapters are often as short as two to three pages, whereas McDonnell's chapters sometimes extend to twenty pages. The distribution of narrative voice in *Girl Soldier* is a quantifiable representation of the battle being waged offstage between survivors and other antislavery activists in the twenty-first century. McDonnell's sections ostensibly serve to fill in the blanks left by Akallo's fragmented recounting of her experience; however, the contexts McDonnell supplies do not correspond

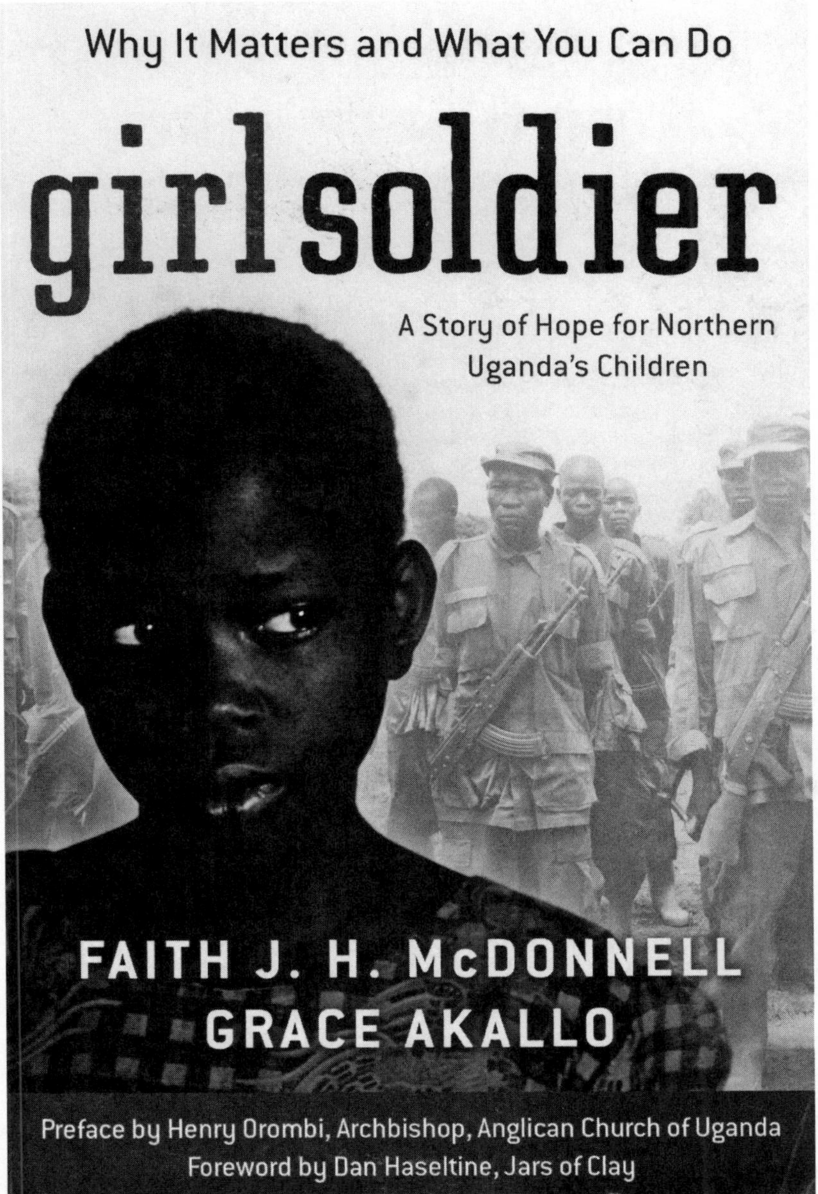

Why It Matters and What You Can Do

girlsoldier

A Story of Hope for Northern
Uganda's Children

FAITH J. H. McDONNELL
GRACE AKALLO

Preface by Henry Orombi, Archbishop, Anglican Church of Uganda
Foreword by Dan Haseltine, Jars of Clay

FIGS. 3.1.–3.2. Front and back covers of Faith McDonnell and Grace Akallo's *Girl Soldier: A Story of Hope for Northern Uganda's Children* (2006) reveal the bifurcation of narrative voice into seemingly mutually exclusive roles of experience and expertise.

More than 30,000 children have been kidnapped in Uganda. Now one of them has a voice.

When Grace Akallo was fifteen years old, rebels from the Lord's Resistance Army raided her school. Thus began her nightmarish existence as one of northern Uganda's thousands of child soldiers. Forced to endure savagery, starvation, abuse and other horrors with only her faith to sustain her, Grace eventually escaped to share her story with the world.

Faith McDonnell is an American activist and writer with a special concern for the future of the vulnerable Acholi people of northern Uganda. In *Girl Soldier,* Grace's personal account and Faith's historical and spiritual insights are woven together to tell the story of Uganda's forgotten children. Be inspired by this heartfelt account and moved to do your part in making sure that these children will not be forgotten.

"A precious gift from two women, both uniquely qualified to speak for the suffering children of Uganda, one an eloquent survivor and the other a fearless advocate. It is no coincidence that their names are Grace and Faith."
—**Michael Card**, Bible teacher and musician

"*Girl Soldier* is not fiction, yet that fact becomes harder to believe with every page we turn. This book is more than just a call to action. It is a challenge to our moral compass."
—**Adrian Bradbury**, founder and director, GuluWalk

"A much-needed reminder of the suffering and faith of the people of northern Uganda. Both have gone largely unnoticed for too long."
—**The Rt. Rev. Robert W. Duncan**, bishop, Episcopal Diocese of Pittsburgh; moderator, Anglican Communion Network

"A poignant reminder that the darkness of the soul and the cruel behaviors it leads to are more devastating than we could imagine. This is an incredible account that demands a hearing and invites a response."
—**Steven W. Haas**, vice president, World Vision International

www.chosenbooks.com

B0013L88GA
Girl Soldier: A Stor
AMZN63

FIGS. 3.1.–3.2. (*continued*)

to Akallo's narrative impulse, and, in fact, the two voices seem to work in tension with or as distractions from each other. The distribution of voices in *Girl Soldier* and the tensions between them provide a unique opportunity to understand the very different ways African victims of human rights violations and Christian evangelical political activists frame the same events as they shape a narrative of enslavement.

In the case of *Girl Soldier*, Akallo's authority extends only to her personal experience of soldiering and slavery, whereas McDonnell is authorized as the "humanitarian hero" in the text to serve as a "proxy witness" for Akallo and claims she can more adequately address the history and politics that made such an experience possible.[45] Of course, this usurpation of the narrative's messaging is reminiscent of Douglass's situation among the Garrisonian abolitionists. McDonnell writes that her part offers "the historical context for the current crisis in Uganda and provides the resources for prayer and activism."[46] In addition, McDonnell fills in the gaps created by Akallo's displacement strategies with the melodrama and the spectacular violence that the white activist perceives to be central to the narrative of Ugandan history and the narration of slavery. McDonnell includes numerous graphic stories of children who were mutilated or raped in her narratives to exemplify the horrors that Akallo typically turns away from. By the end of the book, however, McDonnell turns her attention from the religious salvation that Akallo prescribes and focuses it on "rescue" and political intervention strategies, providing the political framing for U.S. engagement in the region and producing recommendations for how churches, communities, and individuals might encourage interventionist U.S. foreign policy.

BLACKFACE ABOLITION

McDonnell is the director of Religious Liberty as well as of the Church Alliance for a New Sudan at the Institute for Religion and Democracy (IRD), a nonprofit think tank whose self-proclaimed conservative Christian mission is to "work to reaffirm the church's biblical and historical teachings, strengthen and reform its role in public life, protect religious freedom, and renew democracy at home and abroad."[47] The IRD contends that "the most fundamental of all human rights is the freedom of religious faith and practice," and their publications and social media postings explore a number of political issues through the lens of religious freedom, by which they typically mean specifically Christian religious freedom. McDonnell's work is particularly focused on what evangelicals call the "persecuted church," which is largely grounded in co-opting violence against Christians abroad to enhance their claims regarding the perceived suffering of Christians in the United States.

As McDonnell appropriates Akallo's narrative for her own political ends, she quickly employs the mechanisms of blackface described earlier. As is true of most blackface performances, McDonnell's representation and understanding of Africa are limited to the stereotypes that grow out of an exoticized, colonial imaginary of the continent. Her fantastical conception of Uganda is summed up in the following passage: "A raw and savage grief fills the air in Uganda. The sadness in that grief is overlaid with an evil so irrational and unfiltered that it seems like the stuff of folk tales. It belongs to a nether world of ogres, monsters, and demons of the night that come in the dark to snatch the innocent."[48] This familiar exoticization that depicts an entire African nation as plagued by indigenous and irrational evil appears throughout the text and her writings on the IRD blog, where she admits to never having visited Uganda until long after the book was published.

The vast majority of *Girl Soldier* is consumed by McDonnell's interpretation of the history of Uganda. She reduces a complicated regional conflict—driven by the need for resources, legacies of colonial oppression and discrimination, ethnic tensions, and border disputes, all exacerbated by Western interventions and covert financial and military support— to merely a centuries-long "struggle between Christianity, Islam and spiritism that is still going on."[49] McDonnell employs the discursive strategies of a historian, including footnoting her sources, but her sources are drawn almost exclusively from Christian webzines and books like F. A. Forbes's 1927 *Planting the Faith in Darkest Africa*. In her amateur history, when Christians arrived in Uganda in the 1880s, they "soon threatened powerful witch doctors and Arab Muslims who operated the slave trade and promoted Islam."[50] The insidious parallel structure she employs here equates the sale of human beings with the promotion of the Islamic religion, allowing her to fashion an indictment of Islam's role in the history of Uganda and completely ignore the role that Christians played in the slave trade in Uganda and elsewhere. She focuses instead on a vague and incomplete lineage of Ugandan rulers, whom she characterizes (as if homogeneous) as responsible for the "persecution and death of hundreds of Christians."[51] She writes, "They have 'channeled' evil to steal, kill, and destroy God's children in Uganda."[52] Throughout her indictment of Ugandan indigenous rule, there is no moment of circumspection regarding the role Christians played in destabilizing Ugandan politics through religious missions. When she does refer to British colonial policies that privileged the South and divided the people of the region, she does not condemn them. She even justifies colonial discrimination by insisting that "war and competition among tribes and ethnic groups existed before Africa was divided into colonies," again asserting the indigeneity of discord and violence.[53] Her largely American Christian readership, educated in Euro- and U.S.-centric values and historical concepts, are likely to consume this racist narrative of Ugandan history with little critical judgment.

Although Akallo's part of the narrative is silent on the question of her captors' religion (they were Christian) and does not suggest that religion played a significant role in her own personal experience as a child soldier (though she does use "Muslim" and "Arab" interchangeably for Sudanese in one very brief section), and, as we have seen, she shies away from anger or blame, McDonnell's depiction of the conflict is quite different. For McDonnell, the crisis is entirely driven by the "demon seed" of Muslim war-mongering aggression and financial funding, which makes the region "vulnerable to the spread of radical Islam."[54] McDonnell's nightmare depictions of otherworldly terrors support her narrative of a Uganda under the sway of Joseph Kony, whom she indicts as a Christian apostate and pagan maniac supported by the allegedly satanic Islamists in Khartoum.[55] McDonnell's monolithic vision of Islam takes center stage and is the focus of all her condemnation, despite the fact that Akallo's narrative shares none of the same vitriol.

There is no doubt that Sudan's support of Kony enabled him to expand his power and extend the viability of the conflict, nor will I offer any debate regarding whether Kony's tactics were legitimate or appropriate. However, the sensational insistence upon the indigeneity of evil in Uganda, grounded in the essentialized malevolence of Islam, works to naturalize violence as inherently African and Muslim, thereby justifying and exonerating all who might intercede against that evil. In this depiction, the reasonable but faithful Christian West (which teams up with people practicing traditional religions) is pitted against the irrational and demonic forces of Islam (which is joined by the so-called pagans). This blackface-style caricature of Ugandan history allows McDonnell to valorize generations of Christian missionaries as saviors within the narrative of Ugandan history and politics.

The image of African conflict that McDonnell inscribes in the text is drawn straight from the Samuel Huntington "clash of civilizations" school of thought.[56] It is no coincidence that many of McDonnell's colleagues at the IRD and other similar groups were Huntingtonian cold warriors before they became antislavery activists. McDonnell's version of the clash of civilizations theory pits the Christian West against pagan, Islamic Africa, but it is rhetorically framed as a mission to deliver the "protection of love" to Uganda children. In *Girl Soldier*, McDonnell commends Invisible Children, Uganda Conflict Action Network (now the Resolve), GuluWalk, and World Vision, all organizations founded by or sponsored by Christian faith-based groups, because they "urge activism by U.S. citizens to push for more political involvement by the U.S. government."[57] The "love" that McDonnell prescribes takes the form of peace talks and negotiations but also demands International Criminal Court indictments, the murder of Joseph Kony, and U.S. military intervention in the region. Huntingtonian logic justifies U.S. intervention in the Ugandan conflict because Christians in the West are called into battle against the enemy of their purported ally—in this case, persecuted Ugandan Christians. As a result, the Ugandan conflict reinforces and justifies aggressive American attitudes and policies toward Islam and toward the region. These intervention strategies are underwritten by the "unwarranted faith in the benign nature of a human rights presence" that David Kennedy warns is at the heart of so much of the "emancipatory intervention" justified by human rights law and discourse.[58] Indeed, McDonnell's co-optation of Akallo's narrative is revelatory of the way in which "the interventions and exercises of state authority" that human rights vocabulary "legitimates are more likely to track political interests than its own emancipatory agenda."[59]

Despite these overt calls to political action and what seems to academic readers as explicitly racist and Islamophobic discourse, the book does not fashion itself as a tract on the Islamic oppression of women and children or a political treatise on American intervention, and most readers would not recognize it as such. Indeed, it is Akallo's first-person slave narrative interspersed in the text that provides a unique vehicle through which McDonnell can disguise and justify her mythological depictions of Africa and Islam. In an interesting twist on the traditional slave narrative, which typically is understood to be validated by the white interlocutors appended to the text, Akallo's own autobiographical sections are appropriated to validate McDonnell's political positions. By mobilizing the truth value of a first-person narrative, McDonnell utilizes Akallo's very real experiences as a blackface of African insider knowledge through which she can justifiably attack (seemingly from the inside) African Islam and the supposedly indigenous evil that taints Kony's version of Christianity.

Even as McDonnell's crusade politics posit Christian heritage as the diametrical opposite to the monstrous African cultures caricatured in the narrative, she has to confront the problem of Akallo's own Africanness. McDonnell manages this tension by holding up Akallo as an exception to this pervasive African evil and as a sign of hope for a new promise of Christian revival on the continent. The Christian imagery of Akallo's own story makes her the perfect victim for the conjuring of a Christian persecution narrative. While she does not invoke the Islamic menace of McDonnell's sections, she does highlight her own persecution, resurrection, and escape through the desert in recognizable biblical imagery that appeals to the Christian reading audience that the book is intended to engage. *Girl Soldier* employs the familiar tropes of Christian suffering to successfully bridge the geographic and cultural divides to evoke sympathies for the distant suffering of Ugandan girls. In this way, McDonnell can depict Akallo dualistically as both the benighted African and the redeemer, and thereby she exempts her from the damnation of the rest of the country. Though once a child soldier fighting other children in a violent conflict, Akallo "now fights to call the world to the difficult task of helping return emotional, physical and spiritual peace to the people of northern Uganda."[60] She creates a melodrama of an innocent and naïve Christian victim by setting her against the backdrop of a caricatured African landscape. As was the case for the blackface performers of the nineteenth century, the new slave narrative provides an opportunity for McDonnell to adorn herself and her politics with Akallo's suffering and at the same time allows her to pit herself and her fellow Christian advocates—as well as their racial whiteness itself—as radically other from the malevolent Africa of their imaginations. She does this through creating an identification between the reader and Grace that transcends Grace's African origins.

THE IMPULSE TOWARD FIRST-PERSON IDENTIFICATION

Since the publication of the earliest slave narratives, the first-person narration of captivity has provided readers an opportunity to engage in an imaginative identification process that encourages them to act against human rights violations. The voice that speaks intimately of rights violations calls out to us and asks us to intuit suffering, to identify with it for just long enough to attempt to comprehend, and then to act. Reading a first-person narrative is a willful engagement with another person and thus with their dignity and rights, freedom and reason. As we read "I" in our own minds, that subjectivity becomes our own for just a moment, even if it is always mediated by the page and our material realities.

Akallo's narrative works in this way—it is a heart-wrenching narrative of extraordinary suffering that we can hardly imagine, but imagine it we do through the identification with her subjectivity, with her "I" voice. Even when Akallo only obliquely gestures to the persistent rape she suffered at the hands of a man forty years her senior, we fill in the silences left by her traumatic abuse and imagine what she has implied. We do the work to conjure those horrific moments and identify with her horror and suffering. The ambition of the narrative is that we are, in turn, motivated by this rendering of human suffering, if only insofar as it shapes our morality and judgment.

Human rights as a universal project relies on our empathizing with others in this way; it implies that each of us must see each and every other human being as a rational, individual subject who, like us, can suffer. As Thomas Laqueur suggests, this recognition of inherent similarity encourages and indeed compels us to "regard the suffering of distant humans as making the same sort of claim on us as the suffering of proximate ones."[61] The human rights movement so often employs the first-person narrative precisely because it encourages us to contemplate others' suffering as if it were our own, and through that process, we imagine a tangible, knowable other who does not deserve to suffer.

It is this very process of identification at the foundation of human rights discourse that has been co-opted by some faith-based antislavery activists and organizations to mask their crusade politics. In McDonnell's sections of *Girl Soldier*, readers are explicitly urged to identify with those innocent African Christians who profess faith in a Christian God but who are unable to escape purportedly endemic African brutality. Throughout the book, McDonnell uses identificatory strategies to encourage this process. In one particularly direct moment, she asks her readers to "imagine being abducted in the middle of the night. Imagine a friend or a sister or a brother forced to march barefoot through a wilderness of rocks and thick trees for days at a time with no food or water. Imagine that it is your daughter or son who must make a decision between killing another child, perhaps one of their own playmates, or being killed."[62] McDonnell explicitly asks us to identify with the child soldier's experience, to make it our own. She later celebrates the work of Invisible Children, who "encouraged public identification with the Acholi."[63] In his preface, Christian singer Dan Haseltine reinforces this mechanism of the book, suggesting that it might help us to see "God or ourselves in the story of Uganda" by putting "ourselves in the place of the story's characters."[64] He describes the difficulty of motivating readers to take action because "we will not readily find ourselves in the numbers and words of information"; instead, we are to listen to stories that effectively communicate the "cruel things that could happen to our own children."[65] Here, the external authorities, not the first-person narrative voice of Akallo, attempt to force the identification. In so doing, McDonnell explicitly describes the implicit work that first-person narratives tend to do and takes it as her own responsibility as the third-person, outsider expert to instruct the reader on precisely how to engage in a very particular sentimental reading practice.

The prescribed identificatory structure built into the dual-voiced text of *Girl Soldier* powerfully encourages the American Christian reader to imagine him or herself as a feminized, innocent, persecuted Christian in Uganda. As an African female child, Akallo is a model victim who cannot be reproached or held responsible for her own victimization. This figure is one that is exonerated from the many evil forces that clearly infect the rest of McDonnell's imagined "ogres" of Uganda. From this space of innocence, the white Christian readers are instructed to imagine their very selves in Akallo's position, taking that identification back with them into the comfortable library space, pondering the possibility of their very own suffering. This is precisely the structure of sentiment that McDonnell is shaping through her interventions in the text. As McDonnell instructs us to imagine ourselves as an innocent child soldier, we are given permission to appropriate Akallo's oppression instead of sympathize with it.

In light of the radical difference between Akallo's experience and that of the armchair Christian humanitarian, McDonnell's call to don the mask of African suffering effects another aspect of blackface. When McDonnell explicitly calls on us to identify with Akallo, asking us to "imagine being abducted in the middle of the night" or "imagine that it is your daughter or son," she asks her Christian readership to imagine themselves and their loved ones as child soldiers.[66] Instead of that radical empathy for and imagination of another, she recruits the readers' self-concern and familial bonds. Readers do not have to imagine the suffering African girl; they are asked to imagine *themselves* as suffering Africans. By identifying with an imaginary Akallo and wearing the blackface for a moment, readers are able to project their imagined construction of African suffering onto their own life narratives, which allows McDonnell to maintain the idea of the mythologically evil Uganda that the intervening chapters describe. This aspect of blackface also has political implications for McDonnell, who is deeply concerned with what she calls "Christian persecution." By putting on the blackface of an irreproachably innocent child, Christians are able to perceive themselves as persecuted through their identificatory process. The fear for the global persecuted church that pervaded evangelical discourse in the decade and a half since the World Trade Center bombings is born of this kind of appropriation of others' suffering. Akallo's black face of Christian suffering serves as justification of a global Christian crusade against Islam.

THE APPROPRIATION OF PERSECUTION

McDonnell's co-optation of the narrative attempts to effect what I call a transitive property of suffering: if Akallo is a Christian, and she is suffering, then Christians worldwide are suffering. The appropriation of Akallo's suffering lends credence to the imagined persecution of Christians domestically. Read in the context of the crusade politics espoused by McDonnell and others, the character of a child soldier becomes a metaphor for global Christian persecution rather than a voice representing a particular experience of human oppression or a unique individual seeking human rights recognition and intervention.

McDonnell published Akallo's particular story because, as the IRD website attests, "IRD's Religious Liberty Program highlights the connection between the situation of Christians in the Islamic world and the effect and influence of global jihad/radical Islam on Western civilization in order to both support our brothers and sisters in their ongoing struggle and to learn from their experience."[67] In this reach toward global solidarity, the IRD evokes that cosmopolitan discourse that Costas Douzinas critiques: "Cosmopolitical space turns all relations into domestic affairs. . . . Liberal aggression is justified because liberalism provides the universal standard of decency, while the indecent character of the rogues makes war against them just."[68] The projection of black suffering onto Western Christianity constitutes a blackface abolitionism that calls on readers to make an intervention in the lives of Ugandans at least in part because of the implication of the need for a domestic defense of the Western Christian tradition and the church's Western membership. In this way, their anti-trafficking discourse echoes Bush-era post-9/11 sentiments that justify U.S. intervention in the world through a mirage of self-defense rhetoric that hinged on the defense of innocents abroad.[69]

Far more nefarious than any of the appropriations evidenced in Douglass's experience is McDonnell's employment of the African former slave as the example while the politics are driven by the interests dictated by the Christian conservative think tank that supported the publication of the book. Through the processes of identification with black suffering, McDonnell centers the conflict within the otherwise safe-seeming boundaries of the American Christian home and makes the reader a crusader in a conflict against an evil Muslim other that is presumably hell-bent on oppressing Christians worldwide. We might then reread the structure of the book and Akallo's brief and unintegrated chapters as a sign that it is, in fact, Akallo's story that is interspersed in brief minichapters amid McDonnell's history in order to act as a convenient metaphor for the larger claims of global persecution and divinely promised salvation of Christians that McDonnell is elaborating.

As Eric Lott suggests of nineteenth-century blackface performance, "The narratives . . . are riveted by the moment of cultural expropriation, and we should look to them . . . as much for what they do not say as for what they do—the way they construct, and then sometimes blur, racial boundaries."[70] In the blurring of racial and geographic boundaries through mobilization of the term "the persecuted church," the American religious Right appropriates the suffering of Christian people in Africa. It is their common experience as Christians that allows the white activists to appropriate the suffering of Christians anywhere in the world and wear it as their own, which, in turn, allows them to shed their racial responsibility for regional conflict. Whatever racial tensions might exist and whatever responsibility Christians might have for conflict in the region are erased in their appropriation of persecution. As Leshu Torchin argues of similar identificatory strategies designed to address the Armenian genocide, these efforts represent "the more broadly ecumenical appeal of the project in which the visual and narrative traditions of Christian suffering convert the faraway violence into a shared cause for injustice, compassion, and concern."[71] American evangelical groups today promote their cause through websites like persecution.org, persecution.net, persecution.com, and christianfreedom.org. They run an online radio station, Voice of Martyrs Radio (vomradio.net), the tagline for which is "Hear the Voice of Your Persecuted Christian Family." There is a dedicated segment of *Christianity Today*'s website devoted to essays on Christian persecution. Articles on that site celebrate Christian martyrdom, document the international confinement of Christians, rank the top offending nations for Christian persecution, raise awareness about international Islamic threats, and explicitly incite Christian rage.[72] At one and the same time, this wearing of a black face indicates the desire to wear the mask of suffering and the terrifying fear that what happens in that other place might, in fact, happen to them. Add that to a diminishing number of Christians worldwide at the same time as there is an increase in global (read: black and brown) Christianity, leading evangelicals to fear that they will grow increasingly insignificant on the global stage and will have less control over the messaging and practice of the church. The persistent dread is that they may themselves become other, marginalized.

In the face of these supposed threats, human rights discourse is being exploited as a language through which thinly veiled racial and religious discrimination can be justified. This formal appropriation of the identity of the victim helps American Christians to imagine a worldwide conspiracy against their own people (suddenly framed by a religion that transcends race), further exonerating them for whatever privilege and guilt they inherit from colonialism, neocolonialism, Western dominance in the world economy, and the forced conversion of people all over the world—the very historical realities that led to the conflicts in Uganda but which McDonnell entirely erases in her narrative. Saidiya Hartman writes of white abolitionist

John Rankin, who tried to imagine himself as an enslaved black person on a coffle, that his "efforts to identify with the enslaved [are thwarted] because in making the slave's suffering his own, Rankin begins to feel for himself rather than for those whom this exercise in imagination presumably is designed to reach. . . . In making the other's suffering one's own, this suffering is occluded by the other's obliteration."[73] Akallo's ability to be God's soldier in her fight to save child soldiers is clearly an enviable role for McDonnell. But in the process of identification, she has erased Akallo, Akallo's voice, Akallo's politics.

Evoking the discourse of human rights allows political groups to mobilize for their own causes a language that is designed for universal appeal and universal power. It is the very process of identification, so integral to human rights activism, that makes the suffering of individuals so easily co-optable for larger political causes. Human rights claims to that vague and much-contested universality obfuscate the ideological foundations of McDonnell's project and obscure both the financial support that makes the publication of the book possible and the religious mission she is trying to defend. "Human rights is the only universally available moral vernacular that validates the claims" of people against oppressive practices and cultures, and thus, people "seek out human rights protection precisely because it legitimizes their protests against oppression."[74] Organizations like the IRD, in turn, co-opt the moral power of human rights language and the oppression of others to legitimize their own ideological battles.

The valence of domination is shifting as a result of global human rights culture, and privileged Western Christians reflect those changes in their understanding of themselves. Domination in the religious marketplace once was read as a sign that Christianity was true and endorsed by God. Today, domination is so explicitly and intimately linked to oppression in public discourse that privileged members of cultures of domination ironically desire the cultural cachet attached to suffering. The position of the oppressed begins to be seen as desirable because it is a sign of one's status as just, innocent, and chosen by God. Because it is ethically untenable to deny another person's suffering, especially that of an African female child, McDonnell and her colleagues don a blackface of African suffering and appropriate the discourse of human rights to describe their own perceived persecution and as a formal means of exonerating themselves for centuries of religious domination and oppression all over the world.

I evoke the specter of blackface not as a reductionist argument about racism in the renewed antislavery movement (though, as is evidenced here, there is certainly a strain of very traditionalist, neocolonial racism present). But the concept and practice of blackface resonate so well in this context because they require that we interrogate the complicated political terrain around race that emerges in moments of heightened binaristic tension in which the black community and black experiences suddenly become emblematic of crises in American culture. As Yogita Goyal contends in her reading of Francis Bok's slave narrative, "Assign[ing] Africa to tragedy and the U.S. to promise" allows American readers to imagine that they have "transcended their own history, rather than encouraging them to think more deeply about how events in the U.S. and Sudan have common politically entangled roots."[75] The white evangelical abolitionists that constitute perhaps the most politically powerful arm of the contemporary antislavery movement exonerate themselves for the oppression of African people through participation in an abolitionist project through which they co-opt the suffering of enslaved Africans as a way of eliciting sympathy for their own contrived persecution. This allows them to obfuscate their own participation and complicity in the legacies of slavery that are a part of everyday life in the United States as well as in Africa. They identify with global black oppression rather than examine its root causes and take responsibility for it.

A POPULAR FACADE

It is the irrefutability of black suffering behind which this segment of the antislavery movement hides its anti-Muslim agenda. It is no coincidence, then, that so many of the new slave narratives focus on African scenes of subjection and that they began to flourish in the first years of the twenty-first century. The new antislavery movement is a curious coalition that emerged out of a unique post-9/11 political atmosphere that was charged with religious messaging and Islamophobia. As Allen Hertzke contends, activist causes like the antislavery and the Sudan genocide campaigns united "evangelicals into coalition with the Congressional Black Caucus, Catholic bishops, Jews, Episcopalians, and secular activists appalled by the indifference of the West toward this humanitarian tragedy."[76] Many (though not all) of these groups utilized similar abolitionist blackface tactics to hold up African oppression as a justification of their own political agenda against Islam.

Anti-Islamic sentiments might be an easy target in *Girl Soldier*, but identifying McDonnell's appropriation of Akallo's narrative guides us in reading other narratives and in locating these politics within antislavery discourse. One narrative that notably echoes the anti-Islamic agenda is Francis Bok's, the publication of which was encouraged and supported by the American Anti-Slavery Group and Bok's "American father," Charles Jacobs. Charles Jacobs persistently focuses his sights and the work of his organization on an unvariegated, monolithic "Muslim world" that is purportedly unchecked by the human rights establishment. According to Jacobs, in that world, "there are millions of blacks, women, gays, apostates, atheists, labor leaders, freedom fighters and racial and religious minorities who live without basic human rights and who desperately need help from the human rights community."[77] Jacobs positions himself and the American Anti-Slavery Group as the only activists who rise above the fear of being labeled racist, or worse, "Islamophobic," a dread that he diagnoses as endemic among the "decent middle-class white people" who make up the human rights community. He claims he and his colleagues are a vanguard who lead the charge against "evil done by non-Westerners."[78] Jacobs, ignoring America's long history of disproportionately holding people of the Global South to account for their rights abuses, touts himself as the unusual white middle-class American man who will denounce people of color who dare enslave other people of color. According to Bok's narrative, the Sudanese survivor of slavery was coached and promoted by Jacobs and his colleague Jesse Sage as part of Jacobs's campaign to reveal injustice in Sudan. Sage told Bok, "We want to help you tell your story," and he encouraged Bok to add details to his story that would pique audience interest, including asking him "What were you thinking?" and "What was going on in your mind when that happened?"[79] Their coaching assisted him in developing his narrative for audiences and publication.

It is no coincidence, then, that while Bok's narrative is otherwise largely uninterested in religion or Islamic oppression, it ends with a long treatise on Islamic radicalism in Sudan. The American Anti-Slavery Group focus their work primarily on Sudan and Mauritania, Islamic countries they argue the Western human rights industry is neglecting. Bok's discussion of the Sudanese conflict, which he describes in a footnote as having been learned from two books by Sudanese experts in addition to the coaching he received from Jacobs, Sage, and Eibner of Christian Solidarity International,[80] focus on the North-South religious divide and northern Sudan's politics of jihad that were encouraged by successive regimes over the course of the 1980s and '90s. While the religious tensions in the region are indisputable, Bok's discussions of politics, guided by the coaching of Jacobs, mobilizes Americans' fears of their own vulnerability to Muslim attacks by making repeated recourse to comparisons to the U.S. fear of Osama bin Laden and the Taliban after the 9/11 bombings. Bok recounts that "audiences were even more interested—and better informed—about Islam and *jihad*" after 9/11.[81] People at his events would pepper him with questions about the Sudanese civil war as anxiety about Muslim global political power was increasing, and his popularity as a speaker against Sudan increased as that fear increased. Through the co-optation of a largely unrelated narrative of Bok's enslavement, Jacobs and his colleagues were afforded an authentic Sudanese voice that could promote their political agenda regarding the global threat of Islam.[82]

A wide variety of radical anti-Islamic groups exploit the new slave narrative as evidence of their claims. JihadWatch.org suggests that Mende Nazer's slave narrative should be of interest to those who "who are concerned about the equality of rights of all people in Islamic societies as an example of the fact that Muslim radicals will enforce Sharia in its fullness, including its institutionalized discrimination against non-Muslim dhimmis and women."[83] In their hurry to condemn Islam, these Christian jihad monitors overlook the fact that Nazer's enslavers were not known to be radicals, and Nazer is herself a Muslim instead of an oppressed non-Muslim woman. For these pundits, Nazer, like Ayaan Hirsi Ali, represents an insider black African voice that aligns with the critiques that Western Christian groups level against Islam's practitioners. Incited by fear mongering, American Christians have virally circulated factoids drawn from Peter Hammond's *Slavery, Terrorism, and Islam: The Historical Roots and Contemporary Threat*, which proposes that "the most convulsive conflict of the past century, and indeed the most convulsive conflict of the past millennia, has undoubtedly been between Islam and Civilization; it has been between Islam and Freedom; it has been between Islam and Order; it has been between Islam and Progress; it has been between Islam and Hope."[84] The book also uses Mende Nazer's autobiography as evidence, in this case in the service of his larger argument that slavery in Africa is intrinsically Islamic. In Hammond's brief history of slavery, told from an explicitly Christian perspective, the relative harm of the Christian-led slave trade in Africa is weighed against that of the Islamic, finding the Islamic in all respects more brutal and deadly. Hammond traces a narrative from "the pagan origins of slavery" to "the Christian roots of liberty" to exonerate Christians for the role they played in the history of enslavement around the globe and placing Christians as the victims of Islamic slavery.[85] It relieves Christians of any responsibility they may have had for slavery because Christian missionaries "set [Africans] free to serve Christ," and his use of Nazer as an example is evidence that there is still much work for missionaries to do.[86]

In the 2010s, as Western governments turned their focus to the Islamic State as the most powerful Islamic adversary, the narratives of Yazidi women rose in popularity. Farida Khalaf's *The Girl Who Escaped Isis: This Is My Story* (2016) and Nadia Murad's *The Last Girl: My Story of Captivity and My Fight Against the Islamic State* (2017) suggest a recent turn in the anti-Islamic antislavery agenda, wherein young women in the Middle East are now used to effect the same transitive property of suffering seen in Akallo's narrative. As non-Muslims, the Yazidi women's narratives provide fertile ground for the antislavery imagination and for emphasizing the need for military interventions in the region. Narratives of Boko Haram's kidnapping of the girls from the Chibok region of Nigeria are functioning in the same role. Both likewise invite the sympathy for military intervention that is endemic in this strain of the new slave narrative, as they typically suggest that this particular form of oppression is one that cannot be abided.[87] What is always missing from the published narratives and the discussions that surround them is a systemic critique of the political mechanisms that maintain global inequality as regards income, welfare, and quality of life—in particular for women in the Global South—or of the local Islamic antirepression activists who prove that slavery and oppression are not endemic to Islam.

The narratives that contain anti-Islamic sentiment do not represent the majority of the new slave narratives. They are, however, indicative of a powerfully vocal part of the anti-trafficking movement that promotes militarized agendas through the publication of slave narratives, appropriating the life experiences of African (and now Arab) children as a means of supporting anti-Islamic agendas abroad. It is not that opposing oppression at the hands of some Muslims is unwarranted. But we must pay attention to how

this strain of the antislavery movement focuses on Christian-Muslim conflict. Organizations use African survivors of slavery as the poster children
for the detrimental effects of radical Islam to mask their Islamophobia in
the legitimizing garb of suffering. Thus, it is critical that we note the cultural
and political contexts within which slave narratives emerge. And given the
preceding critical analysis of the anti-Islamic threads that appeared in the
early years of the new slave narrative, we must continue to carefully analyze the ways the specter of international sexual enslavement continues to
be mobilized by conservative Christian organizations as a means of evoking sympathy for Western military and political intervention in the Global
South as these crises continue and new ones emerge. Our critical reading
of these literary texts helps expand our understanding of antislavery activism and the uses and abuses of human rights discourse.

Antislavery movements are often depicted as monolithic, as singular
entities that share a particular commitment, the same ideological motivations, and the same means for addressing labor exploitation.[88] Instead, when
we look to the narratives and the contexts in which they are written, we
begin to see unfolding a larger picture of the current antislavery movement.
Many forces are at play here, all of which are seeking the eradication of slavery, perhaps, but many of which have other motivating factors that we
might not otherwise detect. The narratives, in their individual differences,
allow us to see those politics at work and understand better how the different motivations for abolition are expressed in the very language used to
describe the horrific experience of slavery.

LESSONS FROM GARRISON

William Lloyd Garrison was an extraordinary activist. Few of us could
claim that we give of ourselves to any cause—especially a cause that does
not directly affect our own personal lives or families—with such vigor, conviction, and generosity. Nevertheless, if we are to take Douglass at his
word, Garrison fell prey to his pride, allowing his own message to over-
whelm the voice and "philosophy" of the people for whom he ostensibly
worked, the enslaved. He sought out but did not attain that "black heart"
to which so many of today's antislavery activists likely aspire.

The end goal of any critical approach to the slave narrative should not be
to indict the contemporary antislavery movement as if it were a monolithic

enterprise. Indeed, I am very much engaged on both a personal and a political level with the movement to eradicate contemporary forms of slavery, and much of my larger project of analyzing the new slave narrative is meant to act as a megaphone for the work that survivors of slavery are doing to address this human rights violation. What this analysis reveals, however, is that any human rights project must be vigilant not to ask survivors to perform as a minstrel act, replicating Western stereotypes and desires. As a black man, Douglass was being asked to perform the distorted white image of blackness. The concern about being a black man used for blackface troubled Douglass so much that he broke free from the Garrisonians. And the same will be true of survivors of contemporary slavery if their own politics, messages, and experiences are not privileged, and especially if they are asked to perform the politics of others.

Chapter Four

SEX PROBLEMS AND ANTISLAVERY'S COGNITIVE DISSONANCE

If the aftermath of 9/11 presented an opportunity for Western organizations to exercise an Islamophobic political agenda in the name of abolition, the influences on the new slave narrative have taken a distinct turn since 2010. The religious fervor that provided the impetus for some of the early narratives' publication did not disappear altogether; instead, it took a new target, one as ancient as unbelief. That target was sex.

After 2010, when the United States began including a review of its own policies in its Trafficking in Persons report, advocates in the United States grew increasingly cognizant of the reality of forced sex work domestically, and they were especially focused on the issue of child sexual exploitation. Early estimates of the number of people being forced into the sex trade in the United States were egregiously misleading (but nonetheless widely disseminated),[1] and scholars have produced no reliable alternative estimate to date. Nonetheless, recent research suggests that attention to forced sex work was warranted and still is. It is clear that people who would commercially exploit others for sex (loosely called "traffickers" in the United States) target people who otherwise lack resources to meet their basic needs.[2] Studies suggest that homeless youth and youth exiting foster care are particularly at risk of being coerced or forced into the sex trade because they have few options for work in the formal economy and lack a significant system of support.[3] LGBT youth are disproportionately vulnerable because of discrimination in the workplace and sometimes at home.[4] Though studies have not been able to clearly demonstrate the case due to limitations regarding the subjects included in studies, many researchers suspect that because traffickers target the poor and disenfranchised and because poverty is raced in the United States, impoverished African American women and men are likely more at risk of being forced into trading sex than other groups. Though these factors have always made American youth vulnerable to people who would exploit them, there was a distinct shift in the discourse around 2010 that led people to think of young people engaged in the sex trade less as tainted wild children or wayward criminals and more as "victims" of sexual exploitation.

The consequences of this shift remain avidly debated. As reports of what came to be called "domestic minor sex trafficking" (DMST) or "commercial sexual exploitation of children" (CSEC) emerged in scholarly articles and, more importantly, in the public media, the diverse factions that made up the twenty-first-century U.S. antislavery movement seemed to turn their attention almost in unison to the rapidly swelling anxieties that American girls would be made "sex slaves" in various "hubs for human trafficking" that were purportedly emerging in major cities across the United States. According to media reports and nonprofit communications, women were being "trafficked" across state borders on major highway thoroughfares, such as Interstates 10 and 95.[5] Municipal governments, church groups, and activists rushed into action when major sporting events visited their cities, mobilized by the pervasive (though largely misinformed) notion that the Super Bowl "is commonly known as the single largest human trafficking incident in the United States."[6] Grounded in punitive strategies, similar to the 1980s War on Drugs, a veritable war on sex trafficking emerged across the United States, guided largely by inflated fears of a trafficking epidemic that was suddenly affecting the average American girl.

While there is no doubt that some women and men—adults and minors alike—are forced into sexual labor in the United States, much as they are forced into all forms of labor, sex in particular was suddenly perceived as a pervasive danger to American girls, even in cities where police could locate few if any actual traffickers to arrest or prosecute. Activists blamed pornography, rap music, films, and other popular culture for glamorizing and romanticizing both sexual exploitation and sex itself. Organizations and universities held conferences with themes devoted to critiquing the commodification of women during which they ironically trucked in sensationalized, violated images of (primarily white) women's bodies. The transitive property of suffering (discussed in the previous chapter) was no longer necessary—the suffering was located right here "in our backyards," and, to many people's horror, it was affecting "our girls." A diverse array of antislavery and anti-trafficking organizations proliferated in the United States, all providing local solutions to the problem—from awareness campaigns and billboards to increased punitive sentences for traffickers to women's empowerment programs to religious conversion therapy to addiction recovery models—much of which focused exclusively on rescuing young women from the perceived predations of the sex trade.

In response, sex worker advocates, labor trafficking activists, and international feminist groups protested against these campaigns. Concerned about labor exploitation in the sex industry (and in general) but convinced that the anti-trafficking movement was myopically focused on legislating morality around sex, critics argued that anti-trafficking feminists ignored women's agency in the sex trade. At the same time, critics claimed, they relied on discriminatory punitive strategies that were ineffective in reducing labor exploitation and violence and indeed increased the vulnerability of impoverished women. They provided indisputable evidence that sex workers were being arrested indiscriminately in the name of human trafficking busts that rarely yielded any women or girls who had actually been forced into the trade. Critics perceived the emerging "prostitution abolitionist" movement driven by self-proclaimed "radical feminists" as an even greater threat to women's well-being, social mobility, and safety at work than trafficking. The feminist debates of the late 1970s and early 1980s seemed to be reawakened by the reemergent antislavery movement.

These popular and legal debates regarding contemporary slavery and human trafficking in the United States were accompanied by—and sometimes initiated by—first-person narratives of domestic minor sex trafficking written by survivors, which represented a similarly radical shift in the life of the slave narrative genre. In the early years of the slave narrative's reemergence, between the passing of the earliest anti-trafficking legislation in the United States in 2000 and this turn in 2010, eleven slave narratives had been published. Four of those narratives were about enslavement for sexual purposes; the others focused on the first-person experiences of survivors of labor trafficking and child soldiering abroad. As established in chapter 3, the vast majority of those narratives were written by and about people from Africa or of African descent. The conventions of the new slave narrative were, for the first twenty years, much more reminiscent of the more familiar aspects of the nineteenth-century slave narrative tradition. Indeed, the new slave narratives were often deliberately shaped, sometimes with the encouragement or insistence of ghostwriters or nonprofit advocates, to conform to the pervasive American cultural understanding regarding antebellum slavery and the slave narrative tradition.[7] As a result, the earliest narratives were diverse and global, primarily depicted forced labor other than sexual labor, and often focused on black lives.

Briefly consumed with forced child labor, child soldier conscription, and undocumented immigrant labor migration, the antislavery movement and the new slave narrative genre retrained their focus on a more proximate and certainly more intimate set of concerns. The girl next door became the nearly exclusive object of concern. Like their earlier counterparts, these exclusively female narrators—regardless of race, culture, or geographic origin—mobilized the word "slavery" as well as its history in the United States and the conventions of the slave narrative tradition to describe their experiences of forced sexual labor in the Unites States.[8] Of the twenty-five new slave narratives published between 2010 and the summer of 2018 (when this book was submitted for publication), only four recounted experiences of labor trafficking.[9] Twenty-one (or 84 percent) of them recounted first-person experiences of forced sex work, but only six of those "sex slavery" narratives depicted the lives of women from the Global South.[10] In all, the period of 2010–2018 saw the publication of at least eleven new slave narratives that depicted domestic minor sex trafficking described as slavery that were set in the United States and another four set in the UK (and there are many more narratives of sex trafficking that do not describe the sexual exploitation as "slavery," but for the purposes of this study, I do not include them as I remain committed to the analysis of the discourse of "slavery" in this project). What is more, whereas only two of the 2000–2009 narratives were written by white American or British women, eleven of the narratives written since 2010 were written by that demographic. Changes in U.S. discourse around slavery had a particularly strong impact on the publishing industry, which now almost exclusively publishes new slave narratives depicting the domestic sexual exploitation of female minors, with the exception of a few additional narratives of sexual enslavement of women who are exploited by American antagonists such as the Islamic State.

This chapter is the only one in this book that focuses on narratives of U.S. domestic minor sex trafficking because, despite the seemingly myopic attention given to that demographic in much American media currently, the popularity of that particular strain of slave narrative is still a relatively new development in the constantly changing terrain of the global antislavery movement, even if the issue of forced sexual labor itself is not. While there are several other narratives of forced sex work from Britain and Syria, in particular, that are relevant to the development of the genre, I am going to focus this chapter on the remarkable set of narratives of sexual enslavement in the United States because, read together, these narratives reveal particular nuances in the U.S. antislavery movement that require critical attention. Those complex and diverse narratives provide significant insight into the range of ideological positions that have emerged in the debates around slavery and trafficking in the United States today, and they also provide a unique set of perspectives on the future of the antislavery movement in the United States that is grounded in survivor experiences and survivor expertise.

What these narratives demonstrate is the that the diverse and often conflicting logic that pervades the controversial and divisive sex trafficking debate is replicated through a sort of narrative cognitive dissonance that inflects the construction of survivors' life narratives. Though far from resolved in the first-person narratives of survivors of sexual bondage, that dissonance is, at its heart, a conflict in the competing characterizations of freedom and agency that the narrators explore in the process of writing about their most intimate and most traumatic experiences. They write in very personal language and tell unique, individual stories; however, as is the case with all authors of life narratives, the myriad conventions for self-definition and subjectivity that they have encountered in their lives inform their memories and interpretations of their experiences. They construct their narrative voices from the many competing generic devices and ideological positions that are available to them. In the process of reading their narratives with deliberate attention to the various discursive conventions that emerge, we might reveal the impulses of the anti-trafficking movement and the role that survivors play in both articulating and shaping antislavery discourse.

Though this analysis, I argue that the new slave narratives that depict domestic minor sex trafficking in the United States after 2010 respond to the conflicting notions of agency and freedom with a fairly unified call to action. Indeed, despite the apparent intellectual conflicts between and within them, the narratives consistently originate in and finally return to a search for the substantive freedoms that have been denied to the narrators both in slavery and in freedom. In an attempt to provide a way forward, the narrators point to a necessary but missing collective and community response to the systemic problems that lead young women to be vulnerable to enslavement in the United States. In this way, new directions for advocacy emerge from the interstices of those narrative tensions to describe a rarely recognized but nearly unanimous survivor-generated alternative to the conflicts around victimization, responsibility, agency, and freedom that fracture antislavery activism otherwise.

SEX PROBLEMS

The concern regarding the newly dubbed "human trafficking" began to circulate in international legislative arenas in the 1990s in response to women's advocacy groups in the Global South protesting labor conditions for migrant women. In the United States, however, the concern about "trafficking" was taken up primarily as a problem regarding sexual labor. The complicated philosophical debates regarding the relationship between labor and sex and the level of women's agency within the labor market that brewed in international human rights circles were largely limited in the early years of human trafficking activism in the United States to a reductive narrative of women's vulnerability to sexual exploitation. As Yvonne Zimmerman contends, "A perception that sex is the central problem of human trafficking has been a staple of anti-trafficking activism in the United States virtually from day one."[11] When Senators Paul Wellstone and Christopher Smith led congress to a compromise on the original Trafficking Victims Protection Act (TVPA) in 2000, for instance, they, too, had as a primary motivating factor this "sex problem." The final TVPA legislation included provisions to protect all people who are compelled to engage in the sex trade or in any form of labor through force, fraud, or coercion, but in practically every iteration of the bill, all other forms of labor are subordinated to sexual labor. For instance, in the first section of the TVPA, where it describes the premises of the law, the bill reads:

(1) As the 21st century begins, the degrading institution of slavery continues throughout the world. Trafficking in persons is a modern form of slavery, and it is the largest manifestation of slavery today. At least 700,000 persons annually, primarily women and children, are trafficked within or across international borders. Approximately 50,000 women and children are trafficked into the United States each year.

(2) Many of these persons are trafficked into the international sex trade, often by force, fraud, or coercion. The sex industry has rapidly expanded over the past several decades. It involves sexual exploitation of persons, predominantly women and girls, involving activities related to prostitution, pornography, sex tourism, and other commercial sexual services. The low status of women in many parts of the world has contributed to a burgeoning of the trafficking industry.

(3) Trafficking in persons is not limited to the sex industry. This growing transnational crime also includes forced labor and involves significant violations of labor, public health, and human rights standards worldwide.

The sex industry is unmistakably described from these first paragraphs as not merely one of a vast array of possible sites of trafficking but as the primary form of trafficking, and it is posed as if it were exclusively a problem that originates in other parts of the world. The authors define the international sex trade as inherently exploitative, and they thereby conflate voluntary sex trade with involuntary forced labor. Correspondingly for its authors, "women and children" are figured as the primary victims of trafficking, with both groups figured as equally vulnerable to predation. The subordination and obfuscation of all other forms of labor (including men's labor) continues throughout the bill.

This was no mistake. Despite Wellstone's lonely resistance to this narrowed focus, the TVPA was based in large part on the Freedom from Sexual Trafficking Act of 1999, originally introduced by Senator Christopher Smith, which focused explicitly on abolishing all forms of sexual labor—not just sexual exploitation. Nearly all the testimonies solicited for the Senate hearings were provided by victims of sex trafficking, and advocates presented composite sketches of harrowing exploitation in the sex trade.[12] For most Americans, including those in Congress, this redefinition of the

word "trafficking," which only in this new iteration included sexual exploitation, was meant to address a "sex problem" that was emerging all around
the world. As many critics have noted, a moral panic about the commercial sexual exploitation of women and children worldwide was revivified
in the first years of the twenty-first century, akin to the "white slavery"
scares of the 1910s that led to the creation of the Mann Act and the racially
biased policing of women's sex and sex work that resulted from it.[13]

In the early years of the TVPA, legislators and media attended largely to
this "sex problem" as an international and immigration issue, and there was
still little emphasis on the sex trafficking of U.S. citizens domestically.[14] For
a decade, the United States legislature signaled that this was an international
and immigration problem by excluding only one country—the United
States—from its analysis in its yearly international Trafficking in Persons
(TIP) report. This focus on the international sex trade reflected a willful
blindness to the existence of forced labor in the United States, grounded in
the belief that slavery, as well as the gender-based violence that characterizes much of forced sex work, was endemic to the Global South but practically impossible in the United States.[15]

In 2010, however, recognizing that the United States had been exonerating itself for slavery by imagining that the end of the Civil War had obliter-
ated all forms of forced labor within its borders, the U.S. government began
assessing itself in the TIP report. With the entry of the Obama administration, Hillary Clinton as secretary of state, and Luis CdeBaca as head of
the Trafficking in Persons Office, the American anti-trafficking industry
largely retrained its focus. Luis CdeBaca announced this shift in attention
at the Center for American Progress, arguing, "Human trafficking is not
an issue in which we can implement policies of American 'exceptionalism.'
We must not only enforce the 13th Amendment and meet our international
obligations—we also have to assess our efforts as we would assess others."[16]
Over the course of a couple of years, a seemingly surprising sound bite
quickly emerged—"slavery exists in our own backyard." The year before
CdeBaca's announcement, David Batstone's Not for Sale campaign began
promoting its organizers as "backyard abolitionists," and scholar Kevin
Bales offered a new book focused on slavery in the United States titled *The
Slave Next Door*.[17] After a decade of attention to the brothels, supply chains,
fields of battle, and agricultural fields of the Global South, U.S. legislators,
media, scholars, and activists began to turn their gaze inward.

Seemingly overnight, reports of sexual exploitation of American women and children were of interest to legislators and average citizens alike, even though sexual exploitation itself was certainly not a new phenomenon in the United States. In February 2010, the Senate Judiciary Committee held a hearing titled "In Our Own Backyard: Child Prostitution and Sex Trafficking in the United States" in which survivor-activist Rachel Lloyd soberly testified about the harm done to young women in the sex trade as well as the harm done when people deny the reality of commercial sexual exploitation in America, in contrast to other advocates at the meeting who promoted inflated factoids and sensationalized tales of horror.[18] During those same years, a deluge of films and television shows depicting the sexual enslavement of American girls flooded the screens, sentimentally encouraging American citizens to personally and financially engage in anti-trafficking efforts.[19] While the infamous Liam Neeson film *Taken* depicted young American women trafficked abroad, new documentaries revealed sexual enslavement closer to home. The 2010 MSNBC documentary called "Sex Slaves in America: Minh's Story," for instance, depicted the enslavement of Minh Dang, who had been traded for sex by her parents in Berkeley, California. After the success of that episode, MSNBC had regular programming on the subject, advertised with salacious titles such as "Sex Slaves in the Suburbs" and "Sex Slaves: The Teen Trade." While the United States' recognition of its own role in the exploitation of human labor in the sex trade marked a critical turning point in the antislavery movement, this sudden shift in discourse sold American audiences a sensationalized narrative of women's vulnerability that brought the issue of trafficking much closer to home and, in turn, encouraged an interest in first-person narratives that would testify to the gravity of the situation for American girls.

The new slave narratives that were published during this period sometimes adopted the sensationalized tropes that antislavery organizations were developing during this period, but they were grounded in the lived experiences of people who did not necessarily need to embellish to reveal the depravations of forced sex work. Many of the first-person narratives of domestic minor sex trafficking that were published during this period are emblazoned with titles that focus explicitly on the anxieties about the vulnerability of the American girl child that were common after 2010—including Carissa Phelps's *Runaway Girl* (2012) and Barbara Amaya's *Nobody's Girl* (2015)—an indicator of the near-exclusive focus on innocence of minor girls.

Whereas the international new slave narrators opened their memoirs with their idyllic though poor origins, in the post-2010 narratives of sexual enslavement, the origin myth that precedes the recollection of slavery's horrors is that of the consummate American good girl, innocent and sweet, unknowing of the horrors of the world. That originary girl, in survivor narrator Alice Jay's experience, "loved dancing and writing songs . . . climbing trees and going to church . . . was a good student who loved school and loved to learn."[20] The narrative settings, however, turn away from the idyllic but poor environs of the earlier international narratives toward the dark, intimate spaces of the impoverished and abusive homes and neighborhoods of the United States, where young girls lose their innocence through incest or rape long before they are introduced to the sex trade.

Other titles, such as Rebecca Bender's *Roadmap to Redemption* (2013), Brook Parker-Bello's *Living Inside the Rainbow: Winning the Battlefield of the Mind After Human Trafficking and Mental Bondage* (2013), Alice Jay's *Out of the Darkness: A Survivor's Story* (2014), and Annie Lobert's *Fallen: Out of the Sex Industry and Into the Arms of the Savior* (2015) point to the redemptive rise from oppression to Christian salvation that is also typical of these narratives. The narrative of sexual enslavement varies widely in its generic structure—from diary to self-help workbook to "academic" text— but the majority of these (with a few notable exceptions) are influenced by evangelical Christian testimony and addiction recovery rhetoric. As I will suggest throughout this chapter, the new slave narratives published in the United States in this period reflect the proliferation of contemporary and conflicting Christian conversion narratives within antislavery discourse. This particular strain of sexual conversion narratives—almost all of which are self-published—relate stories that testify to "God's goodness," the return to a true self found in God's grace after a fall, and the vocation to proselytize about the power of Christian redemption. However, they often refract the different claims to salvation to which the authors subscribe. Neoliberal personal responsibility, evangelical submission, and recovery from addiction all feature prominently in the narratives. Because of their attention to the long road of recovery from both trafficking and addiction, these conversion narratives are often grounded in the logic of Alcoholics Anonymous (AA) and Narcotics Anonymous (NA), programs that require a conversion process all their own, including the adoption of an entirely revised worldview aligned with the values of the group.[21] The domestic minor sex trafficking narratives that dominated the new slave narrative market after 2010 refract these important trends in the discourses of slavery and recovery that were developing in response to this seemingly emergent problem in the United States.

In this chapter, I zoom in on these domestic minor sex trafficking narratives published since 2010 in the United States. In addition to those already mentioned, this chapter also considers Wendy Barnes's *And Life Continues: Sex Trafficking and My Journey to Freedom* (2015), Katariina Rosenblatt's *Stolen: The True Story of a Sex Trafficking Survivor* (2014), Jasmine Grace Marino's *The Diary of Jasmine Grace* (2016), and Mimi Crown's *Stuck in Traffic* (2016). All the narrators use the rhetoric of "modern slavery" to ground their claims in the rights framework that was developed by antislavery activists in the first years of the twenty-first century, and they also take up the language of "victimization" familiar to anti-trafficking efforts, which allows them to reject any sense of personal guilt they may have harbored in response to their abuse. At the same time, the narrators also reveal the influence of a very different logic of freedom that emerges from conservative "family values" and "Radical Feminist abolitionist" politics as well as from Christian evangelical traditions and self-help discourse. These widely divergent discursive scripts create intellectual tensions in the texts that, I will suggest, are impossible to reconcile but which reflect a transparent fissure in the antislavery movement. It reveals what is essentially an open secret—that the anti-trafficking "movement" is a fragmented coalition of activists so diverse and divided in its membership and ideologies that it should not even be understood to be a single social movement, and those tensions have real effects on survivors' lives and self-perceptions.

FROM PROSTITUTION TO TRAFFICKING

Barbara Amaya was watching the 10 p.m. local news broadcast when she heard the story of young girls who had been wooed into gangs and forced into selling sex. "Hearing those words shook me out of my sleepy daze," she reports. "Now I began to see the truth: I had been a victim. A walking target. I had been trafficked, and now I had a name for it."[22] Amaya immediately had an "epiphany" and began speaking about her experience and conducting outreach efforts to homeless youth.

Jasmine Grace Marino was visiting a church group where a "cute little Christian lady [was] talking about how she goes into strip clubs and befriends the dancers." She learned that this group helped people exit the sex trade. Marino was surprised to recognize the clubs, hotels, and highways that the outreach team frequented. She realized when the young women who worked there were being described as "trafficked" that it was also an apt characterization of what had happened to her.[23]

Katariina Rosenblatt serendipitously visited the office of a professor in the field of human trafficking at a law school while she was considering returning to school. The professor explained to her the definition of human trafficking, and Rosenblatt remembers, "Although I didn't tell her, I thought, *That's me!*"[24] She didn't have the courage to admit her victimization that day, but she enrolled in the law school and then a PhD program and eventually wrote her thesis on the vulnerability of American youth to traffickers.

The narrators of the domestic minor sex trafficking narratives provide detailed accounts of their recruitment into the sex trade as children or young adults. They depict their experiences of forced sex work over the course of years, typically accompanied by increasing drug addiction and other forms of self-harm. After leaving the men who held them mentally and physically captive, they describe years of living with the resulting trauma and a haunting sense of self-blame for their experiences of sexual exploitation. For much of their lives, they pointed to their own childhood flaws, desires, and mistakes as the source of their pain, because, as Rebecca Bender suggests of trafficked children, "It takes TIME to convince us that we have even been trafficked."[25] But as if suddenly called by a forgotten name, these survivors heard the stories of trafficked youth and recognized themselves in the gruesome details. And with that newfound articulation of their experiences—"child sex trafficking"—their narratives depict a radical transformation from the cowering, drug-addled, and traumatized sleep in which so many of them felt they had been walking into driven, studious, anti-trafficking warriors.

Throughout most of the narratives, survivors tend to utilize the terminology they employed to describe their experiences before they became acquainted with the concept of "trafficking." Many of the narrators use the word "prostitution" throughout their narratives to describe their engagement in the sex trade, though they often did not initially recognize what they were doing as such when they were first traded for sex, usually by a trusted adult. Rebecca Bender calls it "selling my body"; Marino refers to herself as a "working girl" who kept returning to "work" even after her abuse; Jay talks about "work[ing] the track" and "work[ing] the club" when she was in "the game."[26] Using language common in the sex industry, these narrators reflect the way sex is exchanged as labor for many who perform that work. Rosenblatt refers to it as a "lifestyle," suggesting (inadvertently perhaps) it is a choice that people make and can change.[27] In Mimi Crown's atypically graphic book, which is sometimes categorized as "erotica" on sales sites, she refers to the "lifestyle" as well, but she also says that she "sell[s] pussy," and "hooked up with people," and she calls herself a "bad whore," reflecting the sexually explicit language of the street and the way she was trained to understand herself by the violent man for whom she worked.[28] All these colloquial usages describe the trade of sex as an active, agentic form of labor and capitalist exchange.

When these survivor-narrators begin to translate their experiences through the lens of "child sex trafficking," however, they activate a logic and a language of victimization. Brook Parker-Bello suggests that survivors must embrace the term "victim" even though it may not feel apt: "I was once a victim, and some believe that we are never victims, but that isn't true. A victim is defined as 'someone or something sacrificed or preyed upon.' That is exactly what happens."[29] She says that in her experience, she was reduced to "a distorted, slave-minded, having-to-please-others-all-of-the-time mind set."[30] The first step to recovery for Parker-Bello was admitting to being victimized, to being prey, to being completely subordinated to another. She believes that accepting one's experience as "victim" assists survivors in avoiding the cycle of victimization that results from remaining "broken" and not healing.

Narrators dramatize their burgeoning realization that what they had understood as their own bad behaviors cannot be internalized in that way and must be externalized as force and victimization, especially for those who were coerced into the trade as children. Rebecca Bender suggests that the colloquial language that is used in street sex work inappropriately invokes the notion of choice. There is sometimes a "choosing fee" when a woman first works with a pimp. Engaging or being engaged by a new pimp, regardless of the lack of any material or social mobility or even agency attached to the move, is colloquially called "choosing up" within the sex trade, as if even the choice between two abusive pimps represents a legitimate choice. Bender writes, "The use of the word 'choose' has had a subtle, yet impactful way on how we as victims have agreed with the lie that our situation is our choice."[31] Before she began to "identify as a trafficking victim," Bender thought "my problem was drugs and that I chose a bad boyfriend who abused me—he happened to be a pimp and I chose a life of prostitution."[32] But once Bender escapes her trafficker, she shifts to the passive voice to mark the realization that she had in fact been unwittingly "chosen" by someone who "deceived" her because she was "vulnerable to a pimp."[33] Rosenblatt similarly makes the shift from understanding the sex trade as a choice she had made as a child to the passive-voiced recognition that a recruiter "had chosen me because she knew I was vulnerable and lonely."[34] Jasmine Grace's recollections turn to the passive voice as well: "I would lie to myself because I always felt that I was the one in control. . . . In reality, I was being purchased, abused, and controlled. Even though I created a sense of control, I lived in fear."[35] These narratives suggest that the limited range of "choices" available to impoverished and abused young women leaves little room for an argument to be made that their alternatives— return to their abusive homes, live on the street, starve to death—could be considered legitimate alternatives to the "choice" that the pimps presented to them. By adopting the logic provided to them by the anti-trafficking advocates and counselors with whom they interacted, however, they began to realize that what had once seemed to be a choice was, in fact, abuse.

As Elizabeth Bernstein's research suggests, for the most marginalized of sex workers, poverty, youth, and sometimes drug use limit access to meaningful "informed consent," given that both internal factors (mental health, urgency of survival, sense of empowerment) and external factors (history of abuse, job opportunities, discrimination) radically restrict the range of choices they may have before them.[36] At the very most, impoverished youth who engage in the sex trade are often making what Alexandra Lutnick calls "the least worst choice" from a range of entirely negative choices.[37] For many of the narrators, then, the recognition of the limited range of choices that led to their victimization allowed them to free themselves (at least temporarily) of the self-condemnation that resulted from their sense of having chosen to work in the sex trade. As victims of forced commercial sexual exploitation, they realized that they were duped into thinking that they were responsible for their abuse at the hands of traffickers who were their trusted

All but one of the domestic sex trafficking narratives are written by women who describe being sexually abused before they were coerced into the sex trade, and the one exception—Rebecca Bender—mentions that she did experience childhood violence of some sort but withholds the details. Previous sexual assault is figured not merely as a first violation but essentially as a cause of (or a "pipeline" to) sexual exploitation later in life. These new slave narrators depict their familial molestation as creating a radical vulnerability that practically invited future predation. As a result, they tend to suggest that they did not have the capacity to escape later abuse and trafficking because they had essentially been psychologically compromised by childhood sexual assault.[38]

The depiction of trafficking as victimization tends to focus on the criminal exploitation that the narrators experienced, their childhood vulnerabilities, and the mechanisms by which traffickers exploited those vulnerabilities. Through a transformation in their self-images, these new slave narrators train their narrative focus on the ways they were sexually victimized, rather than on their bad behaviors, as they internalize the language and ideas employed by those counselors, activists, educators, journalists, lawyers, and social workers who first introduced them to their new self-image as a "trafficking victim." Including childhood sexual assault in one's published life narrative, then—and perhaps even one's own personal psychological narrative—is one of the ways new slave narrators have resisted the stigma of the "wild child" who engaged in prostitution and instead have embraced the logic of victimization that is prevalent in antitrafficking discourse. These narratives of domestic minor sex trafficking all point to this early victimization as a route to self-exoneration as well as to acceptance into a community of survivors and activists rather than the community of criminals and addicts to which they previously felt confined. In this way, the transition from understanding their life experiences as "prostitution" to thinking of them as "child trafficking" allowed them a language and a context in which they could move from criminal to victim in their own minds and begin the process of healing from that abuse.

FROM TRAFFICKING TO SLAVERY

Over the course of the narratives, these new slave narrators also begin to express their experiences as "slavery," which allows them to articulate a somewhat different approach to their life narratives.[39] When they invoke the discourse of "modern slavery," their arguments about their experiences often stress victimization less and align more with the sociological arguments typically expressed by academics such as Kevin Bales and organizations such as Free the Slaves, who have both been influential among survivors. The narrators' logic correspondingly shifts from a discourse of victimization to a discourse of rights (and rights violations), including notions of ownership, commodification, and disposability. Indeed, in the moments when they invoke the language of modern slavery, the narrators adapt the language and tropes that are more common to the international slave narratives discussed earlier. This discourse tends to, as Alison Brysk and Austin Choi-Fitzpatrick put it, "move the conversation from sex to slavery, from prostitution to power, and from rescue to rights."[40]

Like the new slave narratives from the first decade of the genre's reemergence, most narratives of domestic minor sex trafficking explicitly cite nineteenth-century slave narrators and employ metaphors of historical slavery to emphasize the gravity of their own experiences. Many of the narrators refer to the metaphorical "chains" and "shackles" that kept them from escaping even when literal chains were not employed.[41] Reinforcing this notion of psychological bondage and giving it historical roots, Marino reminds us of the (commonly misattributed) quote of Harriet Tubman's in which she purportedly claimed that she would have freed thousands more enslaved African Americans "if only they knew they were slaves."[42] Here, Marino does more than conjure slavery's gravity, she makes a claim of false consciousness for all those youth engaged in the sex trade who do not yet self-identify as enslaved. By this logic, if even Tubman had known African Americans who did not recognize their own captivity and needed to be rescued from bondage, then it is no surprise that people enslaved today might be unable, as the narrators previously were, to articulate their experiences as slavery and understand their need to escape. As was the case with the logic of "trafficking," this awakening from the misapprehension of their experiences runs throughout the texts and continues to exonerate the narrators from the sense of personal responsibility that previously made it difficult to recognize their oppression as "slavery." However, with the introduction of the idea of slavery, the narrators reinscribe their experiences with a broader set of concerns regarding rights. Parker-Bello, for instance, employs the historical slave trade as an entrée to critique the civil rights that are denied to people who are enslaved today. She quotes Sojourner Truth's claim that she "feels for her rights, but der ain't any dare" to suggest that "even now, many of us do not know of or are not acquainted with our rights."[43] The narrators demonstrate throughout their narratives the ways in which they have been exiled from knowledge of and access to their rights to human dignity, to freedom of movement, and to freely choose and be paid for their work while held in forced sexual labor.

These white and black slave narrators do not invoke the language of "slavery" only to connect themselves with a history of oppression or to appropriate the gravity of nineteenth-century slavery. The authors point to salient aspects of contemporary slavery that exhibit the larger structural and ideological injustices in the United States that they were only able to recognize when they began to come to terms with their experiences of forced sexual labor as slavery. Through mobilization of the concept of "slavery," they move the target of their critique from interpersonal violence to structural violence. For instance, the denial of rights is crystallized in the way commercially sexually exploited people are often treated as if they are "owned" by their traffickers. Despite the fact that there is no legal right to ownership of another human being in the United States or anywhere else in the world, child trafficking victims have often been treated as if they are the property of someone else. If we think of the 1926 League of Nation's Slavery Conventions definition, which indicates that "slavery is the status or condition of a person over whom any or all of the powers attaching to the right of ownership are exercised," it becomes clear that the individual exercise of power implying ownership, even in a context in which contractual or legal ownership is impossible, is indeed considered slavery globally (as the Bellagio-Harvard Guidelines on the Legal Parameters of Slavery reiterate).[44] New slave narrators recognize the way perceptions of ownership act as coercive psychological bonds in slavery. Amaya's pimp told her, "You belong to me now," and Alice Jay's exploiters told her, "You're mine."[45] They both felt compelled to work for men who exercised the rights of ownership over them. But as they began to be enmeshed in the discourse of antislavery, they came to see how this was a significant violation of their rights rather than simply an abusive boyfriend. They began to interrogate how the cultural objectification of women and sex was complicit in the denial of their rights. Though human rights are generally considered the domain of the state, individual actors commit the "private wrongs" that constitute human rights violations at the interpersonal level.[46] These private wrongs are thus held up by survivors as the symptoms of a larger societal refusal of the female child's right to her own body and labor.

As survivors begin to think of their experiences as slavery, another level of critique emerges from the reconceptualization of the treatment of their bodies as property. If a person can "sell her body" (as so many of the narrators phrase it) or if her body or labor can even be perceived to be owned by another person, then bodies are being exploited as a commodity to be traded and consumed. The narrators adopt a critique of labor commodification that is widely employed by social scientists and some activists working to articulate the societal structures that undergird and even encourage slavery in the twenty-first century. Rosenblatt takes up this discourse in the way she describes the mechanisms of enslavement in her chapters "Enslaved . . . Again" and "Unsuspected Predators," recalling, "To these men, I wasn't a person, I was a commodity. I was a piece of meat, not even a child. I had lost my childhood innocence, dignity, and self-respect before I started going on 'dates.' In time, I began to see myself as the customers saw me—as nothing. And that's what I felt I was: nothing."[47] Rosenblatt points here to her belief that the sexual economy in which she and other women were forced to work reduced them to a commodity and thereby reduced their access to human dignity. She suggests that commodification leads to a sense of degradation of the self that is central to the maintenance of power in slavery. Echoing, perhaps, Kevin Bales's notion of "disposable people," Alice Jay tells us that pimps treat women as if they are "dispensable," and she elaborates, saying, "It is slavery! . . . There is no honor or glory in this type of thinking that somehow makes another human being's life expendable."[48] Here, Jay taps into a powerful economic critique of contemporary slavery, which suggests that because it is relatively easy and inexpensive to coercively or forcefully extract a person's labor within the current global economy, people who are enslaved in this way are treated as if they are disposable. Bales's popular academic work provides a more expansive, global economic viewpoint on this issue, but Jay and the other slave narrators zoom in to the everyday violence that results from notions of women's disposability in the U.S. economy.[49] The commodification of labor power is an essential part of capitalism, but these writers focus specifically on the commodification of the body, not simply its labor.

After connecting to survivor networks, reading the scholarly literature on contemporary forms of slavery, attending conferences, and even pursuing advanced degrees in law and related fields, these empowered survivors invoke a critique of the capitalist commodification and consumption of sex to condemn the exploitation of sexual labor. Through shifting the language from victimization to disposability, they point to the fundamental violations of human dignity and rights that survivors of slavery have undergone. By connecting to the history of slavery in the United States, they suggest the responsibility of the state to protect the rights of its citizens, and by localizing it in individual experience, they target everyday acts of commodification that are allowed when women's rights are not more stringently protected and, indeed, when cultural trends encourage this violation of women's dignity. From their discrete, individual, intimately personal examples, the narrators make claims regarding the way women's disposability, commodification, and curtailed rights point to a larger systemic crisis that positions the economy and culture of the United States as structurally supportive of the gender-based objectification and violence they experienced.

Through the discourses of "trafficking" and "modern slavery" that the authors invoke, a lack of choice is central to the characterizations of exploitation. Whether that lack of choice has to do with victimization or commodification, whether the perpetrator is an individual or a culture's oppressive structural inequalities, the question of choices made by the authors is moot within these frameworks. The authors depict trafficking as victimization against one's will and slavery as the commodification of human life and the absolute control of another that precludes any choice in the matter. Though they sometimes risk in these particular moments suggesting an essential lack of female agency, the authors suggest that their own individual wills are not what is at stake in defining their experiences in the sex trade.

THE IRONIC IMPERATIVE OF PERSONAL RESPONSIBILITY

The compelling tapestries of sexual victimization and labor commodification that are woven into the narratives begin to fray at the edges as new anxieties about personal responsibility interrupt the narratives. While all the narrators devote significant time to undermining their own personal and societal propensity for victim-blaming when it comes to the trafficking of children in the sex trade, there remains a powerful specter of self-blame that haunts the narratives. Early sexual assaults taught the young women to think of themselves as responsible for the abuse inflicted on them by family members and neighbors. Their adoption of the victimization lens assists them in eschewing that responsibility. Ironically, however, the thread of an insidious, compulsory sense of personal responsibility is incongruously woven into the discourse of recovery from slavery and victimization.

In the final pages of *And Life Continues*, for instance, Wendy Barnes insists that her recovery from trafficking and subsequent drug abuse depended on her acceptance of her complicity in her own and others' abuse. Convicted, imprisoned, and labeled a sex offender as a result of living in a household in which minors were trafficked (despite the fact that she was being trafficked as well), Barnes cites the charges against her as undeniable proof of her criminality. She reminds herself that the court was correct in the assessment of her behavior: "I had been a horrible mother to my children. It wasn't what I planned or wanted, or that I felt I had no other choices. I had exposed them to hell."[50] She extends her sense of personal responsibility by admitting to herself and her readers that she harmed both her children and the other young trafficked women whom she "had helped [the trafficker] victimize by not standing up for what was right." Through court hearings and meetings with her parole officer, she slowly came to believe that "doing nothing was a choice and an action in itself and that my 'action' of doing nothing to protect the girls had hurt many children over the years. The fact that I had been one of those children was not a mitigating factor in the jurisprudence system."[51] Following the lead of the judicial system that held her criminally liable for her own victimization, Barnes continued to admit no mitigating circumstances for her behavior and held herself responsible for the acts she witnessed but did not prevent. Countering much of the argument for trafficking as victimization that she makes throughout her memoir, she reflects in the final pages on the legitimacy of the sex offender label she was assigned: "If I hadn't made the choices I made, this wouldn't be happening. It's a consequence that I need to learn to face." Her brother, sympathetic to and encouraging of this attribution of responsibility, responds, "Wendy, I am so proud of you right now. You're taking responsibility for your actions and facing the consequences. This shows me how much you have grown and matured. I am so proud to have you as my sister."[52] In this culminating moment of triumph over adversity and apparent growth that essentially concludes her life narrative, Barnes suggests that recovery from the trauma of trafficking requires a recognition of the role one played in one's own victimization. She must frame her experience in terms of her own responsibility both because of and in spite of the fact that the judicial system has marked her as a social pariah by compelling her to make public declarations of responsibility through the sex offender registration system, which not only altered her self-conception but also delimited the spaces in which she could reside, the jobs for which she was eligible, and the kind of relationship she could share with her children. Clearly, it also circumscribed her ability to understand herself as a commodified victim who can be entirely exonerated from self-blame. Barnes sometimes resists the requirements of the sex offender label and its attendant constrictions on her life in "freedom," but, following the logic of the legal conviction, her family, and the social workers she encountered, Barnes frames these excruciating outcomes as her own responsibility. Relegated either to helpless victim or complicit criminal, Barnes lands on the latter.

Despite all the overt rejections of self-blame for victimization found throughout the narratives, admitting personal responsibility for one's own choices is a recurring theme of the recovery sections of the new slave narratives published after 2010. If the narrators invoke the logic of victimization and commodification to describe their experiences of sexual exploitation, they harken to a very different logic to describe their roads to emotional and intellectual emancipation. Ironically, whereas considering oneself "enslaved" by definition suggests that the narrator was forced to engage in the sex trade against her will, much of the logic of how the narrators exited the sex trade relies on embracing the emancipatory potential of "making good choices," implying that one's experience in the sex trade was a result of making bad choices.

These narrative tensions make it difficult to parse the narrators' conceptions of choice. Though Bender condemns the logic of choice that is pervasive in the sex trade,[53] her book, framed as a self-help manual, is largely designed to help survivors explore and defeat the negative psychological effects of making bad choices.[54] She suggests to her survivor readers, "The way our minds work has only got us into trouble. . . . You must admit to yourself that the way you think has got you into the situation you're in. . . . YOU MUST CHANGE YOUR MINDSET."[55] Framing the recovery process in terms of choices and change locates it in a different and contradictory discourse than that of victimization. Bender suggests that one must begin to change one's behaviors and mindsets because previous choices have resulted in terrible consequences. She advances this claim without regard to the fact that the troubling outcomes that victims of trafficking experience are not commensurate with the choices they individually made. She writes in an atypically large font, in capital letters: "IT'S EASY TO CHOOSE THE GAME, IT TAKES A STRONG PERSON TO CHOOSE TO DO THE RIGHT THING."[56] Here, she explicitly suggests that engaging in the sex trade ("the game") was a choice for her and her readers, and it is a choice they can refuse to make in the future. Like Barnes, she has come to terms with her own victimization in many parts of her narrative but only to the extent that it does not rob her of the opportunity to escape it. By framing the sex trade as a choice, even when it contradicts her own revelations of victimization and commodification, survivors retain the power to make the choice to escape a cycle of future exploitation and slavery. In this way, the two competing ideas are both empowering and unreconciled.

Unlike Barnes, whose commitment to a logic of personal responsibility grew from her engagement with the judicial system, however, most of the narrators are compelled to address their own responsibility because of drug and alcohol recovery programs that they attended as part of their self-emancipation from people who exploited them. Many of the post-2010 new slave narrators struggled with drug addiction as a result of their exploitation in the sex trade. At least seven of them narrate their path to emancipation as one that intertwines recovery from both trafficking traumatization and drug addiction. They tended to use their recovery programs as a first phase in addressing the harms done to them through childhood sexual abuse and commercial sexual exploitation. For instance, at one point during detox and recovery, Alice Jay returned to selling sex but immediately felt ashamed. She writes, "I realized that for the last eight years it was me exploiting me and degrading me." She then sought counseling that would attend to both her addiction to drugs and her engagement in the sex trade. She wanted to concentrate her efforts "on my behavior, the choices I made, and the things I was accountable for. It was time I stopped blaming everyone else for my life. . . . I was responsible for my actions and my future. . . . I would have to make better choices."[57] Only a few pages earlier, Jay indicated that she was enslaved at twelve years old and that she felt she had no choice but to submit to a man who traded her for sex. As part of her recovery, however, she believes it to be essential that she take responsibility not only for her drug addiction but for her engagement in the sex trade and even for the choices that led her to being exploited. Notions of personal responsibility then reaffirm the idea that people make choices—often bad choices—that lead to justifiably negative consequences. Within this framework of personal responsibility, even consequences that are entirely incommensurate with their horrific outcomes are attributable to the bad choices of the victim. According to recovery logic, however, in order to heal from those bad choices—whether abusing drugs, engaging in the sex trade, or taking part in criminal activity—one must recognize her responsibility for the choices *and* the consequences. The idea is that once someone recognizes that she can choose to inject heroin or, by extension, choose to work in the sex trade, then she can choose *not* to do those things.

The addiction script that many of the narrators have adapted in their processes of recovery from trafficking is grounded in this conflicted notion of choice. The addict is compelled by her body to do a certain thing (and in the trafficking parallel, compelled by another person), but she must choose *not* to do it in order to recover. This framework is inherently contradictory because it tells a survivor that she is a "slave" to the addiction or trafficker, but it also tells her that she has a personal choice to stop and that she is personally responsible for the damage she has caused when engaging in these behaviors. In the context of childhood or forced sexual exploitation, this framework puts responsibility for sexual exploitation on the shoulders of the victim, often using the same terminology of "slavery," but this time in the literal sense. When the script shifts to personal responsibility, then, the only way for a woman to avoid sexual exploitation is through self-regulation, and, indeed, self-regulation is the path to recovery prescribed for and by these female new slave narrators.

The recognition of one's ability, and even responsibility, to exercise one's agency outside the coercive control of another is no doubt an important shift in a survivor's thought patterns. It is entirely justifiable that survivors would foreground the importance of personal decision-making. However, a societal imperative toward "personal responsibility" grew out of several decades of cultural and political discourse that treated impoverished women's lives and victimization as a burden on the state. As Nancy Bumiller writes in *In An Abusive State*, beginning in the 1970s and 1980s, with the dissolution of the social safety net, "the call for state responsibility for preventing and treating victims was in direct contrast to the new ethics of personal responsibility that was the cornerstone of the neoliberal agenda."[58] By the 1990s, insistence on personal responsibility in the realm of sexual behaviors found great traction in the legislation of women's bodies. In Bill Clinton's 1996 Personal Responsibility and Work Opportunity Reconciliation Act (which codified the idea of "workfare"), citizens were called upon to take full responsibility not only for their employment (or lack thereof) but for their sexual activity and reproduction.[59] So-called welfare queens were denounced as irresponsible predators on the social safety net at the same time as sex education was reduced to "abstinence only" programs. George W. Bush institutionalized this sentiment in an election stump speech in which he promoted his Faith-Based and Community-Based Initiative, saying, "You see, some of the problems that people face are really problems of the heart. And Government can't change hearts, but hearts can be changed by loving individuals who are inspired by something greater than Government. Take, for example, alcohol and drug abuse. We want to save people's lives in America. And sometimes it requires a higher power to help change somebody's life. You change their heart; they change their habits."[60] That effort put a significant portion of the government's funding for the alleviation of poverty in the hands of religious groups and paved the way for regulations that would disallow abortion counseling, promote abstinence, and refuse assistance to sex workers. Thus, over the course of thirty years, women's sexual lives were consistently imagined as requiring Christian social controls, and the government social programs that could reduce their vulnerabilities to poverty, gender-based violence, and other forms of discrimination that were the roots causes of sexual exploitation were set aside in favor of changing their "hearts and minds." In the early 2000s, as anti-trafficking efforts were ramped up, these self-help mandates were transferred from the drug addiction counseling environments to the emergent anti-trafficking setting. As Yvonne Zimmerman notes, "religiously based anti-trafficking interventions tend to attempt to 'fix' the sexual morality of trafficking victims. Freedom from trafficking is in this way intimately connected to correct sexual values."[61] Changing women's sexual choices was posited as imperative in shifting the economic terrain in which they lived (instead of the other way around) and in shifting the burden of protection and support from the state to individual women. Thus, the impulse to have trafficking victims improve their morality and their capacity to make better choices emerges in the discourse.

Like other supposed "sexual epidemics" before it (prostitution, teenage pregnancy, homosexuality, pornography), human trafficking and sexual enslavement are figured as a terror that can only be stopped through the regulation of sexual practices and the constriction of individual choices.[62] This notion that women are always responsible for sexual decisions they make—whether it results in pregnancy or poverty and regardless of the exercise of choice associated with the sexual encounter—continues to permeate American culture. As these new slave narratives attest, these powerful ideas pervade the messaging that marginalized women receive from the very people who are ostensibly meant to support them and help them escape exploitation, including legal advocates, drug dependency programs, social workers, child protective services, and probation officers. These trends are reflected in the complex and contradictory ways the new slave narrators depict their own experiences. Despite the fact that the logic of personal responsibility stands in stark contrast to the language of victimization and commodification that emerges in other parts of their narratives, these judicial and societal frameworks for regulating women's bodies unmistakably influence the way survivors conceive of their own role in their victimization. Forced through juridical requirement as well as through recovery and other social programs to admit their own complicity and commit to change in order to be deemed a worthy citizen and to gain access to state services, the narrators are compelled to integrate a sense of personal responsibility into the narrative arcs of their lives, regardless of the resulting cognitive dissonance.

DELIVERED FROM BONDAGE, RESURRECTED BY GOD'S GRACE

The complex balancing act of victimization and responsibility, force and choice, slavery and complicity, described in these narratives is troubled further by a pervasive trope of submission drawn from the Christian conversion narratives and addiction counseling testimonial conventions upon which the narrators frequently rely. If the social service and judicial regimes require women to take personal responsibility for their choices, the Christian recovery models that the narrators encounter demand that survivors surrender their wills once again—but this time to a higher power. Within the rigid, faith-based drug recovery regimes in which they often enroll, survivors find it inadvisable to stray from the narrative scripts of choice and surrender that are predetermined for them by the generic conventions prescribed by the programs.

Having first recognized their victimization, then having taken personal responsibility for their complicity in it, many of the narrators then surrender themselves not to a trafficker but this time to God. Following instructions that are fairly typical of Alcoholics and Narcotics Anonymous programs as well as victim assistance programs developed in the era of personal responsibility, the authors recognize their bad choices only to relinquish their freedom once again. As part of this rhetoric of recovery, the new slave narrators typically revert to passive language to describe their emancipation, allowing Jesus to be the agent. As Jesus "broke off the shackles of bondage" and "achieved the victory, even for us!" the narrators are "given redemption, forgiveness, deliverance, a new life, and a new birth."[63] They are "freed from prostitution, addiction, shame, and guilt" when they are "called chosen, redeemed, forgiven, beloved and a child of God."[64] These passive constructions are complex articulations of an emancipatory process that is simultaneously willful and submissive. The new slave narrators *choose* the path of God only to *conform* to his will and *surrender* to his power. With their souls infused with God's forgiveness, they are no longer responsible for their own exoneration, they no longer have to release themselves from the burden of complicity. The narrators repeatedly articulate a sense that for all future decisions, they are free to surrender themselves to a higher power's will that will guide them to a positive future. Many of the narrators describe their experiences of trafficking as a sign of spiritual warfare, a struggle between God and Satan over control of their spirits, and they frame their enslavement as an evil that had control over them for a time before God took the reins.[65] Crown concludes, "There was a time where I was very lost, and the devil did not want to see me with anything. . . . God brought me through; he delivered me and saved me from myself."[66] In contrast to both the idea that control rests in their abuser and that control rests in themselves, in this mode, the narrators suggest that it was Satan that had control, and while "only I can release me, only God can restore me."[67] The primary choice they had to make on the road to freedom, then, was to choose God, who had already chosen them.

Though it certainly does not seem deliberate, there is no mistaking the way this new commitment and submission to God echoes the narrators' previous submission to their abusers. God expects his followers to "choose" him as he chose them, much as coercive pimps did according to the narratives.[68] Under this new supernatural power regime, the narrators feel they have no choice but to submit to God's will.[69] In a special offset text box, Bender instructs her readers to "think of Jesus as your man now. But a good man, a man that only has great plans for you. Follow, listen, and obey him with as much desire! He deserves more respect than anyone!"[70] Referring to the etymology of the word "know" in the Bible, she makes the connection even more explicit in suggesting that the "know" in the sense of sexual relations and the "know" in the sense of knowing God's love are the same sense of intimacy. She says that God "wants to be intimate with you, like a husband and wife."[71] Despite a categorical announcement that God is "nothing like your pimp," this reference to sexual intimacy in the context of submission and obeisance is eerily reminiscent of the process of cultivating artificial consent that a trafficker used on Bender when she was a young person.[72] Brook Parker-Bello says that to truly submit to God, people have to become like children: "He is no longer speaking of a physical child but also an adult who has surrendered to Him and is *His* child. Wow! I get to be his baby girl, and it's like starting over, like starting life for the first time."[73] This sentiment very much echoes Bello's and others' claims that abused children are so desperate for mother and father figures that they are vulnerable to traffickers.[74] Here, though, the women surrender not to a "daddy" but to the "holy Father," who similarly expects her to play the role of a submissive child. Marino condemningly writes that "the addiction to love and money" made it so that she did not know her own worth, and that allowed her to believe anything a trafficker told her. In the very next paragraph, she says she is "so grateful that I know my worth today. It is based solely on Jesus and what He did for me, what He did for all of us."[75] This ironic juxtaposition suggests that there is great comfort in the act of surrendering to a God that displays qualities so similar to those of a pimp. After all the suffering they have survived, the narrators release their will to a power that is animated by supernatural goodness. This iteration of surrender relieves an individual of both the lifelong expectation that submission necessarily leads to victimization and equally releases them from the imperative of full responsibility for charting their own futures. One is neither responsible nor irresponsible, neither willful nor victim, when guided by God's will. In this formulation, one must make the first move to accept, embrace, and surrender to God's will, but once there, there is great relief that he will be the shepherd. This cooperative will, to simultaneously choose and be chosen, reminiscent though it is of their entry into the sex trade, is what animates many of the writers in their emancipation and comes to serve as the main prescriptive route to freedom for survivor readers of many of these texts.

These new slave narratives adapt tropes of Christian submission that circulate in addiction counseling discourse. Much of the rhetoric of addiction counseling in the last thirty years is drawn from the published history and doctrine described as Alcoholics Anonymous's Big Book and the public testimonies required of those attending AA group meetings. As the Big Book reminds its adherents, "The central fact of our lives today is the absolute certainty that our Creator has entered into our hearts and lives in a way which is indeed miraculous. He has commenced to accomplish those things for us which we could never do by ourselves."[76] The sense of helpless victimization and the burden of personal responsibility are both released when a person allows a higher power to take control and make possible a freedom that is understood to be outside the realm of one's power to grasp alone. Freedom—that treasured intangible that slavery withheld—is practically guaranteed if one surrenders. "Rarely have we seen a person fail who has thoroughly followed our path. Those who do not recover are people who cannot or will not completely give themselves to this simple program, usually men and women who are constitutionally incapable of being honest with themselves."[77] This rhetoric of "surrender" to a prescribed path, guided by the grace of a higher power, is an integral aspect of the addiction counseling that the majority of the narrators who have suffered sexual enslavement undergo on their paths to freedom.

Embracing God's power guides the narrators to a sense of what they repeatedly describe as the "true self," which allows them to psychologically and ontologically dissociate themselves from the selves who sold sex. Whereas their enslaved selves made unhealthy decisions that inevitably led to exploitation and self-destruction, the new slave narrators' "true selves" make good decisions, follow God's chosen path, and are free to live in his grace. This change of heart, soul, and habit leads to a successful return to an originary, authentic self that preceded the abuse and oppression that the narratives are meant to bring to light. Jay says that her life in the sex trade meant that "I died to who I was in order to survive," but she insists that survivors need to return to family values and God's law in order to come "out of the darkness," as her book is titled.[78] Parker-Bello says that "in these severe abuses, the minds have been manipulated to an altered state that is not a true self."[79] Slavery "robs us, through abuse and other forms of sin, of the authenticity, of who God created me to be."[80] She "had to die after all. I had to die to what I thought was desirable, and die to all the pain and rapes that I had experienced. . . . I had to die to self so that I could be reborn again and again and again, in Him."[81] By the end of her (admittedly much less spirituality-oriented) narrative, Amaya "was finally doing what I was supposed to be doing and becoming who I was supposed to become."[82] She had been waiting so long to "discover the real me who had been waiting inside, waiting to come out."[83] For each of the narrators, the specter of her trafficked self still haunts her psyche, and her recovery requires her to create a sense of a separate, true self that is distinct from that tainted self. These spheres of life separated, she is able to start fresh, regain her childhood innocence, and be born again in God's reflection.

These tropes of rebirth are, of course, part of a discursive script of evangelical Christianity in the United States. As Susan Harding writes of evangelical rebirth, "As God restored man to himself by sacrificing his son on the cross, so the unsaved may restore themselves to God by dying to their old selves and being born anew in Christ."[84] Being born again is not merely a matter of going to church or being baptized but is grounded in the narrative process of witnessing, which "involves an unconscious willingness to join a narrative tradition, a way of knowing and being through Bible-based storytelling and listening."[85] The narrative conventions of rebirth are then imbedded in the process of returning to a life of faith, and it thereby functions as an unspoken prerequisite for a true recovery from sin. Thus, while the psychologically coercive refrain of predatory pimps insists on a profitably enforced consistency ("once a ho always a ho"),[86] the postemancipation narrator consistently bifurcates her life. Her identity—and not merely her history—thus divided, she phrases her experience of trafficking as occurring to a "past self" that is in radical opposition to the redeemed and present self. And that redeemed present self is a reflection of her original pre-sex-trade self, the "true self" that has been resurrected. Many of the narratives of sexual enslavement (though admittedly not all—the few narratives published by major presses are not as explicitly Christian) are an extension of the public testimonies that they participate in as born-again Christians and recovering addicts. As with other Christian models of therapeutic counseling (I am thinking here in particular of homosexual conversion therapy), change occurs individually but within a protective community of others who equally shape their life narratives within the generic conventions of Christian rebirth and deliverance from previous "falls" from God's grace.[87]

ANTISLAVERY'S COGNITIVE DISSONANCE

In many ways, the uplift narrative that is driven by a journey out of destitution or up from a fall from grace that is animated by personal responsibility, good choices, and Christian redemption is typical of what Leigh Gilmore calls the "neoliberal life narrative." This common form of autobiography "features an 'I' who overcomes hardship and recasts historical and systemic harm as something an individual alone can, and should, manage through pluck, perseverance, and enterprise. The individual transforms disadvantage into value."[88] Neoliberal life narratives are quite familiar to the reader of American autobiography. Most nineteenth-century American slave narratives follow a similar trajectory, in fact. Autobiographical genre conventions encourage the portrayal of an individual remarkable life, and the slave narrative, in particular, typically illustrates inspiring tales focused on one man's path to subjectivity, grounded in a sense of self-reliance that triumphs over even the most horrific of hardships—slavery. The slave narrative celebrates the triumph of the will, independence, and hard work. The neoliberal life narratives that are grounded in recovery models integrate conventions of the conversion narrative and situate that unusual level of perseverance as ultimately inspired and assisted by God's fortitude. Like the conversion narrative and the addiction testimony, the slave narrative—past and present—provides hope and inspiration and a call to action based not on the example of ordinary collective action but on the example of an individual's extraordinary suffering and even more extraordinary escape.

That persuasive teleological imperative encounters a conflict when paired with the rhetoric of personal responsibility in the context of slavery. Slave narrators of the nineteenth century were never called upon to take responsibility for the suffering inflicted upon them in slavery. Though they were likely to embrace Christianity as a route to salvation both on earth and in the afterlife, their conversion narrative traditions did not include the imperative that they admit that they "had a problem" or that they contributed to their own declines. Their narratives of victimization, commodification, and disposability were recorded without reference to their own complicity in it (though they did often point to enslaved overseers who may have been complicit). On the other hand, the new slave narrators who write about sexual servitude after 2010 attempt to do both—they recognize their own victimization but return to the language of choice and personal responsibility as part of their narratives of emancipation and salvation. These competing demands create a certain cognitive dissonance—if not for the narrators, then certainly for the narratives. Putting those questions of complicity and God's will into conversation with the notions of commodification and victimization that form the foundation of their claims to enslavement creates nearly unresolvable tensions in this particular group of new slave narratives.

The cognitive dissonance that shapes these new slave narratives is indicative of larger cultural trends that have divided the budding U.S. antislavery movement in the last twenty years. As the recent new slave narratives demonstrate, two overarching, powerfully explanatory discursive constructs regarding choice and freedom inform and entangle those who write about escape from sexual captivity. First, there is the definition of choice that emerges from the revivified antislavery discourse to which these authors subscribe. In this model of choice, one is free when one is not burdened by external strictures that would hinder one's ability to make a reasonable and desirable choice, in particular within the realm of work. It would be impossible to consider forced sexual labor that is performed under force or coercion a legitimate, reasonable, and desirable choice. A trafficker who would make a claim to ownership or to full control over one's labor and profits would thus represent a stricture on freedom. That stricture would undermine one's ability to exercise free will or to make the choices that one might desire. In this model, a person is only free when she is free of those violent or coercive strictures that an external party might impose.

The other conception of choice—emerging from the Christian regime of recovery and redemption that pervades both addiction programs and political and cultural life in the United States since the 1980s—suggests the existence of a radical, inherent individual freedom to make choices even under significant constraints. By this logic, a person's freedom is defined by the sum of all the choices she has made. In order to accept who she truly is and become the most exalted self she is capable of becoming, she must accept her mistakes as her own, even (or especially) when they lead to horrific outcomes. A person embraces her freedom when she accepts responsibility for her past life and creates a future dedicated to changing her past negative behaviors. Freedom is entirely contingent upon recognizing one's ability to choose in all circumstances.

This division is somewhat difficult to parse because the perception of choice and freedom in these two communities is premised on two very different motivating questions. For those who work to address slavery, the primary concern is what constitutes free labor and the fair use thereof. Within the discourse of evangelical therapeutic models, the animating question concerns how to lead an appropriate life on earth and hence gain salvation for the spirit in the hereafter. Thus, responsibility for the choices that lead to an experience of slavery is determined in very different ways by these two groups. If the concern with responsibility is grounded in a slavery approach focused on labor practices, the source of the lack of freedom is clearly external—the enslaver is to blame. If the question of responsibility is grounded in the logic of recovery and salvation, the source of the lack of freedom is internal, individual, personal. In the first, the victim maintains no individual responsibility for being forced into labor against her will. In the second, she must account for and set aside her previous bad choices in order to access her true self in the present, build a future free of bad choices, and guarantee salvation in Christ after victimization.

In this cacophonous symphony of competing ideological constructs, it is the language and logic of the slavery paradigm that most quickly gets lost in the narratives and, not coincidentally, in the advocacy efforts more broadly. "Slavery" is employed to help explain the confusing jargon of "trafficking." But even more crucially, it is mobilized to suggest gravity, to describe the extraordinary extent of the limitation on personal freedom in forced labor. Painting the problem in large brush strokes, however, the writers bring this structural analysis into focus by concentrating their evidence at the level of personal experience and degradation. Indeed, the modern slavery paradigm is taken up through individualist terms that negate much of the larger frame of rights. Though, as Brysk suggests, personal wrongs can constitute the field of human rights violations, the proclivity of these authors, likely driven by the narrative impulses of autobiography, is to keep the focus of those wrongs on the personal. They briefly link their personal enslavement to a larger community of oppressed people through the language of commodification and disposability, but the narratives, shaped as they typically are as memoirs or self-help books, consistently return to the question of personal recovery from exploitation. In focusing this human rights violation on a personal wrong inflicted on an individual, the narratives tend to favor the personal freedom to pursue individualized solutions to the problem. As the central conversion event of the narrative takes shape, the impulse to take responsibility for bad choices grows, as does the investment in an individual model of recovery and salvation. As Rebecca Bender's use of the workbook format suggests, each survivor reader is meant to learn how she can individually return to her true, free self. The conventions of addiction and conversion narratives guarantee this will be the case—they rely on the individual woman's personal journey to redemption as a testament not only to her own individual will but to the potential for other individuals to make the same change. When they localize the concept of commodification to the individual—to the rights violations of the individual—they often lose sight of the structural critique that is available when they invoke the human rights framework that is associated with the slavery paradigm. In the process of describing the narrator's personal journey to emancipation, the logic of victimization and commodification is drowned out by the ideological imperatives of the Christian conversion narrative, as the personal responsibility angle provides an opportunity for redemption, hope, and empowerment to change her own existence in a world that has sorely failed her.

AGENCY DEBATES

This analysis of the unresolved conflicts that complicate the narratives writ-ten by survivors of sexual enslavement in the United States is not meant to be condemnatory of the survivors themselves or to suggest that their recov-eries are not significant, personal, and valuable to others. However, careful attention to the cognitive dissonances that pervade these narratives is quite productive for thinking about contemporary antislavery discourse and the uses and abuses of survivor testimony. First and foremost, the narratives reveal a fissure in conceptions regarding choice and responsibility that are endemic in antislavery discourse today and that no doubt increase the post-traumatic anxieties of survivors. Much academic and journalistic writing on domestic minor sex trafficking conflates these significantly divergent ideas about freedom and choice, wavering unconsciously between victim naming and victim blaming, in large part because many advocates and sur-vivors do as well, as evidenced by these narratives. As this chapter has demonstrated, the cognitive dissonance described here is not the invention (or the unique plight) of survivors—it is an ongoing debate inscribed even in the founding documents of the anti-trafficking field. It is a debate that has burdened conversations regarding the rights of people working in the sex trade since the incarnation of the idea of "sex trafficking" and the fears of a growing "sex problem" emerged. It is no surprise, then, that it creates significant dissonance in the life narratives produced by survivors.

Another way this dissonance is illuminating is that it suggests that the monolithic "anti-trafficking movement" described by its critics is slightly more complex than most would admit. I submit that this literary critical reading of survivors' narratives highlights another problematically con-stricted, binaristic, and constructed popular conception of agency, a con-ception that radically divides many advocates who work with those who are voluntarily engaged in the sex trade from anti-trafficking activists.[89] The pro-sex-worker advocates and scholars who have critiqued the anti-trafficking movement have condemned it as overwhelmingly plagued by a Christian, conservative view of women's sexuality and agency. To be sure, most of the narratives discussed here could be used as evidence to support those claims, and it would be easy to reduce them all to the neoliberal ideologies embedded in their pages. In the end, however, the narrative cognitive dissonance analyzed here can also point us to a much more complicated perspective on women's agency than the U.S. anti-trafficking movement is typically understood to support.

Popular and academic pro-sex-work advocates convincingly critique the overwhelmingly antisex stance of many antislavery advocacy efforts. They lodge a pointed criticism of anti-trafficking through a rigorous discursive analysis of the sensationalized, fear-mongering rhetoric that circulates in the West. Scholars interested in the law have unpacked the discriminatory and sexist agendas at the heart of the new legislation that has been drafted since the late 1990s.[90] Historians and literary critics (myself included) have provided cultural histories and analyses of the paternalistic, racialized "white slavery" scares of the 1910s that have reemerged in twenty-first-century discourse around sex trafficking.[91] Pro-sex-work advocates and scholars dissect pervasive narratives of "our girls" being victimized and commodified by the sex industry and suggest they provide an intentional distraction from global economic inequality and unequal negative effects of Western neoliberal policies on women in the Global South, displaced people, people of color, sexual minorities, and migrant laborers.[92] Elizabeth Bernstein aptly demonstrates the way white women, in particular those who have launched a moral crusade against sex trafficking, have grown attached to a "carceral feminism" that makes the security state the center of their response to violence against women and have thereby contributed to the mass incarceration of black men.[93]

Those critiques are all quite applicable to these narratives of U.S. domestic sex trafficking and certainly are not admitted adequate entry into the conversations among anti-trafficking advocates. I want to focus here, in particular, on one critique made by sex worker advocates that points right to the heart of the cognitive dissonance reflected in these narratives. Many scholars who are critical of the anti-trafficking movement condemn anti-trafficking's negation of women's agency in the decision to engage in sex work. They argue that anti-trafficking discourse denies the fact that many women choose to work in the sex trade, elides the choices that people who are trafficked make, and obfuscates the economic conditions that make sex work the most feasible opportunity for many women in the United States. It is on this point that these first-person narratives of slavery, while very much engaging in anti-sex-work discourse, may nonetheless add nuance to common perceptions within the anti-trafficking movement, given the complexity of lived experience they depict.

To wit, most critics of the anti-trafficking movement point to the way forced sex work and consensual sex work are consistently conflated by most advocates as a sign of the denial of any agency within sex work.[94] Indeed, the first-person narratives studied here largely lend credence to these concerns. Brook Parker-Bello and Katariina Rosenblatt, for instance, explicitly indicate that all sex trade is tantamount to force because, they argue, no woman could submit to such torment willingly.[95] Sex work scholars—and empirical evidence—firmly suggest otherwise. Not only does research show that some women do engage in the sex trade voluntarily and, in fact, feel empowered by it, it also suggests that some women who do not actually enjoy sex work choose it over other unenjoyable, demeaning, demoralizing, and underpaid labor.[96] This data suggests that there is indeed significantly more agency exhibited in sexual labor than most of the new slave narrators can represent based on their own experiences of extraordinary subjugation or their generalized sense of all people with whom they interacted in the sex trade. There is no doubt whatsoever that reliable social science suggests there is more agency in sex work than many activists in the anti-trafficking movement would admit when they claim, as Rosenblatt does, that any women who think they are engaged in the sex trade voluntarily are "brainwashed by their pimps."[97] For most of the new slave narrators writing in the United States after 2010, sex work is necessarily slavery, and all people who engage in it are victims.

The paradigmatic "helpless victim" of trafficking that many of these narratives depict is also a contested category among anti-trafficking critics. Kamala Kempadoo argues, for instance, that the anti-trafficking movement frames women as essentially innocent until proven victim and men as agentic actors who have the unique capacity to create victims.[98] She further argues that the notion of this particular strain of the "woman-as-victim" emerged at least as early as the 1970s as a way for so-called Radical Feminists to oppose what they considered the patriarchal objectification of women through sex work.[99] This false equation of women with fragility in need of protection erases and obfuscates women's agency, and it dominates justifications for anti-trafficking advocates to take as their central task the complete legislative abolition of prostitution. Carol Vance suggests that anti-trafficking rhetoric "diverts attention from larger structures of exploi-tation. It focuses instead on individual actors: an innocent female victim crying out for rescue from sexual danger and diabolical male villains intent on her violation. The plot may feature excess, extremity, and sensation, but what is at stake—as in the sexual purity campaigns of the early twentieth century—is normative heterosexuality and its sexual arrangements."[100] Often, anti-trafficking rhetoric encourages a rescue mentality, which sug-gests that women are incapable of escaping sexual subordination and there-fore must be saved by organizations or a supernatural power in order to ever be free of bondage to the generalized, overwhelming male libido that leaves individual women helpless. As we have seen in the titles, packaging, and content of the texts, the helpless girl child victim trope is pervasive throughout the text, and narrators often depict their rescue from the clutches of evil men and their perverse sexuality by government programs, the criminal justice system, and the church. In this formulation, their recov-ery from victimization requires an individualized therapeutic response that does nothing to undo the misogynist structures that subordinated her but instead reinforces normative domestic relations and insists that women make better sexual choices. This individualized approach undermines women's agency and ignores structural inequality and discrimination.

However, when sex-worker-rights scholars critique the absence of agency in anti-sex-trafficking discourse, they tend to focus on those situations of sex work that allow for the most significant expression of individual agency as the counterpoint to the sensationalized images of extraordinary victim-hood. To prove that anti-trafficking advocates are inappropriate in denying women's agency and empowerment in the sex trade, sex worker advocates typically narrow their own focus to women for whom the choice to engage in sex work is one among many other reasonable choices. The examples of agency often involve sex workers who are middle class, who work indoors, who have the opportunity to go to college, who migrate for expanded work opportunity, or who possess the self-efficacy that would allow them to pursue work other than sex work. These women do, in fact, choose to pursue sex work despite what many anti-trafficking activists would sug-gest. Thus, critics convincingly make the case for women's agency, but in the process, they very often ignore legitimate examples of impoverished, street-level sex workers that would complicate their portrait of agency within the sex trade. Pro-sex-work scholars recognize the economic realities that commercially sexually exploited youth face, but they routinely dismiss the anti-trafficking movement's description of their victimization as nothing more than sensational Christian sentiment. In the process, they create a monolith of the anti-trafficking movement, conflating all the different activist agendas described in this book, as if all the players in this diverse discursive terrain adhere to a single ideological project. As a result, many anti-anti-trafficking scholars and activists end up denying certain forms of exploitation experienced by the very people for whom they are advocating. Where the anti-trafficking movement tends toward obfuscation of agency, the anti-anti-trafficking movement tends toward the obfuscation of slavery.

While much of the anti-sex-work rhetoric contained in the pages of the new slave narratives would certainly seem anathema to pro-sex-work scholars and activists, it is important to recognize that the effect of shaping the narratives of sexual enslavement around conflicting models of choice is that they represent a much more complex vision of agency than any of the aforementioned schools of thought would admit. Their narratives meander through phases in which they describe feeling empowered by their work in the sex trade only moments after they depict horrific scenes of captivity. Their individual lives represent the incredibly complicated relationship to agency experienced by people enslaved in a society in which slavery is not enshrined in law or compulsory for any group of people and, therefore, remains unseen and unrecognized. As we have documented here, these new slave narrators sometimes take responsibility for their actions, but they also provide evidence of the multitude of reasons they felt personally, economically, psychologically, intellectually, and emotionally compelled to enter the sex trade. Some of them describe returning to the work out of desperation even after realizing the extent of the harm inflicted by traffickers. They lament feeling compelled by the economy and not a coercive individual to return to trading sex when they realize they cannot afford to take other low-paid jobs in the formal economy. They describe their emotional bonds with their traffickers and the other women with whom they worked, which make it difficult to walk away from abuse. They impress upon us the radical disempowerment of being forced to work against their wills while still conveying the sense of self-worth that they first encountered in the sex trade and the power that the sex trade provided over their abusive pasts. Their narratives reveal people who have a sophisticated relationship to their own agency, rejecting the simple binaristic logic of force versus agency, to forge a path that includes elements of agency that nonetheless lead to unjustifiable and reprehensible exploitation.

For many of the authors, their first sense of their own agency was, in fact, discovered within the sex trade. This is relatively typical of young women who engage in street-level sex trade. As Sharon Oselin (one of the few scholars who study both impoverished and middle-class sex workers) found in interviews with sex workers that minors tended to enter the sex trade as a result of abuse because "they had little control over their lives and decided to escape their home situations in order to take care of themselves."[101] They described entering the sex trade as a way of taking control of their lives and escaping the abuse they had suffered within their homes. Thus, the discovery of subjectivity and agency, a central generic requirement of the neoliberal life narrative, ironically occurs in the scenes in which they are recruited into the sex trade and, by their own accounts, into the very bondage that would undermine their free will.

However, we must not lose sight of the fact that these experiences of agency are consistently recast in light of their later recognition that they were duped and abused within the sex trade. For those women who have written of their lives in the sex trade as slave narratives (which is not to say all women in the sex trade), the experience of the sex trade did not remain empowering for long. Those who engaged in the street trade, as children, while addicted to drugs, or through force encountered a higher incidence of violence than other people engaged in the sex trade.[102] The narratives provide readers with a clear sense of the constraints on freedom that are attendant to the adverse childhood experiences that lead impoverished young people into the sex trade. While survivors do indeed depict a certain sense of agency—often driven by their desire to escape their lives subjected to abusive families and poverty—that agency is circumscribed by a lack of viable, desirable options. The new slave narrators who depict their experiences of forced engagement in the sex trade are writing about the act of consenting to a choice that is limited to extremes: either engage in the sex trade or starve in the street; get beaten by a brutal pimp or return to a broken home. They submit to the violence and coercion of another person. Their freedom is indeed constrained; their agency is overridden. Unlike the middle-class and upper-class street-level sex workers described by Elizabeth Bernstein, for whom work in the sex trade provided a "sense of choice and

volition . . . despite the evident dangers and even if they might also have preferred the luxury of a better set of vocational possibilities" or the "overwhelmingly white, native-born, and relatively class-privileged women and
men" who engage in what she calls "post-industrial forms" of sex work,[103]
these new slave narrators depict a life of physical and emotional abuse, drug
addiction, and lack of viable employment options that ultimately make them
feel they have no choice other than remaining in the sex trade. In the end,
the narratives reveal the illusion of choice that haunts the labor market and
the sexual economy for the poorest people in the United States. Their
engagement in the sex trade often provided a sense of agency initially when
they "chose" the sex trade over the abusive family, but those choices led to
abuse—both in terms of sex and labor—and thus were not legitimate choices
in the first place. In this way, the conflation in their narratives of choice and
victimization, of agency and subjugation, is appropriate—they encountered
both in the very same formative moments in their lives.

These survivors are not necessarily the "perfect victims" of the antislavery imaginary, nor are they the radically empowered sex workers of the pro-
sex-work camp. They are conflicted women who made difficult decisions
in their escape from childhood poverty and abuse, who engaged in culturally taboo behaviors, and who are still assimilating those experiences in
their larger life narratives. Indeed, this may explain why so many of these
books are self-published—perfect victim status and good presses are posi-
tively correlated, so the more complex or conflicted the sense of agency
exhibited is (and hence, the truer to the complex human experience of
choice the narrative is), the more likely someone is to need to self-publish
if she wants to tell her story. The new slave narrators who write about the
commercial sexual exploitation of children represent an antidote to the typically polarized debates that pit empowerment against victimization as
they explore through writing their ambivalent relationship to choice in the
context of the poverty, misogyny, and rape culture to which they were subjected as youth.

Despite the compelling critiques of the anti-trafficking movement's
approach to agency and choice, I want to suggest that the new slave narrative reveals the ways this critical debate is based on a false binary of choice
and force that is grounded in rigid neoliberal definitions of freedom.
Whether the speaker is a Christian antiprostitution advocate, a rights-based
antislavery activist, or a sex-positive, progressive sex-worker advocate, the

terms of the debate are often constricted by this inadequate conception of consent that suggests that a person's life can be described either in terms of rights or objectification, agency or victimization, personal responsibility or submission. In the end, what this bifurcation does is force advocates to deny either women's agency or their exploitation when, in fact, the narratives of survivors reveal to us that both are always at work.[104] In an economy that has historically and structurally devalued women's labor to the point where sex work is one of the only options for marginalized women who seek living wages, these narratives reveal that the commodification of women's lives restrains the field of possible choices, such that when they do make choices that will support their survival, they are more vulnerable to exploitation. As the narratives of sexual enslavement suggest, both empowerment and exploitation are hallmarks of the sex trade for economically marginalized women who engage in the trade.

The debate between sex worker rights and prostitution abolition, between rights-based antislavery activists and Christian recovery counselors, is thus something of a red herring that both nominally and intellectually divides the antislavery movement in such a way that we are unable to address collectively the structural violence against women that is at the heart of the problem. Both sides claim to be fighting the rabid discrimination against and exploitation of women. What is at the heart of that exploitation is an endemic, systemic, economic injustice and inequality that often gets ignored when critics claim either that all women who engage in the sex trade are exploited or that all women who engage in the sex trade are empowered agents. A recognition of this structural violence, which the slave narratives implicitly and explicitly reveal, will allow us a more nuanced, collaborative, collective approach to addressing systemically the way in which the most vulnerable women are being exploited.

SYSTEMIC RESOLUTIONS

While these narratives of sexual enslavement reveal the ideological fissures in the community of antislavery advocates, they also offer possible alternatives for thinking about the structural causes of sexual enslavement and trafficking in the United States. All the narratives of commercial sexual exploitation pursue a deliberately activist agenda that exceeds the conventions of the individual conversion narrative and that cleaves more closely to the nineteenth-century slave narrative tradition of activism. Most do so by adopting a critical stance toward the structural issues that made them vulnerable to slavery in the first place. Whereas typical neoliberal life narratives, conversion narratives, and antislavery melodramas myopically "distill politics and social change to an *n* of one,"[105] book-length new slave narratives wend their way back to the larger ethical demands they are making of U.S. society, even as they are replicating the modes of neoliberal discourse that are endemic to the genre conventions they have employed. In the end, these narratives consistently exceed the strictures of the religious conversion narrative, the AA testimony, and the individual trauma narrative as they critique the systemic injustices that are the "root causes" of slavery in the twenty-first century.

While a workbook like Bender's necessarily focuses on the work that an individual must do to recover from the trauma of trafficking, a book like Brook Parker-Bello's represents a clear integration of the personal responsibility to make better choices and the larger societal changes that must occur to facilitate those choices for women. Throughout her narrative, Parker-Bello points to the societal impediments to women's freedom that made her vulnerable to trafficking. From the very first pages, she demands that we "go deep, to examine the root causes [of human trafficking], which are found in discrimination, of all kinds, and negative and destructive societal pop culture. From focusing too much on self, to gender issues, to ethnic discrimination, economic discrimination, classism, unresolved child abuse, too much unrelenting media violence, evil, and lust without conscience or respect for innocence any more—it seems that many of these discriminations are at an all-time high."[106] While a reader may not be willing to condemn every one of the items Parker-Bello has listed here, her aim is to zoom out to the structural level in order to think about how larger economic and societal trends impact young women's lives. She is indebted, no doubt, to some of the same conservative impulses to blame sex (which she defines as a sacred intimacy) that inaugurated the anti-trafficking movement in the United States. In addition to that, however, she is keenly aware of the role that language plays in determining our response to women's victimization, remarking that even terms like "human trafficking, forced prostitution, abuse, incest, molestation, and child sex slavery/sex slavery" sterilize the abuse of female children to such an extent that people are unable to consider the prevalence of it and its roots in accepted cultural practices.[107]

She repeatedly points to the ways in which race, gender, and class determine the opportunities women have for exercising their agency. Writing from the perspective of a woman of color, she is wary of white Christianity because she connects late twentieth- and twenty-first-century slavery to the transatlantic slave trade and recounts how religion has long been used as an attempt to sedate enslaved people's desires for emancipation in this life.[108] Nevertheless, she admonishes us not to relegate the movement to the "Christian Right" or to any other particular group, but "to come together, to forgive, and to *work together* on all of these issues . . . whether Black or White or any ethnic group or religious creed, it really doesn't matter."[109] Collective action addressing the systemic issues that make young people vulnerable to being compelled to engage in the sex trade is her prescription.

Unlike the majority of nonprofits that address domestic minor sex trafficking through aggressively punitive sentencing or radical increases in law enforcement attention or the cultural policing of women's sex and sexuality, the new slave narrators suggest that local, grassroots, collective, community-based action that accounts for the structural inequalities in our society is crucial to addressing slavery on the ground. To varying degrees, they reveal that they believe that economic salvation is nearly as important as Christian salvation in allowing women to escape exploitative situations. Marino repeatedly reflects in her diary-style memoir that it was a lack of economic opportunity that thwarted all her attempts to escape traffickers and exit the sex trade.[110] She says that the one thing that links all the women she has worked with who are exiting the sex trade is that they lack the financial resources for a successful exit and legitimate routes to self-sufficiency.[111] She makes a plea to business owners to play a role in changing women's economic opportunities by creating jobs for women who have a criminal record or addiction.[112] She also calls for educational scholarships, safe shelters, and employment opportunities.[113] For her, these are the underlying crises that women cannot overcome when fleeing exploitation. She started an organization that addresses the hunger and hygiene of homeless women, since those are the basic needs they seek to fill that make them vulnerable to the sex trade.[114] Taking a critical approach to the criminal justice system instead of the lack of a social safety net, Barnes's story illustrates the way female victims of sexual abuse and domestic violence are so misunderstood that they can be criminalized for their own victimization. She shows how the criminal justice system is designed to punish rather than to identify and protect victims. Amaya, Rosenblatt, and others train law enforcement to relinquish their discriminatory outlook on women who are engaged in the sex trade in order to assist them in recognizing victims.

Even where the authors rely on Christian salvation and paternalistic modes of outreach to exotic dancers as their prescription for eradicating sex trafficking, their narratives all belie a much more complicated set of circumstances that encourage the exploitative aspects of this economy. Their memoirs all point to the abysmal support system that American girls have when they are sexually abused and the way in which their experiences are ignored and stigmatized culturally. The same goes for addiction to drugs and alcohol, for which they rarely find adequate solutions and are regularly criminalized instead of provided with the help they need. Their narratives point to the way in which impoverished women struggle to find formal work and thereby struggle to define themselves within an economy that valorizes the worker. And they all expose the way stigma regarding the sex trade results in women being ignored when they are abused and having little recourse when they decide they want to escape traffickers. Essentially, a close reading of the post-2010 new slave narrative reveals a culture and an economy that support the commercial sexual exploitation of children instead of one that prevents it.

This is why survivor voices must be foregrounded in efforts to address contemporary forms of slavery and trafficking. As Brook Parker-Bello astutely surmises, "What one non-survivor lacks in theory, we are able to communicate, from our neck-down experience—and the neck-up as well, for that matter. Anyone can be taught a neck-up theory, but the neck-down exposure and experience cannot be taught. Thus, we must be at the leaders' table."[115] What the new slave narrative contributes to the movement is that complexity of the human experience that both is informed by and exceeds theory. The complicated (and even sometimes productively contradictory) intellectual contributions of survivors are essential if we wish to transcend the divisive decades-long battles that have created fragments in the movement to end the abuse and enslavement of women engaged in the sex trade. Recognizing the gray areas between and intersections of consent and victimization, choice and force, freedom and slavery, is critical to that cause. The new slave narrative gives us a window into that complex terrain.

Unfortunately, the very act of writing a new slave narrative to provide that expertise to the movement is more likely to inadvertently encourage suspicious reading rather than garner an invitation to serve as leadership. In the next chapter, Somaly Mam's rise to celebrity-survivor status and precipitous downfall are analyzed in light of what we have uncovered about the conflicting impulses of the new slave narrative. In the conclusion, however, I will synthesize those theories drawn from the new slave narratives to present an ethic for scholars and activists working in the contemporary antislavery movement, one that emerges from both the theories and experiences of the new slave narrators.

Chapter Five

WHAT THE GENRE CREATES, IT DESTROYS
The Rise and Fall of Somaly Mam

The narratives of contemporary slavery that have been dissected through-out this book reveal a powerful drive on the part of the formerly enslaved to recount their experiences. Those narratives work in concert as well as in conflict with activists' impulses to shape those narratives in ways that motivate audiences toward their own political ends. But as Douglass testified about being asked to put on a bit of "the plantation manner" in order to be believed by audiences, adherence to convention can be used as a gauge of veracity, even when conformity might force a narrator into literary contortions or into betraying one's own experience or expertise. The rise and fall of Somaly Mam—one of the most widely known of the new slave narrators—reveals the power of the genre (and the veracity tests that accompany it) to propel a survivor into the limelight and, just as rapidly, to precipitate her fall from grace.

Solomon Northup's 1853 narrative of captivity and enslavement in the bayous of Louisiana was made into a major motion picture in the United States and provided an unprecedented visibility for the genre of the slave narrative. Directed by Steve McQueen, the film version of *12 Years a Slave* (2013) grossed $172 million worldwide and won three Oscars including Best Film and Best Adapted Screenplay as well as the Golden Globe for Best Drama.[1]

Oprah Winfrey said the film represented "where the root of the problem started . . . and . . . how much further we need to go."[2] Sean "Diddy" Combs urged his fans to see the film, calling it "very painful but very honest and . . . a part of the healing process."[3] Academics embraced the film as a turning point in the representation of slavery as well. Salamishah Tillet called the film "masterful," saying, "by privileging the testimonies and voices of the slaves themselves, it gives us a new cinematic story of slavery as exceptionally violent and quintessentially American."[4] Winfrey, Combs, and Tillet saw McQueen's portrayal of the horrors of nineteenth-century slavery as a long-awaited sincere effort to contend with the racial inequalities that are a contemporary legacy of slavery in the United States and an acknowledgement that the healing process had nonetheless only just begun.

Antislavery organizations also mobilized around this depiction of the nineteenth-century narrative, not to describe slavery's long reach for African Americans but to leverage the film's depiction of historical bondage to their own cause of fighting global slavery in the twenty-first century. Somaly Mam, an international spokesperson for the anti-sex-trafficking movement in Cambodia and a self-described survivor of child sexual enslavement, published a piece called "My Own 'Twelve Years a Slave'" in the *Daily Beast*, capitalizing on Hollywood's depiction of slavery by comparing her own life story—and her slave narrative—to that of Northup's. She writes,

Despite time and place, both Solomon and I were tricked and trafficked, and endured years of servitude, torture, and abuse, at the hands of men and women who saw us as nothing more than a commodity. Yet, we were determined to live, and we sought to share our stories with the world in the hopes that our stories could prevent this crime from happening to anyone else. In 1853, Solomon published *Twelve Years a Slave*. Over 150 years later, I published my story in *The Road of Lost Innocence*.[5]

In connecting her new slave narrative to Northup's as well as to the U.S. abolitionist movements of the 1850s and 1860s, she laid personal claim to the legacy of suffering that the word "slavery" conjures for American readers. At the same time, the Northup connection allowed her a new avenue through which to bring the issue of contemporary forms of slavery to the attention of more wealthy Americans, as many had already responded enthusiastically and generously to her nonprofit organization's wretched depiction of slavery in the sex trade in Cambodia for a decade. Like so many narrators, legislators, and journalists who write about sexual enslavement, when Mam reminded readers in her Northup piece that slavery was happening "not just in remote parts of Southeast Asia, but in your hometown, in your backyard," she made the issue present for those "educated people [who] believe that slavery ended in 1863," evoking a similar transitive property of suffering as we saw exhibited in chapter 3 by the Institute for Religion and Democracy through *Girl Soldier*. Mam's powerful evocation of the grievous history of nineteenth-century slavery allowed her to tap into the gravity that the word "slavery" conveys in the United States while provoking the fear cultivated among many white Americans that their daughters might be kidnapped into the sex trade, as is discussed in chapter 4. It was the brilliant combination of sensationalized media and humanitarian gravitas that Somaly Mam was known for.

Mam's work as leader of perhaps the most powerful and well-funded anti-sex-trafficking organization in Southeast Asia taught her that stories were at the center of any successful social justice movement. Her life narrative of slavery, escape, hope, and activism was lauded in the media by the likes of *New York Times* reporter Nick Kristof, featured on the *Tyra Banks Show*, and adopted as a cry for justice by a vast array of feminist public figures including Hillary Clinton; actors Susan Sarandon, Angelina Jolie, and Meg Ryan; designer Diane von Furstenburg; and social media maven and author of *Lean In*, Sheryl Sandberg. For courageously speaking out on behalf of so many exploited women, Mam was named *Glamour*'s Woman of the Year and a CNN Hero in 2006 as well as one of *Time* magazine's 100 Most Influential People in 2009, the *Guardian*'s World's Top 100 Women in 2011, *Fortune* magazine's Most Powerful Women of 2011, and *Fast Company*'s 2012 League of Extraordinary Women. She was awarded the Prince of Asturias Award for International Cooperation, the Roland Berger Human Dignity Award, and the World's Children's Prize for the Rights of the Child, and she has been officially commended by the U.S. Department of State and Homeland Security for her anti-trafficking leadership. Mam even carried the Olympic flag in the opening ceremonies of the 2006 Winter Olympics.

Kirkus Review called her book "An urgent, though depressing, document, worthy of a place alongside Ishmael Beah's *A Long Way Gone*, Rigoberta Menchú's autobiography and other accounts of overcoming Third World hardship."[6] *Publishers Weekly* reported that the book was "a moving, disturbing tale" that was a "cry for justice and support for women's plight everywhere."[7] Indeed, for a time, Mam's refusal to remain silent made her the standard bearer for anti-trafficking efforts as she brought sorely needed attention to a then largely unrecognized global crime against women, children, and humanity.

When I first began research on the new slave narrative, it seemed as if Mam's narrative might be the Platonic form of the new slave narrative. Thinking along the lines of James Olney's use of Frederick Douglass's narrative to outline the conventions of the genre,[8] I turned to Mam's narrative of childhood commercial sexual exploitation because it exhibits nearly every single genre convention that I was delineating in this project. In addition to fulfilling many of the main conventions outlined here in chapter 1—the poor origins set in an idyllic landscape, the violent recognition of enslavement, the character sketch of the brutal master, the suicidal ideation, the escape with the assistance of a benevolent Westerner, the activist vocation, the call to action, etc.—Mam's narrative also elegantly displays many of the more nuanced aspects of the new slave narrative described in chapter 1. For instance, though Mam suggests that her story is meant to "make visible the lives of so many thousands of other women" and allow reading audiences the opportunity to probe the dark underbelly of the sex trade, Mam uses many of the strategies of displacement that allow her to remain silent about her most gruesome experiences.[9] Intentionally controlling which aspects of her life are revealed and which remain shrouded, Mam is explicit about the challenge of making slavery legible without revealing more of herself than she wishes. She writes instead about the silences that are enforced on Cambodian women, which caused her to remain silent when she saw other women brutalized, when she was subjected to violence herself, and even when she was in recovery. Mam tells us in her narrative, "There is one law for women—silence before rape and silence after. We're taught when we're little to be like the silk-cotton tree: *dam kor*. Deaf and dumb. Blind too, if possible."[10] She is particularly open about the way her cultural upbringing encouraged her silence and regularly explained her reluctance to give in to the repeated demands from journalists and advocates for a tell-all narrative. "Perhaps journalists will stop asking me to recount my story over and over again," she writes, "because it is very difficult to keep repeating it."[11] Writing her story, she claims, was an investment in the comfort of future silence. One of the reasons she wrote the book was that "perhaps it will stop me from having to tell my story over and over again."[12] Her narrative is as much a documentation of her life of silence and her attempts to shield herself from the gaze of the media and others as it is a record of her exploitation.[13]

A simultaneous claimant to voice and silence, Mam's story is evocative of both the ambivalences and the ambiguities of being in control of one's own narrative. Mam uses the strategies of displacement—familiar from Jean-Robert Cadet's, Mende Nazer's, and Grace Akallo's narratives—to maintain her right to silence and to eschew the voyeurism of the human rights industry. Even in the epigraph of the book, Mam turns to statistics (loose and perhaps exaggerated as they may be) and the experiences of others to avert the gaze from her own experience, dedicating her book to "the thousands of little girls who are sold into prostitution every year."[14] Instead of describing the sexual and physical assaults she endured, she immediately turns her writerly gaze upon the women she serves, deflecting from her own bodily experience in an effort to suggest that her individual story can be read as representative of the collective thousands of women who are experiencing what she escaped. Indeed, she writes that her story "isn't important. The point is not what happened to me. I'm writing about it to make visible the lives of so many thousands of other women. They have no voice, so let this one life stand for their story."[15] Mam projects her voice into the silences that slavery keeps in the new slave narrative, and by telling her story, at least this once, she hopes to allow others to keep their silence while still having the opportunity to escape and heal. Nonetheless, Mam utilizes strategies of displacement to deflect from her own experience while still managing to make the enslavement of those "tens of thousands" of others legible for international readers.

Further conforming to the conventions of the new slave narrative, Mam describes her sense of the precarity and perhaps even the inaccessibility of freedom after emancipation, remarking that she still feels "dirty" and is psychologically haunted by nightmares and flashbacks as well as by social stigma.[16] The last chapters of her memoir focus on the lives of young women who have been aided by her organization, Agir Pour Les Femmes en Situation Précaire (AFESIP), and she trumpets the typical call to action familiar to the long-form slave narrative, past and present. In these ways, Mam's narrative checks nearly every box on the emerging list of new slave narrative genre conventions that I have outlined in the preceding pages.

I argue, however, that while Mam's fulfillment of the genre conventions of the new slave narrative was what catapulted her into the spotlight and garnered her so many accolades and sponsors, it was precisely that same adherence to the conventions that brought her narrative into question. Mam's narrative of sexual enslavement and its attendant violence conform so successfully to the demands of the genre that she was held up as a poster child and elevated to the status of a celebrity. Her narrative was well received because it met readers' expectations for a slave narrative and confirmed public sentiments (misinformed as they sometimes are) about sexual enslavement. As a representative of the suffering masses of enslaved sex workers, however, she was required to testify to much more than her own experience can encompass—to have her "life stand in for their stories" as she put it. Those who encouraged her to tell her story—advocates, ghost-writers, and journalists who were inured to the tropes of the Western human rights industry—imposed upon Mam's experiences the dueling generic expectations of the slave narrative to represent subject and object, individual and collective, servant and celebrity, victim and savior, and even a whole social movement, conventions that are so contrary that no memoirist or autobiographer could possibly conform to them. The contradiction of those conventions encouraged Mam to invent and embody a composite narrative of extraordinary mass suffering, which was doomed to fail the veracity tests to which it was subjected by her critics. In this chapter, I synthesize the tropes, conventions, and politics described in the earlier chapters to focus on the tangible consequences of activists' interference in and reception of the new slave narrative. In the end, I suggest that Mam's precipitous decline was fated by the competing expectations that are defined and demanded by the very industry—and genre—that lifted her up.

THE PERFECT VICTIM

Perhaps Mam's narrative adherence to all the generic conventions of the new slave narrative should have raised my suspicions and alerted me to the possibility that it was only lauded because it performed so compellingly the mythological "perfect victim" narrative. The perfect victim narrative emerges when human rights advocates, the media, and legislators look for representatives who can speak to the lived experience of contemporary slavery or other rights violations. Wary of naysayers and often lacking in a nuanced understanding of contemporary slavery themselves, advocates seek out the "perfect victim" who conforms to a misinformed definition of slavery and a stereotypical portrait of the kind of person who can be held up as the victim of such a violation. As Robert Uy described this type in 2011 (before the rise of the U.S. minor sex trafficking narrative described in chapter 4), advocates "often envision a 'third world,' if not primarily Asian, woman or a child in deplorable conditions, being brought across borders, and being forced into commercial sex acts."[17] The presumption of innocence is perceived to be critical to avoid victim blaming, and so child victims tend to be favored over adults, and women over men, in the search for a representative, as women and children are lumped into the same category of feeble, agency-less objects. Indeed, in the passage of the Trafficking Victims Protection Act in the United States, legislators and advocates utilized images and stories of powerless, poor, foreign-born, passive victims of sexual assault and smuggling who desperately needed the assistance of benevolent Western benefactors to escape the horrors of sexual enslavement.[18] Though the narratives of sexual slavery leave no doubt as to the fact of human rights violations, these sensationalized portraits of agency-less children held captive in brothels dominated the earliest discussions of victim protections and continue to play an outsize role in antislavery discourse today.

The idea of the perfect victim suggests that there are some who are more "deserving," as Jessica Elliott notes.[19] Different forms of trafficking and slavery as well as people who are smuggled or immigrate irregularly or those who are seen to be complicit in their exploitation are simply considered undeserving.[20] This stereotype of the deserving, nonconsensual victim is used pervasively by a wide range of actors with varying, often divergent political agendas for several reasons. First, the "perfect victim" image separates survivors of slavery from economic migrants—both may appear in the United States without proper documentation, but the trafficking victim is figured as having committed no crime. The "perfect victim" is one who was smuggled against her will, allowing advocates and legislators to continue to condemn economic migrants who enter a country by choice.[21] Even more sympathetic is the victim who remains in her own country, never penetrating vulnerable Western borders and thus better able to penetrate the formidable walls of our concern. This image conveniently allows us to ignore much forced labor because its reliance on a nonconsenting migrant or nonmigrant laborer disqualifies those who immigrated to the country seeking paid work but found themselves in forced labor. Furthermore, this portrait of nonconsenting sexual labor excludes victims of forced labor and makes a case for the victimization of all women engaged in sex work by suggesting that all sex work is akin (or even equivalent) to slavery. And as Jayashri Srikantiah argues, "perfect victims" are typically foreign, born in places where Americans tend to assume male domination and female subordination as a cultural norm, exonerating themselves for their own paternalistic behaviors in the name of saving the helpless women of other countries.[22] This image of the perfect victim creates an opportunity for a "white savior" to appear to have great effect through legislation and nonprofit advocacy, to enact that racist paternalism that Spivak dubbed "white men saving brown women from brown men."[23] Through these tactics, conservative lobbies, in concert with progressive human rights advocates, rally around the very same images of helpless international victims of sexual exploitation, creating an unusually powerful coalition around a narrow and misinformed mythology of contemporary slavery and a coercive mandate for survivors' narratives to conform to the expected conventions.[24]

The consequences of this victim paradigm are stark and tangible—making it difficult to identity victims and making it possible to deny relief to those who do not fit the mold—but the stereotype is nonetheless embraced and replicated by most advocates in the field. "Victim scripts" as Pardis Mahdavi calls them, encourage victims to conform certain aspects of their experience to gain assistance or attention from the judicial branches of governments and from nonprofits.[25] Claudia Cojocaru critiques this stereotype, arguing that as a survivor-scholar, she is often reduced simply to her experience as a victim. She recounts a time when she was asked to perform the "survivor" role at a public lecture, writing, "It was easy, because this narrative is a well-trodden path that almost anybody can walk down—regardless of whether what they are talking is the truth, the near truth, or complete fabrication. My suspicion is that all such varieties are present in the circus of salvation—where performativity, rather than experience, is what is rewarded."[26] Cojocaru concludes from this experience, "There is absolutely no interest in the salvation and rehabilitation of undeserving victims, the ones whose self-description does not include the perfect victim features—the one worthy of saving, but rather a campaign to reinforce colonial and ethnocentric values around class, race and access to resources, and to increase influence of the privileged."[27] For survivor-advocates who

do not fit neatly within the paradigm of the "perfect victim," the consequence can be that their stories and expertise are willfully ignored, even
by those scholars, advocates, and legislators who are ostensibly fighting for
their rights.

Mam's husband, Pierre LeGros, who had previously worked with other
NGOs, including Médecins sans Frontières, recognized the power of these
tropes of victimhood as well as the pornographic voyeurism of the media
and urged Mam to be a spokesperson and to write her memoir. He con-
fessed, "I wanted to draw a lot of attention to get funds from international
institutions. Somaly is beautiful, sexy, charismatic, and determined. Every
NGO dreams of having its Somaly, and every media wants her on camera.
We soon became very much high profile, and we welcomed a lot of journalists. They all wanted to make something sexy, to draw attention and mark
everyone's mind."[28] Despite Somaly's constant refuge in silence, LeGros
knew that she could be an icon for a movement because her physical appearance would appeal to cameramen and her story of stolen childhood innocence would confirm the portrait of depravity that was becoming de rigeur
in journalistic exposés of the Southeast Asian sex industry. Her story resonated with both academic and popular presses because it carried both the
gravity of her brutal victimization and the uplift of her role as savior and
surrogate mother to the young women she served.

Mam, for her part, conformed perfectly to the paradigm—she was a shy
Asian woman who was first exploited as a child and who continued to critique a patriarchal regime that rewarded her silence instead of her activism. For that she was fêted around the world. But Mam was not only the
"perfect victim" for media and nonprofit representations; in many ways, she
was a researcher's "perfect victim" because, as much as she conformed to
all the reductive categories that made her a perfect victim for the media,
she also conformed to all the displacement and identification strategies and
political impulses that make the new slave narrative a compelling and complicated subject for rigorous analysis. As a result, for the first several years
of research on this project, Mam's narrative was essential in the development of my understanding of the form of the slave narrative, and it still is.
My approach to what precisely she represents changed, however, when she
was accused of being a fraud and her activist projects were shuttered by critics who were quick to turn their backs on her before she had a chance to
defend herself.

THE SAINT AND THE SINNER

In May 2014, less than a year after she announced herself in the *Daily Beast* as a slave narrator akin to Solomon Northup, Somaly Mam's work ground to a halt when journalist Simon Marks, writing for *Newsweek*, revealed to the magazine's 1.5 million U.S. readers what he had been arguing in the Cambodian press since 2012: Mam's claims regarding her traumatic life and her benevolent work were not only exaggerated but outright fabricated.[29] For his cover article titled "Somaly Mam: The Holy Saint (and Sinner) of Sex Trafficking," Marks delved deep into Mam's past to determine whether her narrative was to be trusted. He reported that Mam's neighbors remembered her living with her parents and not held captive by the abusive and enslaving "Grandfather" figure she describes in her book. The neighbors remembered Mam as a "happy, pretty girl with pigtails," not the lonely, brooding, traumatized child that Mam describes in her autobiography. Marks spoke with Mam's high school director, who stated Mam was enrolled in school at the time when she reports being forced into a brothel. In addition, he pointed to significant discrepancies in the stories Mam had told publicly of her captivity: "Not even Mam can keep the story straight. In February 2012, while speaking at the White House, she said she was sold into slavery at age 9 or 10 and spent a decade inside a brothel. On *The Tyra Banks Show*, she said it was four or five years in the brothel. Her book says she was trafficked when she was 'about 16 years old.'"[30] These serious allegations called into question foundational aspects of Mam's narrative, suggesting that she was otherwise occupied and accounted for during the moments she recalled as characterized by inhumanly brutal sexual enslavement.

More disconcerting, however, was evidence Marks provided that suggested Mam had used her newfound role as benefactor to convince young, impoverished Cambodian women into auditioned, coached, and rehearsed performances meant to deceive the public into thinking they had been enslaved in the sex trade even though they had not. One woman, Meas Ratha, who claimed she had been forced into sex work as a child, later told Marks that she had actually been brought to AFESIP with her sister because her parents felt incapable of providing for their large family.[31] Another young woman, Long Pross, who told the media that her right eye had been surgically removed after an attack by a brothel owner, had her story refuted by her own father, who told Marks that she had not been enslaved at all but had actually suffered from a large benign tumor that had been removed just before she enrolled in a vocational course at Mam's shelter. Marks cited the medical records and hospital staff to prove it.[32] Both women had been featured in Western media as victims of child sexual enslavement, including in features by the *New York Times*' Nicholas Kristof.[33] According to Marks's reporting, the two women had been convinced by Mam that they should use their commanding self-confidence to share the stories of other genuinely exploited women. In his reporting in the *Cambodia Daily*, Marks wrote that Meas Ratha told him, "Mam had told her that the story she was to recount for the filmmakers was true, but was the life-story of another young girl, Sokha, who had been too traumatized to speak about her past." Marks claimed that a girl named Sokha's appearance in the same film is evidence to the contrary.[34]

In light of the government allegations, medical records, neighbors' memories, clients' testimonies, and even the disavowal of her former husband and cofounder, evidence against Mam seemed damning as did Mam's resignation from her eponymous foundation and then the eventual shuttering of the U.S.-based charitable organization. Still, many supporters felt they could discount the significance of these inaccuracies by recalling the way traumatic memory functions and malfunctions and by speculating as to the political or personal motivations that neighbors and teachers might have to deny that such abuse could have happened to someone in their own community. Even what seemed to be factual inaccuracies had seemingly reasonable explanations. For instance, if the director of her school is correct in saying that Mam attended his school between 1981 and 1987, that would mean that she left the school when she was about sixteen, about the time she says she was sent to the work in the sex trade. When journalist Abigail Pesta went to Cambodia to investigate Marks's claims for *Marie Claire*, the director of Mam's school told Pesta that while Mam attended his school for several years, she disappeared before her graduation. Pesta also reinterviewed the community elder cited by Marks, who recanted his claim that Mam was a happy child in pigtails and said instead that she was a "silent and sad child."[35] In regard to the coaching of the young women, Long Pross denied her father's claims and continued, along with many other clients, to support Mam and her work. When Pesta visited the doctor and medical clinics cited in the *Newsweek* takedown, staff claimed there were no records of Pross's surgery. Pesta also found receipts that might confirm that Meas

Ratha (who is now married with a child) was literally sold to a broker for $100.[36] It seems possible that both Pross's father and Ratha would have an investment in erasing the parts of their pasts that might be considered shameful. Indeed, Ratha openly admitted that she came forward because she had had grown tired of being falsely maligned as a prostitute, evidence of the shame attached to that designation. Further exonerating evidence was found in the fact that Mam's daughter defended claims regarding her own kidnapping as a teenager, a claim her father had disputed.[37] And for her main evidence of Mam's exoneration, Pesta turned to Mam's clients. Some of the survivors who worked with Mam were so offended by the vague accusations and the final decisions of the Somaly Mam Foundation board that they collectively resigned from the organization, and some moved into Mam's home. Pesta depicts the suffering visages of these women as irrefutable proof of Mam's claims.

On the other hand, Mam was publicly silent for months before she spoke out about Marks's claims, which led people to believe that she was guilty or hiding something. Her silence, so central to both the structure of the text and the representation of her gendered oppression, was now read as a corroboration of her fraudulence. The generic demands for a narrative of self-defense were just as compulsory as the narrative conventions of her life story. She was required to doggedly fight the accusations regardless of the power dynamics, political futility, or personal/emotional expense. Silence was read essentially as a confession instead of as a sign of oppression as it had been in her narrative. Nonetheless, Mam circumvented the demands of the defense-against-fraud genre by redoubling her efforts in her work and by refusing to engage with the accusations. She renewed her activism after her board dismissed her and terminated operations through what she called the New Somaly Mam Foundation: Voices for Change, the name of which reflected her ever-growing sense of the importance of survivor narratives. Mam continued to run her shelter and training programs with the continued support of Susan Sarandon, Diane von Furstenburg, and others (by 2018, AFESIP was primarily funded by Together1Heart, a foundation run by actress Anna McCord, with significant cooperation from Mam). When she granted an interview to *Marie Claire*, she explained the vagaries of traumatic memory, its impact on a formerly enslaved person, and what she saw as the true stakes of her story: "I was a domestic slave, then I was in a brothel.

How do you count? So I was in the brothel two years, twenty years, twenty days? I was a slave."[38]

Supporters of her nonprofit might be suspected of having defended her because, through her, they defended their financial investments and endorsements. Those who have benefited from Mam's programs are committed to seeing their patron—and not insignificantly, the programs that have assisted them out of poverty—survive this onslaught regardless of potential inaccuracies. Her daughter's defense can be attributed to filial duty. The testimony of the director of Mam's former school is perceived as tainted because he reportedly now works for Mam's foundation. Mam's husband still refutes her claims about the daughter's kidnappings and insists that all nonprofits, including the Somaly Mam Foundation, exaggerate for journalists.[39] Furthermore, there have been accusations (notably made by her husband and by Simon Marks) that Mam's supportive clients have intimidated and threatened people in the community to keep them silent.[40] And Pesta's Western reporter's gaze undermines her own authority when she suggests that at least some of her determination of her subjects' veracity is based on their "tribal roots," impoverished environment, or naïve confusion about the nature or purpose of journalism, which to her signaled their inherent authenticity.[41] All these concerns keep many antislavery advocates at a distance from Mam and her work.

Competing narratives pathologizing Mam emerged immediately: either she was a sociopath who viciously duped people to generate emotional support, or she suffered from posttraumatic stress syndrome that undermined her capacity to remember. Some claimed that Mam had always been a transparent liar and mercenary opportunist. Others claimed that she had been victimized by the media's desires for a sexy story. Still others maintained that she had been unjustly maligned, that Marks had focused on the wrong aspect of the sex trafficking story, that PTSD was to blame for the mistakes she had made in her narrative.[42] In the end, most critics, activists, and journalists did not feel Mam could be redeemed. Elizabeth Nolan Brown of Reason.com even dubbed Mam "the James Frey of anti-sex trafficking activism," referring to the author of *A Million Little Pieces*, who was made infamous for his fabrication of events in his memoir.[43] Indeed, the life of Mam's narrative can tell us as much as Frey's can about the limits of authenticity and the crisis of autobiography. Mam's narrative is instructive, in particular, in unpacking the specific ways the new slave narrative comes in conflict with expectations for veracity placed upon the first-person narrative of rights violations.

DOES IT MATTER?

Throughout this highly public attack on Somaly Mam, journalists fixated on the question of whether or not Mam had lied. In the end, this complicated "he said–she said" narrative cannot tell us much about what is actually true about Somaly Mam's life. But one question, which did circulate among some journalists and nonprofit organizers and that echoed the one that was featured on the *Newsweek* cover (though it remained unanswered in its pages) seems most significant: "Does it matter that key parts of her story aren't true?"

Does it matter? What harm is there if parts of Mam's story are fabricated or exaggerated? What role does veracity play in one individual's story when the work to address human rights violations affects millions of people?[44]

Those who dared to ponder the question of the significance of fraud had some compelling answers, many of which pointed to an answer of "yes, it does matter." United States Embassy workers in Cambodia had apparently long fretted that a revelation of Mam's fraudulent story and mismanagement of the organization would have negative effects on other organizations in the region doing similar work.[45] Anti-trafficking nonprofit leaders suggested that malingering could lead to distrust in the entire nonprofit sector and, worse, encourage the concerned public to question the credibility of all survivors of trafficking.[46] Kristof and other pundits warned (reminiscent of William Lloyd Garrison's plea when James Williams's narrative was found to be a fraud) that journalists and activists should be more cautious in reporting the stories of oppressed subjects, expressing their concern that controversy would overshadow the plight of forced sex workers or even give credence to naysayers who deny the very existence of sexual enslavement.[47]

Pro-sex-work advocate journalists such as Elizabeth Nolan Brown suggested, on the other hand, that what mattered was that these lies about human rights violations would continue to lead to legislation built on "boogeymen."[48] Anne Elizabeth Moore and Melissa Gira Grant agree, suggesting that it has been Mam's malingering all along that has been the impetus for Draconian, patriarchal policies that employ antiterrorism tactics to oppress sex workers in Cambodia and around the region and that this supposed scandal will only continue to obscure the oppressive garment industry "alternatives" presented to women exiting the sex trade.[49] The polarized debates between the anti-sex-trafficking activists and pro-sex-work advocates dominated the conversation regarding the scandal.

As an activist, I harbor similar anxieties about the veracity of claims made by anti-trafficking advocates and pro-sex-work advocates alike; however, as an academic, I am much less concerned about whether or not one individual is telling the truth. Instead, what matters to me about Mam's story is that it reveals clearly how truth claims are shaped within human rights discourse and how generic conventions help authorize certain kinds of narratives and deauthorize others. At least part of what these concerns point to is the power of genre. When the denial of veracity in one person's narrative has the effect of denying the reality of millions of people's experiences, the stakes are high. And when our understanding of what constitutes the truth is dependent on conformity to generic conventions, the question of how genre functions to legitimize and delegitimize rights claims is critical. If Leigh Gilmore is correct in suggesting that "we can interpret autobiography as re-presentation, that is, a structuring of events, motives, and so on in an effort to position one's story within a discourse of truth and identity—in short, as an attempt to authorize the autobiography,"[50] then Mam's narrative is constrained and produced by the very structures of truth suggested by the genre of the autobiography (and the slave narrative, more particularly). The controversy surrounding Mam's authenticity helps us to frame the limits of human rights narration and understand the real and significant risks of generic expectations. It reveals the voyeuristic demands of human rights defenders, and it uncovers the ways cultural notions of the truth in the West undermine international activists' positions of authority and their ability to maintain any one version of their lives as "truth." As we saw in chapters 3 and 4, neoliberal, Christian activists have utilized contemporary slavery (and its narratives) as a facade for their political agendas. But it is not simply that segment of the movement that constrains the voices of the slave narrators by demanding spectacularized, first-person accounts of slavery and binaristic notions of good and evil that flatten the experiences of the formerly enslaved into politically and ethically consumable simulacra. The liberal human rights industry's drive toward "humanitarian pornography" equally violates the agency of survivors to shape the narratives of their own lives.

Mam's narrative is compelling *because* of, not in spite of, the questions regarding its veracity. Narratives that have been called into question like hers have helped us to learn more about the narratives of slavery that exist, the ways slavery is narrativized by those who experience it, and the ways it is co-opted by those who utilize the narratives to fight injustice. Suspect narratives can be used as a limit test for authenticity and can inform our understanding of how narratives invest in formal legitimating techniques, how the narratives must elicit and quell doubt, and how amanuenses and coauthors affect the reception of a text's authenticity. In any movement, there is likely to be a case of fraud or two—the twenty-first-century antislavery movement is in no way immune to that. A scholarly approach to this issue, however, allows us to critique the way veracity is packaged and sold as well as the demands it places on the survivors who come forward to tell their stories.

THE BURDENS OF THE PROPER NAME

Who is the Somaly Mam that we have come to know through her life, through her narrative, and through her activism? Are they necessarily the same? Must they be?

Philippe LeJeune writes that it is "in relation to the *proper name* that we are able to situate the problems of autobiography,"[51] and the case of the name "Somaly Mam" is no different. As Mam writes in her first memoir published in France, "My name is Somaly. At least, that's the name I'm wearing now. . . . I do not remember my childhood. I do not know much about my origins, and I have reconstructed after the fact, from vague memories, this little bit of history."[52] Structuring a narrative, and thus a name, from the fragments of the past is the work of autobiography—for the enslaved narrator or otherwise. LeJeune reminds us that while the proper name is linked to "the pledge of responsibility of a *real person*" to which that name refers, this does not suggest that the author named on the cover is merely or precisely the living person to which the name refers. The author "is a person who writes and publishes. Straddling the world-beyond-the-text, he is the connection between the two."[53] If the author is the connection between the text and the world-beyond-the-text, it does not necessarily follow that the textually represented first-person narrator is the precise equivalent of the "real person" who lives in the world-beyond-the-text.

Whose name is it, then, that is printed on the cover of the book? Is it the living person, is it the textual representation of that person, or is it the author? In fiction, these questions are typically moot; the name on the cover refers to the author, who is generally not represented in the text (though we often find ourselves searching for signs of the author embodied in a character). In autobiography and memoir, however, the author is the producer of a textual life that represents the lived life of a verifiable person, whose name is printed on the cover. However, the "Somaly Mam" who is produced in the text is not necessarily the unmitigated, unmediated, absolutely verifiable truth of the life of Somaly Mam, the living person; in fact, the subject of autobiography never is. Thus, while the name on the cover refers to all three—the living person, the author, and the representation—none of those is necessarily synonymous with the others.

A problem arises when people who refer to "Somaly Mam" conflate the three—the person, the author, and the representation—typically understanding the textual representation to characterize all three. Because readers primarily have access to the written product, the textual "Somaly Mam" is imbued with a certain power of representation, such that what is written in the text is considered the definitive "Somaly Mam" that then comes to define not only the representation but also the author and the living being. The textual "Somaly Mam" is persistently imposed upon the living Somaly Mam, who then must account for all details printed in the books' pages. Furthermore, as Mam's ghostwriter, Ruth Marshall, puts it "What happens when you ghostwrite somebody's book [is that] you put words on the page that aren't really exactly right, and they think, 'Yeah, yeah. It was like that.' "[54] Marshall's experience is that narrators often begin to tell their life stories as their ghostwriters present them in their autobiographies rather than from their own memories. As a result, their lived lives and personal memories are subordinated to the textual representations of themselves not only in the minds of readers but even in their own minds, and our access to the living person is thereafter always mediated by the representation contained in the text, even when speaking directly to the living person.

However, to literary scholars—and, I would suspect, to most anyone who has tried to tell a "true story" of her own life—the concern with errors and fractures in life narratives is not so much a question regarding production as it is of reception. The storyteller always knows that the story she tells can never be a perfect representation of the past. It is in the reception of the text that the three aspects become conflated and veracity becomes a crisis. LeJeune (and practically all others who write on life narrative) admits to the "errors, the distortions, the interpretations consubstantial with the elaboration of personal myth in all autobiography." In fact, he suggests that genuine, intentional, and total fraud is "extremely rare" and that the autobiographical pact is not undermined by the omissions and necessary slippages of memory over time and the necessity of the author of the autobiography to narrate his or her life in spite of the knowledge of the frailty of memory.[55] Essentially, all scholars of first-person narratives recognize that the representation of a life can never precisely and accurately represent the living person and that the three aspects of the name remain distinct. By contrast, in a court of law, the three aspects of the name must be conflated, and the representation of self is bound by the premise that humans are capable of telling "the whole truth and nothing but the truth." It appears that in the court of public opinion, the same judicial standards of veracity are expected of life narratives. When first-person narratives are condemned for containing slippages and misrepresentations, then, the reader's conflation of the three burdens of the name becomes particularly relevant. When readers expect the first-person representation of a life to accurately and precisely reflect the lived experience of a person, narrators are almost inevitably going to fail.

Challenges to authenticity based on a refusal to recognize the constructed nature of narrative for formerly enslaved people are pertinent to each aspect of the proper name in autobiography—the living person, the author, and the representation—each of which reveals how it is that genre destroyed Somaly Mam. At the level of the living person, the slave narrator is required to understand and represent his or her life experience first and foremost as "slavery," which creates a problem of legibility when the very notion of slavery in the twenty-first century is unrecognized. At the level of authorship, the identity of the slave narrator is often necessarily a compound voice— that of the narrator and her amanuensis or ghostwriter—which adds another burden to the weight the name must carry. And at the level of the textual representation, the slave narrator must be constructed as a unique individual worthy of autobiography at the same time as she stands as a composite figure of suffering masses, for which she is not merely a single example but also their victim-savior. These additional generic pressures on the proper name of the slave narrator create unavoidable fissures that, I argue, lead inevitably to the crisis of authenticity that both the living and the represented Somaly Mam have suffered. In the following sections, I take up each of these burdens individually.

Mam as Enslaved Subject

As discussed in chapter 1, the anxieties of legibility inherent in representing contemporary slavery present a genuine challenge to the new slave narrator, as representation of one's authenticity as a formerly enslaved person compels the narrator to first establish that slavery still exists and that the concept of slavery is indeed one that can be used in relation to the contemporary experiences of forced labor described by the narrators. In addition to that crisis of legibility, Mam's narrative reveals to us the way in which the subject of the narrative of slavery is in a unique bind in terms of the generic conditions of autobiography. If, as John Paul Eakin reminds us, "the final object of every autobiographical quest . . . is the impossible search for one's birth," then the slave narrator likely feels that futility even more sharply.[56] At a literal level, the search for origins is challenging for the international slave narrators in particular because they are often unable to remember their birthdates or recount details of their early experiences beyond the landscapes and cultural practices of their childhoods because their enslavement has removed them from those settings and others with whom they might share early memories. As such, the slave narrator is distinctly burdened with an impossible task of finding his or her origins—there are voids, absences, and gaps that can never be recovered precisely because of the experience they are writing to depict. In many ways, the living person being represented is a cipher, a ghost, and her origin is even more so. In Mam's case, her childhood experiences have been left behind in the murky haze of memory, and reports suggest that her hometown is now so transformed by her own generosity that its earlier manifestation has been reduced to a blurry shadowland to which she can never return.

Although those aspects of the search for one's origins may be common to many experiences of geographical displacement, we might think more figuratively about the notion of origins to which Eakin points here in order to understand it as a return to the birth of subjectivity. A recounting of the birth of one's own subjectivity, the early recognition of the individual self, is no doubt a generic convention of the Western autobiography, but that conception of origins is particularly alienating for people who have been enslaved. By convention, the slave narrator establishes her own recognition of subjectivity in her inherent right to freedom before slavery *and* to convince readers that she was disenfranchised as a subject in bondage. In returning to that moment of preslavery subjectivity formation, the slave narrator establishes herself as a subject worthy of autobiography. Moments later, however, when the narrator depicts her enslavement, narrative convention requires that she differentiate her agency from that of the enslaver; to wit, she is typically expected to prove her complete lack of agency or choice in her own enslavement. To cement a claim to enslavement in a slave narrative, agency—seemingly the soul of subjectivity—is often erased or elided in the scene of subjection; to have it otherwise would risk suggesting one's own culpability in one's own subordination. That is to say that any sign of agency may suggest to suspicious readers that one's own subordination is his or her own choice, and as we have seen, formerly enslaved people personally confront this accusation through self-blame quite often. As we saw in the narratives of domestic minor sex trafficking, that tension between emphasizing one's own agency in changing one's life and convincing readers that the narrator had no complicity in her own subjection to bondage is one that slave narrators find themselves navigating quite regularly.

Mam and so many other narrators write their way out of this bind through depicting a rise to glory that is necessarily dependent on their work as liberators, revealing a teleological narrative trajectory that begins with inherently free origins but then moves from the depths of supposed agencyless subordination to the heights of altruistic commitment to liberation for all. Nonetheless, to meet the demands of the genre, the name of the slave narrator must simultaneously evoke both the Enlightenment subject imbued with free will and capitalism's abject object, the unfree laborer—a dichotomous individual identity that, by definition, should be a paradox. Thus, to conform to the conventions of the slave narrative, the search for origins must necessarily describe a story of the narrator's birth as an object much more so than as a subject if she is to prove that she was, in fact, a person who was enslaved. The name "Somaly Mam," then, must represent both a free-willed, self-possessed subject and the captive, possessed object.

Mam manages this delicate balance by representing the originary freedom of her youth to wander the forest "like a little savage,"[57] an absolute
freedom that was stolen from her when she was held against her will as a
forced laborer for "Grandfather," which marked the birth of her life as
a "slave."[58] The "blood-stained gate" represented by the terrorizing violence
she endured at the hands of Grandfather marks the recognition of that other
origin, one that is diametrically opposed to the simple origins or the birth
of the subject typical of the autobiography. Throughout her narrative, she
walks this generic tightrope—exploring her willful insistence on the freedom of all Cambodian women while insisting on the reality of sexual
captivity for both herself and the women she interacts with (sometimes even
to the point of suggesting that all women in the sex trade are agency-less
captives). The very existence of an enslaved subject calls into question the
inherent freedom at the origin of all Enlightenment autobiography and is
thus, in itself, a contradiction that cannot be countenanced by the genre.
That such dissonance in values would inspire readerly scrutiny of Mam's
agency in moments she has depicted as subordination is not a surprise.

Mam as Compound Author

While Rachel Lloyd's narrative and some of the self-published narratives
are single-authored works written exclusively by the formerly enslaved
person named on the cover (sometimes with little even in the way of copyediting), more than half of the narratives considered here are either cow-
ritten or ghostwritten by professional writers who are sometimes named
on the covers or on the copyright pages. It is nearly impossible to tell which
aspects of a narrative represent the direct recollections of the person who
is named on the cover and which have been conjured in the imagination of
the coauthor, so throughout this project, I have read these texts as, at the
very least, *authorized* by the named slave narrators on the covers. However,
when the question of authenticity arises, it is unwise not to consider the
"oxymoronic status" of the coauthorship of these narratives, which, according to Thomas Couser, is "always in danger of breaking, exposing conflicts
of interest that are not present in solo autobiography."[59]

When Western coauthors work with non-Western new slave narrators
to represent non-Western settings, in particular, it often results in conservative Western values and misinformed imaginations of the Global South

coming to the fore in the narratives, as we saw in chapter 3. In the case of Mam, the Western political influence can be located in a brief critique of the Khmer Rouge and the underlying emphasis on Cambodian patriarchy as distinct from and exceeding the norms of the ubiquitous global patriarchy we all live under. Perhaps more significant, however, is the generalized influence of the Western autobiographical tradition. The market demands of such a narrative, which would recount a little-known and hardly understood phenomenon of oppression in another country, no doubt requires a savvy and attentive coauthor who can shape a story into a package that will be consumable by and inspiring to Western audiences. In these pursuits, Ruth Marshall, Mam's amanuensis for the American edition of Mam's autobiography, is indeed incredibly successful. Nielsen BookScan reports that *The Road of Lost Innocence* has sold ninety thousand copies in the United States alone (far more than any other narrative examined in this study), a feat that would be entirely impossible for Mam without an amanuensis, given the fact that Mam's English and French are rudimentary. Despite the fact that her story could not possibly be told without the skills of a writer like Marshall, readers—in particular, critical readers and journalists—of her narrative receive it as if she were the sole author of the text.

From the very beginning of Mam's narrative to the very last pages, the impulse of the amanuensis to conform to the norms of the Western slave narrative/humanitarian narrative form predictably and necessarily comes in direct conflict with the normative silences that Mam feels persistently confined by in her telling of her story. Mam's retreat to silence and her consistent reminder of the cultural mandates for women to maintain silence around sexual assault demonstrate her understanding of a normative Cambodian approach to life narrative. On the other hand, the tell-all expectations of the first-person narrative in the West produce a conflict in the very concept of identity in these coauthored narratives.

Is the "Somaly Mam" of the narrative the culturally constituted, living person whose storytelling style reflects her own society's expectations for her behavior and generic conventions for her life narrative? Or is "Somaly Mam" the textual representation produced by a culturally determined, generically conforming amanuensis who shapes the fragments of Mam's memories into a narrative? More often than not, the slave narrative leans toward the latter in its structure and conventions, but it is always necessarily both. What would it mean for "Somaly Mam" to be a hybrid of the two? While the text is a mutually agreed upon product and has the imprimatur of the person named on the cover, the narrative conventions are determined by the ghostwriter's and publisher's cultural expectations regarding genre and the reception of the book.

Marshall is not unique in her influence on the text, of course; all ghostwriters process their collaborators' lives through the learned conventions of the genre as well as through their own life experiences, politics, and knowledge. Speaking of the nineteenth-century slave narrative, John Blassingame notes, "An editor's education, religious beliefs, literary skills, attitudes toward slavery, and occupation all affected how he recorded the account of the slave's life."[60] Briton Hammon's slave narrative of 1760 was shaped by his editors at Green and Russell to conform to the captivity narratives that were popular at the time of his publication. So closely did it conform, in fact, that it appears to be a near replica of another captivity narrative published by a collaborating press.[61] When the 1785 slave narrative "of the Lord's Wonderful Dealings" with John Marrant was "arranged, corrected, and published" by William Aldridge, it was explicitly told in the form of the religious conversion narrative, exalting a God who provided salvation from the subordination of slavery (interestingly echoed in recent "sex slavery" narratives in the United States).[62] Hammon's or Marrant's stories might have been told entirely differently had they lived seventy or ninety years later and worked with Lydia Maria Child or William Lloyd Garrison instead of Green or Aldridge. James Olney suggests that amanuensis David Wilson imposed the stylistics of the sentimental novel on Solomon Northup's narrative, for instance.[63] For a more recent example, we might turn to Malcolm X's autobiography, which Alex Haley almost refused to complete because X was so committed to telling his life narrative by extolling the virtues of Nation of Islam rather than telling the rags-to-riches neoliberal life narrative so familiar to American audiences. Haley won; despite the fact that X understood his subjectivity and indeed his own story in different terms than those Haley himself accepted, the narrative that Haley produced nonetheless conformed to the conventions of the autobiography as Haley understood them. The cultural differences—even between a member of the Nation of Islam and a nonmember African American— were great enough that Haley believed he had to significantly "domesticate" the form and content of X's narrative in order for audiences to understand it as a life narrative at all—and, more crucially, for X's life to be incorporated into the American national mythology.[64]

Mam's own reticence to speak about certain aspects of her life—in particular those aspects about sexual abuse—is a window into the details that are most likely to be questioned by people who doubt her in Cambodia. As Mam's narrative depicts the events related to her sexual exploitation (and that of her poster children) to conform to the requirements of the tell-all memoir, Cambodian cultural norms for storytelling and silence are necessarily challenged. These details in particular are the ones that Marks's investigation turned up to be considered false by neighbors of Mam's. In conforming to Western expectations for the slave narrative, even with its deployment of strategies of displacement, Mam's story reveals too much; it challenges the cultural silences and patriarchal values she describes, and thus it is made the subject of scrutiny by her peers. The inherent contradictions between the narrative that the amanuensis has to tell to sell books and the narrative that the living slave narrator wants to tell undermine any possibility that the name "Somaly Mam" can maintain its coherence as an individual author's name.

In the moments where Mam reminds us that she hates telling this story, we witness the fissures in the proper name. She explains explicitly that the effects of Pol Pot's reign significantly diminish Cambodians' propensity to discuss their lives: "The more you let people know about yourself—the more you speak—the more you expose yourself to danger. It was important not to see, not to hear, not to know anything about what was happening. This is a very Cambodian attitude toward life."[65] When culturally enforced silences are exposed, the stakes of speaking out are higher, and there arise abundant opportunities for claims of fraud to emerge from the very people who profit or benefit from the silence. Essentially, this puts all international memoirists at risk because they have told the story that matters to their communities at home, and then they collaborate with others to tell the story that matters to donors and human rights organizations and media in the United States. These can be two different stories, and nonetheless, both can be true to a person's experience. However, these stories are translated in terms of language, culture, religion, gender, caste/class, politics, and indeed storytelling conventions in such a way that they can be comprehensible and consumable by Western audiences. This might give the appearance of discrepancies in a person's life narrative, and, in the worst-case scenario, this process of translation can produce a fitting narrative that does not fit the actual events of a person's life. Thus, compound authorship, so common to the slave narrative, is inherently compromising, especially in the cases of transnational translation.

Mam as Representation

Whereas the autobiography of the average person (if there is such a thing) is subject to the autobiographical pact that connects the subject of the text to the name of the individual on the cover, the new slave narrator (and other human rights autobiographers) is required to play a dangerous double-naming game. Simultaneously, the name on the cover indicates that the events in the text are a representation of a unique individual and that the story told in its pages will perform a representation of hundreds or thousands more like her. Thus, the name "Somaly Mam" no longer stands only for the one verifiable woman named on the cover. Instead, as Mam repeatedly suggests of her relationship to all other women held in sexual bondage, "It's as if we are the same person." As such a representative, Mam feels she has to "wear the scars" of the other women she hopes to protect and rescue from sexual enslavement, even though acting as a verifiably authentic representative of such a mass of diverse women is impossible.[66]

As a result, the narratives of these few chosen slave narrators must act as representative samples of a diverse array of forms of victimization and slavery. As Vincent Carretta argues of Olaudah Equiano's use of composite narration, "Print allows him to resurrect not only himself publicly from the 'social death' enslavement had imposed on him, but also the millions of other diasporan Africans he represented. By combining his own experiences with those of others he refashioned himself as *the* African."[67] The same can be said of Somaly Mam's complicated narrative negotiations. Mam was catapulted into a position that encouraged her to forge an identity that would speak for all Cambodian victims of sexual enslavement. Her impulse to, perhaps, include some composite portraits of slavery that she witnessed and her encouragement of other young women to tell composite stories is much like what Carretta ascribes to Equiano. And there is no doubt that Equiano's narrative was central to the success of the abolitionist movement in Britain in the late eighteenth century precisely because he was able to represent so many African lives lost to the slave trade, just as Mam's story has brought much-needed attention to contemporary forms of slavery.

Insofar as the witness testimony is meant to elevate the status of a single experience to that of the collective, there is no question that the genre's narrative conventions and the demands of nonprofit supporters practically require the kind of composite narration that Mam is accused of creating. As Lara Langer Cohen writes of the nineteenth-century abolitionists' influence on the construction of the traditional slave narrative, "Less concerned with individual life stories than with establishing a unified picture of slavery, they jettisoned or massaged details in favor of representative experience. Even when abolitionist editors did not directly intervene in slaves' narratives, the movement's public relations imperatives and the conventions of white literary culture almost inevitably mediated their production."[68] Fraud and authenticity were, thus, "instrumentalized categories, not definitive ones."[69] Since all slave narratives were manipulated to one degree or another to meet the expectations of the abolitionist audiences, the specter of politically expedient claims of fraud prompted vociferous performances of authenticity in legitimizing letters, extensive "written by himself" proclamations, and apologia introductions. Like the nineteenth-century narrators, Mam was confronted with the burden of representation, which required that she both represent her own individual story and allow her life to stand in for the thousands of women that her organization hoped to save. This inevitably led to "massaging" a life narrative in favor of a collective voice that had the capacity to represent wounds that she herself had not suffered.

In addition to those strategies of displacement previously discussed, then, Mam brings our attention to another strategy of displacement, one that is critical to the genre of the new slave narrative. She creates what Sidonie Smith and Julia Watson call the "composite I"—a first-person narrative voice in which the narrator speaks not only for herself but on behalf of other people who have suffered the same traumatic fate.[70] This "composite I" may be most familiar from the Rigoberta Menchú controversy of the 1990s.[71] When scholar David Stoll made his own name synonymous with attempting to dismantle Guatemalan activist Rigoberta Menchú's story (as Carretta did with Equiano and Marks did with Mam), he was forced to admit and was repeatedly reminded that the *testimonio* genre testified to the experiences and politics of the collective. When Menchú narrated her experiences, she included moments that she did not personally witness, but the stories she told nonetheless represented what was true for the people whom her narrative was meant to represent—"all poor Guatemalans." Her composite narrative catapulted those oppressed masses onto the global political map and helped to end a government war against them. As Mary Louise Pratt noted of testimonio, "The category of 'experience' is thus ruled simultaneously by paradigms of individualism (uniqueness) and of collectivity (exemplarity)."[72] That the unique and exemplary aspects of experience may come into conflict or require a composite portrait is undeniable, and that these two models for representation come from two different cultural traditions reinforces the problem of the ghostwriter as cultural translator. Furthermore, for women of color, it is practically impossible to speak without being read as representative of entire demographics in any case because of the extraordinary limitations on the diversity of women and people of color who gain access to political platforms. No matter how Mam's book was written, it would have been read as representative even if she had not figured herself as such. Moreover, as Leslie Barnes suggests, Mam is held up as representative of all women who are engaged in the sex trade in Cambodia, whether they are working voluntarily or by force, which leads to the problematic conflation of trafficking and sex work that is so common to anti-sex-trafficking advocacy efforts. Her status as representative thus endangers women who are engaged in the sex trade consensually but who are subject to the raids and arrests that have resulted from Mam's advocacy efforts.[73] This hyper-representativeness increases the skepticism regarding Mam's veracity.

Of course, Mam is not and cannot be representative of all the women who are trafficked in Cambodia. Her story—even if every word of it is true—is unique to her experience and, at this point, is more than twenty years in the past. Even her experience of escaping and her elevation as a celebrity survivor place her outside the bounds of the vast majority of those who are enslaved in Cambodia today. And yet authors like Mam are held to account for any contradictions that can be easily attributable to this generic tension. In the court of public opinion, there are no evidentiary standards, no judge or jury, no lawyers, no cross-examination, no necessary or equal right of the defendant to face her accusers, no equal standing in the court, no right to a defense, no calling of one's own witnesses, no equal access to the medium of presentation utilized by one's accuser. People who are tainted with the brush of fraud carry that weight and have no adequate recourse. As Leigh Gilmore suggests, while the timeline of scandal is short, the timeline of justice is long.[74] Those who seek to clear their names may never have a chance at adequate representation, and if they do, it takes significant time to gain traction, but the sound-bite-worthiness of scandal reaches a fever pitch quickly and can mark a person's story and life with immediate and long-lasting rabidity.

THE SURVIVOR-SAVIOR AND THE AUTOBIOGRAPHICAL MOVEMENT

As representative of such an extraordinary range of identities, Mam's name is further expected to carry the role of the survivor-savior. This convention positions the survivor as an exemplar of the call to action at the center of the long-form new slave narrative. Smith and Watson's description of the "composite I" not only incorporates others like the narrator but also "blends the highly stylized victim-voice with those of the social worker, the editor-ghost-writer, the publishing house more generally, and the rescue mission."[75] In Smith and Watson's formulation, sometimes those highly stylized voices are not the author's own—as would be the case for ghostwritten books but also for those that include prefaces and other legitimating documents penned by other writers and activists. However, as new slave narrators ground their proposal for action in the activism they have themselves engaged in before writing their narratives, they describe their own efforts to advocate before legislators (Bok), care for the needs of victims (Lloyd), or run international nonprofits (Cadet, Akallo, Bok) and thus take on the role of the social workers and the activists themselves. In the process of describing their work as activists, the first-person gaze of the narrative turns from the inward description of the development of their own subjectivity in freedom to the humanitarian gaze of one who must compellingly describe the plight of others. Of course, survivor-centered strategies, survivor-led organizations, and survivor-grounded discourses are critical to effective advocacy against slavery and for victims. This demand for the survivor-savior within the genre, however, inherently presents a conflict, again at the level of the name. The victim Somaly Mam must gain the readers' trust by evoking sympathy for her individual suffering and weakness; at the same time, the savior Somaly Mam requires her readers' trust in her fortitude and generosity so that they will entrust her with donations. This balancing act between strength and weakness, empowerment and suffering, victim and savior, can create fissures in a narrative and in the expectations for the narrative that narrators struggle to bridge. As critics of Frederick Douglass wondered how someone so articulate could be a former slave, critics of Mam wondered how someone so powerful and well connected could have truly been enslaved in Phnom Penh's brothels. Mam's narrative, constantly walking the fine line between revealing her most gruesome sexual traumas and maintaining the power to tell only the story that she authorized, is haunted by this additional, weighty duality of survivor and savior that was expected to be carried by the name "Somaly Mam."

As Mam's then husband, Pierre LeGros, predicted, when the trope of the victim-savior is employed most successfully, the public often elevates the narrator to celebrity status. Inasmuch as the narrator uses her individual story to indicate the millions of people suffering like her, the publication of the narrative that bears her name—along with the awards, speaking tours, and journalistic attention to her individual suffering and bravery that accompanies it—often forces the narrator into the limelight and makes it seem like she is *individually* the center of the suffering universe. Dina Francesca Haynes critiques film celebrities who take on social justice mantles in her article "The Celebritization of Human Trafficking," writing, "A 'sexy' topic, human trafficking is not only susceptible to alluring, fetishistic, and voyeuristic narratives, it plays into the celebrity-as-rescuer-of-victim ideal that receives a huge amount of attention from the media and the public."[76] The same can be said of the celebritization of the survivors themselves, especially those who become slave narrators and public activists. This victim-savior turned celebrity and his or her individual experiences then animate debates regarding the prevalence, scope, types, locations, and even existence of contemporary slavery. Legislators and advocates appropriately turn to survivors for their advice, but only a few celebrity survivors gain the highest levels of access and garner the most resources for their cause. As a result, the new slave narrative is driven by a tendency to situate the activism of the narrator in these celebrity-like terms and to package the narratives with the testimonies of celebrity companions, like Kristof or Clinton or Sarandon, who can attest to the societal ascendency of the narrator.

The higher Mam's star rose, the more it was guaranteed that scrutiny over her life and narrative would emerge. Her name became more than a marker of the meek Cambodian girl who was silent for so long—it became a brand and a cause. "Somaly Mam" became a social movement. When Mam's name became synonymous with a social movement, the pressure was even higher to represent the masses *and* represent the humanitarian approach to ending forced sex work—all in the body of a person who is singled out as exceptional, a celebrity. Once an autobiographical social movement emerged through her eponymous foundation and through the prizes that were awarded in her name, not the name of AFESIP, any perception of fraudulence in Mam's story could be equated with the fraudulence of her entire organization, indeed, the entire movement. The gaps and fissures and screen memories that are typical of life narrative were then all too easily transferred to accusations of gaps in AFESIP's services, cooked books, and trumped-up successes. The result is that when the name of the survivor-savior is compromised, the autobiographical social movement is compromised as well.[77]

THE VULNERABILITY OF THE SLAVE NARRATIVE

Essentially, the slave narrator's conformity to genre conventions is treated as a veracity test. Adherence to genre conventions implicitly advances truth claims. Ironically, this veracity test increases significantly the responsibility of the author to conform to sensationalized, composite, and representative notions of truth, which will satiate the demands of the donors for stories that they recognize and that organizations can sell. As Leigh Gilmore has written, "Testimonial accounts are anchored in experience, but they do not simply draw their authority from how well or fully they comport with verifiable fact. . . . Testimony acquires meaning and authority from the historical force of genre."[78] The genre conventions of the slave narrative enabled Mam and her amanuensis to structure a story line that would provide a sense of legitimacy and authority that would compel audiences to take heed through its utter familiarity. Her narrative and those she encouraged her clients to tell provided organizations with the poster children that would fuel a movement and the humanitarian porn that would compel donations. Mam was the subject of those voyeuristic impulses, which compelled her and her colleagues to shape her experience and her work to conform to nonprofit desires and strategies. In the search for the perfect victim and the compelling lede, organizations and their donors impose implicit expectations that those who seek to be read as victims should conform to conventions of testimony that circumscribe the experience of enslavement instead of revealing its complex or surprising contours. Thus, generic conventions come to be understood not as writerly strategy but as requirements to which narratives must conform or else be illegible or unrecognizable and, in the end, unfundable. And in an environment where the very existence of slavery is in doubt, legibility is of the utmost importance for survivors who wish to make a case for addressing injustice and exploitation. Indeed, humanitarian narratives are expected to be *more true* than any other memoirs or life narratives written by people whose lives are less public, less traumatized.

As we have seen, those conventions also put pressures on the narrative that create fissures. The name Somaly Mam on the cover of *The Road of Lost Innocence* is thus an expansive one that is inclusive of all the identities she has to adorn in order to be recognized as a slave narrator—"slave," survivor, savior, celebrity, fundraiser, social movement. These compulsory and nonetheless competing narrative demands are doomed to fail any test of veracity that is based on a neoliberal, "pull yourself up by your bootstraps" model of the individualist autobiographical compact.[79] As a result, the narrative of the enslaved and oppressed always lives in the shadows of suspicion, doubted by those with a much more prominent platform and political and social cachet. This is evidenced by the fact that so many of the most prominent slave narrators of the nineteenth century were doubted (Douglass, Jacobs, and Equiano to name a few). The "parasitic" nature of the fraud hunter is seen most vividly in the fact that scholars are practically required to cite Vincent Carretta's name and his suspicions of fraud any time we discuss Equiano (or David Stoll's any time we discuss Rigoberta Menchú), even when the critic's supposed evidence is easily discredited or explained away. In this same way, Somaly Mam's name is now intimately intertwined with her doubter, Simon Marks—a journalist who has no other claim to fame than his take-down of Mam. Whether allegations stick or not, the new slave narrative cannot escape the demands of the genre, nor can it escape what Watson and Smith call the "suspicious reading" practices that turn readers of rights narratives into pseudo detectives.[80] Lejeune suggests, in fact, that the very promise that the book is autobiographical inspires readers to search for dissonance between the subject of the text and the life to which it refers.[81] Essentially, there is an inherent, implied detective reader of all autobiography—and, we must conclude, the reader of the slave narrative is no exception.

The nineteenth-century slave narrators were no strangers to the doubts that Mam encounters now. Even Harriet Jacobs's narrative *Incidents in the Life of a Slave Girl*, one of the most revered and widely disseminated of all the narratives, was considered fraudulent not so long ago. People assumed that Lydia Maria Child, Jacobs's editor and friend, authored the text. In an effort to stave off the inevitable doubt regarding her authorship and the veracity of her long escape from slavery, Jacobs wrote in her introduction, "Reader, be assured this narrative is no fiction. . . . I am aware that some of my adventures may seem incredible; but they are nevertheless, strictly true. I have not exaggerated the wrongs inflicted by Slavery; on the contrary, my descriptions fall far short of the facts."[82] There were also accusations that Mam's role model, Solomon Northup, had misrepresented his experiences, as people claimed that he was a collaborator of his captors when he was abducted into slavery—questions again of agency that would ostensibly refute his claims of enslavement.[83] Frederick Douglass, taking up Northup's cause, said of his narrative, "Its truth is far greater than fiction."[84] William Wells Brown, in an effort to represent the vast diversity of experiences of slavery and to entertain his white abolitionist audiences, went so far as to produce a patchwork of plagiarized stories from both black and white authors in the creation of his fictional and nonfictional texts alike. Critic Geoffrey Sanborn has recently dubbed him "the most original artist of nonoriginality in American history."[85]

What seems most useful from these historical protests against readerly doubt is the slave narrators' continued insistence on accepting the challenge of writing both a true-sounding and a true-to-the-facts narrative—not because they felt they had to fabricate events but simply because of the impossibility of capturing the enormous horrors of slavery. Like William Wells Brown, who keenly observed, "Slavery Has Never Been Represented— Slavery Can Never Be Represented,"[86] slave narrators (whether writing in the nineteenth or twenty-first centuries) are in a bind of representation that calls for them to express, in full, the most unintelligible experiences of suffering—truth that is stranger than fiction. The result is a genre that cannot but be doubted because of the near impossibility of capturing in language such depths of depravity, and where the slave narrator is able to provide a glimpse, we cannot fathom it and are not willing to face our complicity in it.

Where does that leave the narrators who use writing as a liberatory practice? They are left to be devoured by the very public that promoted them in the first place—at times because they call into question the very foundations of our economy as well as our complicity in it. While readers often embrace the critique of the gendered oppression that Mam describes as happening in faraway Cambodia, readers often do not recognize the ways those structures of oppression—gendered and otherwise—are endemic in the West as well. Slave narratives critique Western capitalism for its propensity for violence and exploitation. They call into question the very aspects of our economy and social relations that make readers' lives comfortable. They undermine notions of uplift and individual subjectivity inherent in the neoliberal life narrative and thus the foundations of our own subjectivity. And so finding gaps and holes in the fabric of those testimonies allows readers to redeem or extract themselves from responsibility for slavery, allows them to disavow the discomfort of complicity. Acknowledging complicity requires sacrifices that most are not willing to make, so we sacrificed Somaly Mam instead.

Thus, slave narratives seem doomed to be haunted by suspicious reading, perhaps even more than other human rights narratives. To make a case for social justice or human rights is to insist on a particular version of the truth—one that tends to be a counternarrative to the master discourse, which emerges through recollection, through memoir. Thus, the truth is always going to be mediated through genre and will generate suspicion. And when that counterdiscourse calls into question the very foundations of freedom that the Western economic imagination is grounded upon, the doubt that the written word inspires is magnified infinitely. Marks domesticates Mam; he shames her, shrinks her, silences her, erases her—and her enslavement. By doing so, he suggests to Western readers that they need not worry about the capitalist structures that allow for labor and sex exploitation in the global economy. Instead, he focuses his attention on this one subject, whose story was made to represent millions, and thereby elevates his own diminution of her to that level of representativeness as well. If we need not concern ourselves with Somaly Mam anymore, then we can lazily conclude that we need not concern ourselves with the systemic structures that facilitate sexual exploitation.

Ultimately, Mam was created by the genre of the slave narrative, and she was destroyed by it as well. What the genre created was simply a narrativized, composite version of the verifiable person whose name was on the cover; however, what the genre destroyed were the woman, her reputation, and her ability to help others. Whether or not Mam was telling the truth is less relevant than how the generic demands of the slave narrative shaped her capacity (and other formerly enslaved people's capacity) to tell the truth, her ability to control the exposure of her violated body and those of the women with whom she worked, and, in the end, her capacity to extend global wealth and resources to the victims of forced sexual labor. Those generic demands required that Mam reveal the everyday violence of sexual slavery—precisely the same moments of violence that were then questioned by journalists and activists. Indeed, her conformity reveals how generic conventions that require voyeuristic "humanitarian pornography" of violence are, at the one and the same time, the best route to garnering the attention of the human rights establishment and the litmus test for veracity that dooms slave narrators to the proverbial dustbin of history. Somaly Mam's extraordinary rise to fame and tumultuous fall from grace are indicators of the way in which the generic demands of human rights discourse actually commit a kind of assault on survivors' agency and control over their own narratives, even long after they are freed from bondage and slavery.

The point is not whether Somaly Mam told the truth. If we agree that the slave narrative empowers formerly enslaved people not only to write themselves into existence but to rewrite the narrative and discourse that has shaped their lives and expression, then we must look to the way the new slave narrative is doing more than simply recalling a factual account of abuse. We must look to these narratives not for the truth of a single person's experience but for what they can tell us about slavery as well as what they can tell us about the current movement against slavery. The conclusion ahead critiques our seeming inability to hear the voices of survivors of contemporary forms of slavery through the noise of our demands upon them and proposes a way forward guided by the ethics we can glean from the new slave narrative.

CONCLUSION
Collegial Reading

Read together, new slave narrators challenge us to interrogate the cultural expectations for veracity that encourage suspicion of their claims, to sympathize with any narrator's inevitable internal contradictions and dissonances, to recognize the complex interplay between individual experience and representation of a larger community of survivors, to integrate the diversity of their voices into our own newly complicated perspectives, and to adopt a systemic approach to our interpretation of institutions that support slavery. In the course of this study, however, we have seen that the lived experiences of the new slave narrators (and of the survivor community more broadly) have been co-opted, sidelined, ignored, and even berated and pathologized. Survivors nonetheless boldly resist reexploitation and persist in their efforts to shape the discourse around slavery and to effect change in collaboration with (and at times in spite of) organized antislavery efforts. Even when they find their stories appropriated to fit unfamiliar purposes, new slave narrators often break through the conventions of the genre to insist that each individual slave narrator is "more than a survivor" (as a recent survivor-led art exhibit announces), to prove that they have substantive ideas to contribute to efforts developed to protect others from similar suffering.[1] As a collected body of protest literature, the new slave narrative certainly represents a battle cry against slavery, but it is also a politicized critique of the institutions of capitalism that precipitate the forms of exploitation under which vulnerable people suffer and a bold indictment of those who would minimize their experiences for profit or politics. Simultaneously, new slave narrators call on readers to see them as experts not only in their own experiences but in the structures that maintain global inequalities and, thereby, slavery.

Reading these narratives closely for the transcripts of oppression that accompany both slavery and not-yet-freedom reveals a much more intractable set of institutional and societal structures than most activists are prepared to address. The narratives are a testament to the fact that slavery is not an exception of capitalism and democracy but is endemic to it. The new slave narrative makes slavery real, present, legible, even mundane, though antislavery activists and scholars often sensationalize it. Despite the shocking declarations of horror on the covers of the books or the disorientation of the in medias res beginnings in the midst of capture or violence, the content of these narratives serves as a testament to the everydayness of not necessarily slavery itself but the conditions that make slavery possible today and have for centuries. They reveal the crises of everyday living for the most marginalized people: the precarity of human life, human dignity, and human potential that results from systemic misogyny, racism, classism, and xenophobia.

The language- and narrative-centered approach that this book employs situates survivor voices at the forefront of the discussion regarding contemporary forms of slavery and our (inadequate) response to the structures they deem responsible for contemporary forms of slavery and unfreedom. This approach provides a critical, survivor-centered angle from which to approach a particular moment in the history of abolition, which is still nascent, still adaptable. There is still the opportunity to alter the antislavery landscape in response to the revelations of the new slave narrative. In this effort, we can heed Rosemary Jolly's call to "see our complicity in ways of framing victim-survivors and their suffering as strange . . . [and] begin to envisage and potentially inhabit an uncomfortable world *with* the victim-survivor who testifies, rather than being complicit in the one from which she is estranged."[2] The work of privileging the voices of the enslaved is not as easy as it sounds. To start, most enslaved people do not have access to platforms that allow their ideas to be disseminated. When they do gain access to the publishing industry, their ideas are significantly mediated by editors, amanuenses, other activists, and the ideological constructs in circulation. Even then, their contributions do not always conform to "academic discourse" or meet the standards of "professionalism" in the nonprofit industry and are thus all too quickly disregarded by many who purport to work on their behalf. Even more daunting for some is the fact that privileging slavery's victims as experts means unleashing a radical critique of the very foundations of democracy and capitalism that can upset basic assumptions. Though slavery does not constitute a critical aspect of the global economy, admitting that new slave narrators are telling the truth about their enslavement means that we have to accept that the freedom and equality that many of our societies hold dear are fragile promises at best, impossible dreams at worst. But if we want to know what slavery and freedom mean in the twenty-first century, we have to accept as our intellectual colleagues the very people for whom those two concepts are most urgent and intimately known.

To this end, there is nothing necessarily unethical or voyeuristic about the desire to hear the true stories of people who have been oppressed in the world. To the contrary, a daily reckoning with the suffering of others might be a route to an ethical relationship with those who do not share our own privilege, so long as we are also prepared to engage with their critiques and solutions as well. Reading the first-person narrative is one such intimate form of reckoning. In the process of resisting the spectacle, the bodily detail, the flesh and blood, in writing narratives that at times seem underwhelmingly sober and distant, however, the narrators revise our reading practices. If we consider these autobiographies as guides to the legibility of slavery in our contemporary context, as instruction manuals in the interpretation of the signs of slavery and in reading alongside the survivor, then the new slave narratives can be understood as teaching the lessons necessary to shape an informed collegial reading practice.

In that educational effort, the new slave narrative often employs an identificatory process that has long been a staple of human rights narratives. Scholars of the humanitarian narrative from Adam Smith to Martha Nussbaum have remarked on how literature creates an "imaginative identification" between narrators and readers that allows them to empathize with the suffering of others as if they were themselves suffering. Lynn Hunt suggests that it was this literary imaginary that inspired nineteenth-century abolitionists to urge formerly enslaved people to pen their life narratives.[3] Those identifications purportedly prompted people to be more concerned about the rights of enslaved people in the United States and to fight to eradicate an institution that supported an entire economy. According to Martha Nussbaum, this kind of "sentimental education" provides opportunities for more engaged, humanitarian citizenship through the reading of literature, which "wrest[s] from our frequently obtuse and blunted imaginations an acknowledgement of those who are other than ourselves, both in concrete circumstances, and even in thought and emotion."[4]

Whether these identificatory schemes actually mobilize readers to action beyond a mere momentary consideration is debatable. Elaine Scarry remarks that those generous imaginings of others are difficult to attain and inadequate to the task of ensuring rights.[5] There is the risk, in promoting a sentimental education, that structures of power that have marginalized the voices of the enslaved will be replicated, that the armchair activist will merely feel a false or fleeting affinity for those who suffer around the world, that such imaginative identifications more often reiterate the comfortable distance between a Western, privileged us and an impoverished, suffering other. There is the problematic basic premise that the most widely circulated human rights narratives are written specifically for American and British audiences by/about people who are largely not of those cultures and that their stories thus become spectacles of otherness, sedimenting notions of "natural" difference and inequality. Saidiya Hartman argues that this kind of humanitarian distance has historically led the abolitionist to "feel for himself instead of for those whom this exercise in imagination presumably is designed to reach."[6] These are all concerns regarding the function of the human rights life narrative and its reception that animate this study.

It is clear that despite these anxieties, the authors of the new slave narratives themselves often inscribe their expectations of a sentimental reading practice into their narratives. Bok, Lloyd, Nazer, Amaya, Phelps, Bello, and many others end their narratives with accounts of the powerful influence of their storytelling on others. But that influence does not precisely require identification; it requires action. When the new slave narrators describe the desired effects of sharing their life narratives and their expertise on the subject of slavery, they call upon their audiences to use the positions and platforms to which they have access to employ their message as an impetus for informed engagement. Bok recalls of his early experience on the lecture circuit, "I not only managed to get the audiences to understand what I was saying. I was able to move them."[7] And he celebrates the fact that his testimony "played a role in getting the American President to speak out against Sudan for the first time ever."[8] Lloyd reflects on testimony she gave with the clients of her Girls Education Mentoring Service program, which she indicates was "all about survivor voices, survivor achievements, survivor leadership," that acted as "a stunning affirmation that offers a rebuttal to all the people who didn't believe in us, in me, in any girl who has been sexually exploited,"[9] and she celebrates how their recommendations led to substantive, survivor-centered legislation in New York and nationally. Many of the narratives end with sections on what the reader can do next or a list of organizations that can support activist efforts inspired by reading the book. New slave narrators understand themselves not as alienated warriors but as ambassadors for change, and their narratives are thus characterized by an optimistic purposiveness to move nonsurvivors to individual and collective action.

The new slave narrators thus call upon us to engage their narratives as *collegial readers*, readers who stand alongside the narrator rather than remain distanced critics, who read with the grain instead of against it, who humble ourselves by amplifying rather than professing, and who embrace the potential of belief rather than skepticism. They ask us not to speak *for* them but to engage with them so that we can locate and embrace our own responsibility for interrogating and dismantling the structures that provide access to freedoms for some but not all. They ask us to set aside our politics and our skepticism and our pride, for just a moment, to read generously so that we might be convinced by a survivor of human rights violations of something otherwise largely illegible. But the narrators do not remain neutral, nor do they ask us to be. They ask us to identify with their intellectual positions—though not necessarily their positionality—and to let their politics guide ours, even if only for the time it takes to read and contemplate their words. It is a necessary act of humility for us to listen instead of stridently interpret for just a moment, and it is an act of courage on the part of the narrators to assume the readers' trust at all.

A collegial literary critical approach to modern slavery differs from the quantitative or social science approaches typical of much of the current research on slavery in that it does not employ big data or a deliberately distanced approach in its efforts to account for or describe the terrain of contemporary slavery; instead it lends us a more receptive ear for the intimate language people use to describe slavery and the way that differs among survivors, scholars, journalists, and other writers. The idea is to adopt a collegial reading practice that will deepen our understanding of slavery and freedom, grounded in the individual perspectives of survivors as well as in the (sometimes harmonious, sometimes dissonant) voice of the collective. Given the high value placed on suspicious reading practices in the academy and in some arenas of public discourse, however, the danger is that in the pursuit of our intellectual agendas, we ironically risk appropriating the narratives of survivors of human rights violations to engage in our own internal culture wars and political infighting. We have seen how divisive and destructive that can be. Thus, inasmuch as a collegial reading practice is meant to amplify the ideas and expertise of the narrators, it calls on us to perform a sympathetic reading of the text, akin, perhaps, to Stephen Best and Sharon Marcus's calls for literary critics to attend to that which is "evident, perceptible, apprehensible in texts; what is neither hidden nor hiding . . . [that which] insists on being looked at rather than what we must train ourselves to see through."[10] This is not to suggest that the critic remain personally neutral in regard to the oppression depicted in the pages of the new slave narrative (quite the opposite is intended, in fact) or act as an undiscerning ally, but she need not play the antagonist or the skeptic in regard to the text either. A collegial approach would allow the reader to engage intimately and humanely with a life narrative in an effort to better understand and represent how survivors of human rights violations overtly articulate their perceptions and responses to the violence enacted upon them and the politics that those experiences inspire in them rather than to locate the meanings, pathologies, or ideologies hidden in the interstices of the text, as literary critics tend to do. A collegial reading requires that significant emphasis be placed on understanding and unpacking the complexity of thought and perspective that is available in a close, committed reading of an individual text or a field of related texts.

The aims of collegial reading may be particular to nonfictional life narratives in which there is an implied and politicized connection between a real living narrator and a real living reader. There is an additional ethical imperative involved in engaging with human rights narratives in particular, which suggests that even the most faithful "surface reading" of an individual text is not in itself sufficient nor entirely possible. Regarding the impossibility, we can neither identify entirely with the narrator or even represent the "surface" of the text with perfect precision because the act of reading itself is as mediated as the text's production. It is impossible to simply "indicate what a text says about itself" in a way that removes it from the context in which it is produced or, more to the point, in which it is being consumed. We are not essential to the work the narratives do, but we are supplemental. When we merely describe, we also supplement, add, mediate, arrange, re-present. In aligning one's analysis with the impulses of the text, the critic nonetheless must identify the difference between analysis and text to introspectively interrogate the discourses that inform our own reading and writing practices. This should not be a deterrent to reading or writing about the narratives, but it is a caution that requires us to be explicit about our own interactions with the texts and thoughtful about the influences on our own readings of the narratives.

The new slave narratives also repeatedly suggest that the aim of our collegiality as readers should not stop at repeating, reproducing, and describing their stories (though these are all valuable) but that we should extend our platforms, privileges, and opportunities to the antislavery work led by survivors. In addition to amplifying the experiences and expertise of survivors, the collegial reader can also elucidate the contexts, histories, and structures within which the authors operate and about which the authors have contributed their individual perspectives. A collegial reading approach may assist in identifying and critiquing the currents of thought and debates into which survivors are sometimes thrust and the ways those contexts circumscribe survivors' own opportunities to describe and interpret their experiences. A collegial reading practice can also increase the figurative synapses between networks of knowledge production to connect the impulses radiating from individual narratives to other potential colleagues—with one another, with other narratives of human rights violations, with other memoirs, with other theories of slavery and oppression—thereby expanding the discourse community in which survivor lives and ideas make meaning.

In order to forge such a collegial reading environment, we need not come to a consensus on all issues related to human rights or on our interpretations of the narratives that address them. Indeed, collegiality is characterized by productive and respectful debate. Many of the new slave narrators are evangelical Christians, while I am a committed agnostic. Some of the narratives reveal homophobic beliefs, and a couple of them condemn the whole ethnic group from which their captors descend, and, of course, I do not endorse those aspects of their texts. Some of the narrators believe that it is inappropriate to describe engagement in the sex trade as work, and after careful consideration of their arguments as well as the arguments of others—survivors of slavery and sex workers alike—I respectfully disagree. I know that many of my survivor-collaborators in the antislavery movement would not be my colleagues on many other issues that I hold dear. Nonetheless, the conversations that these differences elicit are productive and engaging, and they should animate collaborative progress rather than the seemingly unbridgeable divisions that now plague the academic and activist communities who work on contemporary forms of slavery. It is my hope that where this study takes critical turns, it is read not as an oppositional polemic but as a constructive commentary on our current discourse around slavery and that it provides avenues for further discussion and change inspired by and led by survivors of slavery.

The new slave narrative represents an avenue through which survivors challenge the limits of political expression, combat the structures that maintain slavery's illegibility, critique the limits of freedom, contradict the political narratives imposed upon them, and promote social justice activism among the reading public. Reading alone may not be sufficient to effect change, but as colleagues of those who write of rights violations, we affirm our commitment to engage in their struggle. The new slave narrative challenges us to transform our critical reading practices into the "NGO *avant la lettre*" that Wai Chee Dimock describes, which employs analytic and political powers derived from the transhistorical, transnational, nongovernmental potentials of scholarship.[11] These narratives empower us as readers and scholars to engage in contemporary political discourse through acting as a megaphone for the critiques that survivors make available and which our practices of close reading can reveal. They also encourage us to move from scholarship to activism, through which we not only describe, historicize, and contextualize the mechanisms of oppression but take it as our responsibility to undo them. Through that scholar activism, we amplify the challenges that marginalized people make against the normative rhetorics to which they are subject. Collegial readings can thus have real influence on the way laborers around the world are read and regarded.

LIST OF NEW SLAVE NARRATIVES

Below is a list of all first-person primary sources that were included in this study. With different parameters, this list might include several other books, including several child soldier narratives that clearly conform to most definitions of contemporary slavery but whose authors do not articulate their experiences as slavery. I consider this list to include the core book-length texts of the new slave narrative tradition thus far, which allows us to begin a discussion of the reemergence of the genre, but I expect that most other studies of the genre will be more inclusive.

NEW SLAVE NARRATIVES

Akofa, Henriette. *Une Esclave Moderne.* With Olivier Broca. Paris: Michel Lafon, 2000.

Amaya, Barbara. *Nobody's Girl: A Memoir of Lost Innocence, Modern Day Slavery, and Transformation.* Pittsburgh, PA: Animal, 2015.

Amony, Evelyn. *I Am Evelyn Amony: Reclaiming My Life from the Lord's Resistance Army.* Madison: University of Wisconsin Press, 2015.

Barnes, Wendy. *And Life Continues: Sex Trafficking and My Journey to Freedom.* Self-published, 2015.

Bender, Rebecca. *Roadmap to Redemption.* Self-published, 2013.

Bok, Francis. *Escape from Slavery: The True Story of My Ten Years in Captivity—and My Journey to Freedom in America.* With Edward Tivnan. New York: St. Martin's, 2003.

Cadet, Jean-Robert. *My Stone of Hope: From Haitian Slave Child to Abolitionist.* Austin: University of Texas, 2011.

——. *Restavec: From Haitian Slave Child to Middle-Class American.* Austin: University of Texas Press, 1998.

Crown, Mimi. *Stuck in Traffic.* Self-published, 2016.

Fatima. *Esclave a 11 Ans: Temoignage.* Paris: Flammarion, 2011.

Fernando, Beatrice. *In Contempt of Fate: The Tale of a Sri Lankan Sold into Servitude Who Survived to Tell It.* Self-published, 2005.

Flores, Theresa L. *The Sacred Bath: An American Teen's Story of Modern Day Slavery.* New York: iUniverse, 2007.

——. *The Slave Across the Street: The True Story of How an American Teen Survived the World of Human Trafficking.* With Peggy Sue Wells. Boise, ID: Ampelon, 2010.

Forsyth, Sarah. *Slave Girl.* London: CPI Bookmarque, 2009.

Hall, Shyima. *Hidden Girl: The True Story of a Modern-Day Child Slave.* With Lisa Wysocky. New York: Simon & Schuster, 2014.

Hayes, Sophie. *Trafficked: My Story of Surviving, Escaping, and Transcending Abduction into Prostitution.* London: Sourcebooks, 2013.

Jackson, Emma. *The End of My World: The Shocking True Story of a Young Girl Forced to Become a Sex Slave.* London: Ebury, 2010.

Jay, Alice. *Out of the Darkness: A Survivor's Story.* Southfield, MI: Manifold Grace, 2014.

Jinan. *Esclave de Daech.* With Thierry Oberle. Paris: Fayard, 2015.

Khalaf, Farida. *The Girl Who Escaped ISIS: This Is My Story.* New York: Atria, 2016.

Kim, Eunsun. *A Thousand Miles to Freedom: My Escape from North Korea.* With Sebastien Falletti. Trans. David Tian. New York: St. Martin's Griffin, 2015.

Lloyd, Rachel. *Girls Like Us: Fighting for a World Where Girls Are Not for Sale, an Activist Finds Her Calling and Heals Herself.* New York: Harper Collins, 2011.

Lobert, Annie. *Fallen: Out of the Sex Industry and into the Arms of the Savior.* Brentwood, TN: Worthy, 2015.

Luecha, Monluedee. *Child Sex Slave: A Memoir.* Self-published, 2012.

MacKenzie, Emily. *Runaway: Wild Child, Working Girl, Survivor.* London: Thistle, 2015.

Mam, Somaly. *Le Silence de L'Innocence.* Paris: Editions France Loisirs, 2005.

——. *The Road of Lost Innocence: The True Story of a Cambodian Heroine.* New York: Spiegel & Grau, 2008.

Marino, Jasmine Grace. *The Diary of Jasmine Grace: Trafficked. Recovered. Redeemed.* Self-published, 2016.

McDonnell, Faith and Grace Akallo. *Girl Soldier: A Story of Hope for Northern Uganda's Children.* Grand Rapids, MI: Chosen, 2007.

Muhsen, Zana. *Sold: One Woman's True Account of Modern Slavery.* With Andrew Crofts. London: Time Warner, 1991.

Murad, Nadia. *The Last Girl: My Story of Captivity, and My Fight Against the Islamic State.* New York: Tim Duggan, 2017.

Nagy, Timea. *Memoirs of a Sex Slave Survivor.* Toronto: Communication Dynamics, 2010.

Nazer, Mende. *Freedom: The Sequel to Slave.* With Damien Lewis. London: Endeavor, 2012.

——. *Slave: My True Story.* With Damien Lewis. New York: Public Affairs, 2003.

Okpara, Tina. *My Life Has a Price: A Memoir of Survival and Freedom.* With Cyril Guinet. Trans. Julie Jodter. Dakar: Amalion, 2012.

Oriola, Bukola. *Imprisoned: The Travails of a Trafficked Victim.* Self-published, 2009.

——. *A Living Label: An Inspirational Memoir and Guide*. Self-published, 2016.

Parker-Bello, Brook. *Living Inside the Rainbow: Wining the Battlefield of the Mind After Human Trafficking and Mental Bondage*. Self-published, 2013.

Phelps, Carissa. *Runaway Girl: Escaping Life on the Streets, One Helping Hand at a Time*. With Larkin Warren. New York: Viking, 2012.

Prum, Vannak Anan. Dead Eye and the Deep Blue Sea: A Graphic Memoir of Modern Slavery. With Jocelyn Pederick. New York: Seven Stories, 2018.

Rosenblatt, Katariina. *Stolen: The True Story of a Sex Trafficking Survivor*. With Cecil Murphey. Grand Rapids, MI: Revell, 2014.

NOTES

A NOTE ON LANGUAGE

1. Julia O'Connell Davidson recently edited an entire issue of *Anti-Trafficking Review* on the misappropriation of transatlantic slavery to describe contemporary forms of forced labor. See Julia O'Connell Davidson, "The Presence of the Past: Lessons of History for Anti-Trafficking Work," *Anti-Trafficking Review*, no. 9 (2017).

2. Tryon P. Woods, "Surrogate Selves: Notes on Anti-Trafficking and Anti-Blackness," *Social Identities* 19, no. 1 (January 2013): 126, 122, https://doi.org/10.1080/13504630 .2012.753348.

3. See, for instance, Laura María Agustín, *Sex at the Margins: Migration, Labour, Markets and the Rescue Industry* (London: Zed, 2007), 36–41; Kamala Kempadoo, "Abolitionism, Criminal Justice, and Transnational Feminism: Twenty-First-Century Perspectives on Human Trafficking," in *Trafficking and Prostitution Reconsidered: New Perspectives on Migration, Sex Work, and Human Rights*, ed. Kamala Kempadoo (Boulder, CO: Paradigm, 2012), xxvii; Joel Quirk, *The Anti-Slavery Project: From the Slave Trade to Human Trafficking* (Philadelphia: University of Pennsylvania Press, 2011), 157–63.

4. See, for instance, Elizabeth Bernstein, "Militarized Humanitarianism Meets Carceral Feminism: The Politics of Sex, Rights, and Freedom in Contemporary Anti-trafficking Campaigns," *Signs: Journal of Women in Culture and Society* 36, no. 1 (2010): 49–51; Gretchen Soderlund, "The Rhetoric of Revelation: Sex Trafficking and the Journalistic Exposé," *Humanity: An International Journal of Human Rights, Humanitarianism, and Development* 2, no. 2 (September 8, 2011): 193–211, https://doi.org/10.1353/hum.2011.0013; Jo Doezema, *Sex Slaves and Discourse Masters: The Construction of Trafficking* (New York: Zed, 2013), 77–105.

5. See, for instance, Michael Dottridge, "Eight Reasons Why We Shouldn't Use the Term 'Modern Slavery,'" OpenDemocracy, October 17, 2017, https://www

.opendemocracy.net/beyondslavery/michael-dottridge/eight-reasons-why-we
-shouldn-t-use-term-modern-slavery; Elena Shih, "Not in My 'Backyard Abolitionism': Vigilante Rescue Against American Sex Trafficking," *Sociological Perspectives* 59, no. 1 (2016): 66–90.

6. Claude Meillassoux, *The Anthropology of Slavery: The Womb of Iron and Gold* (Chicago: University of Chicago Press, 1991), 21–22.

PREFACE

1. Peter Landesman, "The Girls Next Door," sec. Magazine, *New York Times*, January 25, 2004, https://www.nytimes.com/2004/01/25/magazine/the-girls-next-door
.html.

2. Olaudah Equiano, *The Interesting Narrative of the Life of Olaudah Equiano*, ed.
Werner Sollors (New York: Norton Critical Editions, 2000), 41.

3. Ephraim Peabody, "Narratives of Fugitive Slaves," *Christian Examiner* 47, no. 1
(1849): 61–93.

4. Sidonie Smith and Julia Watson, "Witness or False Witness: Metrics of Authenticity, Collective I-Formations, and the Ethic of Verification in First-Person Testimony," *Biography* 35, no. 4 (2012): 596.

5. Rachel Banner, "Surface and Stasis: Re-reading Slave Narrative via *The History of
Mary Prince*," *Callaloo* 36, no. 2 (Spring 2013): 303.

INTRODUCTION: THE REEMERGENCE OF THE SLAVE
NARRATIVE IN THE TWENTY-FIRST CENTURY

1. Francis Bok, *Escape from Slavery: The True Story of My Ten Years in Captivity—and
My Journey to Freedom in America* (New York: Macmillan, 2003), 12.

2. Bok, 29.

3. Bok, 81.

4. Bok, 221.

5. Frances Smith Foster, *Witnessing Slavery: The Development of Ante-Bellum Slave
Narratives* (Madison: University of Wisconsin Press, 1979), ix.

6. Three collections of short narratives have been published that introduce the notion
of the new slave narrative, and they begin to suggest the conventions of the new
slave narrative. In addition to the journal articles I have published that are included
as sections of this book, several academic articles discuss the genre to date as well.
See Kevin Bales and Zoe Trodd, *To Plead Our Own Cause: Personal Stories by
Today's Slaves* (Ithaca, NY: Cornell University Press, 2013); Jesse Sage and Liora
Kasten, eds., *Enslaved: True Stories of Modern Day Slavery* (New York: St. Martin's Griffin, 2006); Laura T. Murphy, *Survivors of Slavery: Modern-Day Slave Nar-
ratives* (New York: Columbia University Press, 2014); Kelli Lyon Johnson, "The
New Slave Narrative: Advocacy and Human Rights in Stories of Contemporary
Slavery," *Journal of Human Rights* 12, no. 2 (2013): 242–58; Yogita Goyal, "African
Atrocity, American Humanity: Slavery and Its Transnational Afterlives," *Research
in African Literatures* 45, no. 3 (2014): 48–71; Abigail Ward, "Servitude and Slave

Narratives: Tracing 'New Slaveries' in Mende Nazer's *Slave* and Zadie Smith's 'The Embassy of Cambodia,'" *Wasafiri* 31, no. 3 (2016): 42–48; Kaelyn Kaoma, "Child Soldier Memoirs and the 'Classic' Slave Narrative: Tracing the Origins," *Life Writing* 15, no. 2 (2017), 195–210; Andrea Nicholson, "A Survivor Centric Approach—The Importance of Contemporary Slave Narratives to the Anti-Slavery Agenda" in *The SAGE Handbook of Human Trafficking and Modern Slavery*, ed. Sasha Poucki and Jennifer Bryson-Clarke (London: Sage, 2018): 259.

7. My use of the terms "the West" and "Western" in this book reflect the ideologically positioned gaze of the United States, Britain, and France—the primary publishers of the new slave narrative—that projects particular interests, discursive demands, and desires on the narratives, experiences, and bodies of women and people from the Global South. As Wendy Hesford argues, "the term *West* denotes a historically and socially constructed category, a locus of power from which some nations have imposed values, norms, and narratives on other parts of the world." Wendy Hesford, *Spectacular Rhetorics: Human Rights Visions, Recognitions, Feminisms* (Durham, NC: Duke University Press, 2011), 4.

8. Leigh Gilmore, *Tainted Witness: Why We Doubt What Women Say About Their Lives* (New York: Columbia University Press, 2017), 85–117.

9. Joe Lockard, "Review Essay: Francis Bok's Escape from Slavery and Contemporary Slave Narratives," *Bad Subjects* (blog), accessed March 1, 2018, https://bad .eserver.org/issues/2004/69/lockard, website has been removed.

10. Joy James has argued that the U.S. "prison democracy" aligns the state with the role of the master and the prisoner with that of the slave and that the narratives produced by its prison population represent "perhaps the world's largest collection of (neo)slave literature" (xxi). I do not disagree that there are aspects of the current privatized prison system in the United States that are tantamount to slavery. However, while James's work levels a powerful critique against the carceral system, the use of the word "slavery" is her own critical apparatus and does not describe the formal qualities of the narratives written by incarcerated people or the language used by them to describe their own experiences, though they often recognize their incarceration as a legacy of antebellum slavery in the United States. For more on prison labor as slavery, see Joy James, *The New Abolitionists: (Neo) Slave Narratives and Contemporary Prison Writings* (Albany: State University of New York Press, 2005).

11. See appendix, "List of New Slave Narratives," for a complete list of works referred to in this book.

12. While I have been able to locate public reports, white papers, children's books, and cautionary tales about contemporary forms of slavery in other parts of the world, I have not found any first-person narratives that suggest that new slave narratives are being produced elsewhere. For more on children's books that depict contemporary slavery, see Esther de Bruijn and Laura T. Murphy, "Trading in Innocence: Slave-Shaming in Ghanaian Children's Market Fiction," *Journal of African Cultural Studies* 30, no. 3 (May 2017): 243–62.

13. See, for instance, Betty De Hart, "Not Without My Daughter: On Parental Abduction, Orientalism and Maternal Melodrama," *European Journal of Women's Studies* 8, no. 1 (2001): 51–65; Alexandra Schultheis, "African Child Soldiers and Humanitarian Consumption," *Peace Review* 20, no. 1 (2008): 31–40; Sissy Helff,

"Refugee Life Narratives—The Disturbing Potential of a Genre and the Case of Mende Nazer," *Matatu: Journal for African Culture & Society* 36, no. 1 (2009): 331–46; Barbara Harlow, "Child and/or Soldier? From Resistance Movements to Human Rights Regiments," *CR: The New Centennial Review* 10, no. 1 (2010): 195–215; Irina Kyulanova, "From Soldiers to Children: Undoing the Rite of Passage in Ishmael Beah's *A Long Way Gone* and Bernard Ashley's *Little Soldier*," *Studies in the Novel* 42, no. 1 (2010): 28–47; Alexandra W. Schultheis, "Global Specters: Child Soldiers in the Post-National Fiction of Uzodinma Iweala and Chris Abani," in *Emerging African Voices: A Study of Contemporary African Fiction*, ed. Walter P. Collins III (Amherst, NY: Cambria, 2010), 13–51; Eleni Coundouriotis, "The Child Soldier Narrative and the Problem of Arrested Historicization," *Journal of Human Rights* 9, no. 2 (2010): 191–206; Stephen Gray, "Rites and Wrongs of Passage: Child Soldiers in African Writing," *English Academy Review* 28, no. 2 (2011): 4–14; Maureen Moynagh, "Human Rights, Child-Soldier Narratives, and the Problem of Form," *Research in African Literatures* 42, no. 4 (2011): 39–59; Mark Sanders, "Culpability and Guilt: Child Soldiers in Fiction and Memoir," *Law & Literature* 23, no. 2 (2011): 195–223; Mitchum Huehls, "Referring to the Human in Contemporary Human Rights Literature," *MFS: Modern Fiction Studies* 58, no. 1 (2012): 1–21; Allison Mackey, "Troubling Humanitarian Consumption: Reframing Relationality in African Child Soldier Narratives," *Research in African Literatures* 44, no. 4 (2013): 99–122.

14. See, for instance, Ishmael Beah, *A Long Way Gone: Memoirs of a Boy Soldier* (New York: Harper Collins, 2008); China Keitetsi, *Child Soldier* (London: Souvenir, 2004). Both Kaelyn Kaoma and I have read child soldier narratives under the rubric of the slave narrative elsewhere because their experiences are typically characterized by forced labor. See Kaoma, "Child Soldier Memoirs and the 'Classic' Slave Narrative"; Laura T. Murphy, "The New Slave Narrative and the Illegibility of Modern Slavery," *Slavery & Abolition* 36, no. 2 (2015): 382–405. Yogita Goyal reads David Eggers's *What Is the What?* and Mohamedou Ould Slahi's *Guantánamo Diary* as revivals or "echoes" of the slave narrative genre even though the authors do not identify their experiences as literal slavery. Goyal, "African Atrocity, American Humanity"; Goyal, "The Genres of *Guantánamo Diary*: Postcolonial Reading and the War on Terror," *Cambridge Journal of Postcolonial Literary Inquiry* 4, no. 1 (2017): 69–87. There are other narratives, such as Emmanuel Jal's *War Child* or Holly Austin Smith's *Walking Prey: How America's Youth Are Vulnerable to Sex Slavery*, that have been considered "slave narratives" by critics, which would not fit the parameters of this project, as the narrators express a deliberate consent to the labor they performed, and Jal even saw joining the war effort as a way to avoid enslavement. Smith's subtitle does, in fact, include the term "sex slavery," but in several places in the book, she indicates that she does not identify with the term because she admits to having briefly felt liberated from her home life by her relationship to a pimp and by working in the sex trade. She reports that her publisher insisted on using the term "slavery" on the cover, though she objected (personal correspondence, April 3, 2018). Emmanuel Jal, *War Child: A Child Soldier's Story* (New York: Macmillan, 2009); Holly Austin Smith, *Walking Prey: How America's Youth Are Vulnerable to Sex Slavery* (New York: St. Martin's, 2014). On the other hand, I do include Rachel Lloyd's *Girls Like Us* as part of the analysis because,

despite her more recent public denouncement of the use of the word "slavery" instead of "commercial sexual exploitation" on Facebook and in public presentations, Lloyd describes forced sex work as "slavery" several times in her narrative. I have chosen to read these texts as they were printed at the time of publication, even if the authors have made different claims in the years since publication.

15. For discussions of nineteenth-century slave narrative conventions, see William Andrews, *To Tell a Free Story: The First Century of African-American Autobiography*, (Urbana: University of Illinois Press, 1986); John W. Blassingame, *Slave Testimony: Two Centuries of Letters, Speeches, Interviews, and Autobiographies* (Baton Rouge: Louisiana State University Press, 1977); Vincent Carretta, ed., *Unchained Voices: An Anthology of Black Authors in the English-Speaking World of the Eighteenth Century* (Lexington: University Press of Kentucky, 2013); Foster, *Witnessing Slavery*; Henry Louis Gates Jr., introduction to *The Slave's Narrative: Texts and Contexts*, ed. Charles T. Davis and Henry Louis Gates Jr. (New York: Oxford University Press, 1985); Dwight McBride, *Impossible Witnesses: Truth, Abolitionism, and Slave Testimony* (New York: New York University Press, 2001); James Olney, "'I Was Born': Slave Narratives, Their Status as Autobiography and as Literature," *Callaloo*, no. 20 (1984): 46–73; Sidonie Smith, *Where I'm Bound: Patterns of Slavery and Freedom in Black American Autobiography* (Westport, CT: Greenwood, 1974).

16. Olney, 50–51.

17. Zana Muhsen and Andrew Crofts, *Sold: One Woman's True Account of Modern Slavery* (London: Sphere, 1991).

18. See also Zana Muhsen, *A Promise to Nadia: A True Story of a British Slave in the Yemen* (London: Little, Brown, 2010); Miriam Ali and Jana Wain, *Without Mercy: A Mother's Struggle Against Modern Slavery* (London: Sphere, 1996).

19. Muhsen and Crofts, *Sold*, 50.

20. Muhsen and Crofts, 7.

21. Venture Smith, "A Narrative of the Life and Adventures of Venture, a Native of Africa: But Resident Above Sixty Years in the United States of America. Related by Himself," in Carretta, *Unchained Voices*; William L. Andrews, *North Carolina Slave Narratives: The Lives of Moses Roper, Lunsford Lane, Moses Grandy & Thomas H. Jones* (Chapel Hill: University of North Carolina Press, 2003).

22. Betty Mahmoody, *Not Without My Daughter* (New York: St. Martin's, 1987). On the popularity of and criticism regarding those sensationalized novels, see Tim Youngs, "'Framed in the Doorway': The *Observer* and the 'Yemeni Brides' Affair," *Media, Culture & Society* 13, no. 2 (1991): 239–47; Betty De Hart, "Not Without My Daughter," 52–53; Vron Ware, "Info-War and the Politics of Feminist Curiosity: Exploring New Frameworks for Feminist Intercultural Studies," *Cultural Studies* 20, no. 6 (2006): 542.

23. In 2002 Nadia Muhsen told Melanie Finn of the *Guardian*, "It was never in my mind that I wanted to leave," though Zana Muhsen vehemently argues otherwise. Melanie Finn, "Nadia's Choice," *Guardian*, March 31, 2002. Though both her desire to be with her children and psychological trauma might have made escape seem impossible, it is difficult to make a definitive assessment of whether she was enslaved. Regarding her hiring of mercenaries, see her own depictions of the events and the aftermath in Muhsen, *A Promise to Nadia*, 128–44.

24. Audrey Fisch, introduction to *The Cambridge Companion to the African American Slave Narrative* (New York: Cambridge University Press, 2007), 2.

25. Jean-Robert Cadet, *Restavec: From Haitian Slave Child to Middle-Class American* (Austin: University of Texas Press, 1998).

26. Mende Nazer, *Slave: My True Story* (New York: Public Affairs, 2003).

27. Sage and Kasten, *Enslaved.*

28. Rachel Lloyd, *Girls Like Us: Fighting for a World Where Girls Are Not for Sale: An Activist Finds Her Calling and Heals Herself* (New York: Harper Collins, 2011).

29. Carissa Phelps, *Runaway Girl: Escaping Life on the Streets* (New York: Penguin, 2013); Barbara Amaya, *Nobody's Girl: A Memoir of Lost Innocence, Modern Day Slavery & Transformation* (Pittsburgh, PA: Animal, 2015); Katariina Rosenblatt, *Stolen: The True Story of a Sex Trafficking Survivor* (Grand Rapids, MI: Revell, 2014); Brook Parker-Bello, *Living Inside the Rainbow: Winning the Battlefield of the Mind After Human Trafficking & Mental Bondage* (self-published, 2014).

30. I have focused this study primarily on the book-length narratives published and distributed in the United States because they constitute the vast majority of the narratives and because it allows a culturally informed, geographically specific interpretation. In a previous book, *Survivors of Slavery: Modern Day Slave Narratives*, I collected and analyzed shorter narratives that were produced by people who have less access to the machinery of the publishing industry in the West. Further work on international and informal circuits of publication and distribution would certainly be an interesting avenue for future scholarship.

31. Kevin Bales, "Testing a Theory of Modern Slavery" (paper, From Chattel Bondage to State Servitude: Slavery in the 20th Century, Gilder Lehrman Center, Yale University, 2004), 15–16, https://glc.yale.edu/sites/default/files/files/events/cbss/Bales.pdf; Sally Engle Merry, *The Seductions of Quantification: Measuring Human Rights, Gender Violence, and Sex Trafficking* (Chicago: University of Chicago Press, 2016), 126, 145–46; "Human Trafficking: Better Data, Strategy, and Reporting Needed to Enhance U.S. Anti-Trafficking Efforts Abroad" (Washington, DC: United States Government Accountability Office, 2006), http://www.gao.gov/assets/260/250812.pdf; David A. Feingold, "Trafficking in Numbers: The Social Construction of Human Trafficking Data," in *Sex, Drugs, and Body Counts: The Politics of Numbers in Global Crime and Conflict* (Ithaca, NY: Cornell University Press, 2010), 46–74.

32. Bok, *Escape from Slavery*, 279.

33. Allen D. Hertzke, "African American Churches and U.S. Policy in Sudan," *Review of Faith & International Affairs* 6, no. 1 (2008): 21.

34. Beatrice Fernando, *In Contempt of Fate: The Tale of a Sri Lankan Sold into Servitude, Who Survived to Tell It: A Memoir* (self-published, 2005).

35. Sage and Kasten, *Enslaved*, 2.

36. For more on the lack of survivor leadership, see Denise Brennan, "Methodological Challenges in Research with Trafficked Persons: Tales from the Field," *International Migration* 43, nos. 1–2 (2005): 38.

37. Dickson D. Bruce, "Politics and Political Philosophy in the Slave Narrative," in *The Cambridge Companion to the African American Slave Narrative* (New York: Cambridge University Press, 2007), 28.

38. "About CAST," CAST LA, http://www.castla.org/about/. See also Jennifer Lynne Musto, "The NGO-ification of the Anti-Trafficking Movement in the United States: A Case Study of the Coalition to Abolish Slavery and Trafficking," *Wagadu: A Journal of Transnational Women's and Gender Studies* 5 (2008): 11–16.

39. "The Victims of Trafficking and Violence Protection Act of 2000," 106th Congress, 2nd Session, H.R. 3244 (P.L. 106–386, January 24, 2000); United Nations General Assembly, "United Nations Protocol to Prevent, Suppress and Punish Trafficking in Persons, Especially Women and Children, Supplementing the United Nations Convention Against Transnational Organized Crime," November 15, 2000, https://www.ohchr.org/en/professionalinterest/pages/protocoltraffickinginpersons.aspx.

40. Anthony DeStefano, *The War on Human Trafficking: U.S. Policy Assessed* (New Brunswick, NJ: Rutgers University Press, 2007), 38–40. See also testimonies collected in Murphy, *Survivors of Slavery*, 27–30, 96–98, 102–6.

41. Bok, *Escape from Slavery*, 273.

42. Faith J. H. McDonnell and Grace Akallo, *Girl Soldier: A Story of Hope for Northern Uganda's Children* (Ada, MI: Chosen, 2007), 21–26, 52–56.

43. Gillian Whitlock, *Soft Weapons: Autobiography in Transit* (Chicago: University of Chicago Press, 2010), 3.

44. Ware, "Info-War and the Politics of Feminist Curiosity," 540.

45. Kamala Kempadoo, "Abolitionism, Criminal Justice, and Transnational Feminism: Twenty-First-Century Perspectives on Human Trafficking," in *Trafficking and Prostitution Reconsidered: New Perspectives on Migration, Sex Work, and Human Rights*, ed. Kamala Kempadoo (Boulder, CO: Paradigm, 2012), vii–xiii.

46. Elizabeth Bernstein, "Carceral Politics as Gender Justice? The 'Traffic in Women' and Neoliberal Circuits of Crime, Sex, and Rights," *Theory and Society* 41, no. 3 (2012): 244.

47. Andrews, "To Tell a Free Story," 102.

48. William Zinsser, *Inventing the Truth: The Art and Craft of Memoir* (Boston: Houghton Mifflin, 1987), 3; Ben Yagoda, *Memoir: A History* (New York: Penguin, 2009), 7; Julie Rak, *Boom! Manufacturing Memoir for the Popular Market* (Waterloo, Canada: Wilfrid Laurier University Press, 2013), 3.

49. Sidonie Smith and Julia Watson, *Reading Autobiography: A Guide for Interpreting Life Narratives* (Minneapolis: University of Minnesota Press, 2010), 125.

50. For more on the relationship between talk shows and therapeutic public disclosure, see Janice Peck, "The Mediated Talking Cure: Therapeutic Framing of Autobiography in TV Talk Shows," in *Getting a Life: Everyday Uses of Autobiography*, ed. Sidonie Smith and Julia Watson (Minneapolis: University of Minnesota Press, 1996), 143–51; Jane M. Shattuc, *The Talking Cure: TV Talk Shows and Women* (New York: Routledge, 2014).

51. Lilie Chouliaraki, *The Spectatorship of Suffering* (London: Sage, 2006), 3.

52. Laura T. Murphy, "On Freedom and Complexity in the (Captive) Nation," *Journal of the African Literature Association* 12, no. 1 (2018): 60–71.

53. Murphy, *Survivors of Slavery*, 259.

54. For the usurpation of human rights narratives, see Paul Gready, "Introduction: 'Responsibility to the Story,'" *Journal of Human Rights Practice* 2, no. 2 (2010): 184.

For the precedent of survivor reappropriation of the narrative in domestic violence activism, see Linda Alcoff and Laura Gray, "Survivor Discourse: Transgression or Recuperation?," *Signs: Journal of Women in Culture and Society* 18, no. 2 (1993): 267–68. For examples of current survivor networks, see Survivors United (https://www.facebook.com/SexTraffickingSurvivorsUnited.USA/); Coalition Against Slavery and Trafficking's Survivor Caucus (http://castla.org/survivors-leadership); the National Survivor Network (https://nationalsurvivornetwork.org); and the Survivor Alliance (https://survivoralliance.org).

55. Gilmore, *Tainted Witness*, 5.
56. Benedetto Croce, *Aesthetic as Science of Expression and of Linguistics in General*, trans. Colin Lyas (Cambridge: Cambridge University Press, 1992); Tzvetan Todorov, *Genres in Discourse*, trans. Catherine Porter (Cambridge: Cambridge University Press, 1990); Jacques Derrida and Avital Ronell, "The Law of Genre," *Critical Inquiry* 7, no. 1 (1980): 55–81.
57. Wai Chee Dimock, "Introduction: Genres as Fields of Knowledge," *PMLA* 122, no. 5 (2007): 1380.
58. Whitlock, *Soft Weapons*.

1. MAKING SLAVERY LEGIBLE

1. Frederick Douglass, *My Bondage and My Freedom* (New York: Dover, 1969), 362.
2. Minh Dang, "An Open Letter to the Anti-Trafficking Movement," in *Survivors of Slavery: Modern-Day Slave Narratives*, ed. Laura T. Murphy (New York: Columbia University Press, 2014), xiii.
3. Kevin Bales, *Ending Slavery: How We Free Today's Slaves* (Berkeley: University of California Press, 2007), 4.
4. It was only during revisions to the final draft of this manuscript that I discovered that Karen Sánchez-Eppler used the term "strategies of displacement" to describe a similar strategy employed by Harriet Jacobs in *Incidents in the Life of a Slave Girl*. For Sánchez-Eppler's usage, see Karen Sánchez-Eppler, *Touching Liberty: Abolition, Feminism, and the Politics of the Body* (Berkeley: University of California Press, 1993), 92.
5. Jean-Robert Cadet, *Restavec: From Haitian Slave Child to Middle-Class American* (Austin: University of Texas Press, 1998), 4–5.
6. Guri Tyldum and Anette Brunovskis, "Describing the Unobserved: Methodological Challenges in Empirical Studies on Human Trafficking," *International Migration* 43, nos. 1–2 (2005): 18.
7. Gillian Whitlock, *Postcolonial Life Narrative: Testimonial Transactions*, 1st ed. (Oxford: Oxford University Press, 2015), 17.
8. Francis Bok, *Escape from Slavery: The True Story of My Ten Years in Captivity—and My Journey to Freedom in America* (New York: Macmillan, 2003), 252.
9. Cadet, *Restavec*, 4.
10. Nadia Murad, *The Last Girl: My Story of Captivity, and My Fight Against the Islamic State* (New York: Tim Duggan, 2017), 122–23.
11. Rachel Lloyd, *Girls Like Us: Fighting for a World Where Girls Are Not for Sale, an Activist Finds Her Calling and Heals Herself* (New York: Harper Collins, 2011), 163, 97.

235

12. Janet Neary, *Fugitive Testimony: On the Visual Logic of Slave Narratives* (New York: Oxford University Press, 2016), 5.
13. James Olney, "'I Was Born': Slave Narratives, Their Status as Autobiography and as Literature," *Callaloo*, no. 20 (1984): 50.
14. Wendy Hesford, *Spectacular Rhetorics: Human Rights Visions, Recognitions, Feminisms* (Durham, NC: Duke University Press, 2011), 1.
15. Hesford, 126.
16. Saidiya V. Hartman, *Scenes of Subjection: Terror, Slavery, and Self-Making in Nineteenth-Century America* (New York: Oxford University Press, 1997).
17. Bok, *Escape from Slavery*, 1.
18. Mende Nazer, *Slave: My True Story* (New York: Public Affairs, 2003), 1.
19. Faith J. H. McDonnell and Grace Akallo, *Girl Soldier: A Story of Hope for Northern Uganda's Children* (Ada, MI: Chosen, 2007), 27.
20. Olney, "'I Was Born,'" 52.
21. As Kelli Lyon Johnson points out, shorter new slave narratives do not typically begin with birth or origins because they are brief and are often told with specific practical purposes in mind. Nonetheless, she estimates that 10 percent of the shorter narratives she analyzed did begin with the story of the narrator's origins. Johnson, "The New Slave Narrative: Advocacy and Human Rights in Stories of Contemporary Slavery" *Journal of Human Rights* 12, no. 2 (2013): 248.
22. Somaly Mam, *The Road of Lost Innocence: The Story of a Cambodian Heroine* (New York: Spiegel & Grau, 2009), 2.
23. Beatrice Fernando, *In Contempt of Fate: The Tale of a Sri Lankan Sold into Servitude, Who Survived to Tell It: A Memoir* (self-published, 2005), 63.
24. Nazer, *Slave*, 9.
25. Evelyn Amony, *I Am Evelyn Amony: Reclaiming My Life from the Lord's Resistance Army* (Madison: University of Wisconsin Press: 2015), 3.
26. Jerome S. Handler, "Survivors of the Middle Passage: Life Histories of Enslaved Africans in British America," *Slavery and Abolition* 23, no. 1 (2002): 25–56.
27. Bok, *Escape from Slavery*, 3.
28. Farida Khalaf, *The Girl Who Escaped ISIS: This Is My Story* (New York: Simon & Schuster, 2016), 5–8, xi–xiii.
29. Amony, *I Am Evelyn Amony*, 3–5.
30. Bok, *Escape from Slavery*, 34.
31. Bok, 4.
32. Mende Nazer, *Freedom: The Sequel to Slave* (London: Endeavor, 2012), 108–9.
33. Hartman, *Scenes of Subjection*, 3.
34. Kelli Lyon Johnson catalogues the slave conventions in 149 narratives. Johnson, "The New Slave Narrative."
35. Cadet, *Restavec*, 5, 10, 44, 54.
36. Cadet, 15–16.
37. Bok, *Escape from Slavery*, 31.
38. McDonnell and Akallo, *Girl Soldier*, 106.
39. Frederick Douglass, *Narrative of the Life of Frederick Douglass, an American Slave* (New York: Broadview, 2018), 16.
40. Tina Okpara, *My Life Has a Price: A Memoir of Survival and Freedom* (Dakar: Amalion, 2012), 79.

41. Paul E. Lovejoy, "'Freedom Narratives' of Transatlantic Slavery," *Slavery & Abolition* 32, no. 1 (2011): 91–107.

42. Thomas Laqueur, "Bodies, Details, and the Humanitarian Narrative," in *The New Cultural History*, ed. Lynn Hunt (Berkeley: University of California Press, 1989), 177.

43. Mario Klarer, "Humanitarian Pornography: John Gabriel Stedman's Narrative of a Five Years Expedition Against the Revolting Negroes of Surinam (1796)," *New Literary History* 36, no. 4 (2005): 560.

44. Sidonie Smith and Julia Watson, *Reading Autobiography: A Guide for Interpreting Life Narratives* (Minneapolis: University of Minnesota Press, 2010), 50.

45. Whitlock, *Postcolonial Life Narrative*, 49.

46. Hartman, *Scenes of Subjection*, 21.

47. William Andrews, *To Tell a Free Story: The First Century of African-American Autobiography* (Urbana: University of Illinois Press, 1986), 7.

48. Andrews, 86.

49. See Harriet Jacobs, *Incidents in the Life of a Slave Girl* (Boston, 1861).

50. See, for instance, Hazel V. Carby, *Reconstructing Womanhood: The Emergence of the Afro-American Woman Novelist* (New York: Oxford University Press, 1987); Franny Nudelman, "Harriet Jacobs and the Sentimental Politics of Female Suffering," *English Literary History* 59, no. 4 (1992): 939–64; Sánchez-Eppler, *Touching Liberty*; Mark Rifkin, "'A Home Made Sacred by Protecting Laws': Black Activist Homemaking and Geographies of Citizenship in *Incidents in the Life of a Slave Girl*," *Differences* 18, no. 2 (September 1, 2007): 72–102; Stephanie Li, *Something Akin to Freedom: The Choice of Bondage in Narratives by African American Women* (Albany: State University of New York Press, 2010); Leigh Gilmore and Elizabeth Marshall, "Girls in Crisis: Rescue and Transnational Feminist Autobiographical Resistance," *Feminist Studies* 36, no. 3 (2010): 667–90; Jasmine Syedullah, "'Is This Freedom?' A Political Theory of Harriet Jacobs's Loopholes of Emancipation" (PhD diss., University of California Santa Cruz, 2014), https://escholarship.org/uc/item/5xz9d2kx.

51. Two notable exceptions are Theresa Flores and Mimi Crown, who elaborate on very specific physical details of sexual assaults while enslaved. Theresa Flores, *The Slave Across the Street: The True Story of How an American Teen Survived the World of Human Trafficking* (Garden City, ID: Ampelon, 2010); Mimi Crown, *Stuck in Traffic* (New Orleans, LA: Khoi, 2016).

52. Hartman, *Scenes of Subjection*, 19.

53. Sidonie Smith, *Where I'm Bound: Patterns of Slavery and Freedom in Black American Autobiography* (Westport, CT: Greenwood, 1974), 11.

54. Claudia Cojocaru, "Sex Trafficking, Captivity, and Narrative: Constructing Victimhood with the Goal of Salvation," *Dialectical Anthropology* 39, no. 2 (2015): 188.

55. Amony, *I Am Evelyn Amony*, 39.

56. McDonnell and Akallo, *Girl Soldier*, 110.

57. Murad, *The Last Girl*, 65.

58. Fernando, *In Contempt of Fate*, 41, 43.

59. Lloyd, *Girls Like Us*, 85–91.

60. Elaine Scarry, *The Body in Pain: The Making and Unmaking of the World* (New York: Oxford University Press, 1985), 4.

61. Eleni Coundouriotis, "You Only Have Your Word: Rape and Testimony," *Human Rights Quarterly* 35, no. 2 (2013): 8.

62. Klarer, "Humanitarian Pornography," 560.

63. Avital Ronell, "The Testamentary Whisper," *South Atlantic Quarterly* 103, nos. 2–3 (Spring/Summer 2004): 492.

64. Lloyd, *Girls Like Us*, 10–11.

65. Lloyd, 1.

66. McDonnell and Akallo, *Girl Soldier*, 68.

67. Cadet, *Restavec*, 14–16.

68. Smith and Watson, *Reading Autobiography*, 30.

69. Bok, *Escape from Slavery*, 221.

70. Elaine Scarry, "The Difficulty of Imagining Other People," in *For Love of Country: Debating the Limits of Patriotism*, ed. Martha Craven Nussbaum and Joshua Cohen (Boston: Beacon, 1996), 103.

71. Bok, *Escape from Slavery*, 196.

72. Joseph Slaughter, "Humanitarian Reading," in *Humanitarianism and Suffering: The Mobilization of Empathy*, ed. Richard Ashby Wilson and Richard D. Brown (New York: Cambridge University Press, 2008), 101.

73. Slaughter, 102–3.

2. THE NOT-YET-FREEDOM NARRATIVE

1. Martin Luther King Jr, "I Have a Dream" (speech, Washington, DC, August 28, 1963).

2. For notable exceptions, see Neil Roberts, *Freedom as Marronage* (Chicago: University of Chicago Press, 2015); Orlando Patterson, *Freedom in the Making of Western Culture*, vol. 1 (London: I. B. Tauris, 1991).

3. Jean Jacques Rousseau, *On the Social Contract: Discourse on the Origin of Inequality; Discourse on Political Economy* (Indianapolis, IN: Hackett, 1983).

4. Hannah Arendt, *Between Past and Future: Eight Exercises in Political Thought* (New York: Penguin, 2006), 143; emphasis added.

5. Zygmunt Bauman, *Freedom* (Minneapolis: University of Minnesota Press, 1988), 4.

6. Patterson, *Freedom in the Making of Western Culture*, 1:xiii.

7. Bauman, *Freedom*, 9.

8. Similar survivor-centric arguments regarding the conception of freedom have been made in Roberts, *Freedom as Marronage*, 15; Andrea Nicholson, Minh Dang, and Zoe Trodd, "A Full Freedom: Contemporary Survivors' Definitions of Slavery," *Human Rights Law Review* 18, no 4 (December 2018): 689–704.

9. Paul E. Lovejoy, " 'Freedom Narratives' of Transatlantic Slavery," *Slavery & Abolition* 32, no. 1 (2011): 91.

10. William Andrews, *To Tell a Free Story: The First Century of African-American Autobiography* (Urbana: University of Illinois Press, 1986), xi.

11. Jean-Robert Cadet, *My Stone of Hope: From Haitian Slave Child to Abolitionist* (Austin: University of Texas Press, 2011), 48.

12. Carissa Phelps, *Runaway Girl: Escaping Life on the Streets* (New York: Penguin, 2013), 98–99; Mende Nazer, *Slave: My True Story* (New York: Public Affairs, 2003), 311.

13. Shyima Hall, *Hidden Girl: The True Story of a Modern-Day Child Slave* (New York: Simon & Schuster, 2014), 63–65.

14. Francis Bok, *Escape from Slavery: The True Story of My Ten Years in Captivity—and My Journey to Freedom in America* (New York: Macmillan, 2003), 48.

15. Timea Nagy, *Memoirs of a Sex Slave Survivor* (Toronto: Communication Dynamics, 2010), 23.

16. Faith J. H. McDonnell and Grace Akallo, *Girl Soldier: A Story of Hope for Northern Uganda's Children* (Ada, MI: Chosen, 2007), 28–29.

17. Bok, *Escape from Slavery*, 85.

18. Bok, 30.

19. Bok, 83.

20. Jeremy Waldron, *Dignity, Rank, and Rights* (New York: Oxford University Press, 2012), 16.

21. William Lloyd Garrison, "Declaration of the National Anti-Slavery Convention," *Liberator*, December 14, 1833.

22. Angelina Grimké, "Letter to Catharine E. Beecher in Reply to an Essay on Slavery and Abolitionism Addressed to A. E. Grimké; Letter 1," June 12, 1837, https://archive.org/stream/letterstocatheri00grimrich/letterstocatheri00grimrich_djvu.txt; emphasis original.

23. Nazer, *Slave*, 335; emphasis added.

24. Nagy, *Memoirs of a Sex Slave Survivor*, 107.

25. Brook Parker-Bello, *Living Inside the Rainbow: Winning the Battlefield of the Mind After Human Trafficking & Mental Bondage* (self-published, 2014), 58.

26. Bok, *Escape from Slavery*, 106.

27. Bok, 96.

28. Bok, 107.

29. Bok, 108.

30. Bok, 108.

31. Eric Foner, "The Meaning of Freedom in the Age of Emancipation," *Journal of American History* 81, no. 2 (September 1994): 460.

32. Douglas A. Blackmon, *Slavery by Another Name: The Re-enslavement of Black Americans from the Civil War to World War II* (New York: Anchor, 2009); Michelle Alexander, *The New Jim Crow: Mass Incarceration in the Age of Colorblindness* (New York: New, 2012); Edward E. Baptist, *The Half Has Never Been Told: Slavery and the Making of American Capitalism* (New York: Basic, 2014); Dennis Childs, *Slaves of the State: Black Incarceration from the Chain Gang to the Penitentiary* (Minneapolis: University of Minnesota Press, 2015); Talitha L. LeFlouria, *Chained in Silence: Black Women and Convict Labor in the New South* (Chapel Hill: University of North Carolina Press, 2015).

33. Arendt, *Between Past and Future*, 148.

34. Cadet, *My Stone of Hope*, 23.

35. Jean-Robert Cadet, *Restavec: From Haitian Slave Child to Middle-Class American* (Austin: University of Texas Press, 1998), 153.

36. Cadet, 147.

37. Cadet, 161.

38. Cadet, 38.

39. Bok, *Escape from Slavery*, 116.

40. Bok, 113.

41. Beatrice Fernando, *In Contempt of Fate: The Tale of a Sri Lankan Sold into Servitude, Who Survived to Tell It: A Memoir* (self-published, 2005), 258.

42. Fernando, 261.

43. Amartya Sen, *Development as Freedom*, (New York: Anchor, 2000), xi–xii.

44. Sen, 73.

45. Nancy J. Hirschmann, *The Subject of Liberty: Toward a Feminist Theory of Freedom* (Princeton, NJ: Princeton University Press, 2009), 121.

46. Roberts, *Freedom as Marronage*, 39.

47. Cadet, *Restavec*, 178.

48. Cadet, 142–43.

49. Cadet, 169, 178.

50. Cadet, 120.

51. Cadet, n.p.

52. Nazer, *Slave*, 318.

53. Nazer, 312.

54. Nazer, 313.

55. Hall, *Hidden Girl*, 115.

56. Cadet, *My Stone of Hope*, 132.

57. Cadet, *Restavec*, 158.

58. Hirschmann, *The Subject of Liberty*, 112.

59. Tina Okpara, *My Life Has a Price: A Memoir of Survival and Freedom* (Dakar: Amalion, 2012), 187.

60. Bok, *Escape from Slavery*, 197.

61. Bok, 225.

62. Nazer, *Slave*, 316.

63. Bok, *Escape from Slavery*, 112.

64. Bok, 141.

65. Bok, 278.

66. Later, Nazer's asylum request was granted, but her first memoir ends with her concern that she will be returned to Sudan where she knows she will be unsafe because of the threats of her former masters and their families.

67. Nazer, *Slave*, 324.

68. Nazer, 335; emphasis in original.

69. Cadet, *My Stone of Hope*, 28.

70. Cadet, 22.

71. Foner, "The Meaning of Freedom in the Age of Emancipation," 451.

72. Nazer, *Slave*, 334–35.

73. Christien van den Anker, "Making Human Rights Accessible: The Role of Governments in Trafficking and Migrant Labor Exploitation," in *From Human*

Trafficking to Human Rights: Reframing Contemporary Slavery, ed. Alison Brysk and Austin Choi-Fitzpatrick (Philadelphia: University of Pennsylvania Press, 2012), 157.

74. Sen, *Development as Freedom*, 233.

75. McDonnell and Akallo, *Girl Soldier*, 181.

76. McDonnell and Akallo, 194.

77. Farida Khalaf, *The Girl Who Escaped ISIS: This Is My Story* (New York: Simon & Schuster, 2016), 196.

78. Martha Craven Nussbaum and Joshua Cohen, *For Love of Country?* (Boston: Beacon, 1996), 10.

79. Nussbaum and Cohen, 15.

3. BLACKFACE ABOLITION

1. John Stauffer, *The Black Hearts of Men* (Cambridge, MA: Harvard University Press, 2009), 46.

2. Frederick Douglass, "The Hutchinson Family—Hunkerism," *Northstar*, October 27, 1848.

3. Stauffer, *The Black Hearts of Men*, 18.

4. Eric Lott, *Love & Theft: Blackface Minstrelsy and the American Working Class* (New York: Oxford University Press, 2013), 15.

5. Lott, 18–19.

6. Stauffer, *The Black Hearts of Men*, 362.

7. The Global Slavery Index, accessed June 7, 2018, https://www.globalslaveryindex .org/.

8. Linda Smith, *From Congress to the Brothel: A Journey of Hope, Healing and Restoration* (Vancouver, WA: Shared Hope, 2007), 22.

9. Faith J. H. McDonnell and Grace Akallo, *Girl Soldier: A Story of Hope for Northern Uganda's Children* (Ada, MI: Chosen, 2007), 26.

10. Makau Mutua, "Savages, Victims, and Saviors: The Metaphor of Human Rights," *Harvard International Law Journal* 42 (2001): 204.

11. Allen D. Hertzke, *Freeing God's Children: The Unlikely Alliance for Global Human Rights* (Lanham, MD: Rowman & Littlefield, 2004), 271.

12. Hertzke, 265.

13. Hertzke, 1.

14. Hertzke, 3.

15. See, for instance, the Institute for Religion and Democracy's blog, *Juicy Ecumenism*, https://juicyecumenism.com/.

16. E. Benjamin Skinner, *A Crime So Monstrous: Face-to-Face with Modern-Day Slavery* (New York: Free, 2009), 50.

17. See the "Issues" drop-down list on the Institute for Religion and Democracy website, http://theird.org/.

18. Hertzke, *Freeing God's Children*, 112.

19. Skinner, *A Crime So Monstrous*, 68–69, 87–92.

20. Hertzke, *Freeing God's Children*, 15.

21. Lott, *Love & Theft*, 18–19.

22. Gillian Whitlock, *Soft Weapons: Autobiography in Transit* (Chicago: University of Chicago Press, 2010), 3.

23. Leigh Gilmore, *Tainted Witness: Why We Doubt What Women Say About Their Lives* (New York: Columbia University Press, 2017), 40.

24. Lott, *Love & Theft*, 27–28.

25. James Olney, "'I Was Born': Slave Narratives, Their Status as Autobiography and as Literature," *Callaloo*, no. 20 (1984): 52.

26. McDonnell and Akallo, *Girl Soldier*, 48.

27. McDonnell and Akallo, 49.

28. McDonnell and Akallo, 105.

29. Elaine Scarry, "The Difficulty of Imagining Other People," in *For Love of Country: Debating the Limits of Patriotism*, ed. Martha Craven Nussbaum and Joshua Cohen (Boston: Beacon, 1996), 98–110; Cathy Caruth, *Unclaimed Experience: Trauma, Narrative, and History* (Baltimore, MD: Johns Hopkins University Press, 2016).

30. McDonnell and Akallo, *Girl Soldier*, 110.

31. McDonnell and Akallo, 113.

32. McDonnell and Akallo, 110.

33. McDonnell and Akallo, 106.

34. McDonnell and Akallo, 111.

35. McDonnell and Akallo, 106.

36. McDonnell and Akallo, 124–25.

37. McDonnell and Akallo, 139.

38. McDonnell and Akallo, 106.

39. Olney, "'I Was Born,'" 52.

40. "About Chosen," Baker Publishing Group, http://bakerpublishinggroup.com /chosen/about-chosen.

41. McDonnell and Akallo, *Girl Soldier*, cover, flyleaf.

42. McDonnell and Akallo, 2.

43. McDonnell and Akallo, 24.

44. McDonnell and Akallo, cover.

45. Gilmore, *Tainted Witness*, 120.

46. McDonnell and Akallo, *Girl Soldier*, 22.

47. "Issues" list, Institute for Religion and Democracy, http://theird.org/.

48. McDonnell and Akallo, *Girl Soldier*, 30.

49. McDonnell and Akallo, 37.

50. McDonnell and Akallo, 41.

51. McDonnell and Akallo, 39.

52. McDonnell and Akallo, 39.

53. McDonnell and Akallo, 71.

54. McDonnell and Akallo, 70, 103.

55. McDonnell and Akallo, 99–103.

56. Samuel P. Huntington, "The Clash of Civilizations?," *Foreign Affairs* (Summer 1993): 22–49. Huntington, in his now infamous essay "The Clash of Civilizations," predicted, "Civilization identity will be increasingly important in the future, and the world will be shaped in large measure by the interactions among seven or eight major civilizations. These include Western, Confucian, Japanese, Islamic, Hindu, Slavic-Orthodox, Latin American and possibly African civilization," 25.

57. McDonnell and Akallo, *Girl Soldier*, 197–98.

58. David Kennedy, *The Dark Sides of Virtue: Reassessing International Humanitarianism* (Princeton, NJ: Princeton University Press, 2005), 24.

59. Kennedy, 26.

60. McDonnell and Akallo, *Girl Soldier*, 26.

61. Thomas Laqueur, "The Moral Imagination and Human Rights," in *Human Rights as Politics and as Idolatry*, ed. Michael Ignatieff (Berkeley: University of California, 2001), 132.

62. McDonnell and Akallo, *Girl Soldier*, 126.

63. McDonnell and Akallo, 208.

64. Dan Haseltine, foreword to McDonnell and Akallo, *Girl Soldier*, 13–14.

65. Haseltine, 12–13.

66. McDonnell and Akallo, *Girl Soldier*, 127.

67. "International Religious Freedom," Institute for Religion and Democracy, https://theird.org/international-religious-freedom/.

68. Costas Douzinas, *Human Rights and Empire: The Political Philosophy of Cosmopolitanism* (New York: Routledge, 2007), 173.

69. Antony Anghie, *Imperialism, Sovereignty and the Making of International Law* (New York: Cambridge University Press, 2007), 273–79.

70. Lott, *Love & Theft*, 39.

71. Leshu Torchin, *Creating the Witness: Documenting Genocide on Film, Video, and the Internet* (Minneapolis: University of Minnesota Press, 2012), 44–45.

72. "Persecution," *Christianity Today*, www.christianitytoday.com/ct/topics/p/persecution/.

73. Saidiya Hartman, *Scenes of Subjection: Terror, Slavery, and Self-Making in Nineteenth-Century America* (New York: Oxford University Press, 1997), 19.

74. Michael Ignatieff and Anthony Appiah, *Human Rights as Politics and Idolatry* (Princeton, NJ: Princeton University Press, 2003), 68.

75. Yogita Goyal, "African Atrocity, American Humanity: Slavery and Its Transnational Afterlives," *Research in African Literatures* 45, no. 3 (2014): 55.

76. Hertzke, *Freeing God's Children*, 238.

77. Charles Jacobs, "Amnesty's Dirty Little Secret," *Jewish Advocate*, February 8, 2007, http://archive.is/vMF3b#selection-569.155-569.398.

78. Jacobs.

79. Francis Bok, *Escape from Slavery: The True Story of My Ten Years in Captivity—and My Journey to Freedom in America* (New York: Macmillan, 2003), 182.

80. Bok, 230.

81. Bok, 228.

82. See also Goyal, "African Atrocity, American Humanity," 55–57.

83. Robert Spencer, "My Life as a Modern-Day Slave," *Jihad Watch* (blog), January 26, 2004, www.jihadwatch.org/2004/01/my-life-as-a-modern-day-slave.

84. Peter Hammond, *Slavery, Terrorism, and Islam: The Historical Roots and Contemporary Threat* (Cape Town, South Africa: Christian Liberty, 2005).

85. Hammond, 2, 4.

86. Hammond, 13.

87. See Laura T. Murphy, "On Freedom and Complexity in the (Captive) Nation," *Journal of the African Literature Association* 12, no. 1 (2018). Most of the Chibok

narratives are currently only available online, but one example of a published book of shorter narratives is Wolfgang Bauer, *Stolen Girls: Survivors of Boko Haram Tell Their Story* (New York: New, 2017).

88. Kamala Kempadoo, for instance, recognizes three strains in the antislavery movement and then argues that they should be evaluated together because, in her estimation, they all equally represent "a neoliberal white chivalrous crusade across the world, born of a moral sense of goodness that shores up the power and subjectivity of the North, with the 'developing' Global South and East as the dumping grounds for helping imperatives involving rescue and charity. They have little effect on the causes of the problem, and the subjectivity and humanity of the Other is secondary." Kamala Kempadoo, "The Modern-Day White (Wo)Man's Burden: Trends in Anti-Trafficking and Anti-Slavery Campaigns," *Journal of Human Trafficking* 1, no. 1 (January 2, 2015): 18.

4. SEX PROBLEMS AND ANTISLAVERY'S COGNITIVE DISSONANCE

1. See, for instance, Richard J. Estes and Neil Alan Weiner, *The Commercial Sexual Exploitation of Children in the U.S., Canada and Mexico: Executive Summary (of the U.S. National Study)* (Philadelphia: University of Pennsylvania, School of Social Work, Center for the Study of Youth Policy, 2001). Estes later retracted these estimates after extensive critiques of his methods.

2. Meredith Dank et al., "Estimating the Size and Structure of the Underground Sex Economy in Eight Major U.S. Cities" (New York: Urban Institute, 2017); Alexandra Lutnick, *Domestic Minor Sex Trafficking: Beyond Victims and Villains* (New York: Columbia University Press, 2016); Jennifer S. Middleton et al., "Youth Experiences Survey (YES): Exploring the Scope and Complexity of Sex Trafficking in a Sample of Youth Experiencing Homelessness," *Journal of Social Service Research* 44, no. 2 (2018): 141–57.

3. Ric Curtis et al., "Commercial Sexual Exploitation of Children in New York City, Volume One: The CSEC Population in New York City: Size, Characteristics and Needs," *Center for Court Innovation* 56 (2008); Elliott Gluck and Rricha Mathur, "Child Sex Trafficking and the Child Welfare System," *State Policy Advocacy & Reform Center, Consultado El* 1 (2014); Meredith Dank, "Surviving the Streets of New York: Experiences of LGBTQ Youth, YMSM, and YWSW Engaged in Survival Sex" (New York: Urban Institute, 2015); Laura T. Murphy, "Labor and Sex Trafficking Among Homeless Youth: A Ten-City Study" (New Orleans: Modern Slavery Research Project, 2017); Makini Chisolm-Straker et al., "A Supportive Adult May Be the Difference in Homeless Youth Not Being Trafficked," *Children and Youth Services Review* 91 (2018): 115–20.

4. Dank; Murphy.

5. These claims are regularly reported in local news outlets and often emerge from law enforcement presentations or guidance. See, for instance, Thom Patterson and CNN, "Inside Houston's Sex Slave Trade," CNN, May 7, 2018, accessed September 27, 2018, https://www.cnn.com/2016/08/11/us/the-hunt-john-walsh-diaz-juarez -texas-sex-slave-human-trafficking/index.html; "Situational Awareness: Possible

Sex Trafficking During Super Bowl XLVIII," U.S. Department of State, January 17, 2014, https://www.state.gov/documents/organization/226277.pdf; Cliff Sims, "The 'Sex Trafficking Superhighway' Most Alabamians Don't Even Realize Runs Through Their State," *Yellowhammer News* (blog), January 29, 2016, https://yellowhammernews.com/the-sex-trafficking-superhighway-most-alabamians-dont-even-realize-runs-through-their-state/.

6. The source for this factoid seems to be nonprofit organizations and law enforcement agencies in cities that hosted the Super Bowl before 2011. However, the idea that the Super Bowl is the "largest human trafficking incident" gained significant traction when then district attorney (later governor) Greg Abbott of Texas made this baseless and vague claim. Rick Jervis, "Child Sex Rings Spike During Super Bowl Week," *USA Today*, February 1, 2011, http://usatoday30.usatoday.com/news/nation/2011-01-31-child-prostitution-super-bowl_N.htm. For critical approaches to the misinformation, see Global Alliance Against Traffic in Women, "What's the Cost of a Rumour: A Guide to Sorting out the Myths and the Facts About Sporting Events and Human Trafficking" (Bangkok: Global Alliance Against Traffic in Women, 2011), http://www.gaatw.org/publications/WhatstheCostofaRumour.11.15.2011.pdf; Eleanor Goldberg, "Super Bowl Is Single Largest Human Trafficking Incident in U.S.: Attorney General," sec. Impact, HuffPost, February 3, 2013, https://www.huffingtonpost.com/2013/02/03/super-bowl-sex-trafficking_n_2607871.html; Kate Mogulescu, "The Super Bowl and Sex Trafficking," *New York Times*, January 31, 2014, https://nyti.ms/1ftLTKI.

7. Maureen Moynagh makes similar claim regarding the demands of amanuenses for child soldier narratives. Moynagh, "Human Rights, Child-Soldier Narratives, and the Problem of Form," *Research in African Literatures* 42, no. 4 (2011): 46.

8. These narratives differ in style and content from many of the earlier new slave narratives as well as from the traditional slave narrative. The conflation of sex trafficking, sex slavery, and sex work in general means that the determination of which of the narrators has been "enslaved" is both definitionally and ethically fraught. The authenticity of some of these narratives has been called into question, sometimes even by other survivors. For these reasons, many critics are hesitant to call domestic minor sex trafficking by the word "slavery." However, for the purposes of this study, I selected these narratives for inclusion precisely because the narrators themselves frame their experiences as slavery. The history of the slave narrative is one that admits to diverse genre conventions—from the earliest conversion narratives to the porch interviews of the WPA, the American slave narrative has taken on a wide variety of forms and has been put to a range of uses. What matters for the purposes of my argument is that the narrators consider themselves to be recounting the experiences of their enslavement, and they shape their life narratives as urgent calls to action. As a result, I am reading these narratives as slave narratives to understand the impulse to articulate one's experience as slavery and to participate in the tradition of activist memoir that is at the heart of the slave narrative.

9. I am not counting here the narratives of survivors who published new or revised editions of their narratives or sequels that were not themselves slave narratives. I have, however, included relevant editions in the bibliography for reference.

10. In this accounting, I am excluding Jean-Robert Cadet's *My Stone of Hope* and Theresa Flores's *The Slave Across the Street* because both of these are largely revised editions of their previously published books from the first years of the century.

11. Yvonne C. Zimmerman, *Other Dreams of Freedom: Religion, Sex, and Human Trafficking* (New York: Oxford University Press, 2013), 60.

12. Anthony DeStefano, *The War on Human Trafficking: U.S. Policy Assessed* (New Brunswick, NJ: Rutgers University Press, 2007), 38–40.

13. Kamala Kempadoo, "Abolitionism, Criminal Justice, and Transnational Feminism: Twenty-First Century Perspectives on Human Trafficking" in *Trafficking and Prostitution Reconsidered: New Perspectives on Migration, Sex Work, and Human Rights*, ed. Kamala Kempadoo (Boulder, CO: Paradigm, 2012); Jo Doezema, *Sex Slaves and Discourse Masters: The Construction of Trafficking* (London: Zed, 2013); Sophie Day, "The Re-Emergence of 'Trafficking': Sex Work Between Slavery and Freedom," *Journal of the Royal Anthropological Institute* 16, no. 4 (2010): 816–34; DeStefano, *The War on Human Trafficking*; Quirk, *The Anti-Slavery Project: From the Slave Trade to Human Trafficking* (Philadelphia: University of Pennsylvania Press, 2011).

14. Julietta Hua, *Trafficking Women's Human Rights* (Minneapolis: University of Minnesota Press, 2011), 51–52, 71–87.

15. Hua, 35–48.

16. Louis CdeBaca, "The Role of the United States in Combating Human Trafficking" (Washington, DC: Center for American Progress, May 12, 2010), https://2009-2017 .state.gov/j/tip/rls/rm/2010/141728.htm.

17. Elena Shih, "Not in My 'Backyard Abolitionism' Vigilante Rescue Against American Sex Trafficking," *Sociological Perspectives* 59, no. 1 (2016): 66–90; Kevin Bales and Ron Soodalter, *The Slave Next Door* (Berkeley: University of California Press, 2009).

18. "In Our Own Backyard: Child Prostitution and Sex Trafficking in the United States," *Hearing Before the Subcommittee on Human Rights and the Law of the Committee on the Judiciary of the United States Senate* (Washington, DC: Government Printing Office, 2010), 14–17, https://www.gpo.gov/fdsys/pkg/CHRG-111shrg58003 /pdf/CHRG-111shrg58003.pdf.

19. "In Our Own Backyard."

20. Alice Jay, *Out of the Darkness: A Survivor's Story* (Fort Worth, TX: Manifold Grace, 2014), 1.

21. Arthur L. Greil and David R. Rudy, "Conversion to the World View of Alcoholics Anonymous: A Refinement of Conversion Theory," *Qualitative Sociology* 6, no. 1 (1983): 5–28.

22. Barbara Amaya, *Nobody's Girl: A Memoir of Lost Innocence, Modern Day Slavery & Transformation* (Pittsburgh, PA: Animal, 2015), 210–11.

23. Jasmine Grace Marino, *The Diary of Jasmine Grace: Trafficked. Recovered. Redeemed* (self-published, 2016), 213.

24. Katariina Rosenblatt, *Stolen: The True Story of a Sex Trafficking Survivor* (Grand Rapids, MI: Revell, 2014), 162.

25. Rebecca Bender, *Roadmap to Redemption* (self-published, 2013), 36.

26. Bender, 35; Marino, *The Diary of Jasmine Grace*, 158; Jay, *Out of the Darkness*, 19.

27. Rosenblatt, *Stolen*, 91, 95.

28. Mimi Crown, *Stuck in Traffic* (self-published, 2016), 13, 33, 27.
29. Brook Parker-Bello, *Living Inside the Rainbow: Winning the Battlefield of the Mind After Human Trafficking & Mental Bondage* (self-published, 2014), 10.
30. Parker-Bello, 39.
31. Bender, *Roadmap to Redemption*, 28.
32. Bender, 29.
33. Bender, 21.
34. Rosenblatt, *Stolen*, 19.
35. Marino, *The Diary of Jasmine Grace*, 144.
36. Elizabeth Bernstein, *Temporarily Yours: Intimacy, Authenticity, and the Commerce of Sex* (Chicago: University of Chicago Press, 2007), 180.
37. Lutnick, *Domestic Minor Sex Trafficking*, 17.
38. Unreliable statistics commonly circulated by antitrafficking activists indicate that 70–90 percent of trafficked women have a history of sexual abuse. Like so many of the numbers paraded as confirmed statistics by antitrafficking advocates, that factoid is unsubstantiated, based as it is on extremely small, localized, and even anecdotal research samples. Though we have reasonable anecdotal evidence that prior sexual abuse is common among women who are trafficked, it is also possible that victims of trafficking feel compelled to fit the mold of the statistic by including this as part of their stories. Certainly, even if we were to accept the commonly believed statistic, survivors who have a history of sexual abuse still have a disproportionate representation in the published narratives as well as among those survivors who are embraced and given a platform by antitrafficking advocates, perhaps because they fit expectations regarding trafficking and because it reinforces the narrative of victimization. This is not to suggest that narrators fabricate sexual abuse but to emphasize prior sexual abuse as a genre convention that narrators likely feel compelled to mention to be considered a legitimate victim. Potentially, any victim of trafficking whose experiences do not conform to the commonly held perception that sexual abuse is a ubiquitous factor in engagement in the sex trade might not be considered representative and, more frightening even, could potentially have her victimization doubted or marginalized.
39. In the majority of these memoirs, the narrators use the terms "human trafficking" and "slavery" somewhat interchangeably and often in tandem, though, admittedly, they use both rather infrequently. Nonetheless, there is a slight distinction in how the two terms are used.
40. Alison Brysk and Austin Choi-Fitzpatrick, *From Human Trafficking to Human Rights: Reframing Contemporary Slavery* (Philadelphia: University of Pennsylvania Press, 2012), 1.
41. See, for instance, Parker-Bello, *Living Inside the Rainbow*, 1, 58; Marino, *The Diary of Jasmine Grace*, 104; Amaya, *Nobody's Girl*, 124; Rosenblatt, *Stolen*, 200.
42. Marino, 128. For an interesting essay about the risks of misattributing this quote to Tubman, see W. Caleb McDaniel, "The Dangers of a Fake Tubman Quote," W. Caleb McDaniel (professional website), March 22, 2016, accessed January 10, 2018, http://wcm1.web.rice.edu/fake-tubman-quote.html.
43. Parker-Bello, *Living Inside the Rainbow*, 104.
44. For full text and commentary on the conventions, see Jean Allain, *The Slavery Conventions: The Travaux Préparatoires of the 1926 League of Nations Convention and*

the 1956 United Nations Convention (New York: Brill, 2008), 31–166. For Bellagio-Harvard legal guidelines, see Members of the Research Network on the Legal Parameters of Slavery, "Bellagio-Harvard Guidelines on the Legal Parameters of Slavery," March 3, 2012, http://www.law.qub.ac.uk/schools/SchoolofLaw/FileStore /Filetoupload,651854,en.pdf; Jean Allain and Kevin Bales, "Slavery and Its Definition," *Slavery Today* 14, no. 2 (Summer/Autumn 2012) 1–8.

45. Amaya, *Nobody's Girl*, 57; Jay, *Out of the Darkness*, 41.

46. Alison Brysk, "Rethinking Trafficking: Human Rights and Private Wrongs," in *From Human Trafficking to Human Rights: Reframing Contemporary Slavery*, ed. Alison Brysk and Austin Choi-Fitzpatrick (Philadelphia: University of Pennsylvania Press, 2012), 73.

47. Rosenblatt, *Stolen*, 109.

48. Jay, *Out of the Darkness*, 77.

49. Kevin Bales, *Disposable People: New Slavery in the Global Economy* (Berkeley: University of California Press, 2012), 14–15.

50. Wendy Barnes, *And Life Continues: Sex Trafficking and My Journey to Freedom* (self-published, 2015), 275.

51. Barnes, 286.

52. Barnes, 344–45.

53. Bender, *Roadmap to Redemption*, 28; Marino, *The Diary of Jasmine Grace*, 36.

54. Bender, 41.

55. Bender, 63, caps in original.

56. Bender, 59, caps in original.

57. Jay, *Out of the Darkness*, 53.

58. Kristin Bumiller, *In an Abusive State: How Neoliberalism Appropriated the Feminist Movement Against Sexual Violence* (Durham, NC: Duke University Press, 2009), 5.

59. For more on this topic, see Elizabeth Bernstein, "Militarized Humanitarianism Meets Carceral Feminism: The Politics of Sex, Rights, and Freedom in Contemporary Antitrafficking Campaigns," *Signs: Journal of Women in Culture and Society* 36, no. 1 (2010): 308–9; Loïc Wacquant, *Punishing the Poor: The Neoliberal Government of Social Insecurity* (Durham, NC: Duke University Press, 2009).

60. George W. Bush, "Remarks in a Discussion at Kirkwood Community College in Cedar Rapids, IA," July 20, 2004, *Public Papers of the Presidents*, George W. Bush, 2004, 2:1368, https://www.gpo.gov/fdsys/pkg/PPP-2004-book2/pdf/PPP-2004 -book2-doc-pg1368.pdf.

61. Zimmerman, *Other Dreams of Freedom*, 7.

62. Bumiller, *In an Abusive State*, 20.

63. Rosenblatt, *Stolen*, 200; Parker-Bello, *Living Inside the Rainbow*, 69, 53.

64. Marino, *The Diary of Jasmine Grace*, 151.

65. Jay, *Out of the Darkness*, 68; Bender, *Roadmap to Redemption*, 75; Crown, *Stuck in Traffic*, 125.

66. Crown, 125.

67. Jay, *Out of the Darkness*, 55.

68. Parker-Bello, *Living Inside the Rainbow*, 74,105.

69. Parker-Bello, 51.

70. Bender, *Roadmap to Redemption*, 98.

71. Bender, 51.

72. Bender, 21, 9.
73. Parker-Bello, *Living Inside the Rainbow*, 122.
74. Parker-Bello, 60.
75. Marino, *The Diary of Jasmine Grace*, 93.
76. *Alcoholics Anonymous: The Story of How Many Thousands of Men and Women Have Recovered from Alcoholism*, 4th ed. (New York: Alcoholics Anonymous World Services, 2001), 25.
77. *Alcoholics Anonymous*, 58.
78. Jay, *Out of the Darkness*, 79.
79. Parker-Bello, *Living Inside the Rainbow*, 161.
80. Parker-Bello, 66.
81. Parker-Bello, 242.
82. Amaya, *Nobody's Girl*, 171.
83. Amaya, 153.
84. Susan Friend Harding, *The Book of Jerry Falwell: Fundamentalist Language and Politics* (Princeton, NJ: Princeton University Press, 2000), 47.
85. Harding, 58.
86. Amaya, *Nobody's Girl*, 112.
87. See, for instance, Tanya Erzen, *Straight to Jesus: Sexual and Christian Conversions in the Ex-Gay Movement* (Berkeley: University of California Press, 2006).
88. Leigh Gilmore, *Tainted Witness: Why We Doubt What Women Say About Their Lives* (New York: Columbia University Press, 2017), 89.
89. Jessica Elliott, *The Role of Consent in Human Trafficking* (New York: Routledge, 2014); Berta E. Hernández-Truyol and Jane E. Larson, "Sexual Labor and Human Rights," *Columbia Human Rights Law Review* 37 (2005): 391; Kara Abramson, "Beyond Consent, Toward Safeguarding Human Rights: Implementing the United Nations Trafficking Protocol" *Harvard International Law Journal* 44, no. 2 (Summer 2003): 473.
90. Wendy Chapkis, "Trafficking, Migration, and the Law: Protecting Innocents, Punishing Immigrants," *Gender & Society* 17, no. 6 (December 1, 2003): 923–37; Yvonne C. Zimmerman, "Situating the Ninety-Nine: A Critique of the Trafficking Victims Protection Act," *Journal of Religion & Abuse* 7 (November 2, 2005): 37–56, https://doi.org/10.1300/J154v07n03_03; April Rieger, "Missing the Mark: Why the Trafficking Victims Protection Act Fails to Protect Sex Trafficking Victims in the United States," *Harvard Journal of Law and Gender* 30 (2007): 231–56; Moshoula Capous Desyllas, "A Critique of the Global Trafficking Discourse and U.S. Policy," *Journal of Sociology* 13, no. 2 (Summer 2012): 243–61.
91. Jo Doezema, "Who Gets to Choose? Coercion, Consent, and the UN Trafficking Protocol," *Gender & Development* 10, no. 1 (2002): 20–27; Gretchen Soderlund, "The Rhetoric of Revelation: Sex Trafficking and the Journalistic Exposé," *Humanity: An International Journal of Human Rights, Humanitarianism, and Development* 2, no. 2 (September 8, 2011): 193–211, https://doi.org/10.1353/hum.2011.0013; Carole S. Vance, "Thinking Trafficking, Thinking Sex," *GLQ: A Journal of Lesbian and Gay Studies* 17, no. 1 (2011): 137–38; Kempadoo, "Abolitionism, Criminal Justice, and Transnational Feminism," xii–xiii; Doezema, *Sex Slaves and Discourse Masters*; Laura T. Murphy, "Narrating 'White Slavery!' in *The Wire*: A Generic Genealogy," *Genre: Forms of Discourse and Culture* 47, no. 2 (2014): 111–40.

92. Kamala Kempadoo, "The Anti-Trafficking Juggernaut Rolls On," in *Trafficking and Prostitution Reconsidered: New Perspectives on Migration, Sex Work, and Human Rights*, ed. Kamala Kempadoo (Boulder, CO: Paradigm, 2012), 249–60; Pardis Mahdavi, *From Trafficking to Terror: Constructing a Global Social Problem* (New York: Routledge, 2013).

93. Bernstein, "Militarized Humanitarianism Meets Carceral Feminism," 313.

94. Jennifer Lynne Musto, "What's in a Name? Conflations and Contradictions in Contemporary U.S. Discourses of Human Trafficking," *Women's Studies International Forum* 32 (2009), 281–87; Elizabeth Bernstein, "The Sexual Politics of the 'New Abolitionism,'" *Differences* 18, no. 3 (2007): 128–51.

95. Parker-Bello, *Living Inside the Rainbow*, 36; Rosenblatt, *Stolen*, 203.

96. See, for instance, Bernstein, *Temporarily Yours*; Lutnick, *Domestic Minor Sex Trafficking*; Alison Bass, *Getting Screwed: Sex Workers and the Law* (Boston: University Press of New England, 2015); Stephanie A. Limoncelli, "The Trouble with Trafficking: Conceptualizing Women's Sexual Labor and Economic Human Rights," *Women's Studies International Forum*, 32, no. 4 (July/August 2009), 261–69.

97. Rosenblatt, *Stolen*, 203.

98. Kempadoo, "Abolitionism, Criminal Justice, and Transnational Feminism," xxix.

99. Kempadoo, xiv.

100. Vance, "Thinking Trafficking, Thinking Sex," 136.

101. Sharon S. Oselin, *Leaving Prostitution: Getting Out and Staying Out of Sex Work* (New York: New York University Press, 2014), 25.

102. Bass, *Getting Screwed*, 66–69; Oselin, 36–40.

103. Bernstein, *Temporarily Yours*, 68, 74–75.

104. Elliott, *The Role of Consent in Human Trafficking*, 108.

105. Gilmore, *Tainted Witness*, 115.

106. Parker-Bello, *Living Inside the Rainbow*, 5.

107. Parker-Bello, 3.

108. Parker-Bello, 132.

109. Parker-Bello, 236, emphasis in original.

110. Marino, *The Diary of Jasmine Grace*, 123.

111. Marino, 128, 124.

112. Marino, 126–28.

113. Marino, 129.

114. Marino, 211.

115. Parker-Bello, *Living Inside the Rainbow*, 237.

5. WHAT THE GENRE CREATES, IT DESTROYS: THE RISE AND FALL OF SOMALY MAM

1. Steve McQueen, dir., *12 Years a Slave* (Los Angeles: 20th Century Fox, 2014).

2. "Oprah 'Happy' at Civil Rights Cycle," sec. Entertainment & Arts, BBC News, November 13, 2013, http://www.bbc.com/news/entertainment-arts-24924888.

3. Revolt TV, "12 Years a Slave," video, YouTube, October 22, 2013, https://www.youtube.com/watch?v=oGOlQETrNds.

4. Salamishah Tillet, "Hollywood Finally Catches Up with History," Root, October 15, 2013, accessed October 2, 2017, http://www.theroot.com/hollywood-finally-catches -up-with-history-1790898482. It is important to note, however, that academics such as bell hooks were critical of the film's betrayal of enslaved women.

5. Somaly Mam, "My Own 'Twelve Years A Slave,'" Daily Beast, November 14, 2013, https://web.archive.org/web/20140323035342/https://www.thedailybeast.com /witw/articles/2013/11/14/somaly-mam-12-years-a-slave-and-the-scourge-of -human-trafficking.html.

6. "The Road of Lost Innocence by Somaly Mam (Review)," Kirkus Reviews, September 9, 2008, accessed October 2, 2017, https://www.kirkusreviews.com/book -reviews/somaly-mam/the-road-of-lost-innocence/. Ironically, both of those narratives have also been called into question by journalists, scholars, and former friends of the authors.

7. "Nonfiction Book Review: The Road of Lost Innocence: The True Story of a Cambodian Heroine by Somaly Mam," Publishers Weekly, August 11, 2008, accessed October 2, 2017, https://www.publishersweekly.com/978-0-385-52621-0.

8. James Olney, "'I Was Born': Slave Narratives, Their Status as Autobiography and as Literature," Callaloo, no. 20 (1984): 46–73.

9. Somaly Mam, The Road of Lost Innocence: The Story of a Cambodian Heroine (New York: Spiegel & Grau, 2009), 290.

10. Mam, 185.

11. Mam, 188.

12. Mam, 189.

13. For a discussion of Mam's use of silence, see Karen Thornber, "Global Health and World Literature: Translating Silences in Cambodian Writing on Sex Slavery," Literature and Medicine 31, no. 2 (2013): 235–55.

14. Mam, The Road of Lost Innocence; for a reading of Le Silence de l'Innocence, an earlier memoir of Mam's life, written in French in conjunction with a coauthor, see Thornber.

15. Mam, 189.

16. Mam, 186–87.

17. Robert Uy, "Blinded by Red Lights: Why Trafficking Discourse Should Shift Away from Sex and the 'Perfect Victim' Paradigm," Berkeley Journal of Gender, Law, and Justice 26, no. 1 (2011): 205.

18. Jayashri Srikantiah, "Perfect Victims and Real Survivors: The Iconic Victim in Domestic Human Trafficking Law," Boston University Law Review 28 (2007): 160.

19. Jessica Elliott, The Role of Consent in Human Trafficking (New York: Routledge, 2014), 24.

20. Wendy Chapkis, "Soft Glove, Punishing Fist: The Trafficking Victims Protection Act of 2000," in Regulating Sex: The Politics of Intimacy and Identity, ed. Elizabeth Bernstein and Laurie Schaffner (New York: Routledge, 2004), 52.

21. Kamala Kempadoo, "Abolitionism, Criminal Justice, and Transnational Feminism: Twenty-First-Century Perspectives on Human Trafficking," in Trafficking and Prostitution Reconsidered: New Perspectives on Migration, Sex Work, and Human Rights, ed. Kamala Kempadoo (Boulder, CO: Paradigm, 2012).

22. Srikantiah, "Perfect Victims and Real Survivors," 201. See also Michael Wilson and Erin O'Brien, "Constructing the Ideal Victim in the United States of America's

Annual Trafficking in Persons Reports," *Crime, Law and Social Change* 65, nos. 1–2 (2016): 29–45.

23. Gayatri Chakravorty Spivak, "Can the Subaltern Speak?," in *Can the Subaltern Speak? Reflections on the History of an Idea* (New York: Columbia University Press, 1988), 50.

24. Julietta Hua, *Trafficking Women's Human Rights* (Minneapolis: University of Minnesota Press, 2011), 35. The myth of the "perfect victim" is not unique to the discourse of modern slavery and human trafficking. For more on this myth in the realm of sexual assault, consult the following: Janice Du Mont, Karen-Lee Miller, and Terri L. Myhr, "The Role of 'Real Rape' and 'Real Victim' Stereotypes in the Police Reporting Practices of Sexually Assaulted Women," *Violence Against Women* 9, no. 4 (2003): 466–86; Jan Jordan, *The Word of a Woman? Police, Rape and Belief* (New York: Palgrave Macmillan, 2004).

25. Pardis Mahdavi, "The Charitable Industrial Complex: Justice, Not Charity, Is What's Needed," HuffPost, June 24, 2014, https://www.huffingtonpost.com/pardis-mahdavi/the-charitable-industrial-complex_b_5503711.html.

26. Claudia Cojocaru, "Sex Trafficking, Captivity, and Narrative: Constructing Victimhood with the Goal of Salvation," *Dialectical Anthropology* 39, no. 2 (2015): 187.

27. Cojocaru, 192.

28. Clothilde LeCoz, "Cambodia: Somaly Mam's Ex-Husband Speaks Out," Public Radio International, October 9, 2014, https://www.pri.org/stories/2014-10-09/cambodia-somaly-mam-s-ex-husband-speaks-out.

29. Simon Marks, "Somaly Mam: The Holy Saint (and Sinner) of Sex Trafficking," *Newsweek*, May 21, 2014; Simon Marks and Saing Soenthrith, "Police Deny Killings at Somaly Mam Center," *Cambodia Daily*, April 21, 2012, https://www.cambodiadaily.com/archives/police-deny-killings-at-somaly-mam-center-3652/; Simon Marks, "Former Afesip Director Denies Claim of Killings," *Cambodia Daily*, April 23, 2012, https://www.cambodiadaily.com/archives/former-afesip-director-denies-claim-of-killings-3648/; Simon Marks and Phorn Bopha, "More Questions over Somaly Mam's Kidnapping Claim," *Cambodia Daily*, April 25, 2012, https://www.cambodiadaily.com/archives/more-questions-over-somaly-mams-kidnapping-claim-1592/; Simon Marks, "Somaly Mam Admits to Inaccuracies in Speech to UN," *Cambodia Daily*, April 26, 2012, https://www.cambodiadaily.com/archives/somaly-mam-admits-to-inaccuracies-in-speech-to-un-1590/; Simon Marks and Khy Sovuthy, "Questions Raised over Symbol's Slavery Story," *Cambodia Daily*, October 26, 2012, https://www.cambodiadaily.com/archives/questions-raised-over-symbols-slavery-story-4809/; Simon Marks and Phorn Bopha, "Sex Slave Story Revealed to Be Fabricated," *Cambodia Daily*, October 12, 2013, https://www.cambodiadaily.com/archives/secrets-and-lies-44964/; Simon Marks, "The Rise of the Somaly Mam Foundation," *Cambodia Daily*, October 13, 2013, https://www.cambodiadaily.com/archives/the-rise-of-the-somaly-mam-foundation-44976/; Simon Marks and Kuch Naren, "Once Coached for TV, Now Asked to Keep Quiet," *Cambodia Daily*, November 4, 2013, https://www.cambodiadaily.com/archives/once-coached-for-tv-now-asked-to-keep-quiet-46510/; Simon Marks, "Aid Worker Claims Fabricated Stories Are Common," *Cambodia Daily*, November 7, 2013, https://www.cambodiadaily.com/archives/aid-worker-claims-fabricated-stories-are-common-46708/.

30. Marks, "Somaly Mam: The Holy Saint (and Sinner) of Sex Trafficking."

31. Marks; Marks and Bopha, "Sex Slave Story Revealed to Be Fabricated."

32. Marks, "Somaly Mam: The Holy Saint (and Sinner) of Sex Trafficking"; Marks and Sovuthy, "Questions Raised over Symbol's Slavery Story."

33. Nicholas Kristof, "If This Isn't Slavery, What Is?," sec. Opinion, *New York Times*, January 3, 2009, https://nyti.ms/2pRjwAM.

34. Marks and Bopha, "Sex Slave Story Revealed to Be Fabricated."

35. Abigail Pesta, "Somaly Mam's Story: 'I Didn't Lie,'" *Marie Claire*, September 16, 2014, http://www.marieclaire.com/world-reports/inspirational-women/somalys-story.

36. Pesta.

37. Pesta.

38. Pesta.

39. LeCoz, "Cambodia."

40. LeCoz; Marks and Naren, "Once Coached for TV, Now Asked to Keep Quiet."

41. Pesta, "Somaly Mam's Story."

42. See comments section of Marks, "Somaly Mam: The Holy Saint (and Sinner) of Sex Trafficking."

43. Elizabeth Nolan Brown, "Somaly Mam, the James Frey of Anti-Sex Trafficking Activism, Resigns from Her Foundation," *Reason* (blog), May 29, 2014, http://reason.com/blog/2014/05/29/sex-slavery-crusader-somaly-mam-resigns.

44. Disclaimer: an interview with Somaly Mam appeared in my own book, *Survivors of Slavery: Modern-Day Slave Narratives*, and an interview with one of her "daughters," Sina Vann, was also included in that collection.

45. Horng Pengly, "U.S. Was on to Somaly Mam," *Phnom Penh Post*, June 1, 2015, http://www.phnompenhpost.com/national/us-was-somaly-mam.

46. Laboratory to Combat Human Trafficking, "The Fall of Somaly Mam from Grace: Deception & Integrity in the Non-profit Sector," *Laboratory to Combat Human Trafficking* (blog), July 29, 2015, http://combathumantrafficking.org/2015/07/education-in-time-of-crisis/; Taina Bien-Aime, "The Somaly Mam Story: What We Still Know About Sex Trafficking," HuffPost, June 2, 2014, https://www.huffingtonpost.com/taina-bienaime/post_7641_b_5425805.html.

47. Nicholas Kristof, "A Woman I Regarded as a Hero, and New Doubts," *On the Ground* (blog), *New York Times*, June 2, 2014, https://kristof.blogs.nytimes.com/2014/06/02/a-woman-i-regarded-as-a-hero-and-new-doubts/; Harry Leibowitz, "Are We Letting the Scandal over Somaly Mam Distort the Realities of Child Trafficking?," HuffPost, June 16, 2014, https://www.huffingtonpost.com/harry-leibowitz/are-we-letting-the-scanda_b_5501356.html. For Garrison's warning to abolitionists, see William Lloyd Garrison, "An Impudent Imposter," *Liberator*, December 25, 1857, 206.

48. Brown, "Somaly Mam, the James Frey of Anti-Sex Trafficking Activism."

49. Anne Elizabeth Moore, "Here's Why It Matters When a Human Rights Crusader Builds Her Advocacy on Lies," Salon, May 28, 2014, https://www.salon.com/2014/05/28/heres_why_it_matters_when_a_human_rights_crusader_builds_her_advocacy_on_lies/; Melissa Gira Grant, "The Price of a Sex-Slave Rescue Fantasy," *New York Times*, May 30, 2014, https://nyti.ms/1ppjM6r. See also Heidi Hoefinger,

"Neoliberal Sexual Humanitarianism and Story-Telling: The Case of Somaly Mam," *Anti-Trafficking Review*, no. 7 (2016).

50. Leigh Gilmore, "Policing Truth: Confession, Gender, and Autobiographical Authority," in *Autobiography & Postmodernism*, ed. Kathleen M. Ashley, Gerald Peters, and Leigh Gilmore (Amherst: University of Massachusetts Press, 1994), 69.

51. Philippe Lejeune, *On Autobiography* (Minneapolis: University of Minnesota Press, 1989), 11.

52. Somaly Mam, *Le Silence de l'innocence* (Paris: A. Carrière, 2005), 9, translation mine.

53. Lejeune, *On Autobiography*, 11.

54. Ruth Marshall, personal interview, October 20, 2017.

55. Lejeune, *On Autobiography*, 26. See also Clayton Koelb, *The Incredulous Reader: Literature and the Function of Disbelief* (Ithaca, NY: Cornell University Press, 1984); Timothy Dow Adams, *Telling Lies in Modern American Autobiography* (Chapel Hill: University of North Carolina Press, 1990); Gilmore, "Policing Truth"; Paul John Eakin, *Fictions in Autobiography: Studies in the Art of Self-Invention* (Princeton, NJ: Princeton University Press, 2014); Leigh Gilmore, *Tainted Witness: Why We Doubt What Women Say About Their Lives* (New York: Columbia University Press, 2017).

56. Eakin, 37.

57. Mam, *The Road of Lost Innocence*, 4.

58. As Kelli Lyon Johnson notes, it is often this "turning point" that replaces the idyllic origins or the statement of one's birth in the shorter new slave narratives. Johnson, "The New Slave Narrative: Advocacy and Human Rights in Stories of Contemporary Slavery," *Journal of Human Rights* 12, no. 2 (2013): 249.

59. G. Thomas Couser, "Making, Taking, and Faking Lives: The Ethics of Collaborative Life Writing," *Style* 32, no. 2 (Summer 1998): 334–35.

60. John W. Blassingame, "Using the Testimony of Ex-Slaves: Approaches and Problems," *Journal of Southern History* 41, no. 4 (1975): 79.

61. Briton Hammon, *A Narrative of the Uncommon Sufferings, and Surprizing Deliverance of Briton Hammon, a Negro Man,—Servant to General Winslow, of Marshfield, in New-England: Who Returned to Boston, After Having Been Absent Almost Thirteen Years. Containing an Account of the Many Hardships He Underwent from the Time He Left His Master's House, in the Year 1747, to the Time of His Return to Boston.—How He Was Cast Away in the Capes of Florida;—the Horrid Cruelty and Inhuman Barbarity of the Indians in Murdering the Whole Ship's Crew;—the Manner of His Being Carry'd by Them into Captivity. Also, an Account of His Being Confined Four Years and Seven Months in a Close Dungeon,—and the Remarkable Manner in Which He Met with His Good Old Master in London; Who Returned to New-England, a Passenger, in the Same Ship* (Boston: Green & Russell, 1760); John Sekora, "Briton Hammon, the Indian Captivity Narrative, and the African American Slave Narrative," in *When Brer Rabbit Meets Coyote: African–Native American Literature*, ed. Jonathan Brennan (Chicago: University of Illinois Press, 2003), 150–52.

62. John Marrant, *A Narrative of the Lord's Wonderful Dealings with John Marrant, A Black* (London: Gilbert and Plummer, 1785).

63. Olney, "'I Was Born,'" 60.

64. Mark A. Sanders, "Theorizing the Collaborative Self: The Dynamics of Contour and Content in the Dictated Autobiography," *New Literary History* 25, no. 2 (1994): 455.

65. Mam, *The Road of Lost Innocence*, 14.

66. Mam, 186.

67. Vincent Carretta, *Equiano, the African: Biography of a Self-Made Man* (Athens: University of Georgia Press, 2005), 367.

68. Lara Langer Cohen, *The Fabrication of American Literature: Fraudulent and Antebellum Print Culture* (Philadelphia: University of Pennsylvania Press, 2011), 103.

69. Cohen, 105.

70. Sidonie Smith and Julia Watson, "Witness or False Witness: Metrics of Authenticity, Collective I-Formations, and the Ethic of Verification in First-Person Testimony," *Biography* 35, no. 4 (2012): 600.

71. Rigoberta Menchú, *I, Rigoberta Menchú: An Indian Woman in Guatemala* (New York: Verso, 2010); David Stoll, *Rigoberta Menchu and the Story of All Poor Guatemalans: New Foreword by Elizabeth Burgos* (New York: Westview, 2007); Arturo Arias and David Stoll, *The Rigoberta Menchú Controversy* (Minneapolis: University of Minnesota Press, 2001); Greg Grandin, *Who Is Rigoberta Menchú?* (New York: Verso, 2011). In her review of Melissa Gira Grant's *Playing the Whore*, Leslie Barnes also briefly connects Mam to Menchú and LeJeune's autobiographical pact. See Leslie Barnes, "Playing the Part, Telling the Tale: A Review of Melissa Gira Grant's *Playing the Whore: The Work of Sex Work*," *Sydney Review of Books*, January 7, 2014.

72. Mary Louise Pratt, "*I, Rigoberta Menchú* and the 'Culture Wars,'" in *The Rigoberta Menchú Controversy*, ed. Arturo Arias (Minneapolis: University of Minnesota Press, 2001), 42.

73. Leslie Barnes, "Exposed: The Scandalous Story of Sex Work in Cambodia," *Contemporary French and Francophone Studies* 22, no. 1 (2018): 40–48.

74. Gilmore, *Tainted Witness*, 67.

75. Smith and Watson, "Witness or False Witness," 604.

76. Dina Francesca Haynes, "The Celebritization of Human Trafficking," *Annals of the American Academy of Political and Social Science*, 653, no. 1 (May 2014): 25.

77. This is not to suggest that claims of fraud, negligence, or mismanagement made by former employees of Mam and observers of the organization are any less credible. Instead, this critique is about the generic factors relevant to credibility.

78. Gilmore, *Tainted Witness*, 14.

79. Gilmore, 89.

80. Smith and Watson, "Witness or False Witness," 596.

81. Lejeune, *On Autobiography*, 14.

82. Harriet Jacobs, *Incidents in the Life of a Slave Girl* (Boston, 1861), 5.

83. Solomon Northup, *Twelve Years a Slave*, ed. Sue Eakin (Woodlands, TX: Eakin, 2013), 215–16.

84. Frederick Douglass, "Literary Notices: Twelve Years a Slave," *Liberator*, August 26, 1853. Douglass's comment is often misquoted as "Its truth is *stranger* than fiction," which echoes the title of a later article in the *Liberator* but is not true to Douglass's original review or its reprint in the pages of Garrison's newspaper.

85. Geoffrey Sanborn, *Plagiarama! William Wells Brown and the Aesthetic of Attractions* (New York: Columbia University Press, 2016), 17.

86. William Wells Brown, *The Narrative of William W. Brown: A Fugitive Slave and a Lecture Delivered Before the Female Anti-Slavery Society of Salem* (Boston: Addison-Wesley, 1848).

CONCLUSION: COLLEGIAL READING

1. Girls Educational & Mentoring Service (GEMS), "More Than a Survivor Campaign," GEMS, accessed October 4, 2018, http://www.gems-girls.org/survivor-leadership/resources/more-than-a-survivor-campaign, page has been removed.

2. Rosemary Jolly, *Cultured Violence: Narrative, Social Suffering, and Engendering Human Rights in Contemporary South Africa*, 1st ed. (Liverpool: Liverpool University Press, 2010), 6.

3. Lynn Avery Hunt, *Inventing Human Rights: A History* (New York: W. W. Norton, 2007), 66.

4. Martha Craven Nussbaum, *Cultivating Humanity* (Cambridge, MA: Harvard University Press, 1997), 111–12.

5. Elaine Scarry, "The Difficulty of Imagining Other People," in *For Love of Country: Debating the Limits of Patriotism*, ed. Martha Craven Nussbaum and Joshua Cohen (Boston: Beacon, 1996), 99.

6. Saidiya Hartman, *Scenes of Subjection: Terror, Slavery, and Self-Making in Nineteenth-Century America* (New York: Oxford University Press, 1997), 19.

7. Francis Bok, *Escape from Slavery: The True Story of My Ten Years in Captivity—and My Journey to Freedom in America* (New York: Macmillan, 2003), 220.

8. Bok, 217.

9. Rachel Lloyd, *Girls Like Us: Fighting for a World Where Girls Are Not for Sale, an Activist Finds Her Calling and Heals Herself* (New York: Harper Collins, 2011), 266.

10. Stephen Best and Sharon Marcus, "Surface Reading: An Introduction," *Representations* 108, no. 1 (Fall 2009): 9.

11. Wai-Chee Dimock, *Through Other Continents: American Literature Across Deep Time* (Princeton, NJ: Princeton University Press, 2006), 8.

BIBLIOGRAPHY

Abramson, Kara. "Beyond Consent, Toward Safeguarding Human Rights: Implementing the United Nations Trafficking Protocol." *Harvard International Law Journal* 44, no. 2 (Summer 2003): 473–502.

Adams, Timothy Dow. *Telling Lies in Modern American Autobiography*. Chapel Hill: University of North Carolina Press, 1990.

Agustín, Laura María. *Sex at the Margins: Migration, Labour, Markets and the Rescue Industry*. London: Zed, 2007.

Akofa, Henriette. *Une Esclave Moderne*. With Olivier Broca. Paris: Michel Lafon, 2000.

Alcoff, Linda, and Laura Gray. "Survivor Discourse: Transgression or Recuperation?" *Signs: Journal of Women in Culture and Society* 18, no. 2 (1993): 260–90.

Alcoholics Anonymous: The Story of How Many Thousands of Men and Women Have Recovered from Alcoholism. 4th ed. New York: Alcoholics Anonymous World Services, 2001.

Alexander, Michelle. *The New Jim Crow: Mass Incarceration in the Age of Colorblindness*. New York: New, 2012.

Ali, Miriam, and Jana Wain. *Without Mercy: A Mother's Struggle Against Modern Slavery*. London: Sphere, 1996.

Allain, Jean. *The Slavery Conventions: The Travaux Préparatoires of the 1926 League of Nations Convention and the 1956 United Nations Convention*. New York: Brill, 2008.

Allain, Jean, and Kevin Bales. "Slavery and Its Definition." *Slavery Today* 14, no. 2 (Summer/Autumn 2012): 1–8.

Amaya, Barbara. *Nobody's Girl: A Memoir of Lost Innocence, Modern Day Slavery & Transformation*. Pittsburgh, PA: Animal, 2015.

Amony, Evelyn. *I Am Evelyn Amony: Reclaiming My Life from the Lord's Resistance Army*. Madison: University of Wisconsin Press, 2015.

Andrews, William L. *North Carolina Slave Narratives: The Lives of Moses Roper, Lunsford Lane, Moses Grandy & Thomas H. Jones*. Chapel Hill: University of North Carolina Press, 2003.

——. *To Tell a Free Story: The First Century of African-American Autobiography*. Urbana: University of Illinois Press, 1986.

Anghie, Antony. *Imperialism, Sovereignty and the Making of International Law*. New York: Cambridge University Press, 2007.

Arendt, Hannah. *Between Past and Future: Eight Exercises in Political Thought*. New York: Penguin, 2006.

Arias, Arturo, and David Stoll. *The Rigoberta Menchú Controversy*. Minneapolis: University of Minnesota Press, 2001.

Bales, Kevin. *Disposable People: New Slavery in the Global Economy*. Berkeley: University of California Press, 2012.

——. *Ending Slavery: How We Free Today's Slaves*. Berkeley: University of California Press, 2007.

——. "Testing a Theory of Modern Slavery." Paper, From Chattel Bondage to State Servitude: Slavery in the 20th Century, Gilder Lehrman Center, Yale University, 2004. https://glc.yale.edu/sites/default/files/files/events/cbss/Bales.pdf.

Bales, Kevin, and Ron Soodalter. *The Slave Next Door*. Berkeley: University of California Press, 2009.

Bales, Kevin, and Zoe Trodd. *To Plead Our Own Cause: Personal Stories by Today's Slaves*. Ithaca, NY: Cornell University Press, 2013.

Baptist, Edward E. *The Half Has Never Been Told: Slavery and the Making of American Capitalism*. New York: Basic, 2014.

Barnes, Leslie. "Exposed: The Scandalous Story of Sex Work in Cambodia." *Contemporary French and Francophone Studies* 22, no. 1 (2018): 40–48.

——. "Playing the Part, Telling the Tale: A Review of Melissa Gira Grant's *Playing the Whore: The Work of Sex Work*." *Sydney Review of Books*, January 7, 2014.

Barnes, Wendy. *And Life Continues: Sex Trafficking and My Journey to Freedom*. Self-published, 2015.

Bass, Alison. *Getting Screwed: Sex Workers and the Law*. Boston: University Press of New England, 2015.

Bauer, Wolfgang. *Stolen Girls: Survivors of Boko Haram Tell Their Story*. New York: New, 2017.

Bauman, Zygmunt. *Freedom*. Minneapolis: University of Minnesota Press, 1988.

Beah, Ishmael. *A Long Way Gone: Memoirs of a Boy Soldier*. New York: Harper Collins, 2008.

Bender, Rebecca. *Roadmap to Redemption*. Self-published, 2013.

Bernstein, Elizabeth. "Carceral Politics as Gender Justice? The 'Traffic in Women' and Neoliberal Circuits of Crime, Sex, and Rights." *Theory and Society* 41, no. 3 (2012): 233–59.

——. "Militarized Humanitarianism Meets Carceral Feminism: The Politics of Sex, Rights, and Freedom in Contemporary Antitrafficking Campaigns." *Signs: Journal of Women in Culture and Society* 36, no. 1 (2010): 45–71.

——. "The Sexual Politics of the 'New Abolitionism.'" *Differences* 18, no. 3 (2007): 128–51.

——. *Temporarily Yours: Intimacy, Authenticity, and the Commerce of Sex.* Chicago: University of Chicago Press, 2007.

Best, Stephen, and Sharon Marcus. "Surface Reading: An Introduction." *Representations* 108, no. 1 (Fall 2009): 1–21.

Bien-Aime, Taina. "The Somaly Mam Story: What We Still Know About Sex Trafficking." HuffPost, June 2, 2014. https://www.huffingtonpost.com/taina-bienaime /post_7641_b_5425805.html.

Blackmon, Douglas A. *Slavery by Another Name: The Re-enslavement of Black Americans from the Civil War to World War II.* New York: Anchor, 2009.

Blassingame, John W. *Slave Testimony: Two Centuries of Letters, Speeches, Interviews, and Autobiographies.* Baton Rouge: Louisiana State University Press, 1977.

——. "Using the Testimony of Ex-Slaves: Approaches and Problems." *Journal of Southern History* 41, no. 4 (1975): 473–92.

Bok, Francis. *Escape from Slavery: The True Story of My Ten Years in Captivity—and My Journey to Freedom in America.* New York: Macmillan, 2003.

Brennan, Denise. "Methodological Challenges in Research with Trafficked Persons: Tales from the Field." *International Migration* 43, nos. 1–2 (2005): 35–54.

Brown, Elizabeth Nolan. "Somaly Mam, the James Frey of Anti-Sex Trafficking Activism, Resigns from Her Foundation." Reason, May 29, 2014. http://reason.com/blog /2014/05/29/sex-slavery-crusader-somaly-mam-resigns.

Brown, William Wells. *The Narrative of William W. Brown: A Fugitive Slave and a Lecture Delivered Before the Female Anti-slavery Society of Salem.* Boston: Addison-Wesley, 1848.

Bruce, Dickson D. "Politics and Political Philosophy in the Slave Narrative." In *The Cambridge Companion to the African American Slave Narrative.* New York: Cambridge University Press, 2007.

Brysk, Alison. "Rethinking Trafficking: Human Rights and Private Wrongs." In *From Human Trafficking to Human Rights: Reframing Contemporary Slavery,* ed. Alison Brysk and Austin Choi-Fitzpatrick, 73–85. Philadelphia: University of Pennsylvania Press, 2012.

Brysk, Alison, and Austin Choi-Fitzpatrick. *From Human Trafficking to Human Rights: Reframing Contemporary Slavery.* Philadelphia: University of Pennsylvania Press, 2012.

Bumiller, Kristin. *In an Abusive State: How Neoliberalism Appropriated the Feminist Movement Against Sexual Violence.* Durham, NC: Duke University Press, 2009.

Bush, George W. "Remarks in a Discussion at Kirkwood Community College in Cedar Rapids, IA," July 20, 2004. *Public Papers of the Presidents,* George W. Bush, 2004, 2:1368. https://www.gpo.gov/fdsys/pkg/PPP-2004-book2/pdf/PPP-2004-book2-doc -pg1368.pdf.

Cadet, Jean-Robert. *My Stone of Hope: From Haitian Slave Child to Abolitionist.* Austin: University of Texas Press, 2011.

——. *Restavec: From Haitian Slave Child to Middle-Class American.* Austin: University of Texas Press, 1998.

Carby, Hazel V. *Reconstructing Womanhood: The Emergence of the Afro-American Woman Novelist.* New York: Oxford University Press, 1987.

Carretta, Vincent. *Equiano, the African: Biography of a Self-Made Man.* Athens: University of Georgia Press, 2005.

——, ed. *Unchained Voices: An Anthology of Black Authors in the English-Speaking World of the Eighteenth Century.* Lexington: University Press of Kentucky, 2013.

Caruth, Cathy. *Unclaimed Experience: Trauma, Narrative, and History.* Baltimore, MD: Johns Hopkins University Press, 2016.

CdeBaca, Louis. "The Role of the United States in Combating Human Trafficking." Washington, DC: Center for American Progress, May 12, 2010. https://2009-2017 .state.gov/j/tip/rls/rm/2010/141728.htm.

Chapkis, Wendy. "Soft Glove, Punishing Fist: The Trafficking Victims Protection Act of 2000." In *Regulating Sex: The Politics of Intimacy and Identity,* ed. Elizabeth Bernstein and Laurie Schaffner, 51–65. New York: Routledge, 2004.

——. "Trafficking, Migration, and the Law: Protecting Innocents, Punishing Immigrants." *Gender & Society* 17, no. 6 (December 1, 2003): 923–37.

Childs, Dennis. *Slaves of the State: Black Incarceration from the Chain Gang to the Penitentiary.* Minneapolis: University of Minnesota Press, 2015.

Chisolm-Straker, Makini, Jeremy Sze, Julia Einbond, James White, and Hanni Stoklosa. "A Supportive Adult May Be the Difference in Homeless Youth Not Being Trafficked." *Children and Youth Services Review* 91 (2018): 115–20.

Chouliaraki, Lilie. *The Spectatorship of Suffering.* London: Sage, 2006.

Cohen, Lara Langer. *The Fabrication of American Literature: Fraudulence and Antebellum Print Culture.* Philadelphia: University of Pennsylvania Press, 2011.

Cojocaru, Claudia. "Sex Trafficking, Captivity, and Narrative: Constructing Victimhood with the Goal of Salvation." *Dialectical Anthropology* 39, no. 2 (2015): 183.

Coundouriotis, Eleni. "The Child Soldier Narrative and the Problem of Arrested Historicization." *Journal of Human Rights* 9, no. 2 (2010): 191–206.

——. "You Only Have Your Word: Rape and Testimony." *Human Rights Quarterly* 35, no. 2 (2013): 365–85.

Couser, G. Thomas. "Making, Taking, and Faking Lives: The Ethics of Collaborative Life Writing." *Style* 32, no. 2 (Summer 1998): 334–50.

Croce, Benedetto. *Aesthetic as Science of Expression and of Linguistics in General.* Trans. Colin Lyas, Cambridge: Cambridge University Press, 1992.

Crown, Mimi. *Stuck in Traffic.* Self-published, 2016.

Curtis, Ric, Karen Terry, Meredith Dank, Kirk Dombrowski, and Bilal Khan. "Commercial Sexual Exploitation of Children in New York City, Volume One: The CSEC Population in New York City: Size, Characteristics and Needs." *Center for Court Innovation* 56 (2008).

Dang, Minh. "An Open Letter to the Anti-Trafficking Movement." In *Survivors of Slavery: Modern-Day Slave Narratives,* ed. Laura T. Murphy. New York: Columbia University Press, 2014.

Dank, Meredith. "Surviving the Streets of New York: Experiences of LGBTQ Youth, YMSM, and YWSW Engaged in Survival Sex." New York: Urban Institute, 2015.

Dank, Meredith, Bilal Khan, P. Mitchell Downey, Cybele Kotonias, Deborah Mayer, Coleen Owens, Laura Pacifici, and Lilly Yu. "Estimating the Size and Structure of the Underground Sex Economy in Eight Major U.S. Cities." New York: Urban Institute, 2014.

Davidson, Julia O'Connell. "The Presence of the Past: Lessons of History for Anti-Trafficking Work." *Anti-Trafficking Review* 9 (2017).

Day, Sophie. "The Re-Emergence of 'Trafficking': Sex Work Between Slavery and Freedom." *Journal of the Royal Anthropological Institute* 16, no. 4 (2010): 816–34.

De Bruijn, Esther, and Laura T. Murphy. "Trading in Innocence: Slave-Shaming in Ghanaian Children's Market Fiction." *Journal of African Cultural Studies* 30, no. 3 (May 2017): 243–62.

De Hart, Betty. "Not Without My Daughter: On Parental Abduction, Orientalism and Maternal Melodrama." *European Journal of Women's Studies* 8, no. 1 (2001): 51–65.

Derrida, Jacques, and Avital Ronell. "The Law of Genre." *Critical Inquiry* 7, no. 1 (1980): 55–81.

DeStefano, Anthony. *The War on Human Trafficking: U.S. Policy Assessed.* New Brunswick, NJ: Rutgers University Press, 2007.

Desyllas, Moshoula Capous. "A Critique of the Global Trafficking Discourse and U.S. Policy." *Journal of Sociology* 13, no. 2 (Summer 2012): 243–61.

Dimock, Wai Chee. "Introduction: Genres as Fields of Knowledge." *PMLA* 122, no. 5 (2007): 1377–88.

——. *Through Other Continents: American Literature Across Deep Time.* Princeton, NJ: Princeton University Press, 2006.

Doezema, Jo. *Sex Slaves and Discourse Masters: The Construction of Trafficking.* London: Zed, 2013.

——. "Who Gets to Choose? Coercion, Consent, and the UN Trafficking Protocol." *Gender & Development* 10, no. 1 (2002): 20–27.

Dottridge, Michael. "Eight Reasons Why We Shouldn't Use the Term 'Modern Slavery.'" OpenDemocracy, October 17, 2017. https://www.opendemocracy.net/beyond slavery/michael-dottridge/eight-reasons-why-we-shouldn-t-use-term-modern -slavery.

Douglass, Frederick. *Frederick Douglass: Selected Speeches and Writings.* Chicago: Chicago Review, 2000.

——. "The Hutchinson Family—Hunkerism." *Northstar*, October 27, 1848.

——. "Literary Notices: Twelve Years a Slave." *Liberator*, August 26, 1853.

——. *My Bondage and My Freedom.* 1855. New York: Dover, 1969.

——. *Narrative of the Life of Frederick Douglass, an American Slave.* New York: Broadview, 2018.

Douzinas, Costas. *Human Rights and Empire: The Political Philosophy of Cosmopolitanism.* New York: Routledge, 2007.

Du Mont, Janice, Karen-Lee Miller, and Terri L. Myhr. "The Role of 'Real Rape' and 'Real Victim' Stereotypes in the Police Reporting Practices of Sexually Assaulted Women." *Violence Against Women* 9, no. 4 (2003): 466–86.

Eakin, Paul John. *Fictions in Autobiography: Studies in the Art of Self-Invention.* Princeton, NJ: Princeton University Press, 2014.

Elliott, Jessica. *The Role of Consent in Human Trafficking.* New York: Routledge, 2014.

Equiano, Olaudah. *The Interesting Narrative of the Life of Olaudah Equiano.* Ed. Werner Sollors. New York: Norton Critical Editions, 2000.

Erzen, Tanya. *Straight to Jesus: Sexual and Christian Conversions in the Ex-Gay Movement.* Berkeley: University of California Press, 2006.

Estes, Richard J., and Neil Alan Weiner. *The Commercial Sexual Exploitation of Children in the U.S., Canada and Mexico: Executive Summary (of the U.S. National Study)*. Philadelphia: University of Pennsylvania School of Social Work, Center for the Study of Youth Policy, 2001.

Fatima. *Esclave a 11 Ans: Temoignage*. Paris: Flammarion, 2011.

Feingold, David A. "Trafficking in Numbers: The Social Construction of Human Trafficking Data." In *Sex, Drugs, and Body Counts: The Politics of Numbers in Global Crime and Conflict*, 46–74. Ithaca, NY: Cornell University Press, 2010.

Fernando, Beatrice. *In Contempt of Fate: The Tale of a Sri Lankan Sold into Servitude, Who Survived to Tell It: A Memoir*. Self-published, 2005.

Fisch, Audrey. Introduction to *The Cambridge Companion to the African American Slave Narrative*. New York: Cambridge University Press, 2007.

Flores, Theresa. *The Sacred Bath: An American Teen's Story of Modern Day Slavery*. New York: iUniverse, 2007.

——. *The Slave Across the Street: The True Story of How an American Teen Survived the World of Human Trafficking*. Garden City, ID: Ampelon, 2010.

Foner, Eric. "The Meaning of Freedom in the Age of Emancipation." *Journal of American History* 81, no. 2 (September 1994): 435.

Forsyth, Sarah. *Slave Girl*. London: CPI Bookmarque, 2009.

Foster, Frances Smith. *Witnessing Slavery: The Development of Ante-Bellum Slave Narratives*. Madison: University of Wisconsin Press, 1979.

Garrison, William Lloyd. "Declaration of the National Anti-Slavery Convention." *Liberator*, December 14, 1833.

——. "An Impudent Imposter." *Liberator*, December 25, 1857.

Gates, Henry Louis, Jr. Introduction to *The Slave's Narrative: Texts and Contexts*. Ed. Charles T. Davis and Henry Louis Gates Jr. New York: Oxford University Press, 1985.

Gilmore, Leigh. "Policing Truth: Confession, Gender, and Autobiographical Authority." In *Autobiography & Postmodernism*, ed. Kathleen M. Ashley, Gerald Peters, and Leigh Gilmore. Amherst: University of Massachusetts Press, 1994.

——. *Tainted Witness: Why We Doubt What Women Say About Their Lives*. New York: Columbia University Press, 2017.

Gilmore, Leigh, and Elizabeth Marshall. "Girls in Crisis: Rescue and Transnational Feminist Autobiographical Resistance." *Feminist Studies* 36, no. 3 (2010): 667–90.

Girls Educational & Mentoring Service (GEMS). "More Than a Survivor Campaign." GEMS. Accessed October 4, 2018. http://www.gems-girls.org/survivor-leadership /resources/more-than-a-survivor-campaign. Page has been removed.

Global Alliance Against Traffic in Women. "What's the Cost of a Rumour: A Guide to Sorting Out the Myths and the Facts About Sporting Events and Human Trafficking." Bangkok: Global Alliance Against Traffic in Women, 2011. http://www.gaatw .org/publications/WhatstheCostofaRumour.11.15.2011.pdf.

Global Slavery Index. Walk Free Foundation. Accessed June 7, 2018. https://www .globalslaveryindex.org/.

Gluck, Elliott, and Rricha Mathur. "Child Sex Trafficking and the Child Welfare System." *State Policy Advocacy & Reform Center* 1 (2014).

Goldberg, Eleanor. "Super Bowl Is Single Largest Human Trafficking Incident in U.S.: Attorney General." *HuffPost*, February 3, 2013, https://www.huffingtonpost.com /2013/02/03/super-bowl-sex-trafficking_n_2607871.html.

Goyal, Yogita. "African Atrocity, American Humanity: Slavery and Its Transnational Afterlives." *Research in African Literatures* 45, no. 3 (2014): 48–71.

——. "The Genres of *Guantánamo Diary*: Postcolonial Reading and the War on Terror." *Cambridge Journal of Postcolonial Literary Inquiry* 4, no. 1 (2017): 69–87.

Grandin, Greg. *Who Is Rigoberta Menchú?* New York: Verso, 2011.

Grant, Melissa Gira. "The Price of a Sex-Slave Rescue Fantasy." *New York Times*, May 30, 2014.

Gray, Stephen. "Rites and Wrongs of Passage: Child Soldiers in African Writing." *English Academy Review* 28, no. 2 (2011): 4–14.

Gready, Paul. "Introduction: 'Responsibility to the Story.'" *Journal of Human Rights Practice* 2, no. 2 (2010): 177–90.

Greil, Arthur L., and David R. Rudy. "Conversion to the World View of Alcoholics Anonymous: A Refinement of Conversion Theory." *Qualitative Sociology* 6, no. 1 (1983): 5–28.

Grimké, Angelina. "Letter to Catherine E. Beecher in Reply to an Essay on Slavery and Abolitionism Addressed to A. E. Grimké; Letter 1," June 12, 1837. https://archive.org/stream/letterstocatherioogrimrich/letterstocatherioogrimrich_djvu.txt.

Hall, Shyima. *Hidden Girl: The True Story of a Modern-Day Child Slave.* New York: Simon & Schuster, 2014.

Hammon, Briton. *A Narrative of the Uncommon Sufferings, and Surprizing Deliverance of Briton Hammon, a Negro Man,—Servant to General Winslow, of Marshfield, in New-England: Who Returned to Boston, After Having Been Absent Almost Thirteen Years. Containing an Account of the Many Hardships He Underwent from the Time He Left His Master's House, in the Year 1747, to the Time of His Return to Boston.— How He Was Cast Away in the Capes of Florida;—the Horrid Cruelty and Inhuman Barbarity of the Indians in Murdering the Whole Ship's Crew;—the Manner of His Being Carry'd by Them into Captivity. Also, an Account of His Being Confined Four Years and Seven Months in a Close Dungeon,—and the Remarkable Manner in Which He Met with His Good Old Master in London; Who Returned to New-England, a Passenger, in the Same Ship.* Boston: Green & Russell, 1760.

Hammond, Peter. *Slavery, Terrorism, and Islam: The Historical Roots and Contemporary Threat.* Cape Town, South Africa: Christian Liberty, 2005.

Handler, Jerome S. "Survivors of the Middle Passage: Life Histories of Enslaved Africans in British America." *Slavery and Abolition* 23, no. 1 (2002): 25–56.

Harding, Susan Friend. *The Book of Jerry Falwell: Fundamentalist Language and Politics.* Princeton, NJ: Princeton University Press, 2000.

Harlow, Barbara. "Child and/or Soldier? From Resistance Movements to Human Rights Regiments." *CR: The New Centennial Review* 10, no. 1 (2010): 195–215.

Hartman, Saidiya V. *Scenes of Subjection: Terror, Slavery, and Self-Making in Nineteenth-Century America.* New York: Oxford University Press, 1997.

Haseltine, Dan. Foreword to *Girl Soldier: A Story of Hope for Northern Uganda's Children*, by Faith J. H. McDonnell and Grace Akallo, 11–14. Ada, MI: Chosen, 2007.

Hayes, Sophie. *Trafficked: My Story of Surviving, Escaping, and Transcending Abduction into Prostitution.* London: Sourcebooks, 2013.

Haynes, Dina Francesca. "The Celebritization of Human Trafficking." *Annals of the American Academy of Political and Social Science* 653, no. 1 (May 2014): 25–45.

Helff, Sissy. "Refugee Life Narratives—The Disturbing Potential of a Genre and the Case of Mende Nazer." *Matatu: Journal for African Culture & Society* 36, no. 1 (2009): 331–46.

Hernández-Truyol, Berta E., and Jane E. Larson. "Sexual Labor and Human Rights." *Columbia Human Rights Law Review* 37 (2005): 391–446.

Hertzke, Allen D. "African American Churches and U.S. Policy in Sudan." *Review of Faith and International Affairs* 6, no. 1 (2008): 19–26.

——. *Freeing God's Children: The Unlikely Alliance for Global Human Rights.* Lanham, MD: Rowman & Littlefield, 2004.

Hesford, Wendy. *Spectacular Rhetorics: Human Rights Visions, Recognitions, Feminisms.* Durham, NC: Duke University Press, 2011.

Hirschmann, Nancy J. *The Subject of Liberty: Toward a Feminist Theory of Freedom.* Princeton, NJ: Princeton University Press, 2009.

Hoefinger, Heidi. "Neoliberal Sexual Humanitarianism and Story-Telling: The Case of Somaly Mam." *Anti-Trafficking Review*, no. 7 (2016).

Hua, Julietta. *Trafficking Women's Human Rights.* Minneapolis: University of Minnesota Press, 2011.

Huehls, Mitchum. "Referring to the Human in Contemporary Human Rights Literature." *MFS: Modern Fiction Studies* 58, no. 1 (2012): 1–21.

"Human Trafficking: Better Data, Strategy, and Reporting Needed to Enhance U.S. Anti-trafficking Efforts Abroad." Washington, DC: United States Government Accountability Office, 2006. http://www.gao.gov/assets/260/250812.pdf.

Hunt, Lynn Avery. *Inventing Human Rights: A History.* New York: W. W. Norton, 2007.

Huntington, Samuel P. "The Clash of Civilizations?" *Foreign Affairs* (Summer 1993): 22–49.

Ignatieff, Michael, and Anthony Appiah. *Human Rights as Politics and Idolatry.* Princeton, NJ: Princeton University Press, 2003.

"In Our Own Backyard: Child Prostitution and Sex Trafficking in the United States." Subcommittee on Human Rights and the Law of the Committee on the Judiciary of the United States Senate. Washington, DC: Government Printing Office, 2010. https://www.gpo.gov/fdsys/pkg/CHRG-111shrg58003/pdf/CHRG-111shrg58003 .pdf.

Jackson, Emma. *The End of My World: The Shocking True Story of a Young Girl Forced to Become a Sex Slave.* London: Ebury, 2010.

Jacobs, Charles. "Amnesty's Dirty Little Secret." *Jewish Advocate*, February 8, 2007. http://archive.is/vMF3b#selection-569.155–569.398.

Jacobs, Harriet. *Incidents in the Life of a Slave Girl.* Boston, 1861.

Jal, Emmanuel. *War Child: A Child Soldier's Story.* New York: Macmillan, 2009.

James, Joy. *The New Abolitionists: (Neo) Slave Narratives and Contemporary Prison Writings.* Albany: State University of New York Press, 2005.

Jay, Alice. *Out of the Darkness: A Survivor's Story.* Fort Worth, TX: Manifold Grace, 2014.

Jinan. *Esclave de Daech.* With Thierry Oberle. Paris: Fayard, 2015.

Johnson, Kelli Lyon. "The New Slave Narrative: Advocacy and Human Rights in Stories of Contemporary Slavery." *Journal of Human Rights* 12, no. 2 (2013): 242–58.

Jolly, Rosemary. *Cultured Violence: Narrative, Social Suffering, and Engendering Human Rights in Contemporary South Africa.* 1st ed. Liverpool: Liverpool University Press, 2010.

Jordan, Jan. *The Word of a Woman? Police, Rape and Belief.* New York: Palgrave Macmillan, 2004.

Kaoma, Kaelyn. "Child Soldier Memoirs and the 'Classic' Slave Narrative: Tracing the Origins." *Life Writing* 15, no 2, 2017, 195–210.

Keitetsi, China. *Child Soldier.* London: Souvenir, 2004.

Kempadoo, Kamala. "Abolitionism, Criminal Justice, and Transnational Feminism: Twenty-First-Century Perspectives on Human Trafficking." In *Trafficking and Prostitution Reconsidered: New Perspectives on Migration, Sex Work, and Human Rights*, ed. Kamala Kempadoo, vii–xiii. Boulder, CO: Paradigm, 2012.

——. "The Anti-trafficking Juggernaut Rolls On." In *Trafficking and Prostitution Reconsidered: New Perspectives on Migration, Sex Work, and Human Rights*, 249–60. Boulder, CO: Paradigm, 2012.

——. "The Modern-Day White (Wo)Man's Burden: Trends in Anti-trafficking and Antislavery Campaigns." *Journal of Human Trafficking* 1, no. 1 (January 2, 2015): 8–20. https://doi.org/10.1080/23322705.2015.1006120.

Kennedy, David. *The Dark Sides of Virtue: Reassessing International Humanitarianism.* Princeton, NJ: Princeton University Press, 2005.

Khalaf, Farida. *The Girl Who Escaped ISIS: This Is My Story.* New York: Simon & Schuster, 2016.

Kim, Eunsun. *A Thousand Miles to Freedom: My Escape from North Korea.* With Sebastien Falletti. Trans. David Tian. New York: St. Martin's Griffin, 2015.

King, Martin Luther, Jr. "I Have a Dream." Speech, Washington, DC, August 28, 1963.

Klarer, Mario. "Humanitarian Pornography: John Gabriel Stedman's Narrative of a Five Years Expedition Against the Revolting Negroes of Surinam (1796)." *New Literary History* 36, no. 4 (2005): 559–87.

Koelb, Clayton. *The Incredulous Reader: Literature and the Function of Disbelief.* Ithaca, NY: Cornell University Press, 1984.

Kristof, Nicholas. "A Woman I Regarded as a Hero, and New Doubts." *On the Ground* (blog), *New York Times*, June 2, 2014. https://kristof.blogs.nytimes.com/2014/06/02/a-woman-i-regarded-as-a-hero-and-new-doubts/.

——. "If This Isn't Slavery, What Is?" Sec. Opinion, *New York Times*, January 3, 2009. http://www.nytimes.com/2009/01/04/opinion/04kristof.html.

Kyulanova, Irina. "From Soldiers to Children: Undoing the Rite of Passage in Ishmael Beah's *A Long Way Gone* and Bernard Ashley's *Little Soldier.*" *Studies in the Novel* 42, no. 1 (2010): 28–47.

Laboratory to Combat Human Trafficking. "The Fall of Somaly Mam from Grace: Deception & Integrity in the Non-profit Sector." *Laboratory to Combat Human Trafficking* (blog), July 29, 2015. http://combathumantrafficking.org/2015/07/education-in-time-of-crisis/.

Landesman, Peter. "The Girls Next Door." Sec. Magazine, *New York Times*, January 25, 2004. https://www.nytimes.com/2004/01/25/magazine/the-girls-next-door.html.

Laqueur, Thomas. "Bodies, Details, and the Humanitarian Narrative." In *The New Cultural History*, ed. Lynn Hunt, 176–204. Berkeley: University of California Press, 1989.

——. "The Moral Imagination and Human Rights." *Human Rights as Politics and as Idolatry*, ed. Michael Ignatieff, 127–40. Berkeley: University of California, 2001.

LeCoz, Clothilde. "Cambodia: Somaly Mam's Ex-Husband Speaks Out." Public Radio International, October 9, 2014. https://www.pri.org/stories/2014-10-09/cambodia -somaly-mam-s-ex-husband-speaks-out.

LeFlouria, Talitha L. *Chained in Silence: Black Women and Convict Labor in the New South*. Chapel Hill: University of North Carolina Press, 2015.

Leibowitz, Harry. "Are We Letting the Scandal over Somaly Mam Distort the Realities of Child Trafficking?" HuffPost, June 16, 2014. https://www.huffingtonpost.com /harry-leibowitz/are-we-letting-the-scanda_b_5501356.html.

Lejeune, Philippe. *On Autobiography*. Minneapolis: University of Minnesota Press, 1989.

Li, Stephanie. *Something Akin to Freedom: The Choice of Bondage in Narratives by African American Women*. Albany: State University of New York Press, 2010.

Limoncelli, Stephanie A. "The Trouble with Trafficking: Conceptualizing Women's Sexual Labor and Economic Human Rights." *Women's Studies International Forum*, 32, no. 4 (July/August 2009): 261–69.

Lloyd, Rachel. *Girls Like Us: Fighting for a World Where Girls Are Not for Sale, an Activist Finds Her Calling and Heals Herself*. New York: Harper Collins, 2011.

Lobert, Annie. *Fallen: Out of the Sex Industry and into the Arms of the Savior*. Brentwood, TN: Worthy, 2015.

Lockard, Joe. "Review Essay: Francis Bok's Escape from Slavery and Contemporary Slave Narratives." *Bad Subjects* (blog). Accessed March 1, 2018. https://bad.eserver .org/issues/2004/69/Lockard. Website has been removed.

Lott, Eric. *Love & Theft: Blackface Minstrelsy and the American Working Class*. New York: Oxford University Press, 2013.

Lovejoy, Paul E. " 'Freedom Narratives' of Transatlantic Slavery." *Slavery & Abolition* 32, no. 1 (2011): 91–107.

Luecha, Monluedee. *Child Sex Slave: A Memoir*. Self-published, 2012.

Lutnick, Alexandra. *Domestic Minor Sex Trafficking: Beyond Victims and Villains*. New York: Columbia University Press, 2016.

MacKenzie, Emily. *Runaway: Wild Child, Working Girl, Survivor*. London: Thistle, 2015.

Mackey, Allison. "Troubling Humanitarian Consumption: Reframing Relationality in African Child Soldier Narratives." *Research in African Literatures* 44, no. 4 (2013): 99–122.

Mahdavi, Pardis. "The Charitable Industrial Complex: Justice, Not Charity, Is What's Needed." HuffPost, June 24, 2014. https://www.huffingtonpost.com/pardis-mahdavi /the-charitable-industrial-complex_b_5503711.html.

——. *From Trafficking to Terror: Constructing a Global Social Problem*. New York: Routledge, 2013.

Mahmoody, Betty. *Not Without My Daughter*. New York: St. Martin's, 1987.

Mam, Somaly. *Le Silence de l'innocence*. Paris: A. Carrière, 2005.

——. "My Own 'Twelve Years A Slave.' " Daily Beast, November 14, 2013. https://web .archive.org/web/20140323035342/https://www.thedailybeast.com/witw/articles /2013/11/14/somaly-mam-12-years-a-slave-and-the-scourge-of-human-trafficking .html.

——. *The Road of Lost Innocence: The Story of a Cambodian Heroine*. New York: Spiegel & Grau, 2009.

Marino, Jasmine Grace. *The Diary of Jasmine Grace: Trafficked. Recovered. Redeemed.* Self-published, 2016.

Marks, Simon. "Aid Worker Claims Fabricated Stories Are Common." *Cambodia Daily,* November 7, 2013. https://www.cambodiadaily.com/archives/aid-worker-claims -fabricated-stories-are-common-46708/.

——. "Former Afesip Director Denies Claim of Killings." *Cambodia Daily,* April 23, 2012. https://www.cambodiadaily.com/archives/former-afesip-director-denies -claim-of-killings-3648/.

——. "The Rise of the Somaly Mam Foundation." *Cambodia Daily,* October 13, 2013. https://www.cambodiadaily.com/archives/the-rise-of-the-somaly-mam -foundation-44976/.

——. "Somaly Mam: The Holy Saint (and Sinner) of Sex Trafficking." *Newsweek,* May 21, 2014.

——. "Somaly Mam Admits to Inaccuracies in Speech to UN." *Cambodia Daily,* April 26, 2012. https://www.cambodiadaily.com/archives/somaly-mam-admits-to-inaccura cies-in-speech-to-un-1590/.

Marks, Simon, and Phorn Bopha. "More Questions over Somaly Mam's Kidnapping Claim." *Cambodia Daily,* April 25, 2012. https://www.cambodiadaily.com/archives /more-questions-over-somaly-mams-kidnapping-claim-1592/.

——. "Sex Slave Story Revealed to Be Fabricated." *Cambodia Daily,* October 12, 2013. https://www.cambodiadaily.com/archives/secrets-and-lies-44964/.

Marks, Simon, and Kuch Naren. "Once Coached for TV, Now Asked to Keep Quiet." *Cambodia Daily,* November 4, 2013. https://www.cambodiadaily.com/archives/once -coached-for-tv-now-asked-to-keep-quiet-46510/.

Marks, Simon, and Saing Soenthrith. "Police Deny Killings at Somaly Mam Center." *Cambodia Daily,* April 21, 2012. https://www.cambodiadaily.com/archives/police -deny-killings-at-somaly-mam-center-3652/.

Marks, Simon, and Khy Sovuthy. "Questions Raised over Symbol's Slavery Story." *Cambodia Daily,* October 26, 2012. https://www.cambodiadaily.com/archives/questions -raised-over-symbols-slavery-story-4809/.

Marrant, John. *A Narrative of the Lord's Wonderful Dealings with John Marrant, A Black.* London: Gilbert and Plummer, 1785.

McBride, Dwight. *Impossible Witnesses: Truth, Abolitionism, and Slave Testimony.* New York: New York University Press, 2001.

McDaniel, W. Caleb. "The Dangers of a Fake Tubman Quote." W. Caleb McDaniel (professional website), March 22, 2016. Accessed January 10, 2018. http://wcm1.web.rice .edu/fake-tubman-quote.html.

McDonnell, Faith J. H., and Grace Akallo. *Girl Soldier: A Story of Hope for Northern Uganda's Children.* Ada, MI: Chosen, 2007.

McQueen, Steve, dir. *12 Years a Slave.* Los Angeles: 20th Century Fox, 2014.

Meillassoux, Claude. *The Anthropology of Slavery: The Womb of Iron and Gold.* Chicago: University of Chicago Press, 1991.

Menchú, Rigoberta. *I, Rigoberta Menchú: An Indian Woman in Guatemala.* New York: Verso, 2010.

Merry, Sally Engle. *The Seductions of Quantification: Measuring Human Rights, Gender Violence, and Sex Trafficking.* Chicago: University of Chicago Press, 2016.

Middleton, Jennifer S., Maurice N. Gattis, Laura M. Frey, and Dominique Roe-Sepowitz. "Youth Experiences Survey (YES): Exploring the Scope and Complexity of Sex Trafficking in a Sample of Youth Experiencing Homelessness." *Journal of Social Service Research* 44, no. 2 (2018): 141–57.

Mogulescu, Kate. "The Super Bowl and Sex Trafficking." *New York Times*, January 31, 2014. https://www.nytimes.com/2014/02/01/opinion/the-super-bowl-of-sex-traffi cking.html.

Moore, Anne Elizabeth. "Here's Why It Matters When a Human Rights Crusader Builds Her Advocacy on Lies." Salon, May 28, 2014. https://www.salon.com/2014/05/28/heres _why_it_matters_when_a_human_rights_crusader_builds_her_advocacy_on_lies/.

Moynagh, Maureen. "Human Rights, Child-Soldier Narratives, and the Problem of Form." *Research in African Literatures* 42, no. 4 (2011): 39–59.

Muhsen, Zana. *A Promise to Nadia: A True Story of a British Slave in the Yemen.* London: Little, Brown, 2010.

Muhsen, Zana, and Andrew Crofts. *Sold: One Woman's True Account of Modern Slavery.* London: Sphere, 1991.

Murad, Nadia. *The Last Girl: My Story of Captivity, and My Fight Against the Islamic State.* New York: Tim Duggan, 2017.

Murphy, Laura T. "Labor and Sex Trafficking Among Homeless Youth: A Ten-City Study." New Orleans: Modern Slavery Research Project, 2017. https://static1 .squarespace.com/static/5887a2a61b631bfbbc1ad83a/t/5a7490fdc8302508d6b76f1c /1517588734590/Labor+and+Sex+Trafficking+Among+Homeless+Youth.pdf.

——. "Narrating 'White Slavery!' in *The Wire*: A Generic Genealogy." *Genre: Forms of Discourse and Culture* 47, no. 2 (2014): 111–40.

——. "The New Slave Narrative and the Illegibility of Modern Slavery." *Slavery & Abolition* 36, no. 2 (2015): 382–405.

——. "On Freedom and Complexity in the (Captive) Nation." *Journal of the African Literature Association* 12, no. 1 (2018): 60–71.

——. *Survivors of Slavery: Modern-Day Slave Narratives.* New York: Columbia University Press, 2014.

Musto, Jennifer Lynne. "The NGO-ification of the Anti-trafficking Movement in the United States: A Case Study of the Coalition to Abolish Slavery and Trafficking." *Wagadu: A Journal of Transnational Women's and Gender Studies* 5 (2008): 6.

——. "What's in a Name? Conflations and Contradictions in Contemporary U.S. Discourses of Human Trafficking." *Women's Studies International Forum* 32, no. 4 (2009): 281–87.

Mutua, Makau. "Savages, Victims, and Saviors: The Metaphor of Human Rights." *Harvard International Law Journal* 42, no. 1 (2001): 201–45.

Nagy, Timea. *Memoirs of a Sex Slave Survivor.* Toronto: Communication Dynamics, 2010.

Nazer, Mende. *Freedom: The Sequel to Slave.* London: Endeavor, 2012.

——. *Slave: My True Story.* New York: Public Affairs, 2003.

Neary, Janet. *Fugitive Testimony: On the Visual Logic of Slave Narratives.* New York: Oxford University Press, 2016.

Nicholson, Andrea. "A Survivor Centric Approach—The Importance of Contemporary Slave Narratives to the Anti-slavery Agenda." In *The SAGE Handbook of Human Trafficking and Modern Slavery*, ed. Sasha Poucki and Jennifer Bryson-Clarke. London: Sage, 2018.

Nicholson, Andrea, Minh Dang, and Zoe Trodd. "A Full Freedom: Contemporary Survivors' Definitions of Slavery." *Human Rights Law Review* 18, no. 4 (December 2018): 689–704.

"Nonfiction Book Review: *The Road of Lost Innocence: The True Story of a Cambodian Heroine* by Somaly Mam." *Publishers Weekly*, August 11, 2008. Accessed October 2, 2017. https://www.publishersweekly.com/978-0-385-52621-0.

Northup, Solomon. *Twelve Years a Slave*. Ed. Sue Eakin. Woodlands, TX: Eakin, 2013.

Nudelman, Franny. "Harriet Jacobs and the Sentimental Politics of Female Suffering." *English Literary History* 59, no. 4 (1992): 939–64.

Nussbaum, Martha Craven. *Cultivating Humanity*. Cambridge, MA: Harvard University Press, 1997.

Nussbaum, Martha Craven, and Joshua Cohen. *For Love of Country?* Boston: Beacon, 1996.

Okpara, Tina. *My Life Has a Price: A Memoir of Survival and Freedom*. Dakar: Amalion, 2012.

Olney, James. "'I Was Born': Slave Narratives, Their Status as Autobiography and as Literature." *Callaloo*, no. 20 (1984): 46–73.

"Oprah 'Happy' at Civil Rights Cycle." Sec. Entertainment & Arts, BBC News, November 13, 2013. http://www.bbc.com/news/entertainment-arts-24924888.

Oriola, Bukola. *Imprisoned: The Travails of a Trafficked Victim*. Self-published, 2009.

——. *A Living Label: An Inspirational Memoir and Guide*. Self-published, 2016.

Oselin, Sharon S. *Leaving Prostitution: Getting Out and Staying Out of Sex Work*. New York: New York University Press, 2014.

Parker-Bello, Brook. *Living Inside the Rainbow: Winning the Battlefield of the Mind After Human Trafficking & Mental Bondage*. Self-published, 2014.

Patterson, Orlando. *Freedom in the Making of Western Culture*. Vol. 1. London: I. B. Tauris, 1991.

Patterson, Thom, and CNN. "Inside Houston's Sex Slave Trade." CNN, May 7, 2018. Accessed September 27, 2018. https://www.cnn.com/2016/08/11/us/the-hunt-john-walsh-diaz-juarez-texas-sex-slave-human-trafficking/index.html.

Peabody, Ephraim. "Narratives of Fugitive Slaves." *Christian Examiner* 47, no. 1 (1849): 61–93.

Peck, Janice. "The Mediated Talking Cure: Therapeutic Framing of Autobiography in TV Talk Shows." In *Getting a Life: Everyday Uses of Autobiography*, ed. Sidonie Smith and Julia Watson, 134–55. Minneapolis: University of Minnesota Press, 1996.

Pengly, Horng. "U.S. Was on to Somaly Mam." *Phnom Penh Post*, June 1, 2015. http://www.phnompenhpost.com/national/us-was-somaly-mam.

Pesta, Abigail. "Somaly Mam's Story: 'I Didn't Lie.'" *Marie Claire*, September 16, 2014. http://www.marieclaire.com/world-reports/inspirational-women/somalys-story.

Phelps, Carissa. *Runaway Girl: Escaping Life on the Streets*. New York: Penguin, 2013.

Pratt, Mary Louise. "I, Rigoberta Menchú and the 'Culture Wars.'" In *The Rigoberta Menchú Controversy*, ed. Arturo Arias, 29–48. Minneapolis: University of Minnesota Press, 2001.

Prum, Vannak Anan. Dead Eye and the Deep Blue Sea: A Graphic Memoir of Modern Slavery. With Jocelyn Pederick. New York: Seven Stories, 2018.

Quirk, Joel. *The Anti-Slavery Project: From the Slave Trade to Human Trafficking*. Philadelphia: University of Pennsylvania Press, 2011.

Rak, Julie. *Boom! Manufacturing Memoir for the Popular Market.* Waterloo, Canada: Wilfrid Laurier University Press, 2013.

Rieger, April. "Missing the Mark: Why the Trafficking Victims Protection Act Fails to Protect Sex Trafficking Victims in the United States." *Harvard Journal of Law and Gender* 30 (2007): 231–56.

Rifkin, Mark. "'A Home Made Sacred by Protecting Laws': Black Activist Homemaking and Geographies of Citizenship in *Incidents in the Life of a Slave Girl.*" *Differences* 18, no. 2 (September 1, 2007): 72–102.

Roberts, Neil. *Freedom as Marronage.* Chicago: University of Chicago Press, 2015.

Ronell, Avital. "The Testamentary Whisper." *South Atlantic Quarterly* 103, nos. 2–3 (Spring/Summer 2004): 489–99.

Rosenblatt, Katariina. *Stolen: The True Story of a Sex Trafficking Survivor.* Grand Rapids, MI: Revell, 2014.

Rousseau, Jean Jacques. *On the Social Contract: Discourse on the Origin of Inequality; Discourse on Political Economy.* Indianapolis, IN: Hackett, 1983.

Sage, Jesse, and Liora Kasten, eds. *Enslaved: True Stories of Modern Day Slavery.* New York: St. Martin's Griffin, 2006.

Sanborn, Geoffrey. *Plagiarama! William Wells Brown and the Aesthetic of Attractions.* New York: Columbia University Press, 2016.

Sánchez-Eppler, Karen. *Touching Liberty: Abolition, Feminism, and the Politics of the Body.* Berkeley: University of California Press, 1993.

Sanders, Mark. "Culpability and Guilt: Child Soldiers in Fiction and Memoir." *Law & Literature* 23, no. 2 (2011): 195–223.

——. "Theorizing the Collaborative Self: The Dynamics of Contour and Content in the Dictated Autobiography." *New Literary History* 25, no. 2 (1994): 445–58.

Scarry, Elaine. *The Body in Pain: The Making and Unmaking of the World.* New York: Oxford University Press, 1985.

——. "The Difficulty of Imagining Other People." In *For Love of Country: Debating the Limits of Patriotism,* ed. Martha Craven Nussbaum and Joshua Cohen, 98–110. Boston: Beacon, 1996.

Schultheis, Alexandra. "African Child Soldiers and Humanitarian Consumption." *Peace Review* 20, no. 1 (2008): 31–40.

——. "Global Specters: Child Soldiers in the Post-national Fiction of Uzodinma Iweala and Chris Abani." In *Emerging African Voices: A Study of Contemporary African Fiction,* ed. Walter P. Collins III, 13–51. Amherst, NY: Cambria, 2010.

Sekora, John. "Briton Hammon, the Indian Captivity Narrative, and the African American Slave Narrative." In *When Brer Rabbit Meets Coyote: African–Native American Literature,* ed. Jonathan Brennan, 141–157. Urbana: University of Illinois Press, 2003.

Sen, Amartya. *Development as Freedom.* New York: Anchor, 2000.

Shattuc, Jane M. *The Talking Cure: TV Talk Shows and Women.* New York: Routledge, 2014.

Shih, Elena. "Not in My 'Backyard Abolitionism': Vigilante Rescue Against American Sex Trafficking." *Sociological Perspectives* 59, no. 1 (2016): 66–90.

Sims, Cliff. "The 'Sex Trafficking Superhighway' Most Alabamians Don't Even Realize Runs Through Their State." *Yellowhammer News* (blog), January 29, 2016. https://yellowhammernews.com/the-sex-trafficking-superhighway-most-alabamians-dont-even-realize-runs-through-their-state/.

"Situational Awareness: Possible Sex Trafficking During Super Bowl XLVIII." U.S. Department of State, January 17, 2014. https://www.state.gov/documents/organi zation/226277.pdf.

Skinner, E. Benjamin. *A Crime So Monstrous: Face-to-Face with Modern-Day Slavery.* New York: Free, 2009.

Slaughter, Joseph. "Humanitarian Reading." In *Humanitarianism and Suffering: The Mobilization of Empathy*, ed. Richard Ashby Wilson and Richard D. Brown. New York: Cambridge University Press, 2008.

Smith, Holly Austin. *Walking Prey: How America's Youth Are Vulnerable to Sex Slavery.* New York: St. Martin's, 2014.

Smith, Linda. *From Congress to the Brothel: A Journey of Hope, Healing and Restoration.* Vancouver, WA: Shared Hope, 2007.

Smith, Sidonie. *Where I'm Bound: Patterns of Slavery and Freedom in Black American Autobiography.* Westport, CT: Greenwood, 1974.

Smith, Sidonie, and Julia Watson. *Reading Autobiography: A Guide for Interpreting Life Narratives.* Minneapolis: University of Minnesota Press, 2010.

——. "Witness or False Witness: Metrics of Authenticity, Collective I-Formations, and the Ethic of Verification in First-Person Testimony." *Biography* 35, no. 4 (2012): 590–626.

Smith, Venture. "A Narrative of the Life and Adventures of Venture, a Native of Africa: But Resident Above Sixty Years in the United States of America. Related by Himself." In *Unchained Voices: An Anthology of Black Authors in the English-Speaking World of the Eighteenth Century*, ed. Vincent Carretta. Lexington: University Press of Kentucky, 2013.

Soderlund, Gretchen. "The Rhetoric of Revelation: Sex Trafficking and the Journalistic Exposé." *Humanity: An International Journal of Human Rights, Humanitarianism, and Development* 2, no. 2 (September 8, 2011): 193–211. https://doi.org/10.1353 /hum.2011.0013.

Spencer, Robert. "My Life as a Modern-Day Slave." *Jihad Watch* (blog), January 26, 2004. www.jihadwatch.org/2004/01/my-life-as-a-modern-day-slave.

Spivak, Gayatri Chakravorty. "Can the Subaltern Speak?" In *Can the Subaltern Speak? Reflections on the History of an Idea*, 21–78. New York: Columbia University Press, 1988.

Srikantiah, Jayashri. "Perfect Victims and Real Survivors: The Iconic Victim in Domestic Human Trafficking Law." *Boston University Law Review* 28 (2007): 157–211.

Stauffer, John. *The Black Hearts of Men.* Cambridge, MA: Harvard University Press, 2009.

Stoll, David. *Rigoberta Menchu and the Story of All Poor Guatemalans: New Foreword by Elizabeth Burgos.* Boulder, CO: Westview, 2007.

Syedullah, Jasmine. " 'Is This Freedom?' A Political Theory of Harriet Jacobs's Loopholes of Emancipation." (PhD diss., University of California Santa Cruz, 2014). https://escholarship.org/uc/item/5xz9d2kx.

Members of the Research Network on the Legal Parameters of Slavery. "Bellagio-Harvard Guidelines on the Legal Parameters of Slavery," March 3, 2012. http:// www.law.qub.ac.uk/schools/SchoolofLaw/FileStore/Filetoupload,651854,en.pdf.

"The Road of Lost Innocence by Somaly Mam (Review)." *Kirkus Reviews*, September 9, 2008. Accessed October 2, 2017. https://www.kirkusreviews.com/book-reviews /somaly-mam/the-road-of-lost-innocence/.

Thornber, Karen. "Global Health and World Literature: Translating Silences in Cambodian Writing on Sex Slavery." *Literature and Medicine* 31, no. 2 (2013): 235–55.

Tillet, Salamishah. "Hollywood Finally Catches Up with History." Root, October 22, 2013. Accessed October 2, 2017. http://www.theroot.com/hollywood-finally-catches -up-with-history-1790898482.

Todorov, Tzvetan. *Genres in Discourse*. Trans. Catherine Porter. Cambridge: Cambridge University Press, 1990.

Torchin, Leshu. *Creating the Witness: Documenting Genocide on Film, Video, and the Internet*. Minneapolis: University of Minnesota Press, 2012.

Tyldum, Guri, and Anette Brunovskis. "Describing the Unobserved: Methodological Challenges in Empirical Studies on Human Trafficking." *International Migration* 43, nos. 1–2 (2005): 17–34.

Uy, Robert. "Blinded by Red Lights: Why Trafficking Discourse Should Shift Away from Sex and the 'Perfect Victim' Paradigm." *Berkeley Journal of Gender, Law, and Justice* 26, no. 1 (2011): 204–19.

Vance, Carole S. "Thinking Trafficking, Thinking Sex." *GLQ: A Journal of Lesbian and Gay Studies* 17, no. 1 (2011): 135–143.

Van den Anker, Christien. "Making Human Rights Accessible: The Role of Governments in Trafficking and Migrant Labor Exploitation." In *From Human Trafficking to Human Rights: Reframing Contemporary Slavery*, ed. Alison Brysk and Austin Choi-Fitzpatrick. Philadelphia: University of Pennsylvania Press, 2012.

Wacquant, Loïc. *Punishing the Poor: The Neoliberal Government of Social Insecurity*. Durham, NC: Duke University Press, 2009.

Waldron, Jeremy. *Dignity, Rank, and Rights*. New York: Oxford University Press, 2012.

Ward, Abigail. "Servitude and Slave Narratives: Tracing 'New Slaveries' in Mende Nazer's *Slave* and Zadie Smith's 'The Embassy of Cambodia.'" *Wasafiri* 31, no. 3 (2016): 42–48.

Ware, Vron. "Info-War and the Politics of Feminist Curiosity: Exploring New Frameworks for Feminist Intercultural Studies." *Cultural Studies* 20, no. 6 (2006): 526–51.

Whitlock, Gillian. *Postcolonial Life Narrative: Testimonial Transactions*. 1st ed. Oxford: Oxford University Press, 2015.

——. *Soft Weapons: Autobiography in Transit*. Chicago: University of Chicago Press, 2010.

Wilson, Michael, and Erin O'Brien. "Constructing the Ideal Victim in the United States of America's Annual Trafficking in Persons Reports." *Crime, Law and Social Change* 65, nos. 1–2 (2016): 29–45.

Woods, Tryon P. "Surrogate Selves: Notes on Anti-trafficking and Anti-blackness." *Social Identities* 19, no. 1 (January 2013): 120–34.

Yagoda, Ben. *Memoir: A History*. New York: Penguin, 2009.

Youngs, Tim. "'Framed in the Doorway': The *Observer* and the 'Yemeni Brides' Affair." *Media, Culture & Society* 13, no. 2 (1991): 239–47.

Zimmerman, Yvonne C. *Other Dreams of Freedom: Religion, Sex, and Human Trafficking*. New York: Oxford University Press, 2013.

——. "Situating the Ninety-Nine: A Critique of the Trafficking Victims Protection Act." *Journal of Religion & Abuse* 7 (November 2005): 37–56.

Zinsser, William. *Inventing the Truth: The Art and Craft of Memoir*. Boston: Houghton Mifflin, 1987.

INDEX

Page numbers in *italics* indicate illustrations.

liberty. *See* freedom

Living Inside the Rainbow: Winning the Battlefield of the Mind After Human Trafficking and Mental Bondage (Parker-Bello): Christian salvation, 145; comparison to gravity of antebellum slaves' situations made in, 152; conflation of forced sex work and consensual sex work, 171; cover, 42; integration of necessary personal and societal changes, 177–78; need to embrace being victim, 148; submission to "holy Father," 162; "true self" found through surrender to God, 164

Lloyd, Rachel: and activism, 14, 219; and readership, 14; testimony before Senate, 144; use of analogies, 33

Lobert, Annie, 145

Lockard, Joe, 6

Long Way Gone, A (Beah), 13, 183, 250n6

Lott, Eric, 103, 127

Lovejoy, Paul, 25, 57–58, 73

Lutnick, Alexandra, 149

Mahdavi, Pardis, 188

Malcolm X, 203–4

Mam, Somaly: as activist, 185, 192; comparing self to Northup, 182; as compound author, 201–5; as destroyed by genre of new slave narrative, 198–99, 214; as enslaved subject, 199–201; as paradigm of "perfect victim," 189; as person, author, and representation, 196–99, 209; on reason for writing book, 1; as representation, 205–8; and sex slavery "in your backyard," 183; as standard bearer for anti-trafficking, 183–84, 186, 194; as survivor-savior, 208–10; as synonymous with social movement, 210; veracity of, 190–95, 196. See also *Road of Lost Innocence* (Mam)

Marcus, Sharon, 220

Marie Claire, 191, 192

Marino, Jasmine Grace, 147. See also *Diary of Jasmine Grace, The* (Marino)

Marks, Simon, 190–91, 204, 211, 213–14

Marrant, John, 203

Marshall, Ruth, 197, 202

Matul, Ima, 22

McBride, Dwight, 29

McDonnell, Faith J. H.: as anti-Muslim, 121–22; appropriation of persecution by, 126–29; cherry picking of history by and promotion of evangelical Christian message, 120–22, 124–26; as director of religious political organizations, 119–20; use of mechanisms of blackface abolition, 120–23, 124–26; as "white savior," 106. See also *Girl Soldier: A Story of Hope for Northern Uganda* (Akallo)

McQueen, Steve, 181–82

Meillassoux, Claude, xiii

Menchú, Rigoberta, 183, 206–7, 250n6

Miller, John R., 40, 116

minstrel shows, 102–3, 127

mobility as right, 53–54

modern slavery, use of term, xi

Moore, Anne Elizabeth, 194–95

Moynagh, Maureen, 244n7

Muhsen, Nadia, 231n23

Muhsen, Zana, 10–11, 12, 36, 64, 231n23

Murad, Nadia, 33. See also *Last Girl: My Story of Captivity, and My Fight Against the Islamic State, The* (Murad)

Mutua, Makau, 106

My Bondage and My Freedom (Douglass), 101

My Life Has a Price: A Memoir of Survival and Freedom (Okpara): captors, 55–56; cover and title, 35, 43; freedom as state-granted, 95; moment of realization of condition, 56; trust in welcoming country, 92

My Name is Evelyn Amony (Amony): future plans, 52; origin story, 51; use of euphemism, 61

"My Own 'Twelve Years a Slave'" (Mam), 182

My Stone of Hope (Cadet): cruelties
of child slavery, 1; freedom as
compromised, 83–85; freedom as
constitutive of his human existence,
75–76; freedom as political rights, 72;
title, 70–71

Nagy, Timea: opening lines of narrative,
49; questioning being free, 79; role of
inherent freedom in escape, 76; use of
legitimating authorities, 64
names: in coauthored texts, 201–5;
as conflation of person,
representation, and author, 197–99;
and demand for survivor-savior,
208–10; and elevation of single
experience to that of collective,
205–7; of pimps, 59; as representation
of free-willed, self-possessed subject
and captive, possessed object,
199–201; synonymous with social
movements, 210
*Narrative of the Uncommon Sufferings,
and Surprizing Deliverance of Briton
Hammon, a Negro Man* (Hammon),
4, 203
narrators. *See* authors and authorship;
survivors
National Survivor Network, 23
Nazer, Mende, 12, 35. See also *Slave: My
True Story* (Nazer)
"Need for Continuing Anti-Slavery
Work" (Douglass), xvii
neoliberals and neoliberalism: and
domestic minor sex trafficking
narratives, 145; and Horatio Alger
myth, 40; life narratives described,
165–66; notions about freedom, 25;
political agenda and new slave
narratives, 6, 105, 106; and women's
rights issues, 20
new slave narratives: and activism of
readers, 218–19; and activism of
survivors, 209; and antebellum slave
narrative conventions, 9–10, 30, 50, 55,
112, 115; anthropological digressions
in, 112; cultural forces aiding, 5–6;

decrease in diversity of type of
enslavement, 14; demands of
antislavery movement on, 26, 123;
demands of conventions on, 195;
demands of human rights industry
on, 12, 26, 123, 195–96, 210–11; early
iterations, 10–14; as elevating single
experience to that of collective, 205–7;
and embodiment of memory and life,
59; as empowering narrators, 8; as
evidentiary foundations of human
rights industry, 104–5; as expressions
of contemporary cultural discourse,
23; frequency of publication, 15; goals,
11, 15; as "neoliberal life narratives," 6,
105, 106; number published, 7, 13;
overrepresentation of African,
anti-Muslim, 105–6; overview, xx; as
political weapons of blackface
abolitionists, 107, 109–10; as
propaganda, 20; publication
locations, 15–16; as spectacles of
otherness, 218. *See also* sex trafficking
narratives
New Somaly Mam Foundation: Voices
for Change, 192
Newsweek, 190, 194
Nivasa, 18
*Nobody's Girl: A Memoir of Lost
Innocence, Modern Day Slavery,
and Transformation* (Amaya):
criminalization for victimization,
179; sense of being owned, 153; stolen
childhood innocence trope, 35; "true
self," 164
North Star, 102
Northup, Solomon, 181, 182, 190, 203, 212,
254n84
Not for Sale campaign, 43
"not-yet-freedom narratives," 25, 74,
79–81, 83, 115
Nussbaum, Martha, 86–87, 99, 100, 218

Obama, Barack, 143
Okpara, Tina. See *My Life Has a Price:
A Memoir of Survival and Freedom*
(Okpara)

Slave Across the Street: The True Story of How an American Teen Survived the World of Human Trafficking, The (Flores), 35, 64
slaveholders, 55–56, 58, 114
"slave mentality," 88–91
Slave: My True Story (Nazer): and anti-Muslim sentiments, 132, 133; and cosmopolitanism, 98; cover and title, 35, 39, 40; freedom after emancipation, 79; freedom as constitutive of her human existence, 76; freedom as state-granted, 94–95, 239n66; opening lines, 49; origin story, 51, 53; paratextual elements, 64; psychological afterlife of slavery, 89, 90; publication of, 12, 13; review, 40; trust in welcoming country, 92
Slave Next Door, The (Bales), 43
slavery: absence of slaves' complicity in, 166; authorities' denial of existence of, 80; as begetting slavery, 80; in binary opposition to freedom, 71–72, 74, 77, 80–81, 82, 85; "breaking-in" process, 55; as endemic to capitalism, 216, 217; ending, as goal of new slave narratives, 11; evolution and renaming of, xvii; experiences designated as, 11; explaining experience of, 29, 49–50, 112, 212–13; extent and types of, in Africa, 105; free will as inherent during, 73; ignorance of existence of, 30, 31, 51; inherent violence of, 56, 112–13; "in our own backyards" trope, 35; issue of responsibility for, 167, 200; labor as necessary condition of, xv; League of Nation's Slavery Conventions definition, 152; perception of, as intrinsically Islamic, 120, 132–33; psychological afterlife of, 88–91; race and conception of, xi, 12, 13, 24, 29; self-identification of narrators with, 8–9, 230n14; and sex trafficking, 167–68; signs of forced labor not read as, 31–32; use of term, xi–xiv, 16–17; use of term for sex trafficking, 151, 246n39

Slavery, Terrorism, and Islam: The Historical Roots and Contemporary Threat (Hammond), 132–33
Smith, Christopher, 141, 142
Smith, Gerrit, 102–3
Smith, James McCune, 102–3
Smith, Linda, 40, 106
Smith, Sidonie: composite "I," 206, 208; increase in interest in memoirs, 21; making body meaningful, 66; materiality of the body linked with memory and subjectivity, 59; survivors' achievement of power by distancing new from old self, 61; on "suspicious reading" practices, 211–12
Smith, Venture, 2
social media campaigns, 22–23
social mobility (postemancipation), 81–82, 83–86, 87, 90
Sold: One Woman's True Account of Modern Slavery (Muhsen, Zana), 10–11, 12, 36, 64, 231n23
Somaly Mam Foundation, 191, 192
"Somaly Mam: The Holy Saint (and Sinner) of Sex Trafficking" (Marks), 190
South Sudan, 12
Spectacular Rhetorics (Hesford), 48–49
spectatorship, as creator of cosmopolitan citizenship, 22–23
Spivak, Gayatri Chakravorty, 188
Srikantiah, Jayashri, 188
Sri Lanka, 18
statistics, as legitimating authority, 65, 185
Stauffer, John, 102
Stolen: The True Story of a Sex Trafficking Survivor (Rosenblatt): conflation of forced sex work and consensual sex work, 171; cover, 40; realization of being reduced to commodity, 153; use of language of sex industry, 148; use of passive voice, 149
Stoll, David, 206–7
strategies of displacement: benefits of, 31; composite "I," 205–7, 208; euphemisms, 61–62, 75, 113; and

evangelical Christian messages, 119; experiences of others, 56, 65–66, 113, 184, 185; legitimating authorities, 34, 64–65, 115–16, 120–21, 125, 185; public, 74; purpose of use of, 24, 63; similes, 61–62; synecdoches, 67–68; tendency toward, 30–31

Stuck in Traffic (Crown), 148, 162

substantive freedoms, 86–87, 91

Sudan, war in, 19

Sudanese People's Liberation Army (SPLA), 108

suffering, transitive property of, 126–30, 133–34, 138

suicidal thoughts, 57, 112–13

"Super Bowl" sex trafficking, 137, 244n6

Survivor Alliance, 23

survivors: as activists, 12, 14, 17–18, 41, 68, 111, 114–15, 179, 185, 188–89, 192, 208, 209; agency of, and human rights industry, 195–96, 214; agency of and paratextual elements, 48; as alienated by origin stories, 199–200; benefits of strategies of displacement to, 31; childhoods' of, 51–52, 111–12; establishment of humanity of, 50, 58, 111–12; impact of testimony on legislation, 19; independent networks and counseling groups, 23; move to West, 92–93; "perfect victim," 187; photos on covers, 41; postemancipation freedom as compromised, 81–82, 83–86, 87, 90; power achieved by distancing new from old self, 61–62, 63, 66; questioning of Western society, 213; readers' establishment of ethical relationship with, 217–22; readers' identification with, 30, 31, 35, 40, 50, 60, 67, 111–12, 124–26; recognition of, 96; as saviors, 208–10; survival and transformation in titles, 35; as theorists of freedom, 72–73; vision of life postemancipation, 78–79

survivors of sex trafficking: absence of legitimate choice for, 149–50; and addiction recovery programs, 157–58;

integration of sense of personal responsibility despite belief in victimization, 159, 160; as not responsible for exploitation, 149–50, 154–55; personal responsibility as part of recovery from sex trafficking, 155–57; realization of being reduced to commodity, 153; "true self" found through surrender to God, 163–64

Survivors of Slavery (Annan), 29

Taken (film), 144

talk shows, 21, 22, 58–59, 183, 190

Tavis Smiley Show, 22

Tillet, Salamishah, 182

titles, 36–39, 117; as aspirational, 70–71; centrality of freedom in, 35; domestic minor sex trafficking narratives, 144; purpose of, 34, 35

Tivnen, Edward, 80

Tooley, Mark, 108

Torchin, Leshu, 128

trafficking, xiv, 20. *See also* sex trafficking

Trafficking in Persons (TIP) reports, 143

Trafficking Victims Protection Act (TVPA, 2000), 141–42, 187

tropes: childhood sexual abuse, 150, 246n38; Christian submission and rebirth, 145, 161–65; Christian suffering, 123; "helpless victim," 171–72; innocent birth and childhood with bright futures, 50–54, 111–12; slavery "in our own backyards," 35; stolen childhood innocence, 35, 184; victim-savior, 198–99, 209

Truth, Sojourner, 152

Tubman, Harriet, 151–52

12 Years a Slave (film), 181–82

12 Years a Slave (Northup), 181, 182, 203, 212, 254n84

Tyra Banks Show, 22

Uganda, 13

United Africans for Women and Children Rights, 111

49; influence on new slave narratives, 202; sensationalized, fear-mongering rhetoric about anti-trafficking movement in, 170; society questioned by survivors, 213; survivors' move to, 57–58, 92–93; use of terms, 229n7; vision of postemancipation life in, 78–79

Whitlock, Gillian, 20, 32, 59, 110

"wild child" stigma, 150–51

Winfrey, Oprah, 182

women: activist Islamic, 41; agency of, choosing sex work, xii, 138, 144, 170, 171–72, 174–75; cessation of government programs to help, 159–60; as disposable, 153–54; as dominant on covers and race, 48–49; evangelical Christian view of

sexuality and agency of, 159, 161–65, 169; and gender discrimination, 52; as "helpless victims," 171–72; individuals as representatives of entire demographic, 207; labor of migrant, in Global South, 141; neoliberals and rights of, 20; as responsible for all sexual choices, 160; violence and gender-based objectification, 154

Woods, Tryon P., xi

Works Progress Administration narratives, 4

Yagoda, Ben, 21

Yazidi sex slave narratives, 20, 33, 133

Zimmerman, Yvonne, 141, 160

Zinsser, William, 21